MY PSALM, MY CONTEXT

Texts@Contexts

Series Editors

Athalya Brenner-Idan
Archie C. C. Lee
Gale A. Yee

MY PSALM, MY CONTEXT

Texts@Contexts

Edited by
Athalya Brenner-Idan and Gale A. Yee

LONDON • NEW YORK • OXFORD • NEW DELHI • SYDNEY

T&T CLARK

Bloomsbury Publishing Plc, 50 Bedford Square, London, WC1B 3DP, UK
Bloomsbury Publishing Inc, 1359 Broadway, New York, NY 10018, USA
Bloomsbury Publishing Ireland, 29 Earlsfort Terrace, Dublin 2, D02 AY28, Ireland

BLOOMSBURY, T&T CLARK and the T&T Clark logo
are trademarks of Bloomsbury Publishing Plc

First published in Great Britain 2024
Paperback edition published 2025

Copyright © Athalya Brenner-Idan, Gale A. Yee and contributors, 2024

Athalya Brenner-Idan and Gale A. Yee have asserted their right under the Copyright, Designs and Patents Act, 1988, to be identified as Editors of this work.

Cover image: "hallelujah" by Lucilla Gardner

All rights reserved. No part of this publication may be: i) reproduced or transmitted in any form, electronic or mechanical, including photocopying, recording or by means of any information storage or retrieval system without prior permission in writing from the publishers; or ii) used or reproduced in any way for the training, development or operation of artificial intelligence (AI) technologies, including generative AI technologies. The rights holders expressly reserve this publication from the text and data mining exception as per Article 4(3) of the Digital Single Market Directive (EU) 2019/790.

Bloomsbury Publishing Plc does not have any control over, or responsibility for, any third-party websites referred to or in this book. All internet addresses given in this book were correct at the time of going to press. The author and publisher regret any inconvenience caused if addresses have changed or sites have ceased to exist, but can accept no responsibility for any such changes.

A catalogue record for this book is available from the British Library.

Library of Congress Cataloging-in-Publication Data
Names: Brenner-Idan, Athalya, editor. | Yee, Gale A., 1949- editor.
Title: My Psalm, my context / edited by Athalya Brenner-Idan and Gale A. Yee.
Description: London ; New York : T&T Clark, 2023. | Series: Texts@Contexts ; 8 | Includes bibliographical references and index. | Summary: "Diverse contextual readings of the Psalms, followed by short reflective commentaries"-- Provided by publisher.
Identifiers: LCCN 2023018499 (print) | LCCN 2023018500 (ebook) | ISBN 9780567710284 (HB) | ISBN 9780567710314 (PB) | ISBN 9780567710291 (ePDF) | ISBN 9780567710307 (ePub)
Subjects: LCSH: Bible. Psalms--Criticism, interpretation, etc. | Bible. Psalms--Commentaries.
Classification: LCC BS1430.3 .M97 2023 (print) | LCC BS1430.3 (ebook) | DDC 223/.207--dc23/eng/20230705
LC record available at https://lccn.loc.gov/2023018499
LC ebook record available at https://lccn.loc.gov/2023018500

ISBN:	HB:	978-0-5677-1028-4
	PB:	978-0-5677-1031-4
	ePDF:	978-0-5677-1029-1
	eBook:	978-0-5677-1030-7

Series: Texts@Contexts, volume 9

Typeset by Trans.form.ed SARL

For product safety related questions contact productsafety@bloomsbury.com.

To find out more about our authors and books visit www.bloomsbury.com
and sign up for our newsletters.

CONTENTS

Series Preface	ix
List of Contributors	xv
Abbreviations	xix

INTRODUCTION
FROM 'AŠREY (BLESSED* – PSALM 1.1) TO HALLELUJAH
(PRAISE YAH – PSALM 150.6)
    Athalya Brenner-Idan and Gale A. Yee   1

PSALM 6: PLEA, PROTEST, ANGER, DISCIPLINE, WEARINESS, DELIVERANCE
    John Goldingay   14

PSALM 8: THE POOR AND THE EARTH CRY OUT
    Nicole L. Tilford   18

PSALM 8: HOW I FELL IN LOVE WITH THE BIBLE
    Francis Landy   23

PSALM 18.35: GIVING DAVID ODYSSEUS' BOW
    Sivan Nir   28

PSALM 19: THE VOICE THAT IS NOT HEARD
    Robert Paul Seesengood and Jennifer L. Koosed   36

PSALM 20: WHEN GOD CROSSES BORDERS
    Roger S. Nam   42

PSALM 23: A MOVING, VERSATILE POEM
    Lieve Teugels   47

PSALM 23: AN AUTOBIOGRAPHICAL
AND INTERTEXTUAL READING
    Musa W. Dube   52

PSALM 37: LIVING FAITHFULLY
  D.N. Premnath   59

PSALM 39: SILENCE THAT SPEAKS
  Mercedes L. García Bachmann   65

PSALM 46: PRESENCE, WAR-LANGUAGE,
AND FEMINIST DIRECTION
  Beth LaNeel Tanner   70

PSALM 49: TWO UNSOLVED RIDDLES AND ONE NEW PROVERB
  Klaas Spronk   75

PSALM 51: A MAN RENEGOTIATING HEROISM
  Mikael Larsson   79

PSALM 68: FURTHER HARMOLODIC MUSINGS
  Hugh R. Page, Jr   85

PSALM 71: DO NOT DUMP ME IN TIME OF OLD AGE
  Athalya Brenner-Idan   90

PSALM 73: BUT I… (*WA'ĂNÎ*)
  Ekaputra Tupamahu   97

PSALM 78.67-72: KING DAVID AND THE CHINESE
'MANDATE OF HEAVEN'
  Archie C.C. Lee   101

PSALM 84: WHERE IS HOME?
  Meira Polliack   109

PSALM 90: IT SOON BECOMES EMPTY –
MY CHINESE READING OF THE PSALM
  Yanjing Qu   116

PSALM 90: IN PRAISE OF PSALM 90
  Jonathan Magonet   120

PSALM 91: LIFE IN THE SHELTER OF THE 'MOST HIGH'
  Susan Gillingham   125

PSALM 100: 'WORSHIP THE LORD
WITH ROUSING ACCLAMATION!'
  Vanessa Lovelace   133

PSALM 104: A DISCOMFORTABLE READING
BY AN IMPLICATED SUBJECT
   Gerrie Snyman   137

PSALM 104: HUMANITY'S FIRM GROUNDING
   Nancy L. DeClaissé-Walford   142

PSALM 104: THE SIGNIFICANCE OF ITS ENDING
   Yairah Amit   146

PSALM 106: BLESSED LIVING AS A MIXED-RACE DESCENDANT
   Lisa J. Cleath   150

PSALM 114: A BEAUTIFUL COUNTER-CULTURAL PSALM
   Marc Zvi Brettler   155

PSALM 117: A HYMN OF STEADFAST LOVE
   Barbara E. Reid   160

PSALM 118: POETRY AND POETICS THROUGH
A PAST IN SCIENCE
   Kevin D. Chau   164

PSALM 121: IN THREE RECEPTIONS
   Gerald West   169

PSALM 121: ASCENDING TO THE HOLY WITH THE PSALM
   Marvin A. Sweeney   175

PSALM 121: AND SYNAGOGUE MUSIC—
HOPE IN A MINOR KEY
   Helen Leneman   180

PSALM 121: WHY THIS PSALM IS POPULAR
IN CONTEMPORARY ISRAEL
   Ora Brison   186

PSALM 123: THE 'FLOW' OF SEEING
   Monica Jyotsna Melanchton   192

PSALM 126: WEEPING, REAPING, AND DINING
   Adele Reinhartz   198

PSALM 126: COMMEMORATING THE DEAD DURING THE
LOCKDOWN, 2020
    Ingeborg Löwisch   202

PSALM 126: THOSE WHO SOW SHALL REAP IN TEARS
    Assnat Bartor   206

PSALM 127.2: HE GIVETH UNTO HIS BELOVED IN SLEEP –
AND WHAT ABOUT ME? A PERSONAL STORY OF PSALM 127
    Sabine Dievenkorn   212

PSALMS 127–128: WHOSE LABOR? WHOSE HANDS?
    Gale A. Yee   216

PSALM 132: LIFEGIVING CONVERSATIONS WITH A PSALM
    Melody D. Knowles   221

PSALM 136: THE POWER OF A LIST
    Diana Lipton   226

PSALM 137: A KAU'I-TALANOA READING
    Nāsili Vaka'uta   231

PSALM 137: EMOTIONS OF THE EXILES IN A FOREIGN LAND
    Wei Huang   236

PSALM 137: SONG OF A BROKEN HEART
    Hemchand Gossai   240

PSALM 139: FULLY KNOWN
    Margaret Aymer   244

PSALM 146: A NATIVE RESTORYING OF THE PSALM
UNDER TSUNAMI AND COVID WAVES
    Jione Havea   249

PSALM 150: HALLELU, HALLELU, HALLELUJAH
    Dominic Mattos   255

Index of Biblical References   261
Index of Authors   268

SERIES PREFACE

> Myth cannot be defined but as an empty screen, a structure…
> A myth is but an empty screen for transference.
>
> — Mieke Bal (1993)

'The Torah has seventy faces' (שבעים פנים לתורה)[1]

The discipline of biblical studies emerged from a particular cultural context; it is profoundly influenced by the assumptions and values of the Western European and North Atlantic, male-dominated, and largely Protestant environment in which it was born. Yet like the religions with which it is involved, the critical study of the Bible has traveled beyond its original context. Its presence in a diversity of academic settings around the globe has been experienced as both liberative and imperialist, sometimes simultaneously. Like many travelers, biblical scholars become aware of their own cultural rootedness only in contact with, and through the eyes of, people in other cultures.

The way any one of us closes a door seems in Philadelphia nothing at all remarkable, but in Chiang Mai, it seems overly loud and emphatic – so very typically American. In the same way, Western biblical interpretation did not seem tied to any specific context when only Westerners were reading and writing it. Since so much economic, military, and consequently cultural power has been vested in the West, the West has had the privilege of maintaining this cultural closure for two centuries. Those who engaged in biblical studies – even when they were women or men from Africa, Asia, and Latin America – nevertheless had to take on the Western context along with the discipline.

---

1. This saying indicates, through its usage of the stereotypic number 70, that the Torah – and, by extension, the whole Bible – intrinsically has many meanings. It is therefore often used to indicate the multivalence and variability of biblical interpretation, and does not appear in this formulation in traditional Jewish biblical interpretation before the middle of the first millennium CE. Its most known appearances are in the medieval commentator Ibn Ezra's introduction to his commentary on the Torah, toward the introduction's end (as in printed versions), in midrash *Numbers Rabbah* (13.15-16), and in later Jewish mystical literature.

But much of recent Bible scholarship has moved toward the recognition that considerations not only of the contexts of assumed, or implied, biblical authors but also the contexts of the interpreters are valid and legitimate in an inquiry into biblical literature. We use *contexts* here as an umbrella term covering a wide range of issues: on the one hand, social factors (such as location, economic situation, gender, age, class, ethnicity, color, and things pertaining to personal biography) and, on the other hand, ideological factors (such as faith, beliefs, practiced norms, and personal politics).

Contextual readings of the Bible are an attempt to redress the previous longstanding, and grave imbalance that says that there is a kind of 'plain' unaligned biblical criticism that is somehow 'normative', and that there is another, distinct kind of biblical criticism aligned with some social location: the writing of Latina/o scholars advocating liberation, the writing of feminist scholars emphasizing gender as a cultural factor, the writings of African scholars pointing out the text's and the readers' imperialism, the writing of Jews and Muslims, and so on. The project of recognizing and emphasizing the role of context in reading freely admits that we all come from somewhere: no one is native to the biblical text, no one reads only in the interests of the text itself. North Atlantic and Western European scholarship has focused on the Bible's characters as individuals, has read past its miracles and stories of spiritual manifestations, or 'translated' them into other categories. These results of Euro-American contextual reading would be no problem if they were seen as such; but they have become a chain to be broken when they have been held up as the one and only 'objective', plain truth of the text itself.

The biblical text, as we have come to understand in the postmodern world and as pre-enlightenment interpreters perhaps understood more clearly, does not speak in its own voice. It cannot read itself. *We* must read it, and in reading it, we must acknowledge that our own voice's particular pitch and timbre and inflection affect the meaning that emerges. Biblical scholars usually read the text in the voice of a Western Protestant male. When interpreters in the Southern Hemisphere and in Asia have assumed ownership of the Bible, it has meant a recognition that this Euro-American male voice is not the voice of the text itself; it is only one reader's voice, or rather, the voice of one context – however familiar and authoritative it may seem to all who have been affected by Western political and economic power. Needless to say, it is not a voice suited to bring out the best meaning for every reading community. Indeed, as biblical studies tended for so long to speak in this one particular voice, it may be the case that that voice has outlived its meaning-producing usefulness: we may have heard all that this voice has to say, at least for now. Nevertheless we have included that voice in this series, in part in an effort to hear it as emerging from its specific context, in order to put that previously authoritative voice quite literally in its place.

The trend of acknowledging readers' contexts as meaningful is already, *inter alia*, recognizable in the pioneering volumes of *Reading from This Place* (Segovia and Tolbert 1995, 2000, 2004), which indeed move from the center to the margins and back and from the United States to the rest of the world. More recent publications along this line also include *Her Master's Tools?* (Vander Stichele and Penner 2005), *From Every People and Nation: The Book of Revelation in Intercultural Perspective* (Rhoads et al. 2005), *From Every People and Nation: A Biblical Theology of Race* (Hays and Carson 2003), and the *Global Bible Commentary* (GBC; Patte et al. 2004).

The editors of the *GBC* have gone a long way toward this shift by soliciting and admitting contributions from so-called Third, Fourth, and Fifth world scholars alongside First and Second world scholars, thus attempting to usher the former and their perspectives into the *center* of biblical discussion. Contributors to the *GBC* were asked to begin by clearly stating their context before proceeding. The result was a collection of short introductions to the books of the Bible (Hebrew Bible/Old Testament and New Testament), each introduction from one specific context and, perforce, limited in scope. At the Society of Biblical Literature's annual meeting in Philadelphia in 2005, during the two *GBC* sessions and especially in the session devoted to pedagogical implications, it became clear that this project should be continued, albeit articulated further and redirected.

On methodological grounds, the paradox of a deliberately inclusive policy that foregrounds differences in the interpretation of the Bible could not be addressed in a single- or double-volume format because in most instances, those formats would allow for only one viewpoint for each biblical issue or passage (as in previous publications) or biblical book (as in the *GBC*) to be articulated. The acceptance of such a limit may indeed lead to a decentering of traditional scholarship but it would definitely not usher in multivocality on any single topic. It is true that, for pedagogical reasons, a teacher might achieve multivocality of scholarship by using various specialized scholarship types together; for instance, the *GBC* has been used side by side on a course with historical introductions to the Bible and other focused introductions, such as the *Women's Bible Commentary* (Newsom and Ringe 1998). But research and classes focused on a single biblical book or biblical corpus need another kind of resource: volumes exemplifying a broad multivocality in themselves, varied enough in contexts from various shades of the confessional to various degrees of the secular, especially since in most previous publications the contexts of communities of faith overrode all other contexts.

On the practical level, then, we found that we could address some of these methodological, pedagogical, and representational limitations evident in previous projects in contextual interpretation through a book series in which each volume introduces multiple contextual readings of the same biblical texts. This is what the Society of Biblical Literature's (SBL) Contextual Biblical Interpretation Consultation has already been promoting since 2005 during the American Annual Meeting; and since 2011 also at the annual International SBL conference. The Consultation serves as a testing ground for a multiplicity of readings of the same biblical texts by scholars from different contexts.[2]

---

2. Since 2010, when this book series was started and the first volume published with this Preface, interest in contextual interpretation has grown considerably. Worth noting is the SBL Press series International Voices in Biblical Studies (IVBS). As can be seen from

These considerations led us to believe that a book series focusing specifically on contextual multiple readings for specific topics, of specific biblical books, would be timely. We decided to construct a series, including at least eight to ten volumes, divided between the Hebrew Bible (HB/OT) and the New Testament (NT). Each of the planned volumes would focus on one or two biblical books: Genesis, Exodus and Deuteronomy, Leviticus and Numbers, Joshua and Judges, the so-called History books and later books for the HB/OT; Mark, Luke-Acts, John, and Paul's letters for the NT.[3] The general HB/OT editor is Athalya Brenner, with Archie Lee and Gale Yee as associate editors. The first general NT editor was Nicole Duran and is now James Grimshaw, with Daniel Patte, Teresa Okure as associate editors. Other colleagues have joined as editors for specific volumes.

Each volume focuses on clusters of contexts and of issues or themes, as determined by the editors in consultation with potential contributors. A combination of topics or themes, texts, and interpretive contexts seems better for our purpose than a text-only focus. In this way, more viewpoints on specific issues will be presented, with the hope of gaining a grid of interests and understanding. The interpreters' contexts will be allowed to play a central role in choosing a theme: we do not want to impose our choice of themes upon others, but as the contributions emerge, we will collect themes for each volume under several headings.

While we were soliciting articles for the first volumes (and continue to solicit contributions for future volumes), each contributor was and is asked to foreground her or his own multiple 'contexts' while presenting her or his interpretation of a given issue pertaining to the relevant biblical book(s). We asked that the interpretation be firmly grounded in those contexts and sharply focused on the specific theme, as well as in dialogue with 'classical' informed biblical scholarship. Finally, we asked for a concluding assessment of the significance of this interpretation for the contributor's contexts (whether secular or in the framework of a faith community).

Our main interest in this series is to examine how formulating the content-specific, ideological, and thematic questions from life contexts will focus the reading of the biblical texts. The result is a two-way process of reading that (1) considers the contemporary life context from the perspective of the chosen themes in the given biblical book as corrective lenses, pointing out specific

the website (http://www.sbl-site.org/publications/Books_IVBS.aspx), seven volumes have been published since 2010. However, the IVBS mission is different from ours, although two of the volumes (Vaka'uta 2011 on Ezra-Nehemiah 9–10 and Havea and Lau [eds.] 2015 on Ruth) do discuss specific texts against contextual, geographical-cultural perspectives. Worth noting too in this connection is the SBL series Global Perspectives on Biblical scholarship (https://www.sbl-site.org/publications/Books_GPBS.aspx), and especially the 2012 volume on postcolonial African interpretation, edited by Musa W. Dube, Andrew M. Mbuvi, and Dora R. Mbuwayesango.

3. At this time, no volume on Revelation is planned, since Rhoads's volume, *From Every People and Nation: The Book of Revelation in Intercultural Perspective* (2005) is readily available, with a concept similar to ours.

problems and issues in that context as highlighted by the themes in the biblical book; and (2) conversely, considers the given biblical book and the chosen theme from the perspective of the life context.

The word *contexts*, like *identity*, is a blanket term covering many components. For some, their geographical context is uppermost; for others, the dominant factor may be gender, faith, membership in a certain community, class, and so forth. The balance is personal and not always conscious; it does, however, dictate choices of interpretation. One of our interests as editors is to present the personal beyond the autobiographical as pertinent to the wider scholarly endeavor, especially but not only when *grids of consent* emerge that supersede divergence. Consent is no guarantee of Truthspeak; neither does it necessarily point at a sure recognition of the biblical authors' elusive contexts and intentions. It does, however, have cultural and political implications.

Globalization promotes uniformity but also diversity, by shortening distances, enabling dissemination of information, and exchanging resources. This is an opportunity for modifying traditional power hierarchies and reallocating knowledge, for upsetting hegemonies, and for combining the old with the new, the familiar with the unknown – in short, for a fresh mutuality. This series, then, consciously promotes the revision of biblical myths into new reread and rewritten versions that hang on many threads of welcome transference. Our contributors were asked, decidedly, to be responsibly nonobjective and to represent only themselves on the biblical screen. Paradoxically, we hope, the readings here offered will form a new tapestry or, changing the metaphor, new metaphorical screens on which contemporary life contexts and the life of biblical texts in those contexts may be reflected and refracted.

The Editors

Bibliography

Bal, Mieke (1993), 'Myth à la Lettre: Freud, Mann, Genesis and Rembrandt, and the Story of the Son', repr. in *A Feminist Companion to Genesis*, edited by A. Brenner; Sheffield: Sheffield Academic Press, 343–78. Originally in *Discourse in Psychoanalysis and Literature*, ed. S. Rimon-Kenan, London: Methuen, 1987: 57–89.

Dube, Musa W., Andrew M. Mbuvi, and Dora R. Mbuwayesango (eds.) (2012), *Postcolonial Perspectives in African Biblical Interpretations*, Global Perspectives on Biblical Scholarship 13; Atlanta: SBL Press.

Havea, Jione, and Peter H.W. Lau (eds.) (2015), *Reading Ruth in Asia*, IVBS; Atlanta: SBL Press.

Hays, J. Daniel, and Donald A. Carson (2003), *From Every People and Nation: A Biblical Theology of Race*, New Studies in Biblical Theology; Downers Grove, IL: Intervarsity Press.

Newsom, Carol A., and Sharon H. Ringe (eds.) (1992, 1998), *The Women's Bible Commentary*, Louisville, KY: Westminster/John knox Press.

Patte, Daniel *et al.* (eds.) (2004), *The Global Bible Commentary*, Nashville: Abingdon Press.

Penner, Todd, and Caroline Vander Stichele (eds.) (2005), *Her Master's Tools? Feminist and Postcolonial Engagements of Historical-Critical Discourse*, Global Perspectives on Biblical Scholarship; Atlanta: SBL Press.

Rhoads, David *et al.* (eds.) (2005), *From Every People and Nation: The Book of Revelation in Intercultural Perspective*, Minneapolis: Augsburg Fortress Press.

Segovia, Fernando F. (ed.) (1995), *Reading from This Place*. Vol. 1, *Social Location and Biblical Interpretation in the United States*, Minneapolis: Augsburg Fortress Press.

Segovia, Fernando F., and Mary Ann Tolbert (eds) (2000), *Reading from This Place*. Vol. 2, *Social Location and Biblical Interpretation in Global Perspective*, repr., Minneapolis: Augsburg Fortress; originally published 1995.

Segovia, Fernando F., and Mary Ann Tolbert (eds) (2004), *Teaching the Bible: The Discourses and Politics of Biblical Pedagogy*, repr., Eugene, Or: Wipf & Stock; originally published 1997.

Vaka'uta, Nasili (2011), *Reading Ezra 9–10 Tu'a-Wise: Rethinking Biblical Interpretation in Oceania*, IVBS; Atlanta: SBL Press.

CONTRIBUTORS

(Details about each contributor's context[s] can be found at the end of each essay)

Yairah Amit

Margaret Aymer

Mercedes L. Garcia Bachmann

Assnat Bartor

Athalya Brenner-Idan

Marc Zvi Brettler

Ora Brison

Kevin D. Chau

Lisa J. Cleath

Nancy L. DeClaissé-Walford

Sabine Dievenkorn

Musa W. Dube

Susan Gillingham

John Goldingay

Hemchand Gossai

Jione Havea

Wei Huang

Melody D. Knowles

Jennifer L. Koosed

Francis Landy

Mikael Larsson

Archie C.C. Lee

Helen Leneman

Diana Lipton

Vanessa Lovelace

Ingeborg Löwisch

Jonathan Magonet

Dominic Mattos

Monica Jyotsna Melanchthon

Roger S. Nam

Sivan Nir

Hugh R. Page, Jr.

Meira Polliack

D.N. Premnath

Barbara E. Reid

Adele Reinhartz

Yanjing Qu

Robert P. Seesengood

Gerrie Snyman

Klaas Spronk

Marvin A. Sweeney

Beth LaNeel Tanner

Lieve (G.M.G.) Teugels

Nicole L. Tilford

Ekaputra Tupamahu

Nāsili Vaka'uta

Gerald West

Gale A. Yee

ABBREVIATIONS

AB	Anchor Bible series
AOAT	Alter Orient und Altes Testament
ASV	American Standard Version
BDB	Francis Brown, S.R. Driver and Charles A. Briggs (eds), *A Hebrew and English Lexicon of the Old Testament* (Oxford: Clarendon Press, 1907)
BHS	*Biblia Hebraica Stuttgartensia* (ed. Karl Elliger and Wilhelm Rudolph; Stuttgart: Deutsche Bibelgesellschaft, 1983)
Bib	*Biblica*
BiOr	Biblica et Orientalia
CBQ	*The Catholic Biblical Quarterly*
CJB	Complete Jewish Bible
CUV	Chinese Union Version
ESV	English Standard Version
EvTh	Evangelische Theologie
FOTL	Forms of Old Testament Literature
HALOT	Ludwig Koehler and Walter Baumgartner (eds), *The Hebrew and Aramaic Lexicon of the Old Testament* (trans. M.E.J. Richardson; rev. W. Baumgartner and J.J. Stamm; Leiden: E.J. Brill, 1994–99)
HB	Hebrew Bible (TaNaKh)
HeBAI	*The Hebrew Bible and Ancient Israel*
HTR	Harvard Theological Review
HUCA	Hebrew Union College Annual
Int	*Interpretation*
IVSP	International Voices in Biblical Studies
JAOS	*Journal of the American Oriental Society*
JBL	*Journal of Biblical Literature*
JNES	*Journal of Near Eastern Studies*
JPS	Jewish Publication Society. *TANAKH: A New Translation of the Holy Scriptures according to the Traditional Hebrew Text* (Philadelphia and Jerusalem, 1985 and later editions. Also known as NJPS).
JRS	*Journal of Religion and Society*
JSIJ	*Electronic Journal for Jewish Studies* [Heb.]
JSOT	*Journal for the Study of the Old Testament*
JSOTSup	Journal for the Studies of the Old Testament: Supplement Series
KJV	King James Version
*LU*17	Neue Lutherbibel 2017, Stuttgart, Germany
LWF	Lutheran World Foundation

LXX	Septuagint, Greek Old Testament
m.	Mishnah
Mid. Teh.	*Midrash Tehillim*
MT	Masoretic Text
NCBC	New Cambridge Bible Commentary
NICOT	New International Commentary on the Old Testament
NIV	New International Version
NKJV	New King James Version
NRSV	New Revised Standard Version
NRSVue	New Revised Standard Version Updated Edition
NT	New Testament
OTE	*Old Testament Essays*
RB	*Revue Biblique*
RSV	Revised Standard Version
SBL	Society of Biblical Literature
SBLDS	Society of Biblical Literature Dissertation Series
t.	Talmud (*b.*, Babylonian Talmud; *y.*, Jerusalem Talmud)
VT	*Vetus Testamentum*
WBC	Word Biblical Commentary
WCS	Wisdom Commentary Series
YJS	Yale Judaica Series
ZAW	*Zeitschrift für die alttestamentliche Wissenschaft*

INTRODUCTION
FROM 'AŠREY (BLESSED* – PSALM 1.1) TO HALLELUJAH (PRAISE YAH – PSALM 150.6)

Athalya Brenner-Idan and Gale A. Yee

At the beginning of 2021 we, the editors of this volume, sent an email letter of invitation to write to numerous friends and colleagues. Parts of that letter, with few modifications, are produced here:

> This is to invite you to write a short piece to be published in an edited volume.
>
> As you may know, Archie C.C. Lee, Gale Yee and Athalya Brenner-Idan have been editing a series of volumes called Texts@Contexts, published by Bloomsbury/T&T Clark. So far, seven volumes have appeared and we're now busy soliciting articles about the book of *Psalms*, and we shall ask the Publishers to produce it as the eighth and final volume of the series.
>
> In all the T@C volumes we've presented essays of regular length (6000 words and over), written by scholars from all over the world, investigating the question of how their own personal membership in synchronous life communities – scholarly and non-scholarly – impacted their understanding of Hebrew Bible texts on the one hand, and their comprehension of their life experiences and contexts on the other.
>
> We had such essays lined up for the presently edited volume as well. But, for the second part of the volume, we wished to introduce another format of essays, and this is what I'm writing to you about, with an invitation to contribute. Meanwhile, The Publishers have agreed with our preference: to have only short essays in the forthcoming volume.

---

* In English and other Bible translations, *'ašrey* is variously translated as 'happy' or 'blessed', with linguistic arguments for other translations, such as 'affirmed', in Psalms scholarship.

We'd like to invite you, together with other invitees, to write a short piece, no more than 1500–2000 words, about a psalm that is your favorite, or that you dislike, or that has had a great influence on your life – a highly personal piece. The choice which psalm it will be is entirely yours. We hope you will present the psalm briefly in a scholarly fashion, then describe the life circumstances, as linked to the communities you inhabit and the identities you assume, that determine your choice. At the end, please mention in one sentence what would have been your second choice. As well, at the end of the piece, please state in a line or two your institutional and your contextual affiliations and your role in them.

We hope that you agree: so far, people we've spoken to have been quite enthusiastic about the idea from both the writing and later reading viewpoint. Having a sizeable collection of such articles, under the general heading 'MY' PSALM, seems to us a suitable finale to a series that is dedicated to scholarly work on the grid of life contexts.

The rationale behind this call is not difficult to uncover. We were hoping for many viewpoints, from many (therefore the essays had to be short!) scholars, about how their work and extra-work, emic and etic, grids interact. We wished to see how their life choices and conditions articulated their scholarly choices and vice versa, how the interpretation and usage of individual Psalms were conditioned by and had conditioned the contributors' lives; in short, we wanted to see what *My Psalm, My Context* (which is now the name of the volume) truly means. There's no dearth of faith-based and scholarly exegesis of the psalms, nor of formal and informal usage in various (semi-)liturgical contexts. However, we were hoping for more in-depth personal statements on the boundary of the professional and personal.

To our delight, most invitees professed interest in this project, and the result is this volume: about 50 essays written by scholars from all over the world and different walks of life, experience and interests, age and gender, location and groups. All the participants are either Jewish or Christians of various degrees or born as such and turned secular[ist]; we regret that we were unable to include essays by contributors from originally other religious affiliations.

Each contributor's 'voice' is of course unique and represents its writer more than the networks this writer occupies or is affiliated with. The views expressed in this collection are not representative of the networks contributors are affiliated with. Our wish as editors was to include as large a variety of viewpoints as possible. Nevertheless, and in spite of vast differences in contributors' self-defined contexts, certain patterns emerge.

Popularity

Some psalms were more popular than others, either as first and elaborated choice, or as second choice. Those are, in the biblical order:

- **8** ('How majestic is Your name throughout the earth');
- **23** ('The LORD is my shepherd; I lack nothing');
- **90** ('O LORD, You have been our refuge in every generation');
- **104** ('Bless the LORD, O my soul; O LORD, my God, You are very great');
- **121** ('I turn my eyes to the mountains; from where will my help come?');
- **126** ('When the LORD restores the fortunes of Zion – we see it as in a dream');
- **127** ('Unless the LORD builds the house, its builders labor in vain on it');
- **137** ('By the rivers of Babylon, there we sat, sat and wept, as we thought of Zion');
- and **150** ('Hallelujah').

(All translations here from the JPS)

Major Themes and Motifs Heightened

Here we shall briefly describe several themes that are repeated by contributors, which overlap community membership and are shared. Such themes or motifs are at times unique to community membership, at others pointing to concerns beyond such communities. To a broad degree, the recurrence of such discussions is inspired by the Psalms texts themselves. However, it will be seen how concerns and issues are shared across milieus. The themes will not be listed in order of importance, and each will be illustrated by a reference to specific articles in this collection.

Contributions may certainly have more than one thematic strand to them, and it may be a matter of individual readerly impression under which heading to catalogue them.

Music: Singing, Melody, Instruments, Libretto as against Recitation and Silent Reading

The non-Hebrew name of this collection, 'Psalms' or 'Psalter' or the like, is highly appropriate, denoting musical poems (poems with melody, can be sung and played). In the Hebrew Bible, the book is not named, although in later rabbinic traditions and further it is referred to as *Tehillim*, 'praises'. In the book itself, only the librettos (so to speak) are preserved; the music, the performance, is largely lost, although much researched over the centuries (not to mention newly composed music to Psalms texts). And yet, the original musical character of the collection is traceable through words in many individual psalms. The verbs שיר, *šīr Qal* and זמר, *zmr Piel* – 'sing' (with music) – appear in many psalms. The nouns מזמור, *mizmōr*, and שיר, *šīr*, even both together, occur in six instances, only in this biblical book.[1] Chapters 121–134 are a block introduced by the superscription

---

1. The noun *mizmōr* occurs 57 times in the whole Bible, all in the Psalms. The noun *šīr* occurs 87 times, mostly in the Psalms. The combined noun phrase, *mizmōr šīr*, occurs 6 times and is unique to psalm superscriptions (Pss. 30.1; 67.1; 68.1; 87.1; 92.1; 98.1). While

שיר המעלות, *šīr hammaʻălōt*, 'song of ascents'.[2] The concentration of information gleaned from the naming of musical instruments, especially string and percussion instruments, expands our knowledge of musical instrumentality in biblical times tremendously,[3] even if we do not always identify fully the instruments themselves. Even superscriptions whose exact meanings elude us point to modes of performance, conductors, and possibly mysterious or lost instruments.[4]

In today's practice, psalms outside liturgical occasions are mostly read and recited without music, unless they are intentionally reworked as such. In this volume, though, we can discern much interest in the musical properties of the psalms for their contemporary consumers: more for their usage today than for the definition of their performances in antiquity.

Many contributors in this collection discuss Psalms as music, not just as 'poetry'. For Athalya Brenner-Idan, Psalm 71 recalls musical renderings that deal with the travails of old age, that plead with the deity not to 'dump' her in her old age. Versions of this psalm have been adapted by a number of Israeli songwriters, and Brenner-Idan finds its British counterpart in Paul McCartney's 'When I'm Sixty-Four'. As a cantor and classically trained singer, Helen Leneman demonstrates how different musical versions of Psalm 121 enhance different aspects of the psalm, focusing particularly on compositions by Shlomo Carlebach and Gershon Ephros. Hugh Page approaches the peculiarities of Psalm 68 through harmolodic theory, a theory of approaching jazz and blues composition that places harmony, melody, and rhythm on equal footing. Applied to this psalm (but also others), this musical theory will open the door into understanding complementary form and structure, rather than relying solely on diagnoses made in traditional Psalms scholarship.

Emphasis on Scholarly Considerations

Like Hugh Page, other scholars too try to suggest new solutions for Psalms issues that occupy them in their life work. Thus, Francis Landy analyzes the poetics of Psalm 8 in detail, and points out how this analysis contributes to the psalm's message and contents, that is, the infinite mystery of the Creation and God's creative power, the magnificence of the world, and the resulting human condition in it. Robert Seesengood and Jennifer Koosed apply their various overlapping personal contexts to Psalm 19. They first supply a short scholarly analysis, then the liturgical context of a mixed Jewish-Christian lifestyle, then into the faith context,

---

it can be argued that psalm superscriptions are editorial and do not belong to the actual psalms they head, the numerous occurrences of 'sing' and stated calls to use accompanying musical instruments are telling.

2. A variation is Ps. 121.1, which reads *šīr lammaʻălōt*.

3. Cf. for instance Pss. 33.2-3; 57.9; 81.34; 92.4; 108.3; 144.9; 149.3; 150.3-5. Various musical instruments are mentioned all over the Bible. However, the only other concentrated parallel is to be found in Dan. 3.5-10.

4. Cf. superscriptions to Pss. 4, 5, 6, 7, 8, 68.

and back into the poetics of the psalm. Klaas Spronk suggests a new interpretation to what he names 'the riddle' of Psalm 49. Yairah Amit looks again at the poetics of Psalm 104. And Susan Gillingham gives us a rich review of Psalm 91's interpretation together with the psalm's afterlives in historical and contemporary Christianity and Judaism. For Marvin Sweeney, the early encounter with Psalm 121 spurred a life-long scholarly career in the Hebrew Bible as an expression of Jewish identity and Hebrew as a living language of the Jewish people.

Ritual and Liturgical Use of Psalms

Vanessa Lovelace picked Psalm 100 to discuss because of its significance as an exuberant call to worship in African American churches as they gather on Sunday mornings. Adele Reinhartz chose Psalm 126 because she has recited this psalm many times. It serves as the introduction to the blessing after meals (*birkat ha-māzōn*) after each of the three Shabbath meals (dinner on Friday evening, lunch and supper on Saturday) and throughout the year on the festivals. According to Ora Brison, the popularity of Psalm 121 is part of the Return to Judaism phenomenon in Israel. Because of its message of divine protection and guidance, it is the psalm most frequently recited, set to music not only in liturgy but also by trendy pop singers. As an observant Jew who has sung Psalm 114 in many Jewish festivals, Marc Brettler loves the way that the psalm resists and protests the stories that the Torah relates. Because of her fascination with the lists she finds in literary works, poems, and fiction, Diana Lipton gravitates toward the lists of God's great deeds that he has done for Israel in Psalm 136. Introducing the *Hallel* psalms (Pss. 113–118) to be sung in her synagogue in Cambridge, Lipton composed a tune for the Great Hallel, Psalm 136, because it cries out to be sung in the repetition of כי לעולם חסדו, 'for His steadfast love is eternal' (JPS), at the end of each verse.

House/Home: Past, Present and Future

As she exclaims in her piece, Musa Dube and Psalm 23 'go back a long way', meeting first in primary school in her home country Botswana. She recalls being a shepherd caring for her parents' sheep and goats on their farm, knowing the dangers that confront a shepherd – but also the assurance of being shepherded, of dwelling in God's house, all the days of her life. Meira Polliack proceeds from 'Even a bird finds a home' (Ps. 84.4 MT) to discuss what a 'home', not only God's home (the Jerusalem Temple, v. 1), means – especially for Jews and migrating Jews, discussing in this framework Freud and Herzl, and the trajectory of ongoing Zionism. In a psalm that begins 'Unless the Lord builds the house, those who build it labor in vain', Sabine Dievenkorn reflects, over the years, on the meaning of *He giveth unto His beloved in sleep* (Ps. 127.2, JPS Tanakh 1917), that became a refrain which her grandmother would offer during Dievenkorn's travails in her childhood home. Gale Yee also sees interconnections among house, home, and family especially with labor in their rural and urban settings in Psalms 127–128. Writing a book-length study on Psalm 132 took Melody Knowles physically to many different places which she would call 'home', both in the US and abroad. Empathizing with the harsh experiences of the exiles in Babylon, Hemchand Gossai resonates deeply with Psalm 137 because of his immigrant memories of a home that brought tears and nostalgia of a time that was lost, snatched away. Psalm 139 served as a life-long support and guide as Margaret Aymer immigrated from one home in the Caribbean to another in New Jersey and many places thereafter. Issues of migration and memories of home and base changes also feature largely in Nāsili Vaka'uta's essay, and in others.

Ecology, Nature and Creation

For Nicole Tilford, Psalm 8 sings of the beauty and vastness of creation but causes her to reflect on the abuse and violence that humans inflict upon it in their God-given 'dominion' over it (Gen. 1.26-28). Because Nancy L. DeClaissé-Walford grew up in a farming community, she too extolls the wonders of nature, as found in Psalm 104. For her, however, before her family farmed the land, this land had belonged to the Shawnee Native American tribe. Long before she encountered the land, it was someone else's 'firm grounding'. Also through Psalm 104, Gerrie Snyman confronts his own complicity as a descendant of white immigrants in post-apartheid South Africa by comparing it with the Indian Mynah, an aggressive alien bird that has also made its own home there in Snyman's own garden.

Prayer as Comfort

Often recited at (Christian) funerals, the simplicity and brevity of Psalm 23 provides a message of comfort for the bereaved. Lieve Teugels focuses on the theme of God as shepherd who provides, restores, and leads, and David as the shepherd boy, who is attributed authorship and is the recipient of God's ministrations.

Finding Strength during the Covid-19 Pandemic, 2020–

Three scholars wrote on psalms from their contexts during the Covid-19 pandemic. For Beth LaNeel Tanner, Psalm 46 offered support while she witnessed multiple deaths in her seminary community outside of New York City. She also uses the Covid-19 pandemic situation as an entry into her discussion of the psalm in the framework of war, social injustice, and feminist direction. As a member of the emergency care team in Hamburg, Germany, Ingeborg Löwisch found that family and friends were not able to visit, care for, or even say goodbye to their loved ones. Her parish decided to perform a ritual commemorating the dead, during which Psalm 126 provided an emotional space for consolation. Through an interpretive lens he calls *reStorying*, Jione Havea relates Psalm 146 with the 15 January 2022 volcanic eruption and the tsunami that followed that wracked the islands Hunga Tonga and Hunga Ha'apai. When these events occurred, Tonga had been free of

Covid-19, but it came in the bodies of the humanitarian aid that flew in to help, reminding the Tongans of their colonial past, 'when the carriers of the Christian good news also infected Pasifika bodies with viruses and pandemics, among many other disgraces and "shitstems".'

Social and Political Concerns

The discovery of Psalm 20 in Papyrus Amherst 63, a fourth-century text written in Demotic script, in the city of Luxor, Egypt, prompts Roger Nam to speculate on the psalm's five-hundred-mile journey from Jerusalem to Luxor, his own family's trans-Pacific immigration history from Korea to the United States, and the traumatic experiences of migrants in today's world. D.N. Premnath reads Psalm 37 through the eyes of his Indian Christian grandmother who lived among a Hindu majority that was often hostile to converts. Through Psalm 106's emphasis on Israel's ancestors, Lisa Cleath reflects on her own mixed-raced ancestral heritage of Chinese and Scandinavian descent and the conflicted histories of both: white immigrants occupying and possessing indigenous land, and the Chinese immigrants trying to assimilate and be accepted by a white culture that marginalizes them. After reading Psalm 121 as a teenager amid anti-apartheid protests, Gerald West revisits it as a linguist and biblical scholar, discovering both a liberative economic-oriented reading of the psalm and its performative appropriations by his West African biblical colleagues in post-apartheid South Africa. For Assnat Bartor, 'those who sow shall reap in tears' (126.4-5) conveys the experiences of Palestinian farmers who see their fields and orchards looted and burned unjustly by Israeli soldiers, police, and settlers. She is one of the farmers' lawyers from a human rights NGO, which argues cases where legal and human rights violations occur against Palestinians in the Occupied Territories.

Issues of Personal Safety, Helplessness, Protest, and Faith

John Goldingay opens our volume with a discussion of Psalm 6, which chronicles a wave of diverse emotions (plea, protest, anger, discipline, weariness, and deliverance) that he reads through the experience of his wife's physical illness. Reflecting on the psalmist's self-imposed silence and his desire to cry out in Psalm 39, Mercedes L. García Bachmann sees parallels between women who may incur death if they speak out in abused relationships and her role as a pastor to help make their voices heard. The challenges of daily life and human temporal existence, and human–God relationship, are the subject of Jonathan Magonet's discussion of Psalm 90, from the viewpoints of a Rabbi, teacher of Bible and former principal of the Leo Baeck rabbinical college. Barbara Reid discusses the unique, shortest, one-verse Psalm 117 as a source of comfort in the changing religious space of her calling and the contemporary cultural scene.

Justice, Life Politics, and Faith

King David's confession in Psalm 51 after raping Bathsheba and ordering her husband's death (2 Sam. 11–12) prompts Mikael Larsson to reflect upon the formation of his own masculinity as a child of missionaries in the Congo. Even encountering and embracing feminism as a call for justice at university and raising his children, he still struggles with that part of toxic masculinity that he shares with David. In Psalm 73, Indonesian immigrant Ekaputra Tupamahu observes the struggle between 'I', the person of faith, with the reality of the wicked who seem to prosper. Amid the messiness of this personal reality, he/'I' will prevail because of his 'nearness to God'. Nāsili Vaka'uta reads Psalm 137 from the standpoint of the Tongan notion of *kau'i-talanoa*, a means of speaking by which the powerless, the excluded, the oppressed, the marginalized, and the ignored tell their stories. Their voices are needed to respond to the violence in their midst, especially against women and children. For Monica Melanchthon, the theme of 'eyes' in Psalm 123 reminds her of the all-seeing eyes of Hindu and Dalit deities whose gaze upon their believers can be favorable or destructive. For Dalit worshippers, the gaze of the psalm's gracious God will equip the worshippers with the power to resist the contempt and scorn that has been poured out upon them.

Comparative Readings with other Literary Works

Archie C.C. Lee, Wei Huang, and Yanjing Qu compare their chosen psalms with works from Chinese literature. Lee reads the royal politics embedded in Psalm 78's narrative of Israel's history with the politicizing of the Chinese Mandate of Heaven to legitimate the changeover from the Shang to Zhou dynasties. Huang compares the powerful emotions conveyed in Chinese ballads, poems, and operas with the passionate cries and longings of Psalm 137. Qu's first encounter with Psalm 90 was its translation in the Chinese Union Version (CUV), which utilizes Chinese words that have rich meanings in a Chinese culture, rooted in Buddhism and the Confucian *Analects*.

Studies of Psalms through other Doors

In Psalm 18, Sivan Nir sees possible allusions to Odysseus' bow through his ventures into both rabbinic literature and Homer. Utilizing his previous background in STEM (Science, Technology, Engineering, Math), Kevin Chau was able to unlock the poetry of Psalm 118. As an Asian American, Chau has found fellowship with other Asian American Hebrew Bible scholars who also had training in STEM.

From the Verbal to the Non-verbal Vocal

It seems like an amazing editorial decision to place, at the end of the Hebrew Bible Psalms collection, a text that calls for Yhwh's praise in the 'voices' of loud and clanky musical instruments: in music, but not in words; in notes, but without libretto – whereas the rest of the collection, even as singing and instrumental music performances are fairly present, is actually devoted to the librettos. In that sense, Psalm 150 is surprising and may even, in some circumstances, deconstruct the necessity of the big collection at whose end it is placed.

Dominic Mattos concludes our volume with a reflection on this final psalm. He writes from the perspective of a professional musician and singer, and from a very personal relationship with an aunt who sang with gusto in a learning disability group. For her and for him, singing this psalm was an act of worship. For all of us, this is a reminder to stop and reflect on the verbal vs. the non-verbal, the wordless vs. the voiced, in the Psalms and beyond.

* * *

Our eighth and final Texts@Contexts volume, then, is an intentionally incomplete mosaic or, if you wish, a complex puzzle of personal views on individual psalms, within diverse communities occupied by Bible scholars. Accordingly, its cover image is a rich tapestry, or collage, of bursting colours in exuberant complexity, much like the volume taken as a whole. It was made by a painter, Lucilla Gardner, with learning disabilities. Like this volume, it can be titled *Hallelujah*.

To sum up, we, the editors, would like to add some personal notes from our own experience of very different contexts (of origin, religion, and location, among other factors) to the general picture. We both share a life-long work in biblical scholarship, and from this shared context would like to add some personal reflections.

Gale was originally Roman Catholic and later became Episcopalian. For her, psalms in the Christian tradition were encountered especially in the chants and antiphons of daily morning prayer at Episcopal Divinity School (EDS), in its eucharistic liturgies, and particularly teaching the psalms to its students, exposing them to the huge variety of psalms set to music. Students would bring their favorite musical renditions of psalms, which she played at the beginning of each class. Some of these included Bob Marley's reggae version[5] and Boney M's Caribbean version[6] of Psalm 137; Bobby McFerrin's feminization of Psalm 23,[7] and U2's rendition of Psalm 40.[8] Kendall Payne belts out a passionate version of Psalm 40 in 'Wait'.[9] One session was taught with the EDS music director who introduced the students to singing various musical modes of psalms. Gale had all students write their own psalms from their particular contexts, giving as a model her own one patterned after Psalm 136 (in the Bible: 'Oh give thanks to the

---

5. See https://www.youtube.com/watch?v=MipmMg-bCPQ (accessed 1 January 2023).
6. See https://www.youtube.com/watch?v=l3QxT-w3WMo (accessed 1 January 2023).
7. See https://www.youtube.com/watch?v=o9fzWq-d8jU&fmt=18 (accessed 1 January 2023).
8. See https://www.youtube.com/watch?v=U_Lc2jtd80Y (accessed 1 January 2023).
9. See https://www.youtube.com/watch?v=z8V7x5fqsB8 (accessed 1 January 2023).

LORD, for he is good', NRSVue), which chronicled the history of Asian Americans in the US context.[10] These psalms were gathered in a publication that Gale gave to the students as a remembrance. Her students also developed a liturgy of lament that was performed at one of the seminary worship services, during which Gale preached on Psalm 137. Gale often spent weekend retreats at Benedictine monastic communities. These monasteries recited or sang the psalms during morning, noontime, and evening prayer. The entire Psalter was prayed every three to four weeks.

It is particularly in music that the psalms make their mark in the Christian tradition. The most notable is Gregorian chant, developed in Europe during the ninth and tenth centuries. Here the psalms were monophonic, sung in Latin, unaccompanied, in male and female choirs of religious orders. Linked here is an example of Gregorian Chant for Psalm 23.[11] The beautiful polyphonic version of Psalm 51 is found in Gregorio Allegri's *Misereri* sung by the Tallis singers.[12] Allegri composed this nine-part *a capella* polyphony for the use in the Sistine Chapel during Holy Week in 1638 CE. During and after Vatican II,[13] Jesuit priest Joseph Gelineau translated the psalmody into the vernacular and provided simple, singable song tones to replace Gregorian chant. The Gelineau version of Psalm 23 is linked here.[14] This is only a sample of the richness of psalms in music in the Christian traditional liturgy.

Athalya is Jewish and a secular[ist] Israeli, which means in her community context that religious texts are known not only as such but as cultural, 'tribal' texts. She makes the following observations.

Many psalms that are used in prayer, for instance those recited in daily and festival prayers or Passover, are encountered by Jews/Israelis before their textual origin as biblical psalms is known. Similarly, much like other biblical passages and especially biblical poetry (such as Song of Songs texts), many psalms are set to popular music, hence we 'know' them (as well as other biblical texts) before we realize their biblical origin. Also, Jerusalem has a central place in the value system of Jews and Israelis (and not only). The same holds for King David. Again: not everybody would recognize lyrics that were lifted from the Psalms as from the actual psalms themselves.

---

10. See the Appendix to this Introduction for Gale's psalm itself. On Ps. 136 see also Lipton's essay in this volume, pp. 226–30.

11. See https://www.youtube.com/watch?v=Qs_VsVSMvak (accessed 1 January 2023).

12. See https://www.youtube.com/watch?feature=player_embedded&v=nKj1iK2WKS8 (accessed 1 January 2023).

13. The second ecumenical council of the Roman Catholic Church, meeting in eight to twelve sessions, each year from 1962 to 1965.

14. See https://www.youtube.com/watch?v=me4utPKJBZA (accessed 1 January 2023).

There certainly is a general if hazy knowledge that psalms are integrated not only into the daily and festival liturgy, but that they also serve many therapeutic, magical, and other functions in orthodox communities, as present in all life events. This seeps into the secular communities. The call for reciting psalms or reading them communally in order to avert illness, bad luck, or catastrophe is shared with many a secular person, in the sense of 'if it doesn't help at least it won't hurt'. The same applies to a daily recitation of individual psalms (as prescribed for specific weekdays or on a monthly cycle), as a quick daily activity, even by people who do not practice daily prayer.

An extended and telling example is the following. Even non-religious Jews mostly resort to religious, that is, Jewish-Orthodox burial ceremonies. Such a ceremony includes a recitation of seven psalms. First Psalms 33, 16, 17, 72, 104, 130 are recited in this order. Then follows a peculiar usage of the long and acrostic Psalm 119 (22 stanzas, each containing eight verses beginning with the same letter of the Hebrew alphabet): the letters of the deceased's first name are highlighted by repeating the relevant alphabetically tagged verses of the psalm – eight verses for each letter that represents a consonant in speech. My father's name was בנימין (pronounced *Binyamin*, English 'Benjamin'). The officiating Rabbi therefore recited 48 verses from Psalm 119 at the grave: eight verses for each of the Hebrew letters /bet/ (ב), and eight verses for /mem/ (מ). And he recited twice, in their order in my father's name, the eight verses beginning with the Hebrew letter /yod/ (י), and twice with the eight verses beginning with the letter /nun/ (נ). All this recitation precedes the prayer for the deceased, the קדיש (*kaddish*): standing at the grave side and listening, while mostly not being aware of the source of such long (or short, depending on the length of the deceased person's name) recitation, results in an uncomfortable affair. Whoever in Israel chooses a Jewish burial, and this is the norm even for secular people (although other options are now available), is exposed to this practice, mostly without realizing that psalms are recited.

And finally: there is a Hassidic story, known in many versions, of the uneducated or autistic boy who cannot pray the words in a synagogue service, but eventually lets out a shout or a wordless melody on a musical instrument, and the Rabbi declares that this action opens the gates of heaven.[15] Another version has a Jewish peddler stranded in a forest on Shabbath eve, without a *minyan* to join for prayer and without knowledge of how to pray, who is called from heaven to simply shout; and there are more. This notion of wordless, silent in a way but not voiceless or soundless, has become a cultural motto of wordless prayer protest.

---

15. This story has many versions and analyses. Cf. for instance https://thegemara.com/article/the-baal-shem-tov-and-the-boy-who-played-flute-on-yom-kippur/; or https://www.jta.org/2019/09/19/ny/the-boy-and-the-flute-the-tale-retold, for a boy who prays by playing the flute for lack of education and ability and the rabbi's approval (accessed 1 January 2023).

This is not a story about performing a psalm, but about voiced but non-verbal prayer. And yet, it fits in perfectly with Psalm 150 and its call: it is no less than astounding that after 149 chapters of verbosity, some with minute instructions for musical performance (that we do not fully understand), we are told, as a climax: just shut up, stop talking, glorify God by playing music. In short: the psalms are in Israeli culture, whether its adherents are aware of it or otherwise.

APPENDIX
AN ASIAN AMERICAN PSALM MODELED AFTER PSALM 136

Gale A. Yee

Give thanks to the Lord for she is good
    For her steadfast love endures forever
Give thanks to the God of gods,
    For her steadfast love endures forever

Who led thousands of men from the coasts of China
    For her steadfast love endures forever
To cross the Pacific to land in Gold Mountain
    For her steadfast love endures forever
To escape the corruption of the Manchu government
    For her steadfast love endures forever
To bring them to settle in California
    For her steadfast love endures forever
And the Pacific Northwest where my granddad ended
    For her steadfast love endures forever
To work in the mines and the coast-to-coast rails
    For her steadfast love endures forever
Becoming houseboys and laundry men
    For her steadfast love endures forever
And 'heathen Chinee' with 'No tickee, no washee'.
    For her steadfast love endures forever
They wept along with their women back home
    For her steadfast love endures forever
And those sexual slaves who were forced into service
    For her steadfast love endures forever
God wept during the Chinese Exclusion Act
    For her steadfast love endures forever
While the men were stereotyped as the Yellow Peril,
    For her steadfast love endures forever
And as Fu Manchu and Charlie Chan
    For her steadfast love endures forever
And as Ming the Merciless from the planet Mongo

    For her steadfast love endures forever
And the women as Dragon Lady and O'Lan,
    For her steadfast love endures forever
And Lotus Blossom and Suzie Wong
    For her steadfast love endures forever.
China doll, exotic mail order bride
    For her steadfast love endures forever
A sexual fetish for white males
    For her steadfast love endures forever

We protested the musical Miss Saigon
    For her steadfast love endures forever
With its white actors in yellow face
    For her steadfast love endures forever
We became model minorities and perpetual foreigners
    For her steadfast love endures forever
But she remembered us in our low estate
    For her steadfast love endures forever
And rescued us from our enemies
    For her steadfast love endures forever

O give thanks to the God of heaven
    For her steadfast love endures forever!
Give thanks to the God of gods,
    For her steadfast love endures forever!

PSALM 6
PLEA, PROTEST, ANGER, DISCIPLINE, WEARINESS, DELIVERANCE

John Goldingay

Psalm 6 is a textbook example of a lament psalm, or protest psalm, as I prefer to call them. While lament is a key element in these psalms, it's not the whole, and lament doesn't need an audience, whereas protest implies that someone is the recipient of the remonstration. These psalms are addressed to someone; people are not just letting it all hang out. Typical of such psalms, Psalm 6 thus begins by addressing God, and urging God to do something; it is a prayer. And it argues and reasons with God. Then, before the end, it suddenly expresses the conviction that God has listened to this plea and is going to answer it. It has a heading with information addressed to the 'leader', that it is a psalm of 'David' and how to sing it; the terms of the description are something of a mystery, but they do indicate that what reads like an individual's prayer found a place in the community's worship.

Fifty years ago, I met a girl, fell in love with her, and in due course married her. But in between those two events we learned that Ann had multiple sclerosis. We then lived with that reality for over forty years. For the last few years, she was wheelchair-bound and unable to do anything or to speak. It was obviously tough for her and for her parents and for our children; and for me. And I learned to pray psalms such as this one. Admittedly, Psalm 6 issues a plea for deliverance from enemies (v. 7 [8]), and although I can occasionally feel resentful towards a reviewer whose critique seems unfair, I don't really have enemies. But the rest of the psalm resonates for me. I know what it's like to be 'weary with my moaning' and to 'melt my couch with my weeping' (v. 6 [7]; translations in this study are my own).

I have used Psalm 6 in classes as a typical lament/protest psalm, and there are one or two questions it then properly raises. One is that its opening talk of Yahweh's anger (v. 1 [2]) doesn't imply that the person praying acknowledges that they've done something to deserve that anger; if it had implied that assumption, it ought to do some confession of wrongdoing. Its implication is more that Yahweh sometimes behaves like someone who is angry, and one doesn't know why. The psalm does ask that Yahweh may not discipline me in a way that suggests anger. In due course I myself had to acknowledge that I couldn't have complained if God had been angry at my waywardness. Although I stuck with Ann through those decades, I got closer to more than one woman than I should have done. So in an odd way, the psalm's initial but incidental reference to anger and its unobtrusive raising of the question about waywardness became important for me.

But the psalm's reference to anger links with its reference to discipline: it urges, 'Don't discipline me in a way that suggests anger' (v. 1 [2]). It thus points to the idea that recurs in Proverbs, that discipline is important if one is to grow. Yahweh is not so much like a judge who punishes Israel, but like a father or mother disciplining and correcting their children with a view to taking them to maturity. Athletes get nowhere if they fail to punish themselves and even subject themselves to punishing regimes from their trainers. Living with Ann's illness disciplined me. It shaped me as a person. If anyone thinks I am a rogue now, they should imagine what I would be if it had not been for that discipline.

During those decades, I might have been appropriately inclined to say to God, 'Give me a break' (and he often did), rather than to say, 'Don't discipline me at all'. I guess I did think, 'Please stop disciplining me', but on a good day I might say, 'Okay, discipline is necessary, but go easy – not in your anger'. As the psalm puts it, 'Be gracious to me, because I'm faint' (v. 2 [3]). Or as it later puts it, 'Deliver me for the sake of your commitment', your *ḥesed*, that faithfulness of yours that never gives up (v. 4 [5]). I didn't assume that Yahweh deliberately sent this hard experience to Ann and thus to me. Psalms and Proverbs, again, do speak of Yahweh deliberately doing such things, but sometimes speak of tough experiences simply being the way life is, without commenting on causation. The scriptures do then suggest that Yahweh can take tough things that happen and turn them into things that have some meaning, by what he achieves through them. He did that for me, and he did it for Ann through the strange ministry she came to have towards people in her disability. But the discipline did become something that made me weary, as the psalm says, and made me weep and made my eyes waste away (v. 7 [8]), with longing for… Well, I don't know what I longed for. I stopped hoping that one day God would miraculously heal Ann, and I wasn't hoping for the day she would die (and when she did die, as far as I can tell I felt as much grief as anyone does when their lover dies).

Deliver me, the psalm pleads, 'because there's no celebrating of you in death; in Sheol who can confess you?' (v. 5 [6]). I am writing in the days after Easter, which for a Christian both does and does not make a difference to that argument of the psalm. The psalmist knew the truth about death. When you die, your family puts your lifeless body in the family tomb, where you join other lifeless people. Israelites hypothesized (perhaps based on occasional experiences of contact with dead people, such as the Saul and Samuel story illustrates [1 Sam. 28]), that your also-lifeless personality joined other lifeless personalities in a non-physical equivalent to the family tomb, called Sheol. You are secure and at rest there in the company of your family, as your outer person is in the tomb. But in Sheol there is no celebrating of Yahweh, partly because you can't worship unless you have a body – it requires hands and feet and a voice. And there is no confessing of Yahweh, because confessing means talking about what Yahweh has done, and Yahweh doesn't do anything in Sheol.

In due course, many Jewish people came to believe that there would eventually be a resurrection and that Sheol would not be the end, and Jesus apparently accepted that assumption in speaking of God being (still) the God of Abraham, Isaac, and Jacob; they must therefore still be alive, then, mustn't they? (Mk 12.26-27). As a Pharisee, Paul would have held that belief, and in due course he became convinced that Jesus has already been resurrected and that his resurrection signifies the beginning of that broad resurrection of Israel, and of other people who get adopted into Israel. It thus makes it possible for anyone who might otherwise be skeptical to believe in the prospect of resurrection. But meanwhile, the psalm is right; if resurrection will come in due course, that doesn't alter the reality of what happens in the meantime. We are all destined for a long sleep.

In connection with Sheol, the psalm likely carries another implication. 'Turn, save, deliver' (v. 4 [5]), the suppliant pleads. When psalms testify to Yahweh having turned, rescued, and delivered, they can say that Yahweh brought me up from Sheol (Ps. 30.3 [4]). It's as if the experience of oppression, persecution, separation from God, or pain is an anticipatory experience of being in Sheol. It wouldn't be surprising if the psalmist implicitly pictures things that way. But three-quarters of the way through, a dramatic change comes over Psalm 6. Suddenly, it urges the enemies to go away, 'because Yahweh has listened to the sound of my weeping. Yahweh has listened to my prayer for grace. Yahweh receives my plea' (6.8-9 [9-10]). When such a change of tone occurs in psalms, occasionally they imply that someone such as a priest or prophet has brought a message from Yahweh, assuring the suppliant that Yahweh has heard the prayer; and I have occasionally been on the receiving end of such a message or been the means of giving one. But more often the sense of having been heard has come to me directly from God rather than via a human messenger, and I imagine the psalm presupposing the same dynamic. One evening at the end of a particularly tough week, after I had helped Ann get to bed, I slumped on the sofa, spent. I can't remember exactly what I said to God, but I do remember then being overwhelmed by a sense of God embracing me, perhaps like a father or mother embracing their child. And I could unwind and in due course sleep in a relaxed way. I picture that as an experience of the kind that took the psalmist from 'my whole body shakes in great dismay' to 'Yahweh has listened'.

While the extraordinary transition that takes place in Psalm 6 could happen within ordinary experience, there is also another version of it. When Ann died, it meant that I was alone, and needed just to get used to it. There was an occasion a year after her death when I took my bike and some *JSOT* Supplements to the beach, and as I lay in the sand reading, I thought to myself, 'I can do this, this being on my own'. A couple of months later I met Kathleen and fell in love and we married, and thus I found a new life. It was another expression of God listening to my prayer for grace.

It also led in due course to my finding new significance in the psalm's reference to enemies. The heading of the psalm points to the likelihood that ideally you don't pray protest psalms on your own; your family and friends pray them with you, maybe when you come to the temple to pray and offer a sacrifice. In that setting, as a member of the family you might pray about the suppliant's enemies as if they were your enemies, because you identify with the suppliant. Thus, protest psalms can become psalms you pray on behalf of other people in need. Kathleen's daughter, Katie-Jay, gave a dozen years of her life to working among Darfuri refugees in Chad, and a psalm such as Psalm 6 became the way we prayed for the Darfuri and against their oppressors. (Katie-Jay and her husband Gabriel were killed in an auto accident in Los Angeles a few months ago, which has given us another reason for protesting in the manner of the protest psalms.)

My second-choice psalm might have been Psalm 30, which pairs nicely with Psalm 6 as a thanksgiving or testimony psalm that could have been the kind you used when you came back to give praise and testify, when Yahweh had answered your prayer. I find students are inclined to think that the person who says 'I will never fall down' (30.6-7 [7-8]) must be showing an inappropriate self-confidence (they like to compare this person with the Pharisee in the parable in Lk. 18.9-14), and I try to get them to see that the psalm is usefully ambiguous and that it is important to recognize that people who are confident that God has made them strong like a mountain are not necessarily wrong to think in that way; it's probably how I felt before Ann got ill.

John Goldingay is a Senior Professor of Old Testament at Fuller Theological Seminary, Pasadena, California and a retired Anglican priest, living in Oxford, England.

We have written further about all this in:

Goldingay, John (2006), *Psalms Volume 1*, Grand Rapids: Baker.
Goldingay, John (2013), *Psalms for Everyone Part One*, Louisville: Westminster John Knox.
Goldingay, John (2011), *Remembering Ann*, Carlisle, UK: Piquant.
Goldingay Scott, Kathleen and John Goldingay (2014, 2015), 'The Sting in the Psalms', *Theology* 117: 403–10.
Goldingay Scott, Kathleen and John Goldingay (2015), 'The Sting in the Psalms', *Theology* 118: 3–9.

PSALM 8
THE POOR AND THE EARTH CRY OUT

Nicole L. Tilford

Every summer, my family vacations in western North Carolina. Among the spots we frequent is Buck Bald, a drivable mountain just across the Tennessee border. Buck Bald has a flat, grassy clearing at the top. On a nice day, you can enjoy 360-degree mountain vistas with very little sign of human habitation. During the summer, you'll frequently find young families rolling in the grass, church groups singing praise and worship, and elderly couples enjoying a quiet night by the campfire. In the evening, the entire sky lights up with brilliant colors, and a calm settles in as visitors still their energies to watch the setting sun. In those moments, removed from the cares of daily life, my mind frequently drifts to Psalm 8, and it is easy to proclaim with the psalmist, 'how majestic'! (8.1).[1]

Against that broad expanse of sky and mountain, it is also easy to feel smaller, insignificant. With the psalmist, I ask myself, 'When I look at your heavens, the work of your fingers… What are humans that you are mindful of them, mortals that you care for them?' (8.3-4). The psalmist provides a comforting answer: despite how insignificant we might feel, God has made each person 'a little lower than אלהים and crowned them with glory and honor' (8.5).[2] A comforting thought, a moment of self-affirmation.

I'd prefer to stop there, to linger in that moment, for what comes next in the psalm is harder to digest. Humans, we are told, are given 'dominion' over the works of God's hands; 'all things [are] under their feet' (8.6). Dominion. Such a

---

1. Biblical translations follow the NRSVue (updated edition 2021), including the verse numbering. For the text of Ps. 8, see for instance https://www.bibleodyssey.org/bibles?SearchText=psalm%208.

2. The Hebrew term אלהים, ᵉlohîm, can be used as a proper name for the Israelite god or as a generic term for deities. The term is grammatically plural, and in later traditions it came to be interpreted as a reference to a divine council that accompanies God and, by extension, as a reference to angels rather than true deities. I leave it untranslated here to allow for this multiplicity of meaning. For a discussion of this term and how it affects New Testament adaptations of Ps. 8, see Childs 1969.

harsh term. From an early age, I have been taught that we are to be stewards of creation, yet here the psalm implies that we are to be its masters.

To understand the discomfort here, we must turn to the first creation story in the book of Genesis. There, in language similar to the psalm, we are also told that humanity is created in the 'image' (צלם) and 'likeness' (דמות) of God. Unlike other animals, humans seemingly possess a divine heritage and share in their creator's glory. Well and good. As in the psalm, humanity is then given 'dominion' (from the Hebrew root רדה) over all plants and animals and told to 'subdue' (from כבש) the earth (Gen. 1.26-28). The Hebrew here is violent. The verb רדה Qal literally means 'to tread upon' and invokes iconographic images of ancient Near Eastern kings stepping upon the heads of foreign peoples.[3] The verb כבש Qal carries similar military resonances, with kings and armies forcefully subduing their enemies (e.g., Josh. 18.1; 2 Sam. 8.11). The first creation narrative may establish an exalted portrait of humanity, but it is one in which humans are seemingly granted the freedom to rule over the rest of creation with an iron fist.

As a so-called hymn of creation, Psalm 8 shares this exalted view, and the nuances of Genesis 1 often influence how interpreters understand the activity described in the psalm. When God 'gives dominion' (from the root משל Hiphil) over creation to humanity in the psalm, is it to be violent? Admittedly, the Hebrew term used here, משל Hiphil, is different than the verb used in Genesis. משל Qal literally means 'to rule' or 'have authority' over, as when an official has authority over the people (e.g., Judg. 8.22) or the king has authority over a region (e.g., 1 Kgs 4.21). The verb lacks the strong connotations of force that the Genesis verbs carry. However, when paired with the next clause, the 'dominion' connotations become clear. God has put all things 'under their feet' (תחת־רגליו, Ps. 8.6), just as all is under the feet of a conquering king. In a sense, then, in both the first creation story and the psalm, God transfers his kingly duties over to humanity to rule in his stead. God turns away, and we are seemingly given free rein. Perhaps this is more a psalm of dominion than of creation.

For much of human history, this dominion mentality seemed natural. Early Christians, for instance, influenced by Greco-Roman ideals, assumed that animals were given to humanity for food, trees were provided for building, and land was given for mining (e.g., Origen, *Cels.* 4.78; Lactantius, *Div. Inst.* 7.4-6; Didymus the Blind, *Comm. Gen.* 1.28).[4] Indeed, this androcentric perspective dominated Chris-

---

3. See, for example, the Victory Stele of Naram-Sim, which depicts the Akkadian king's victory over the Lullubi, or the relief of Ramses II from Abu Simbel, which depicts the pharaoh's victory at the Battle of Qadesh.

4. For a discussion of these and other early thinkers, see Bauckham 2012: 14–62. Some have argued that the modern environmental crisis is rooted firmly in Judeo-Christian tradition. See White 1967. Bauckham and others, however, have argued that the dominion mentality (what Jeanne Kay calls the 'despotism school') is not native to the Hebrew Bible and actually stems from Greco-Roman philosophical influence on early Christian interpretation. See Bauckham 2012; Kay 2001. Here I am not interested in pinpointing the origin of this mentality; rather, I simply wish to illustrate its longevity in Christian tradition.

tian thought well into modernity, and it continues to be used to justify all sorts of negative interactions with the environment: from the simple act of throwing litter out the car window or using harsh chemicals on our lawns, to more invasive practices of injecting livestock with hormones, or stripping minerals and other natural resources from the land without regard for the environmental impact. Even when divorced from biblical foundations, there is a sense that humans, as the highest recognized lifeform in the ecosystem, have the right to do with the planet as they will. Is this really our crown of glory?

There is, however, a growing awareness that such activities are unsustainable and ultimately detrimental to the health of this planet and all who live on it, including humans. This awareness has increasingly worked its way into biblical scholarship, influencing the way scholars read passages like Psalm 8. Some scholars, for instance, use lexical evidence to soften the connotations of משל and תחת־רגליו, while others use theological or ecological perspectives to argue for a more compassionate and environmentally responsible view of kingship.[5]

I am sympathetic to both. Here, however, I would like to use a different lens to reread Psalm 8, that which is provided by *Laudato si'*.[6] *Laudato si'* is an encyclical that was written in 2015 by the leader of the Roman Catholic Church, Pope Francis. It was not the first ecological response from the church hierarchy,[7] but it is the most sustained statement to date on the subject from a papal authority. In this encyclical, Pope Francis calls upon all citizens of the earth to care for what he calls 'our common home'. Like other ecological writers, the pope decries the current environmental situation and laments the indifferent attitudes that contribute to it. He condemns governments and businesses for their destructive behaviors, and encourages individuals and communities to pay attention and take immediate action toward ecological conversion.

What makes the encyclical distinctive is its view of humanity. As one might expect, Pope Francis rejects interpretations that find support within biblical texts for a dominion mentality, arguing that God, humans, and the earth are intimately connected; and that stepping beyond our limitations harmfully disrupts that

---

5. See, for instance, Greenspoon 2008: 177–78; Kim 2016. Similar exegetical moves are made with respect to Gen. 1. See, for instance, Vander Hart 1990; Manus and Obioma 2016.

6. In English, 'Praise to you, my Lord'. The encyclical draws its name from the refrain of *Laudes Creaturarum* ('The Canticle of Creatures', also known as the 'The Canticle of the Sun'), a hymn of creation written by the pope's namesake, Francis of Assisi (thirteenth century CE). Francis of Assisi is known for his spiritual engagement with the natural world and uses the poem to highlight the wonder of different natural elements, including the sun, moon, wind, fire, humans, and even death. In what follows, I will refer to the approved English translation of the encyclical, though I will continue to refer to the encyclical by its Latin title. In using *Laudato si'* as my reading partner, I am not claiming to speak on behalf of the Roman Catholic church, its people, or its hierarchy. Opinions here are my own.

7. Ecological concerns were also raised, for instance, by Pope Paul IV (*Pacem in Terris*, 1971), Pope John Paul II (*Redemptor Hominis*, 1979; 'The Ecological Crisis', 1990), and Pope Benedict XVI (*Caritas in Veritate*, 2009).

connection (*Laudato si'* 66). We may be made 'in the image of God', he says, but 'we are not God'. We are not meant to 'have dominion' but to 'till and keep',[8] that is, to care for the earth and its occupants in a 'relationship of mutual responsibility' (67).

However, the pope places a special emphasis on the role of humanity in the world, not only as agents that affect the environment but also as participants in the planetary ecosystem. As he states, 'Human beings too are creatures of this world… We cannot fail to consider the effects [of environmental degradation] on people's lives' (43). The pope is especially concerned about the environmental impact on 'the most vulnerable people' (48), the economically and socially disenfranchised. 'A true ecological approach', he says, 'always becomes a social approach; it must integrate questions of justice in debates on the environment, so as to hear *both the cry of the earth and the cry of the poor*' (49, emphasis original). *Laudato si'* does not promote ecology for its own sake; it promotes careful stewardship of the earth for all life upon it, especially human life.

The encyclical does not reference Psalm 8, and the psalm's connection to a heritage of dominion remains. But that does not mean we should abandon it. The psalm remains a favorite because it celebrates creation and humanity's place within it. At the same time, the psalm compels me to rethink my own role in creation and how my actions affect the world around me. It challenges me to work with the larger global community toward justice for our common home. Together, humanity can share in the psalmist's wonder; we can question our significance and be comforted by the special distinction humanity is granted. But it cannot stop there. *Laudato si'* encourages us to push through the discomfort of tradition and read verbs of dominion as verbs of care…to step down from the mountains we create for ourselves and embrace humans as part of creation…to move from affirmation into action.

What is humanity that God made them? Mere mortals. But God cares for them. So too must we care for all creatures that share our common home. We are not to dominate; we are not to rule. Rather, we are to look after the beasts of the field, the birds of the air, and the fish of the seas. We are to keep the land and preserve its natural resources. We are to be mindful of what we consume and where the residue ends up. But we are also to be accountable to the babes and infants, earth's human occupants, especially those who are most vulnerable to environmental change, those who are young now and those yet to be. We are to stand in the valleys alongside the disenfranchised and to listen to those who have been silenced. We are to mourn with the mothers whose children have been lost to violence and rebuild with those whose lives have been overturned by environmental disasters. We are to strive for justice and promote human dignity.

---

8. In this, the pope privileges the language of the second creation story (Gen. 2.15), whose divine mandate is given using verbs that are more agricultural and pastoral in tone.

'The poor and the earth are crying out'.[9] Let us hear their call. Only then can we reclaim Psalm 8 as a hymn of creation. Only then will we be in the position to proclaim the majesty of the earth.

Another psalm worth reading alongside Psalm 8 is Psalm 148, a hymn of creation that recognizes humanity, young and old, rich and poor, as but one part in a long litany of creation.

Dr. Nicole L. Tilford is a biblical scholar living in Atlanta, GA. She works as the Production Manager for SBL Press and is a member of the Roman Catholic church.

References

Bauckham, R. (2012), *Living with Other Creatures: Green Exegesis and Theology*, Milton Keynes: Paternoster.
Childs, B.S. (1969), 'Psalm 8 in the Context of the Christian Canon', *Int* 23: 20–31.
Greenspoon, L. (2008), 'From Dominion to Stewardship: The Ecology of Biblical Translation', *JRS*: 159–83.
Kay, J. (2001), 'Concepts of Nature in the Hebrew Bible', in *Judaism and Environmental Ethics*, 86–104, Lanham: Lexington Books.
Kim, J. (2016), 'Psalm 8: An Ecological Reading', *Korean Journal of Christian Studies* 101: 11–30.
Manus, C. and D. Obioma (2016), 'Preaching the "Green Gospel" in Our Environment: A Re-reading of Genesis 1:27-28 in the Nigerian Context', *Hervormde Teologiese Studies (HTS Teologiese Studies/HTS Theological Studies)* 72: a3054.
Vander Hart, M. (1990), 'Creation and Covenant: Part One', *Mid-America Journal of Theology* 6: 3–18.
White, L., Jr (1967), 'The Historical Roots of Our Ecologic Crisis', *Science* 155: 1203–207.

---

9. Excerpted from 'A Christian Prayer in Union with Creation', which is included at the end of *Laudato si'*.

PSALM 8
HOW I FELL IN LOVE WITH THE BIBLE

Francis Landy

²O YHWH our Lord, how magnificent is your name in all the earth,
Which gives/recounts your majesty over the heavens.
³From the mouths of babes and sucklings you have founded strength
On account of your enemies, to make the foe and the avenger cease.
⁴When I look at your heavens, the work of your fingers,
The moon and the stars, which you have established.
⁵What is a human being, that you remember them,
The child of humanity, that you visit them.
⁶You made them a little less than God,
And crowned them with honour and glory.
⁷You made them rule over the work of your hands,
Everything you have placed under their feet.
⁸Sheep and all cattle, and also the beasts of the field,
⁹Birds of the heaven and fish of the sea, those who traverse the paths of the sea.
¹⁰O YHWH our Lord, how magnificent is your name in all the earth.[1]

I read this psalm with Jonathan Sacks[2] and Philip Skelker[3] in Cambridge, some time in 1968–69, in my last year at university. It was a Sunday afternoon. We agreed to read a biblical text on a continuing basis, but I don't think we ever followed up. We saw ourselves as very special, a unique group of Jewish students, who included also Avivah Gottlieb[4] and Freema Gottlieb.[5] For me it was a change,

---

1. Translation my own.
2. Later chief Rabbi of the United Hebrew Congregations of the British Commonwealth and respected Bible scholar. See for instance: https://www.rabbisacks.org/life-of-rabbi-jonathan-sacks/biography/.
3. Jewish educator and scholar, former Head Teacher, Immanuel College, Bushey, UK.
4. A Hebrew Bible and English literature scholar: https://jwa.org/encyclopedia/article/zornberg-avivah-gottlieb.
5. Scholar of Judaism and literature: https://www.freemagottlieb.com/.

even a revelation, after my stuffy bourgeois upbringing, when not an idea penetrated the Shabbat somnolence. For the first time I became aware that Judaism could be vital, that it had something in common with the eastern religions I was tangentially in touch with. Jonathan was a philosophy student, of staggering brilliance, just returned from his life-changing journey to the States and his meeting with the Lubavitcher rebbe. Philip had transferred from Oxford, was doing a teacher's training course, and invited me to talk at the Friends' school in Saffron Walden, where he was undertaking his practicum. He was effervescent, in love with language, with an immediate and unaffected rapport. He was on the threshold of a brilliant career in Jewish and secular education.

But I knew nothing. I had no idea that the Bible could be beautiful. An Orthodox upbringing had left me completely devoid of curiosity. And then we read this psalm. For a long time I thought it was the only psalm that was beautiful, a single touch of genius amid all the pieties. I liked the circularity, the sudden contrast between the divine and the human, the animals, and above all, the personal voice. I read it now with nostalgia, for a lost self, for a certain naivety, as well as for friendships that did not survive. But the essential insights are the same.

The first verse is a puzzle. Is תנה, *tenah*, 'gives, recounts', derived from נתן, 'give', or תנה, 'recite, repeat'?[6] Of course, I was not aware of the problem; I simply noted the anomaly, and assumed it was some kind of poetic language. In either case, it suggests the dependence of heaven on earth. The name is magnified on earth and reflects the divine majesty to the heavens. Another favourite verse at the time was יושב תהלות ישראל, 'who is enthroned on the praises of Israel' (Ps. 22.4): the sense that God inhabited, and only existed through, human language. I was intrigued too, by the preposition על, '*over* the heavens'. The splendour of the heavens is the visible correlate of the divine majesty, which is nonetheless beyond it.

The puzzles increase in the second verse.[7] It is not on any language, but on the mouths of babes and sucklings,[8] that God founds strength. The paradox augments that the heavens are being dependent on the earth: the very weakest members of society are the basis of His power in the cosmic battle. And who are the enemies and avengers? At the time I imagined them as human antagonists, hostile to Israel or to divinely established order. I wondered, however, about the reason for their revanchism, their grudge. The image of Shabbat also intrigued me – להשבית אויב ומתנקם, 'to cause the foe and the avenger to cease'. Was God declaring a pact with his enemies, just as in the sabbatical year there is a truce with the wild beasts (Lev. 25.7; 26.6)? At any rate, they disappear from the rest of the psalm.

---

6. תנה is otherwise found in Judg. 5.11 and 11.40, and may be a northern or archaic variant of שנה. In either case, it refers to ritual speech, either of praise or lament. For the different possibilities for interpreting our verse, see the very full discussion in *HALOT*, pp. 1760–61.

7. Alter (1985: 118) divides v. 3 in two, thus separating the babies and the enemies. However, this reading is not maintained in his translation and commentary (2009: 73).

8. Hunter (1999: 119–21) considers a proposal that these refer to heavenly beings. As he concedes, there is little evidence for this, but he still finds it attractive.

The infants are the future; their cries and verbal play are a primal liturgy. What strength do they found? Just the prospect of new life at its most elemental, despite all the forces that would destroy it, especially in time of catastrophe. However, like the enemies, the babies also disappear from the poem. Verse 3 is a loose end; it is a stage setting for a world without enemies. I wondered what the babies were really doing. Perhaps they contrast with, and reinforce, the divine status of humans two verses later. With my current, deconstructive, self I might see it differently; I like the byways of poems, the paths not pursued.

I look at the skies at night time; it is easy to identify with the poet. I doubt if I noticed the transference from שמך, 'your name', to שמיך, 'your heavens'. However, the next phrase, מעשה אצבעתיך, 'the work of your fingers', still gives me a frisson of pleasure.[9] I imagine the fingers curling down from a great height. The touch of the fingers is the extreme point of contact between creator and creation. We may follow the fingers back, through the muscles and nerves of the divine body, as far as we can see, to invisibility. Wolff (1974: 68) comments that the image suggests delicacy, that the stars are a filagree. It also takes us, however, back in time. 'The moon and the stars which you have established' evokes creation, the subject of the rest of the poem. They are traces of the divine thought and work, sparks of light in all the darkness.

And then we look at ourselves: 'What is a human being (Enosh) that you remember them, the child of humanity that you visit them?' Of course, I knew them as 'man' and 'son of man' respectively, and the plurals were singular. They recalled Adam's grandson, Enosh, and our Adamic heritage. The contrast between the celestial splendour and the human self-reflection is breath-taking, what the poet Paul Celan (1999) calls an *Atemwende*, a turn of breath. Who are we in all this chaos and majesty? The expected answer to the rhetorical question may be, 'Nothing'. The mystery is that as well as creating the moon and the stars, God thinks of us, and remembers us. The thoughts penetrate further than the fingers. I think I took פקד, 'visit', literally in English. We are creatures visited by God.[10] There is the divine memory, when everything else is forgotten, but also the subjective experience of the interconnectedness of humans and God.

It leads inexorably to the next sensational verse: 'And you have made them a little less than God, and crowned them with honour and glory'. Humans are almost God, including me. The stance is one of humility, but also of wonder. It appealed to me because of my sense that God was not a being external to humanity, but an aspect of consciousness. But the niggling detail is the 'almost'. There is a slight, but impassible, gap between humans and God. The human attributes, honour and glory, match the divine majesty and magnificence in the first verse (Alter 1985: 120). God crowns Adam; Adam's sovereignty corresponds to God's. One imagines the diadem, with its gems, reflecting the stars. The parallel lines, so proximate, never meet.

---

9. I have discussed this, in relation to Exod. 31.18 and 32.15-16, in an unpublished paper (Landy 2019).

10. פקד has a very wide semantic range. *HALOT* devotes five pages to it! (pp. 955–59).

YHWH set Adam over the creatures: we are back in the world of Genesis 1–2, presumably entirely at peace. Everything is under Adam's feet: Adam is a cosmic, even comic, figure. That Adam is representative of humanity suggests that the Edenic realm still subsists, that humans live and rule over a perfect world. 'The work of your hands' complements 'the work of your fingers' in v. 4. From transcendence we pass to immanence, God getting his hands dirty while he moulds the soil and shapes everything. It had, I think, something unreal about it, as if everything is made from playdough.

The last lines, up to the concluding refrain, are a list of creatures: 'Sheep and all cattle, and also the beasts of the field; birds of the heaven and fish of the sea, those who traverse the paths of the sea'. It moves outward from the human, domestic sphere to the domains of air and water. I imagined the sheep and cattle grazing peacefully, the wild animals living their wild life, the birds and fish fluttering and swimming. And Adam moving quietly and approvingly among them. I was attracted by the anomalous spelling of צנה, 'sheep' (usually צאן), but did not recognize the pun on אלפים, which means both 'oxen' and 'thousands', suggesting the multitudinousness of creation. At the end, tagged on, there is the final delectable phrase, 'those who traverse the paths of the sea'. The paths of the sea are invisible; fish know them, but humans do not. It is a realm which is foreign to humanity, and yet, mysteriously, is within the human orbit. The paths of the sea lead to unknown destinations, are fluid, opening and closing with the waves. In them the stars are reflected.

And then we go to the final verse, the refrain: 'O YHWH our Lord, how magnificent is your name in all the earth'. Alter (1985: 119; 2009: 74) comments on the sense of totality, that by the end we have encompassed the entire creation; the end is the same but different from the beginning. At the centre there are the twin monarchs, God and humanity. But there is one significant difference: the refrain is incomplete (see v. 2). The incompleteness suggests that something is open, and we do not know what.

If I had to choose a second psalm it would have been Psalm 19, because I like to misread it as suggesting that all speech is infused with the dialogue of night and day.

Professor Francis Landy taught Religious Studies at the University of Alberta for many years. He teaches a weekly *shi'ur* for his local synagogue in Victoria on different books of the Bible.

References

Alter, Robert (2009), *The Book of Psalms: A Translation with Commentary*, New York: Norton.
Alter, Robert (1985), *The Art of Biblical Poetry*, New York: Basic Books.
Celan, Paul (1999), 'Meridian', in *Collected Prose*, 37–56, trans. Rosmarie Waldrop, Manchester: Carcanet.

Hunter, Alastair G. (1999), *Psalms*, London: Routledge.
Landy, Francis (2019), 'Freedom and Responsibility', an unpublished paper presented to the Deconstructive Poetics section of the European Association of Biblical Studies Annual Meeting, in Warsaw.
Wolff, Hans Walter (1974), *Anthropology of the Old Testament*, London: SCM.

PSALM 18.35
GIVING DAVID ODYSSEUS' BOW

Sivan Nir

Introduction: Rediscovering Textual Worlds

My main interest in Psalm 18, which is attributed to King David by its title (and cf. 2 Sam. 22), is in a later implied Homeric contextualization of David's figure, suggested by an almost unknown rabbinic legend used to explain a difficult expression in Ps. 18.35.

In many aspects of my life, I seem to relish the lost and the unknown. It matters not whether these are forgotten sources, as is the focus of this paper, concertos (such as Scharwenka's piano works); or even secrets in video games, *Breath of the Wild* or the insidious *La Mulana*, come to mind. There is something intoxicating in discovery, in feeling like an explorer, proving that the horizon is still endless, and that wonders may yet await beyond to push back one's mortality.

My love for medieval Bible exegesis goes back to high school. Conversely, I arrived at midrashic literature late and quite by chance. During my second year at university, one of my professors in an elective noted my natural affinity for deciphering the textual underpinnings of rabbinic legends. Before me unfurled a new world of alien rabbinic chaos. I was sorely tempted. An offer to 'defect' from biblical studies led instead to abandoning a teen fascination with German philosophy. The burden of a seemingly endless Kant might also have been involved. The choice to focus on later midrashim was but a natural extension of my personal tastes. The texts are generally understudied and, consequently, are as fresh in the eyes of lifelong Yeshiva goers as in the eyes of a scholar whose first brush with the Talmud was at university. They are an equal playing field of the neglected.

The Psalter was another *terra incognita*. For me, as a secular teen in Israel, it was something people whispered on buses in apotropaic prayer. During my Bachelor of Arts studies, I came to regard the Psalter as a repository of alternate documentary hypotheses. As a graduate working on characterization in midrashic literature and medieval Bible commentaries, reading attempts to harmonize David the King with David the psalmist almost but not quite led to a dissertation and inspired papers (e.g., Nir 2021). Read in this harmonistic light, Psalm 18 is a major wellspring of imagined biographical characterizations, a summation of David's career. This was also a start to my career. My first conference appearance turned to the Islamic-Jewish dialogue implicitly inspired by this psalm.

I recognized, but could not broach then, another cultural context hiding beneath the surface: imagine David recast by rabbis not as a midrashic Moses (Shenan 1995: 197–98), or a Hellenic Orpheus (Flesher 1995), but as Odysseus! Here I present this reading preserved in Rashi (R. Shlomo Yitzchaki, d. 1105? CE), conduct a comparison to Homer, and show this interpretation was not singular in Byzantine Eretz Israel, another world mostly lost to the darkness of time. For me, this quest started with Ps. 18.35, where David's military prowess, especially with a bow, is a real riddle.

David's Bronze Bow in Rashi

The Hebrew verb in 18.35b is difficult:

מלמד ידי למלחמה ונחתה קשת נחושה זרועתי

> He teacheth my hands to war, so that a bow of bronze is ונחתה (*wěniḥătāh*) by mine arms' (KJV modified).[1]

The precise imagery is Egyptian (Gunkel 1998: 114) or Assyrian (Berry and Clines 2009: 74) and thus perplexed later unfamiliar generations, who turned to their own contexts. Rashi – pioneering, influential, but midrash oriented and of the northern French school – thus looks to an unorthodox *'aggadah meyashevet* ('settling legend') (Kamin 2000: 64–65):[2]

> 35b 'My arms can bend a bow of bronze'…: 'A bronze bow was drawn by my arms'. *David had bronze bows hung up in his palace. When the kings of the Gentiles saw them, they would say to each other, 'Do you think that David has the strength to draw these?' ['No',' they would say]. 'This [display] is only for the purpose of awing us'. When he would hear them, he would draw them [the bows] in their presence.* (Gruber 2004: 240)

---

1. The poet bends (Goldingay 2006: 1:272), or breaks (Buttenwieser 1969: 465), a bronze bow; or is gifted a divine bow (Dahood 1966–70: 1:115), as in the Ugartic AQHT myth, where a bow designed by the god Kothar is connected to *neḥusha*, 'bronze', in divination. I feel that the rendering 'bend' is superior.

2. See Joseph Kara's commentary on 2 Sam. 22.35. He 'heard' a tradition much like Rashi's. Rashi is usually the one that 'hears' things from Kara and thus suggestive of an unusual source, see Mack 2010: 60–65. Rashi, like Kara there, mentions David drawing and then *breaking* the bow.

Mayer Gruber notes that Rashi's source is based on *Midrash Tehillim* (2004: 243 nn. 30–32); but this interpretation is *neither present* there, nor – to my knowledge – in any known midrash.³ Hence, Rashi presents an alternative not an adaptation (Gray 2014: 146–49).⁴ It seems that here Rashi preserved a lost account, possibly from another version of *Midrash Tehillim*, as evident from other quotes in this chapter and elsewhere.⁵

Comparably, Rella Kushelevsky analyzes a legend found in the thirteenth century Northern French *Sefer Hama'asim* ('Book of Tales') on 'Joab's Valor' (301a–302; Yassif 1979: 22–23; Kushelevsky 2017: 387–89). *Maḥzor Vitry* attributes this legend to *Midrash Tehillim Shoḥer Tov*: 'Shoḥer Tov elaborates on his (Joab's) valor among the Ammonites'. The only place in rabbinic literature where Joab and David catapult themselves as in 'Joab's Valor' is, indeed, in *Mid. Teh.* 18.24, so quoted by Rashi as in *Midrash Tillim* ('in the midrash on Psalms'). However, the version in this midrash is much shorter compared to *Sefer Hama'asim*. Hence, it seems that some enhanced midrash on Psalm 18, which contained both 'Joab's valor' and 'David's bow', might have been in circulation in medieval Northern France.

David's Odyssean Homecoming

And that possibility, of an almost lost midrash and its connections, leads me further. Whereas David 'drawing' of bows has no known sources in Bible or midrash, will it be too far-fetched to try and find a parallel for this in Homer?

Midrash Tehillim also contains a rare mention of Homer in talmudic literature:

> David prayed: 'Let the words of my mouth and the meditation of my heart be acceptable in thy sight, O Lord' (Ps. 19.15). Let them be treasured and graven by the generations, and be read not as one reads the books of *Homer*.⁶

---

3. The midrash for 18.27 proposes three readings, see Braude 1959: 90–91: 'bending', (based on Ps. 65.11), 'arm as strong as a bronze bow' (cf. Briggs and Briggs 1906–1907: 1.148), and Nahshon's 'bow'. See Braude 1959: 258–59.

4. The legend's independence is buttressed by the fact that 'bending' something in Rabbinic Hebrew cannot equate 'drawing a bow'. See Sokoloff 2002: 267, 509; Jastrow 1926: 563–64, 1433. Bow strings are tied, not bent (e.g., *Qoh. Rab.* 1). A search in *Ma'agarim: The Historical Dictionary of the Hebrew Language*, shows that D-R-K (Ps. 11.2) and M-Š-K are common bow drawing and shooting verbs, contra Rashi. K-F-F with קשת, *qešet* (as Rainbow!) occurs in the *Piyyut*.

5. Rashi on Ps. 84.12 implies a different version of *Mid. Teh.* Also see Rashi on Deut. 33.7; Judg. 6.1; 1 Sam. 17.49; Isa. 5.12; 29.12; 30.29; 54.12; 66.21; Zech. 5.11; Pss. 18.30; 34.1; 41.4; 44.2; 64.2; 70.1-2; 78.37-39; 86.2-3; and Qoh. 11.7.

6. The Hebrew here has another ending for 'Homer'. There is a graphic similarity between *s* and *m* at the end of the word (ס-ם) that changes מירס to מירם. And see below.

Instead, let those who read and meditated upon them [the Psalms], be rewarded thereafter as [though they had studied] the treatises of "the signs of leprosy" or of "tents"'. (*Mid. Teh.* 1.8, in Braude 1959: 12, modified)

David wishes the study of the Psalms to grant the same rewards as difficult halakhic topics. However, 'his' psalms clash not with farfetched '*aggadah*, the common rival of the halakhic *Negaʿim we-Oholot* ('signs and tents'),[7] but with the books of Homer (Jastrow 1926: 355, 779).[8] I suggest that David here complains that some Jews are reading his Psalter like reading Homer, not in the recreational or exegetic senses (Niehoff 2012) but *with* Homer. The legend quoted above from Rashi in *Midrash Tillim*, situated *after* David's homecoming, is one such reading.

The legend mirrors the circumstances of the archery contest in the *Odyssey* book 21, where the returning Odysseus proves his identity by stringing and drawing his unique bow in the face of the sneering suitors at home, a feat of literally Herculean strength (Crissy 1997), comparable to David's bow and (Homeric?) hospitality (Feldman 1990: 154–55) towards the hostile kings:

> But Odysseus, master mind in action, once he'd handled the great bow and scanned every inch, then like an expert singer skilled at lyre and song[9] – who strains a string to a new peg with ease, making the pliant sheep-gut fast at either end – so with his virtuoso ease Odysseus strung his mighty bow. Quickly his right hand plucked the string to test its pitch and under his touch it sang out clear and sharp as a swallow's cry... Odysseus looked to Telemachus and said, 'Your guest, sitting here in your house, has not disgraced you. No missing the mark, look and no long labor spent to string the bow. My strength's not broken yet, not quite so frail as the mocking suitors thought'. (Fagles 1996: 21.405–28)

Homeric Jewish Mosaics?

Whereas an association of Odysseus and Polyphemus with David and Goliath would seem tenuous, but less surprising when reoccurring in Josephus (Feldman 1990: 143), *Midrash Tehillim* reimagining David as Odysseus is not unique. This midrash contains other accounts with possible Davidic–Homeric undertones, one of which is nearby (*Mid. Teh.* for 18.30): David's capture under a pillow by the giant Ishby:

---

7. *b. Sanh.* 38; *b. Hag.* 14a; David's studies in *b. B. Metz.* 59a.

8. Corrupted to sound like *hamiram* ('[the Lord] removed them'), hinting at Homer's popularity. Also see *m. Yad.* 4.6.

9. The image of fixing a household by drawing a bow like a minstrel is older than Homer and reflected in Ugaritic epics. See Ready 2014: 250–57. Compare the talmudic David as a musician (*y. Ber.* 1.4-5 [p. 2]; *b. Ber.* 3b-4a; *Mid. Teh.* 28.8; 57.4; 108.2).

> When Ishby saw him (David) at Nob, he said: 'this is the one who killed Goliath, my brother'. He caught him, folded him and placed him under his pillow and sat upon him. He said: 'I shall eat and drink, and play with him as I will'. (Sasson 2010: 27–30)

The feasting and David's position under the pillow might be alluding to Odysseus' captivity and escape from the cyclops under a fluffy ram:[10]

> There was one bellwether ram, the prize of all the flock,
> and clutching him by his back, tucked up under
> his shaggy belly, there I hung, face upward,
> both hands locked in his marvelous deep fleece,
> clinging for dear life, my spirit steeled, enduring. (Fagles 1996: 9.430–34)

Midrash Tehillim is not the only Jewish source from Eretz Israel to read David in this light. One Qumran fragment (4Q373.1) describes Goliath's captured shield 'as a tower'.[11] This simile is Homeric: Ajax wields such a shield in the *Iliad* (σάκος ἠύτε πύργον) (Jacobson 2009).

A mosaic at the Meroth synagogue in Upper Galilee (early sixth century CE) continues this allusion (see Figure 1). David is portrayed reclining on Goliath's tower shield (Xeravits 2018: 72–73). This visual exegesis is from the same period as most *Midrash Tehillim* accounts (Reizel 2011; Kalimi 2004), supporting the authenticity of Rashi's transmission.

Alluding to Odysseus is not unique. His trial by the Sirens was a centerpiece in another synagogue mosaic (Beit Leontis, Beit She'an; mid-fifth century CE), where Odysseus' journeys serve as an allegory for the journey of the soul (Hasan-Rokem 2014: 168, 175–76, 180–88). Similarly, David's implicit crediting of his strength and success in Psalm 18 to God, unlike Odysseus' self-reliance that so soured Poseidon (cf. Homer, *Od.* 1.68-70; 9.500), implies a nuanced Jewish reception that subsumed Homer rather than ignored him.

---

10. Yassif (1999: 86) is convinced that David's captivity is not based on exegesis but on an incorporated independent tradition, much like my reading of Rashi. In some versions David is in an olive press not under a pillow. Even an alteration to 'pillow' implies knowing a Homeric equivalent. Also see the later reception of this tale in *Midrash Al Ythallel* and *Midrash Goliath*, where David's strength is superhuman like in Rashi (Mehlman and Limmer 2017: 81–83).

11. An alternative, but less likely consistent with talmudic tradition, is a reading of this fragment as about Moses' struggle with King Og (Schuller 1992).

Figure 1. Figure (David?) with weapons around it (Ilan and Damati 1985: 48).[12]

Concluding Remarks

The Psalter is a kaleidoscope of voices that resonate with differing audiences due to the inherently subjective contribution of personal contexts to exegesis – some rabbinic Byzantine Jews wanted David to be a better Odysseus, no matter how the tannaitic authorities felt.[13] Was that the result of a decentralized Jewish Byzantine existence? Did Rashi only repeat this legend because of a didactic French fascination with *roman antique*?[14] Did Heinrich Ewald similarly see Ps. 18.35b as

---

12. © Courtesy of the Israel Exploration Society. https://synagogues.kinneret.ac.il/synagogues/meroth/ (accessed 15 May 2022).

13. See the reading of the cognate verse in Dahouh-HaLevi 2014: 237. A medieval Byzantine Yefet ben Eli summary reads as Rashi, 'drawing a bronze bow'.

14. Rashi predates the major Antiquarian French romances, whose sources also do not seem to make the Odyssey's archery influence likely. Cf. the shooting of the dragon: 'And in al hast he bent a sturdy bowe' in Lydagte's fifteenth-century English 'Siege of Thebes' (l. 3492), which is possibly inspired by 18.35b.

Odyssean because of the classical background of biblical studies (1880: 134)? Did I only notice this legend because of my current project, as a 2021–2022 Harry Starr Fellow at Harvard, on tales of late midrash? Had I chosen the even more extensively biographical Psalm 119, which would have been my second choice for this volume, would it have led to Homer too?

Dr. Sivan Nir's dissertation (Tel Aviv University, 2019) is to be published by SBL Press under the title, *From Typology to Mimesis: Characterization in Midrash and Medieval Jewish Bible Commentaries*. He is currently finalizing a second book, on the tales of rabbinic sages in late midrash, which concludes his work as Harry Starr fellow of Judaica at Harvard University. He lives in Giva'tayim, Israel, and defines himself as a born-Jewish liberal.

References

Academy of the Hebrew Language, '*Ma'agarim*: The Historical Dictionary Project', http://maagarim.hebrewacademy.org.il/Pages/PMain.aspx (accessed 4 March 2022).

Berry, D.K. and D.J.A. Clines (2009), *The Psalms and Their Readers: Interpretive Strategies for Psalm 18*, London: Bloomsbury.

Braude, W.G., trans. (1959), *The Midrash on Psalms*, New Haven: Yale University Press.

Briggs, C.A. and E.G. Briggs (1906–1907), *A Critical and Exegetical Commentary on the Book of Psalms*, Edinburgh: T. & T. Clark.

Buttenwieser, M. (1969), *The Psalms*, Library of Biblical Studies, New York: Ktav.

Crissy, K. (1997), 'Herakles, Odysseus, and the Bow: Odyssey 21.11-41', *The Classical Journal (Classical Association of the Middle West and South)* 93 (1): 41–53.

Dahood, M.J. (1966–70), *Psalms*, Anchor Bible 16–17A, Garden City: Doubleday.

Dahouh-Halevi, D. (2014), 'Studies in Hebrew Translation from Byzantium of Yefet ben 'Eli's Commentary on Samuel', MA diss., Tel Aviv University [Heb.].

Ewald, H. (1880), *Commentary on the Psalms*, trans. E. Johnson, London: Williams & Norgate.

Fagles, R., trans. (1996), *The Odyssey*, New York: Penguin.

Feldman, L.H. (1990), 'Josephus' Portrait of David', *HUCA* 60: 129–74.

Flesher, P.V.M. (1995), in P.V.M. Flesher and D. Urman (eds), *Ancient Synagogues: Historical Analysis and Archaeological Discovery*, Vol. II, 346–66, Studia Post Biblica 47/2, Leiden: Brill.

Goldingay, J. (2006), *Psalms*, Baker Commentary on the Old Testament Wisdom and Psalms, Grand Rapids: Baker Academic.

Gray, A.R. (2014), *Psalm 18 in Words and Pictures: A Reading through Metaphor*, Biblical Interpretation 127, Leiden: Brill.

Gruber, M.I. (2004), *Rashi's Commentary on Psalms*, Brill Reference Library of Judaism 18, Leiden: Brill.

Gunkel, H. (1998), *Introduction to Psalms: The Genres of the Religious Lyric of Israel*, completed by J. Begrich, trans. J.D. Nogalski, Macon: Mercer University Press.

Hasan-Rokem, G. (2014), 'Leviticus Rabbah 16, 1 – "Odysseus and the Sirens" in the Beit Leontis Mosaic from Beit She'an', in S. Fine and A. Koller (eds), *Talmuda de-Eretz Israel: Archaeology and the Rabbis in Late Antique Palestine*, 159–90, Studia Judaica 73, Berlin: de Gruyter.

Ilan, Z. and E. Damati (1985), 'Excavation of the Synagogue at Meroth', *Qadmoniot: A Journal for the Antiquities of Eretz-Israel and Bible Lands* 18: 44–50 [Heb.]

Jacobson, H. (2009), 'Two Greek Hero-Types in Ancient Jewish Texts', *Zutot; Perspectives on Jewish Culture* 6 (1): 7–8.

Jastrow, M. (1926), *Dictionary of the Targumim, the Talmud Babli and Yerushalmi, and the Midrashic Literature*, New York: G.P. Putnam's Sons.

Kalimi, I. (2004), 'Midrash Psalms Shocher Tov, Some Theological and Methodological Features and a Case study, The View of God', in J.H. Ellens, D.L. Ellens, R.P. Knierim and I. Kalimi (eds), *God's Word for Our World: Studies in Honor of Simon John De Vries*, Vol. 2, 63–79, London: Bloomsbury T&T Clark.

Kamin, S. (2000), *Rashi's Exegetical Categorization in Respect to the Distinction Between Peshat and Derash*, Jerusalem: Magness Press [Heb.].

Kushelevsky, R. (2017), *Tales in Context: Sefer ha-ma'asim in Medieval Northern France (Bodleian Library, Ms. Bodl. Or. 135)*, trans. R. Avital and C. Naor, with a historical epilogue by E. Baumgarten, Raphael Patai Series in Jewish Folklore and Anthropology, Detroit: Wayne State University Press.

Mack, H. (2010), *The Mystery of Rabbi Moshe Hadarshan*, Jerusalem: The Bialik Institute [Heb.].

Mehlman, B.H. and S.M. Limmer (2017), *Medieval Midrash: The House for Inspired Innovation*, The Brill Reference Library of Judaism 52, Leiden: Brill.

Niehoff, M.R., ed. (2012), *Homer and the Bible in the Eyes of Ancient Interpreters*, Jerusalem Studies in Religion and Culture 16, Leiden: Brill.

Nir, S. (2021), 'David the Pious Musician in Midrashic Literature and Medieval Muslim Sources', in M. Zawanowska and M. Wilk (eds), *Warrior, Poet, Prophet and King: The Character of David in Judaism, Christianity and Islam*, 43–66, Themes in Biblical Narrative 29, Leiden: Brill, 2021.

Ready, J.L. (2014), 'ATU 974 The Homecoming Husband, The Returns of Odysseus, and the End of Odyssey 21', *Arethusa* 47 (3): 265–85.

Reizel, A. (2011), *Introduction to Midrashic Literature*, Alon Shvut: Tevunot Mikhlelet Hertsog [Heb.].

Sasson, G. (2010), 'The Story of David's Captivity in the Hands of Yishbi Be-Nov', *JSIJ* 9: 19–44 [Heb.].

Schuller, E.M. (1992), 'A Preliminary Study of 4Q373 and Some Related(?) Fragments', in J.C. Trebolle Barrera and L.V. Montaner (eds), *The Madrid Qumran Congress: Proceedings of the International Congress on the Dead Sea Scrolls, Madrid 1991*, 516–30, Studies on the Texts of the Desert of Judah 11, Madrid: Universidad Complutenseia; Leiden: Brill.

Shenan, A. (1995), 'David's Character in Rabbinic Literature', in Y. Zakovitch (ed.), *David: From Shepherd to Messiah*, 181–99, Jerusalem: Yad Ben Zvi [Heb.].

Sokoloff, M. (2002), *A Dictionary of Jewish Palestinian Aramaic of the Byzantine Period*, Ramat-Gan: Bar-Ilan University Press, 2002.

Xeravits, G.G. (2018), 'The Reception of the Figure of David in Late Antique Synagogue Art', in G.G. Xeravits and G.S. Goering (eds), *Figures who Shape Scriptures, Scriptures that Shape Figures: Essays in Honour of Benjamin G. Wright III*, 71–90, Berlin: de Gruyter.

Yassif, E. (1979), 'The Story of Joab's Deeds of Valor: The Literary Aspects of the Heroic Tale', *Yeda-'Am* 19: 17–27 [Heb.].

Yassif, E. (1999), *The Hebrew Folktale: History, Genre, Meaning*, trans. J.S. Teitelbaum, Folklore Studies in Translation, Bloomington: Indiana University Press.

PSALM 19
THE VOICE THAT IS NOT HEARD

Robert Paul Seesengood and Jennifer L. Koosed

Context, of course, is everything. Particularly when reading a psalm. Psalms were, and are, liturgy. As words in a liturgy, as song, how should a psalm sound? How might the meaning of a psalm's words be affected – inflected – by music in minor or major keys, of varied tempo and instrumentation? How does the psalm's precise location in the larger liturgy affect its sense; how does a moment of worship affect the way the words are encountered? Do meanings change with contexts, perhaps with the association of the psalm with a holiday season, a jangling and dissonant melody, or a peaceful series of major cords? How does the space in which a psalm is being read or chanted or sung affect the encounter, whether outdoors in the Temple surrounded by the lowing of cattle for sacrifice and the murmurings of children and elders, in an overheated *shul* (synagogue), in an incense-scented cathedral, at a graveside, in a simple whitewashed meeting house repeated by rote in unison or read silently, while alone in a library or study? What we have in a psalm is a trace of a context long lost and forever varied and varying, the skeletal remains; better: the fossil of what once was, leaving only its imprint behind.

We, the authors, approach the psalms from several contexts. We are each, by training, biblical scholars, trained in ancient languages, history, critical theory and history of interpretation. Jennifer spent her childhood nominally Jewish, educated in a Catholic girls' school. She reinvested in her Jewish practice in college and beyond. Rob was raised in a primitivist Protestant tradition, later trained in seminary, and he served seven years as director of religious education for a small New Jersey congregation. We met as graduate students, married years later (the second marriage for each of us). We worked together for over a decade at a small Methodist liberal arts college. Jennifer remains there as professor and department chair. Rob is academic dean of a nearby UMC (United Methodist Church) theological school.

Contexts shift and change. We read psalms as scholars of the ancient world, as specialists in ancient languages and textual criticism. We read psalms within their history of interpretation, both Christian and Jewish. We read psalms alongside contemporary debates and discussion, alongside popular media. We read psalms as congregants, worshippers (however we understand that word), as parents of a *bar mitzvah* student, as the child of a Protestant Christian elder. As the psalms shift and change their context, so do we.

Psalm 19 opens with 'the heavens' and 'the firmament' proclaiming God's glory and deeds (v. 2),[1] words reminiscent of the story of creation in Genesis 1 (vv. 1, 6-7).[2] Echoes of Genesis 1 continue in the next verse (v. 3), as 'day to day' and 'night to night' continue the praise in a call and response both celestial and temporal. Perhaps it is no coincidence that the speaking cosmos of Psalm 19 alludes to Genesis 1, since there God speaks the universe into existence. From the beginning, words and material reality are entangled. Yet, what kind of speaking is uncertain as the words of the created order are undone in the very next verse: 'There is no speech (אמר, *'omer*; the same word used in the previous line to describe the verbal actions of the day) and there are no words' (v. 4a). What kind of speaking is spoken without words; what kind of proclamation is proclaimed without speech, 'without their voice being heard' (v. 4b)? Unless that is not what this verse says. Verse 4 can be translated in two ways, carrying one idea and its opposite (Sommer 2015: 392). The last phrase in v. 4 may say, 'whose voice cannot be heard'. In other words, when something is spoken, who cannot hear it? The praise hymns of the heavens cannot be heard/are audible to all, cannot be heard/are audible to all… in unending and undecidable oscillation.

After the wonders of the sun are lauded in striking imagery (a bridegroom emerging from the *chuppah*; a joyfully running warrior [v. 5]), the poem shifts in theme from creation to Torah, the perfect word of God (v. 7). Generally, scholars concur that Psalm 19 falls into two parts (Craigie 1983: 179; Mays 1994: 96-97), but disagree on the relationship between the parts. Critically, is this the taming of some ancient poem to a sun god, too popular to remove from liturgy, but in need of Torah-scrubbing? In the first half of the twentieth century, critical biblical scholarship did aver that the original hymn celebrated the sun as deity (Weiser 1962: 197; Dahood 1965: 121; see also Craigie 1983: 179). Yet, by the end of the twentieth century this consensus had crumbled as other scholars noted how the imagery of light laces the two halves together; as does the motif of language, whether spoken by creation or inscribed in the Torah. Benjamin Sommer, for example, argues that the psalm is 'highly integrated' (2015: 382, 388-90). As a unit, the psalm presents an argument that creation reveals God in a sort of natural revelation. This cosmic declaration is made explicit (Brueggemann and Bellinger 2014: 101) or supplemented (Sommer 2015: 399) by the teaching of the Torah. Such scholarly readings harken back to rabbinic understandings like those of the medieval commentator David Kimchi (Radak), who 'sees that Torah makes explicit the speech of the sun' (Gillingham 2018: 123). Maybe the light of the sun

---

1. Unless otherwise noted, all translations are our own.
2. Jeffrey L. Cooley argues that Ps. 19 'consciously reflects on the cosmology in Genesis 1' (Cooley 2014: 195), further establishing Sabbath observance and the Priestly role in liturgy.

is a Torah, radiating words we hear with our eyes. Rather than being antithetical (in contemporary theological terms, natural theology versus revelation[3]), the two themes work together in ways that undermine our own dichotomous thinking.

Psalm 19 unites the ancient traditions of natural revelation of deity with the tradition of verbal and textual disclosure. The combination is more than religious syncretism. It is a fusion of various ancient epistemological modes: the biblical God is known in every way knowable. In every sense, the psalm is about *order* (Gillingham 2018: 122). Later Jewish engagement would take the insight even further, seeing rabbinic commentary already imprinted in the biblical text. 'Noting the six appellations of Torah in vv. 7-9 (law / testimony / orders / command / fear / judgments), these are seen to correspond to the six orders of the *Mishnah*; hence in the context of this psalm as a whole, study of Torah surpasses our knowledge of the universe with the aid of scientific research, for only Torah can help us to become who we should be in the cosmos' (Gillingham 2018: 123). Enlightenment Christians would later pick up the rabbinic themes of divine order and reason, albeit without the talmudic cast. Science and learning would reveal God, much more than daydreaming philosophy or speculation. 'The concern for the ordering of the world in this psalm has resulted in its being used from the fifteenth century to the present day as an argument from design for the existence of God' (Gillingham 2018: 128–29).

A few scholars, nearly all Protestant Christians, posit a third movement, as well, in vv. 13-14. These verses, they argue, arise after the psalmist, initially awed by Nature and turned as a result to ponder Scripture, realizes his own unworthiness before God. Craigie (1983: 182) writes, 'In the concluding portion of the Psalm (vv. 13-14), the tone changes once again; the initial praise of God in nature and law evokes in the psalmist a sudden awareness of unworthiness…as his eyes turn back from the double and glorious vision to gaze upon himself, the shock is almost too much'. Mays (1994: 99) knowingly asserts: 'the psalmist realizes he cannot be righteous through *torah* alone'. Mays continues, 'Only by God's pardon and preservation can the psalmist be blameless (in the sense of complete and whole in life under God) and innocent of much transgression' (1994: 100). Goldingay (2006: 285) somehow knows that 'vv 12-14b implicitly lament the supplicant's moral weakness and make a plea with respect to this need'. Indeed, several writers assert this reading is simply obvious, clearly inherent in the text, rather than being influenced by their Protestant Christian context with its concept of human depravity.

Late antique and medieval Christian exegesis of Psalm 19 took perhaps an even more idiosyncratic turn, molding Psalm 19 into Christological doctrine. Reading the bridegroom of v. 5 through allegorical, Christological lenses, instead of the

---

3. Psalm 19 is a crucial part of Karl Barth's argument against natural theology in *Church Dogmatics*, claiming that only Torah not creation reveals God; James Barr (1994) counters in *Biblical Faith and Natural Theology*, arguing that natural theology and revelation are presented in Ps. 19 as complimentary. Sommer analyzes their debate in 2015: 390–99 and calls their arguments 'mirror image[s]' of one another (395).

bridegroom/sun stepping out from under the *chuppah* ('wedding canopy' in the NRSV), the bridegroom/Christ bursts forth from the chamber of his mother's womb. Not only did Augustine read Psalm 19 in this way, but 'this extraordinary link to the Virgin Birth is taken up by several other commentators. Arnobius the Younger speaks of Christ "stepping forth from the Virgin like a bridegroom from the bridal chamber". Bede speaks of David [the presumed author, per Ps. 19.1] as a prophet making the comparison of the Bridegroom and the Chamber to refer to the Incarnation' (Gillingham 2018: 124). In this way, Psalm 19 becomes a prediction of the Virgin Birth; the two parts of the psalm speak to the two natures (human and divine) of Christ.

Psalm 19 proves remarkably adaptable, shaped ever anew in various contexts. In the very contemporary debates over the intersection of religious expression and LGBTQ rights, Psalm 19 has even been read in ways celebrating queer identities, even appearing, in its Polari version, in the liturgy of the Sisters of Perpetual Indulgence in 2003–2004 (Gillingham 2018: 129). The Polari Bible, a translation based on the King James Version, is wildly affirming and, therefore, centrally embedded in the Sisters' liturgy of self-celebration: 'The heavens *screech* the *fabeness* of *Gloria*; and the firmament sheweth *her* handiwork' (italics in the original; www.polaribible.org).

Our liturgical context is much more staid, albeit welcoming nevertheless. Psalm 19 is the first psalm in the Shabbat morning *Pesukey D'zimra* (פסוקי דזמרה), the section that precedes the morning service (שחרית, *Shachrit*) as a kind of warm-up for prayer. For years I (Jennifer) missed Psalm 19. We live only ten minutes from the Conservative synagogue; yet, with a young child our only goal was to arrive for the Torah service. The Torah reading happened right around naptime. As an infant, our son would sleep snuggled in his carrier; as a baby and toddler, curled up in my arms. Sometimes, if restless and cranky, his father would take him for a walk around the park across the street until he fell asleep, head on his shoulder. We imagined the Hebrew wafting into his dreams, imprinting itself in his subconscious, weaving into his very sense of self. As a child, he would play with Lego and other toys between the seats or in the aisle; sometimes I would whisper the *parshah* (weekly Torah portion) in English in his ear as it was read in Hebrew from the *bimah* (dais, central synagogue platform). Do you want me to tell you the story? I would ask. We would catch the fragments of Psalm 19 as verses broke off and wandered into the Torah service.

As our son approached *bar mitzvah* age, we started going to *Chabad*[4] for Shabbat more frequently. We had always attended other *Chabad* services and events, but rarely on Saturdays. But, our son was in *Chabad* Hebrew school and there were more children at *Chabad* than at our *shul*. Somehow, no matter how late, we always arrived right before the service begins. Now, the sounds of Psalm 19 are a part of the rhythms of Shabbat morning.

I (Rob) met this psalm in hymns, but not like those I share in lately. Its words resonated in sermons, ringing and bouncing from the walls of a small,

---

4. https://www.chabad.org/.

spare country church house where religion was presented as the only sensible, 'reasoned' way to engage with the world, and our religion of mind, text and liturgy was far more 'reasoned' than the ecstatic, emotional shouts of the charismatic congregation just down the road. Only a fool could assert there was no God; we went further and avowed it with sober reasonableness and patient biblical interpretation. We rooted through the leaf litter of Romans 1–3 and found in Paul a natural theology, that God was revealed in Creation first, then in Incarnation, now (when the 'perfect' had come) clearly via the infallible Word. We saw that affirmed in Psalm 19. Now I sit with my son among gracious men, praying through Psalm 19 in celebration but more in meditation, letting the pattern of oft repeated words quiet their mind before God even as they speak. I sit to one side, cheating a gaze at my wife through-and-around the *mechitzah* (space divide for women from men), wobbly-tongued by the thick, warm Hebrew vowels in my mouth. My son sits, impassive, head down, unmoved, the consummate tween response to wearing a tie and uncomfortable shoes. I note his lips move over some words as he reads. His Hebrew has long ago surpassed my own, and this text is so familiar, there is little chance he is stumbling. He mouths the words for another reason. I wonder if the words that erupt are his favorites and watch from week to week to see any pattern. So far, I've seen none. The words that he mouths declare something, surely, but the meditation in his heart remains his own, ineffable.

In our contexts beyond Psalms – classrooms, shuls, chapels, divinity schools, dining room tables, car trips, holiday gatherings and more – the Bible appears frequently, even daily. Our lives are permeated with Bible and its language, 'sweeter than honey' (Ps. 19.10 [11 Heb.]), dripping from our lips like the honeycomb. And yet, do we believe in God? The answer could be simple (no) or complex (define 'believe' and 'God'). On the one hand, living in our modern world, the Scylla of scientific discovery and Charybdis of continued inhumanity and suffering make any traditional belief in 'God' strained, at best. On the other hand, how can anyone talk about ideas like hope, forgiveness, grace, meaning or transcendence without reference to the metaphoric and ideological contexts which invoke 'God' as something, somehow 'there'. In the unique category of 'religious but not spiritual', finding meaning in ritual and community, we live in and among an array of devotional contexts, each circling around the Bible and its language about the divine.

Psalm 19 suggests a solution in its union of heavenly wonder and written word, its moments of undecidability, the ways it challenges dichotomies. Both the natural world and the Torah are beautifully and tangibly true, yet also shaped by context and expressed through poetic speech. What could be more scientifically certain than the sun, for example? We feed on its heat, mark time by its passage, marvel at its display as it rises and sets. And yet, we know it is the Earth that is in motion, that the sun does not 'rise' nor 'run its course' eagerly or otherwise. And yet again, how else can we perceive it? The moving sun is core to our very sense of time and space; yet we also know that it cannot be happening. We believe in God in the precise same way we believe in the rising and setting sun. Contexts of sky and earth, of perception and language, of the rejoicing Heavens and Perfect Law fuse. Neither context is, in itself, meaningful nor empty. Their voice is not heard, even as it is. In Psalm 19, with all its contexts in tow, lies a final restorative hope for a post-spiritual, but deeply religious belief in God.

On our choices for a second favorite psalm...

Rob: I might have chosen Psalm 121 for its first two verses ('I lift up my eyes to the hills...'). I was born and raised in the Ozark Mountains and currently live near the Appalachian range. These first two verses often occur to me on quiet hikes.

Jennifer: My two favorite psalms are Psalm 137 for its complicated emotions and visceral images; and Psalm 126 for its expression of an overpowering and transformative joy. (I especially love the phrase 'our mouths were full of laughter', v. 2.)

Robert P. Seesengood served as Director of Religious Education at Chatham Church of Christ, in Chatham, New Jersey for seven years, while completing his Ph.D. He is currently Associate Dean of Academic Affairs at Drew Theological School. His family has a membership in *Kesher Zion* Synagogue and he frequently teaches in their adult education program.

Jennifer L. Koosed is professor of religious studies at Albright College, in Reading, Pennsylvania. Her family belongs to *Kesher Zion* Synagogue, where she has served on the board and as President.

References

Brueggemann, Walter and William H. Bellinger, Jr (2014), *Psalms*, New Cambridge Bible Commentary, Cambridge: Cambridge University Press.
Barr, James (1994), *Biblical Faith and Natural Theology: The Gifford Lectures for 1991: Delivered in the University of Edinburgh*, Oxford: Oxford Academic.
Cooley, Jeffrey L. (2014), 'Psalm 19: A Sabbath Song', *VT* 64: 177–95.
Craigie, Peter C. (1983), *Psalms 1–50*, WBC 19, Waco: Word Books.
Dahood, Mitchell (1965), *Psalms 1: 1–50*, AB 16, New York: Doubleday.
Gillingham, Susan (2018), *Psalms Through the Centuries: A Reception History Commentary on Psalms 1–72,* Vol. 2, Blackwell Bible Commentaries, Oxford: Wiley-Blackwell.
Goldingay, John (2006), *Psalms, Volume 1: Psalms 1–41*, Baker Commentary on the Old Testament Wisdom and Psalms, Grand Rapids, MI: Baker Academic.
Mays, James Luther (1994), *Psalms*, Interpretation, Louisville: John Knox.
Sommer, Benjamin D. (2015), 'Nature, Revelation, and Grace in Psalm 19: Towards a Theological Reading of Scripture', *HTR* 108: 376–401.
Weiser, Arthur (1962), *The Psalms: A Commentary*, The Old Testament Library, Philadelphia: Westminster.

PSALM 20
WHEN GOD CROSSES BORDERS

Roger S. Nam

Anyone who has taken an introductory Hebrew Bible/Old Testament course knows that scholars can obsess over the diachronic development of biblical texts. Psalm 20 has a particularly rich history due to an extraordinary extra-biblical find. But we will get to that soon.

Psalm 20, with its Davidic superscription and its abundant royal language and imagery, has traditionally been classified as a royal psalm (Smelik 1985). The psalm begins with an invocation for divine support during a 'day of trouble' (20.1), calling on the name of the 'God of Jacob' (20.1).[1] The first half of the psalm (20.1-5) repeats the jussive form, invoking YHWH to do the following:

- 'answer you' and 'protect you' (20.1),
- 'send you help' and 'give you support' (20.2),
- 'remember all your offerings' and 'favor (you)' (20.3),
- 'grant you' and 'fill all your plans' (20.4).

The superscription (למנצח מזמור לדוד, 'To the leader. A psalm of David') indicates that the psalmist boldly petitions YHWH on behalf of the king. The opening temporal anchor of a 'day of trouble' hints at Sennacherib's siege as a setting for this audacious prayer, as the same phrase appears in 2 Kgs 19.3 (cf. Isa. 37.3). The repetition of these jussive verbs culminates with the anticipated response 'that we may shout for joy' (20.5). Such a proclamation carries a similar exhortational force as the jussives, but in the first-person form as a cohortative. The verse closes this section with another jussive for God to 'fulfill all your petitions' (20.5).

The second half of Psalm 20 begins with 'Now' (20.6) and shifts from the third person jussive to the first person. Traditionally, this may signal that the text is now drawing from a different source (Tournay 1959: 161–69). Other literary theorists might posit this shift as a stylistic device to show a different

---

1. The English translation, as well as the verse numbering, are from the NRSV.

perspective (Goldingay 2006: 306). Still others suggest that the interplay of perspective demonstrates a liturgical form to be performed among laity and priests (Gillingham 2018: 130). These viewpoints are not mutually exclusive. The psalmist no longer entreats God directly but continues in a self-reflexive posture. The ensuing verses recognize the futility of earthly military strength compared to the faithfulness of God. The prayer closes with a return to jussive forms, calling God to 'give victory' (20.9) and 'answer us' (20.9). The final verb creates an *inclusio* with the first verb of the first verse with a slight change in the pronominal direct object suffix. Instead of the second-person 'answer you' as in the opening verse, it uses a first common plural suffix, 'answer us'. This shift integrates the jussive forms of the first half of the psalm to the first-person perspective of the second half. The Hebrew syntax of the final verse is awkward with the placement of [הושיעה] המלך, 'the king', possibly as the object of the first clause as translated by the NRSV: '[Give victory] to the king, O Lord' (cf. Kraus 1988: 278). Other commentators translate as 'O King', suggesting a vocative form based on the MT, as in the sense of 'save, O king' (DeClaissé-Walford et al. 2014: 218–19). Such a translation implies that YHWH is the true king who will bring relief to the entirety of the community (Weiser 1962: 205).

The superscription ascribing Psalm 20 to David situates it against the narrative of his royal journey, as outlined in 1 and 2 Samuel, and reiterated in 1 Chronicles. The 'day of trouble' is obscure enough that it can reflect a variety of situations during the storied career of David. It also becomes a relatable theme for the descendants of David reading, hearing, or performing this in later contexts to relate to their ancestral narrative. In the opening verse, the call to the 'name of the God of Jacob' is valid for the worshipping communities of Israel and Judah, those in exile, and those in the diaspora during the Persian period. The Psalter resonated powerfully for Judean communities long after the monarchy as a model of prayer in times of distress.

Yet Psalm 20 not only has a lengthy diachronic history, but a broad spatial history as well. In the nineteenth century, in the Egyptian city of Luxor, an explorer discovered a papyrus (Papyrus Amherst 63) in Demotic script which, based on the writing style, is dated to the fourth century BCE. Although the script was recognizable, the contents were non-sensical. Eventually, Egyptologists and Semitic scholars discovered that it was Demotic script used to write in the Aramaic language (Bowman 1944). Within immigration contexts, languages can easily permeate political borders, and pollinate with native dialects. But discovering this combination of Demotic script with Aramaic words within an extant writing sample is remarkable. Once understandable, scholars saw that the document was a combination of three psalms. Two of the psalms were unknown. In the 1980s, two sets of scholars independently recognized the other psalm as a version of Psalm 20 (Nims and Steiner 1983; Vleeming and Wesselius 1983). Later studies refined the impressive historical journey of Papyrus Amherst 63 and its relationship to Psalm 20 (especially Zevit 1990; van der Toorn 2017; 2019; Holm 2022).

But how did Psalm 20 get all the way to Luxor? The ancient Egyptian city lies along the Upper Nile portion of Egypt, over 500 miles from Jerusalem. In addition to the political boundary that separates Egypt from Judah, the inhospitable terrain of the Negev prevents easy border crossing.

Despite these obstacles, the tradition of Psalm 20 crossed the border. During the fifth century BCE, the Persians had fortified their southeastern defenses, which included Luxor. They employed foreign mercenaries to station the different military outposts. Those included Judean mercenaries, who brought their traditions to their new residences. Along the Nile, these Judeans were situated alongside other immigrant communities from Syria, Babylonia, and Phoenician city-states. Traditions were adapted and made more accessible in language and script. Aramaic is a language distinct from Biblical Hebrew. Demotic is not even in the same linguistic family, but a required script for Egyptian daily life. This migration and assimilation of Psalm 20 happened over multiple generations, during which Hebrew language and writing yielded to the Aramaic language and the Demotic alphabet.

As theories of the connection between Papyrus Amherst 63 to Psalm 20 emerged, I immediately thought about my family's own migration experience. My mother and father immigrated from South Korea to San Jose, California in 1967 to escape poverty and political oppression. They were part of the first generation of Asians to take advantage of the 1965 Hart-Cellar Act, which eliminated immigration quotas.[2] My parents found jobs, raised their children, and tried their best to learn English, with limited success. Every Sunday, we would gather with other Korean immigrants at the Korean United Methodist Church of Santa Clara. I do not remember the content of a single sermon as my native language was English and not Korean. But I do remember the weekly rhythm of sitting through Korean language morning worship (bored out of my mind), then being sent off to English language Sunday School (slightly less bored), followed by a Korean lunch (finally!). We attended every Sunday as well as midweek events, so I suspect that at some point we read Psalm 20, though I cannot be sure. As I wrote this paragraph, I browsed at the website of this church. The pictures of the building stimulated all kinds of childhood memories of the sights, sounds, even smells of this church.

The memory of my family's own narrative can connect with different immigration settings. Without being reductive nor anachronistic, one can see broad themes that emerge in immigration experiences both in the present as well as in antiquity. Immigrant experiences are transformative and totalizing. Immigrants forge new and dynamic identities, as they merge aspects of their past history into their present reality.

2. 'This [American Congress] law set the main principles for immigration regulation still enforced today. It applied a system of preferences for family reunification (75 percent), employment (20 percent), and refugees (5 percent) and for the first time capped immigration from within Americas'. Read further in https://immigrationhistory.org/item/hart-celler-act/.

But these immigration experiences can also be traumatic. A sudden displacement to a new culture and new language is stressful. The stress is exacerbated with economic peril and social marginalization. The impact spans multiple generations – whether fleeing from Sennacherib's campaign in the Iron Age, the military dictatorship of Park Chung-Hee in post-war South Korea in the 1960s, or even a war-torn Ukraine in 2022. This trauma would naturally be reflected in religious traditions of these immigrants.

The discovery of Papyrus Amherst 63 compels me to think about the movement of Psalm 20 as a text across borders. I imagine how a community of immigrants could find comfort in a royal psalm that recalls the splendor of David. The Judeans in Egypt faced economic distress as they found themselves in Egypt. They acknowledged this trauma using a heritage text from Judah, adapted for their own use in this new land.

Psalm 20 could help these displaced Judeans engage with God in the realities of their own daily challenges through these same jussive forms. Over time, later generations contextualized the psalm. Without the notion of canon, the text was much more flexible and adaptable to local religious customs. But the core of the text in Psalm 20 remains recognizable. The displaced Judeans in Egypt valued their perceived connections to their homeland God. As an immigrant community, they made bold proclamations for divine rescue.

I do not contest the classification of Psalm 20 as a royal psalm. But alongside, I believe that the comparative studies with Papyrus Amherst 63 merit Psalm 20 as an example of migration literature. Any immigrant community can readily appreciate an invocation that calls God for protection, help, support, remembrance, and favor. The king is figurative for the migrants who bring their origin narrative of the Davidic kingdom to their new land. The symbolism of the priestly language of 'offerings' and 'burnt sacrifices' (20.3) may refer to both powerful collective memory of the Jerusalem temple, or even to a reference to their own local sanctuary, which these diasporic Judeans had constructed in Egypt at Elephantine. The military imagery becomes symbolic for their present immigration struggles. The Korean American community of my childhood church could relate to asking that God may 'fulfill all your places' (20.4) through the anointed one. A liturgical poem that sanctions bold petitions from a worshipping community in the margins. This community can make the same claims to God as if they were of elite royal status on the day of trouble. And in the end, we can anticipate that God will answer us.

My second choice would have been Psalm 18, because of its superscription:

> To the leader. A Psalm of David the servant of the LORD, who addressed the words of this song to the LORD on the day when the LORD delivered him from the hand of all his enemies, and from the hand of Saul. (Ps. 18.1, NRSV)

Roger S. Nam is professor of Hebrew Bible at Candler School of Theology of Emory University. He attends the Korean Community Presbyterian Church of Atlanta (PCUSA).

References

Bowman, R. (1944), 'An Aramaic Religious Text in Demotic Script', *JNES* 3: 219–31.
DeClaissé-Walford, N., R. Jacobson and B. Tanner (2014), *The Book of Psalms*, Grand Rapids: Eerdmans.
Gillingham, S. (2018), *Psalms Through the Centuries: A Reception History Commentary on Psalms 1–72*, Vol. 2, Blackwell Bible Commentaries, Hoboken: Wiley-Blackwell.
Goldingay, J. (2006), *Psalms 1–41*, Grand Rapids: Baker.
Holm, T. (2022), 'Papyrus Amherst 63 and the Arameans of Egypt: A Landscape of Cultural Nostalgia', in R. Kratz and B. Schipper (eds), *Elephantine in Context*, 323–51, Tübingen: Mohr Siebeck.
Kraus, H.J. (1988), *Psalms 1–59*, Minneapolis: Fortress.
Nims, C.F. and R.C. Steiner (1983), 'A Paganized Version of Psalm 20.2-6 from the Aramaic Text in Demotic Script', *JAOS* 103: 261–74.
Smelik, K. (1985), 'The Origin of Psalm 20', *JSOT* 31: 75–81.
Tournay, R. (1959), 'Recherches sur la chronologie des Psaumes (suite)', *RB* 66: 161–90.
van der Toorn, K. (2017), 'Celebrating the New Year with the Israelites: Three Extrabiblical Psalms from Papyrus Amherst 63', *JBL* 136: 633–49.
van der Toorn, K. (2019), *Becoming Diaspora Jews: Behind the Story of Elephantine*, New Haven: Yale University Press.
Vleeming, S.P. and J.W. Wesselius (1982), 'An Aramaic Hymn from the Fourth Century B.C.', *BiOr* 39: 501–509.
Weiser, A. (1962), *The Psalms*, Louisville: Westminster John Knox.
Zevit, Z. (1990), 'The Common Origin of the Aramaicized Prayer to Horus and of Psalm 20', *JAOS* 110: 213–28.

PSALM 23
A MOVING, VERSATILE POEM

Lieve Teugels

Psalm 23 is a beloved and popular psalm due to its accessible, universal and comforting message, and its simplicity and briefness, only six verses. In the Jewish and Christian traditions alike, it is often recited at the occasion of funerals, probably due to some sections deemed relevant, specifically v. 4: 'even though I walk in the vale of death's shadow'; and v. 6, 'And I shall dwell in the house of the Lord for many long days'.[1] Robert Alter does not agree with the fact that the intention of the last verse is eschatological. In line with the previous verse which describes a state of happiness (good food, wine, hair rubbed with oil), he believes 'for many long days' doesn't mean 'forever', but rather a happy life and the good fortune to spend time in the temple, 'a place of security and harmony with the divine' (Alter 2009: 80). I agree that this seems to be the intention of the original poet. Nevertheless, the comforting message seems to suit the needs of the mourning, an important aspect of the reception history of this psalm which should not be ignored.

The main imagery used in Psalm 23 is that of shepherding. God is presented as a shepherd, at least in the first verses. The depiction of God and his representatives as shepherds, and consequently of us humans as sheep, is an ancient trope, stemming from shepherding societies. The Mesopotamian king Hammurabi (c. 1780 BCE) wrote about himself in the conclusion of his code:

> I, Hammurabi, have been called by the great deities.
> I am the shepherd who brings well-being and abundant prosperity; my rule is just.
> So that the strong might not oppress the weak, and that even the orphan and the widow might be treated with justice, I inscribed my precious words on my stele called 'King of Justice' in Babylon.[2]

---

1. All translations are from Alter 2009: 78–90 except when the psalm is quoted in another source, such as the midrash on Psalms.
2. Code of Hammurabi 35 (www.kchanson.com/ANCDOCS/meso/hammurabi.html).

In the Hebrew Bible, being a shepherd was a respectable profession. King David, to whom the psalm is attributed, had himself been a shepherd in his youth and the metaphor of the shepherd for God is found throughout the biblical books (Alter 2009: 78; MacMillan 1983: 35; Brinkman 1995: 117). Today, in our urbanized world, the metaphor of the shepherd is still in use, even though few may identify as sheep when they refer to their clergy as 'pastors'.

In the rabbinic midrashic interpretation, to the contrary, the comparison of God with a shepherd is frowned upon. In the midrash to Psalms, Rabbi Jose bar Hanina is quoted that he wonders:

> In the whole world you find no occupation more despised than that of the shepherd, who all his days walks about with his staff and his pouch. Yet David presumed to call the Holy One, blessed be He, a shepherd! (Braude 1987: 327)

Yet David's words are explained by his following an ancient and respectful example, that of the patriarch Jacob who also called God his shepherd:

> But David said: *I understand more from the ancients* (Ps. 119.100), meaning that Jacob called God shepherd, as it is said, *The God who hath been my shepherd all my life long* (Gen. 48.15); so I, too, call God shepherd. (Braude 1987: 327)

The attribution of the psalm to King David is what spurs the rabbinic sages' largest interest. In this, they do not care much for the poetic context and language. In one line of interpretation, each and every verse is read as referring to an incident in David's life. 'He lays me down in green pastures' (v. 2a), for example, is applied to David's flight from Saul, when he ended up in the forest of Hereth (1 Sam. 22.5). The sages ask:

> Why was it called forest of Hereth? Though it was once dry as a potsherd, the Holy One, blessed be He, covered it with blossoms out of the richness of the world-to-come, as is said 'In a dry and thirsty land, where no water is…my soul shall be satisfied as with marrow and fatness' (Ps. 63.2). (Braude 1987: 332)

In its turn Ps. 63.2 is connected to 23.3a, 'He restores my soul'. This application of the psalm to David's personal circumstances and internal developments is found in many later Jewish commentators, often with respect for the song's poetic qualities.

In a different line of interpretation, the midrash relates all the psalm's verses to incidents in the history of Israel, specifically Israel's forty-year journey through the desert: the prepared table (v. 5a) refers to the quail and the manna etc. (Braude 1987: 332, 334). Yet another midrashic interpretation relates it, typically, to the Torah. The 'staff' and the 'rod' (v. 4b) are thus interpreted as referring to the

Written and the Oral Torah (Braude 1987: 332). Unlike Alter's literary-critical view, the midrash interprets the last verse (v. 6b), 'And I shall dwell in the house of the Lord for many long days', as 'for time never-ending, that is, life in the world-to-come' (Braude 1987: 335).

The question as to how far in the psalm the image of the shepherd and the sheep continues, is one that I discuss with my students when reading this text in my Biblical Hebrew course. The green pastures and the still waters fit the metaphor of God, 'my shepherd', who guides and protects me. Yet with 'my life He brings back', the 'pathways of justice', and in particular 'for His name's sake' (v. 3), it seems that 'the speaker glides from the sheep metaphor to speaking of himself in human terms' (Alter 2009: 78). In v. 4, however, the rod and the staff are again taken from the shepherding world. But what about the set table, the foes, the moistening of the head with oil, and the overflowing cup (v. 5)? We can hardly imagine sheep eating from a table or drinking from a cup? Morgenstern, an exegete of an older generation, concedes that the psalm would have been 'stronger and more direct and effective' if the image of the deity as the good shepherd would have been 'maintained throughout the entire Psalm' (Morgenstern 1946: 15). Some scholars, on the other hand, have tried to relate all the verses to shepherds and sheep. In his Christian bestseller, the Scottish evangelical minister and scholar J. Douglas Macmillan has argued that the entire psalm, including the less evident verses, relates to ancient oriental shepherding practices: sheep would have been given food on small tables, and their wounds would have been treated by the shepherd with oil. He explains v. 6 as referring to the sheepdogs that herd the flock (MacMillan 1983: 116–20). I do not think that we need to go so far to interpret the psalm as one seamless whole. Biblical poetry, like parables, sometimes shift their imagery midway. In an online blog, Tsippora Heller explains the shifts in imagery, even while adhering to its Davidic origin.

> Earlier in the psalm King David compares himself to a sheep following the shepherd. Through the challenges that God, the Shepherd, presented him, David's status has changed. He can no longer be compared to a sheep that eats grass. He is now described as a full human being. He has overcome his baser impulses. A sheep eats continually; a human can control his desire to eat and wait until mealtime. An animal and his food are almost organically insepa- rable. A human will invest his food with spiritual meaning through thanking God for his food, and esthetic meaning by eating at a set table. (Heller 2002)

The change in perspective – sheep or human – intersects with another change, from the third person (vv. 1-3) to the second person (vv. 4-5), and back to the first person. This is of course noticed by all commentators and given many explana- tions (Morgenstern 1946: 14). For me, it fits the style of Jewish blessings. Also the classical ברכות (blessings) formulas switch from second to third person ('Blessed are you, Lord of the Universe, who has commanded us' etc.). This going back and forth from 'you' to 'he' reflects the experience of the Jews with their God: some- times distant, sometimes close, a god you speak about and speak to.

My personal encounters with Psalm 23 in a liturgical setting stem, not surprisingly, from funerals. I became acutely aware of the beauty of the psalm when my friend, a rabbi, sang the song in Hebrew at the funeral of her father. She testified that he had asked her to sing this *mizmor le-David* many times for him on his sickbed. When my own father passed away a few months later, and I took upon myself to select texts that are appealing for both Catholics and Jews, I had my agnostic partner read Psalm 23. He was charmed by the psalm's beauty and imagery. A few months later I discovered the Israeli Singer Ehud Banai's beautiful and simple rendering of *mizmor le-David*, with the same melody as my friend had sung. I had by then been fortunate to have seen Banai twice on stage in Tel Aviv. Ehud Banai in concert is for me an experience of bounty like an overflowing cup.

Last year I was asked to contribute to a permanent education course about Psalms for Protestant ministers, organized by the Protestant Theological University where I teach. The idea was that I would run an evening program, read a psalm with the participants in Hebrew, and teach them something about Jewish uses of psalms. I introduced them to the Hebrew text of Psalm 23, and I taught them the melody of Banai. We sang it slowly and repeatedly until they got the hang of it. One of the students had studied the chords on a piano and we moved to the chapel to sing along with the piano. Because of the late hour, the housekeeper had left and had switched off the light in the chapel, and we did not manage to turn it on. By the light of cellphone torches we sang, gathered around the piano. When the course was over, I left for a drink with my colleague and some participants in the nearby lounge. Suddenly I heard music from the chapel: a number of the students had gone back to practice some more. I was drawn back to the chapel. The atmosphere was mesmerizing: the sound of the Hebrew words sung by three men around a piano, in the half dark, lit only by a telephone light. I never had stronger evidence that my teaching had struck a note.

My second choice would have been Psalm 114. I love its poetic metaphorical qualities, specifically the 'dialogue' with the personified sea ('what is it with you, Sea, that you fled?', v. 5). Grandiose. It is a very different psalm, much more heroic, which is also reflected in its most common melody, sung during the Passover *Haggadah Hallel* ritual.

Lieve (G.M.G.) Teugels is associate professor of Hebrew and Jewish Studies at the Protestant Theological University in Amsterdam. Her favorite research field is Midrash. She is an active member of the Liberal Jewish Communities in Utrecht and in Amsterdam.

References

Alter, Robert (2009), *The Book of Psalms: A Translation with Commentary*, New York: W.W. Norton.

Braude, William G. (1987), *The Midrash on Psalms 1*, New Haven: Yale University Press.

Brinkman, J.M. (1995), *Psalmen: een praktische bijbelverklaring* I. I, Kampen: Kok.
MacMillan, J. Douglas (1983), *The Lord Our Shepherd*, Bridgend, Wales: Bryntirion.
Morgenstern, Julian (1946), 'Psalm 23', *JBL* 65 (1): 13–24.

Online Resources

Ehud Banai, מזמור לדוד ('Mizmor for David'), in his album שיר חדש ('A New Song'). Available for listening at https://www.youtube.com/watch?v=QC3n1uMT-0Q&list=PL18D1381DF8E30FDB&index=7. Banai's official YouTube channel address is https://www.youtube.com/user/EhudBanaiOfficial.

Code of Hammurabi 35, www.kchanson.com/ANCDOCS/meso/hammurabi.html/.

Heller, Rebbetzin Tziporah (3 August 2002), 'The Lord is My Shepherd', *Aish.com* (accessed 28 June 2022).

PSALM 23
AN AUTOBIOGRAPHICAL AND INTERTEXTUAL READING

Musa W. Dube

The opening of Psalm 23 is captivating and remains one of the most memorable citations in the collection of world literature and scriptures. It states that, *'God is my Shepherd, I shall lack nothing'* (v. 1, my translation). The rest of what follows, in my view, elaborates the opening statement, with many more powerful, memorable, and beautiful sentences. The opening statement is, therefore, the theme and meaning of the whole psalm. The power of the statement can be located, perhaps, in three factors for the believing reader who identifies with David the psalmist. First, the assurance that one is not alone; rather one has a shepherd. The image of a shepherd articulates continuous presence of someone or something that looks out for you. Second, the identity of the shepherd, who is named as God, is awesome. While shepherds come in all sorts of classes, genders, ages, and cultures, the idea (generally of low class) that God, the Creator of the universe and the ultimate power of goodness, cares so much so that God takes up the role of being 'my Shepherd' is overwhelmingly humbling, assuring, and powerful. It also asserts the importance of each person of faith who reads the Psalm. The third, and perhaps a logical part, is of course the assertion and assurance that this shepherd cares and ensures that all my needs are met, not just now, but also for the rest of my days – *'I shall lack nothing!'* To fulfill such a role consistently, the shepherd cares for both the flock and its pastures. Psalm 23 is my favorite psalm for reasons stated here and many more. In this essay, I share my historical, autobiographical, and contextual journeys with Psalm 23 and its musical afterlives in Botswana.

My Historical Reading of Psalm 23

Psalm 23 and I go a long way! We first met at primary school, where I was taught to recite the psalm in the early seventies. I was also taught to recite the Lord's Prayer (Dube 1997). Like the rest of the students, we also sang a hymn entitled

'*Kreste yo o Galalelang, Oiponatse mo mahubeng*' ('Shining Jesus show yourself at dawn; break the clouds with your rays'). Save for the rare days when we sang '*Kuna Shango imbuya e ngweno*' ('There is beautiful land there'), we almost always recited the Lord's Prayer and sang '*Kreste yo o Galalelang*' every morning in the assembly. I never knew if these texts and song were in the curriculum, or the taste and choice of our teachers, but most students of my generation were raised with this staple food. Most probably the texts dated back to the days when missionaries started formal Western schools. It took me a long time before I realized that both Psalm 23 and the Lord's Prayer were biblical texts. I did not own the Bible back then. Yes, my mother owned and read her Bible weekly during the Sabbath. But I did not read her Bible because it was in Ndebele, my Zimbabwean mother tongue, while I learnt to read Setswana (Botswana national language) and English language at school. Below are the graphic texts that formed my earliest biblical canon which, as I will demonstrate later, also shaped my interpretation of Psalm 23.

Psalm 23	Lord's Prayer	Kreste yo o Galalelang	My Translation (of the Hymn)
God is my Shepherd; I shall not want.	Our Father Who art in Heaven Hallowed be your name Your will be done On Earth as it is in Heaven	*Kreste yo o galalelang Iponatse mahubeng Phunya maru ka marang Onthabele mo hihing O Lesedi bosigong Le Naledi mo mosong*	Shining Christ Reveal yourself at dawn Break the clouds with your rays Shine for me in the darkness; You are the light in the night; And you are the morning star
God makes me lie down in green pastures. God leads me besides the still waters God restores my soul God leads me into paths of righteousness, for God's name sake	Give us this day our daily bread And forgive us our debts as we forgive our debtors Lead us not into temptation, but deliver us from evil	*Ke nna ke lebeletseng Sedi jele ntshwarelang Se se ntekanyeng ke eng? Se se ntumedisang? Ke Phatshimo ya marang A' go a galalelng*	I am always watching For the Light that forgives me What is suffices for me? What makes me joyful? It is the shining rays Your shining rays

Yea, even though I walk through the valley of death, I shall fear no evil; for you are with me. Your rod and your staff they comfort me.	For thine is the kingdom, the power and the glory, forever and ever. Amen	*Ontekole mo moeng* *Ntlosa bontsho mo pelong* *O nkgolole mo dibeng* *O nkgomotse botlhokong* *O nkgogele tseleng* *Tsatsi je le sa feleng*	Check on my spirit Remove darkness from my heart Set me free from sins Comfort me in pain Lead me back to the path You the unfailing sun
You prepare a table before me in the presence of my enemies; you anoint my head with oil; my cup overflows			
Surely goodness and mercy shall follow me all the days of my life. And I shall dwell in the house of the Lord forever.			

I shall return to these texts and how they informed my interpretation of Psalm 23 below.

Context of Reading: Shepherd Girl Meets Her Shepherd

I grew up on the Dube Farm, my parents' farm. It was not in a village, town, or city. It was in the farming area for Borolong Mpatane villages, in Botswana. My parents chose to live and make their home permanently on the farm, where my siblings and I were raised. There were other farms around us. We ploughed and planted maize, grains, sweet melons, squash, ground nuts, beans, chickpeas, and sweet reeds; but we also kept cows, goats, sheep, chickens, dogs, and cats. Living in a farming area with our domestic animals, being a shepherd was an important role during the planting season, to ensure that our domestic animals do not wander into other people's farms and eat their crops. I remember particularly our neighbor Mmaskota, who had a farm adjacent to ours. Should our goats and sheep wander into her field and eat her crops, she would herd them back to our home and throw herself down and weep that her crops had been eaten and that it jeopardized her food supply for the whole year. It would threaten her with hunger and starvation. So, the last thing I, or any of my siblings who was responsible for shepherding the sheep and the goats wanted, was to lose sight of the flock. For these reasons, one or two animals always had a bell around their neck to help track their movements should they get out of sight.

So, often with a stick, I would take the sheep and goats out of the kraal (corral) to the pastures for grazing. Before letting them out, I checked if any highly pregnant animal was entering labor; if so, I left it behind to give birth. All lambs and kids were also left behind, in case they got lost in the forest. I would normally (culturally) lead the flock from behind. They led me and I followed them, but I also made efforts to direct them to places I wanted them to go. I talked to them with human language saying such things as, 'Hey, don't go that way! Hey! hey, come back here! Where are you going? This way', etc. My stick was part of my communication. I used it to direct the flock where it should go. After reaching a place where it was acceptable for both of us to stop (far away from farms and where the pasture was good) I would sit, sometimes on a rock or under a tree, or sleep on the sand in the stream and watch them grazing. Many times, I also helped myself to wild berries and fruits such as *mogwana, moretwa, morula, moretologa, and morojwa* and carried some home with me.

On a few occasions I would come across the enemy. This was primarily the jackal, which would turn up trying to snatch one of the animals. Wielding my stick, I would shout, scream, and chase it away. Fortunately, the jackal was never confrontational. It would quietly run away and leave me and the flock in peace. On some days, I encountered a slithering snake, prompting me to run a few meters away while I watched it go on its way. But the sight of a snake had a way of leaving me shaken and rattled and jumpy, long after it had disappeared. When the animals had grazed to satisfaction, we headed down to Tlhalogang River, where they would drink from water pools. During times when the pastures were good and the flock got full without much struggle, they sometimes would lie down and rest, ruminating. If any of the animals gave birth, I had to assist by carrying the lamb/kid back home. The day ended with all of us heading back home to the kraal at sunset. I would check if any of them was missing. Any sheep or goat left behind was in danger of being a good meal for the jackals. Consequently, post-harvest, when the goats and sheep were allowed to go grazing on their own, they always came back to the kraal when the sun was setting.

Umchachacha

But then there was *umchachacha*, as we called it in my mother tongue, Ndebele. These were curled pod fruits of a *mosu* tree (*Acacia tortilis*) that rattle. They fall to the ground when ripe. *Umchachacha* must have been the most delicious food for goats and sheep in our area. When *umchachacha* was ripe, it was a nightmare to be the shepherd of the day, for the moment one opened the kraal, the goats and sheep would rush out bleating and running towards the *mosu* trees to eat *umchachacha*. They did not go to one tree, but rather they divided themselves in small groups, rushing to different trees and directions simultaneously. As a shepherd girl, I did not know which group to follow and which one to leave, but one thing I knew was that while they seemed to be running from one tree to another, they would finally turn to Mmaskota's farm and that was serious trouble. *Umchachacha* taught me that while I was a shepherd girl, leading the sheep and goats to pastures, I was not always in control, for when *umchachacha* was ripe, the flock staged a rebellion, one that often left me helpless and crying.

Psalm 23: An Autobiographical and Intertextual Reading

Given this background, Psalm 23 is my favorite psalm. It is pregnant with pleasant memories of a shepherd girl discovering that she too has a shepherd! I read and understood Psalm 23 through the lens of its imagery, which informs me that I too have someone who travels with me, watches over me; one who cares about my wellbeing to the point where 'I shall lack nothing!' Through the eyes of one who was a shepherd girl, it was pleasant knowing that my shepherd leads me to green pastures and to still waters. From my context, I understood still waters as referring to standing waters that have distilled themselves, with all soil and foreign particles settling out, leaving clean and clear water for drinking.

As a shepherd girl, I also knew about the dangers that one can encounter while taking care of the flock, but Psalm 23 assured me that I have a powerful shepherd who restores my soul and who leads me to paths of righteousness. It assured me that when I pass through scary valleys of death I should fear no evil, for the rod and the staff of my shepherd protect me. My enemies, Psalm 23 assured me, will not dare do me any harm due to the strength of my shepherd: 'God set my table before my enemies'. God as my Shepherd cared so much and served me – restoring my soul when rattled; setting my table, pouring oil over my head; and filling my cup till it overflows (v. 5). It seemed a sure thing that 'surely goodness and mercy shall follow me all the days of my life' (v. 6a). Consequently, I agreed with the psalmist that I will dwell in the house of my shepherd in all the days of my life (v. 6b) – where 'I shall lack nothing'. This house of God, understood intertextually, was the whole Earth that I and everyone inhabited.

Intertextuality: Psalm 23, the Lord's Prayer
and Kreste yo o Galalelang

My understanding of Psalm 23 was interwoven with my other key texts. All the above three pieces featured the theme of being led. Whereas the Lord's Prayer petitions God to give us daily bread and to lead us not into temptation but to deliver us from evil, Psalm 23 bangs with assurance. Similarly, while my key hymn petitioned God to break clouds and visit me, to check on me and remove all that brings me down and to lead me back the path, in Psalm 23 this is a given. Psalm 23 tells me: God leads me to green pastures and to still waters; restores my soul; protects me from fear of death; and I will dwell in the house of God all my life. Dwelling in the house of God was a logical choice, for then I remain under the protection of the divine shepherd all my life. It seemed to me that if I prayed the

Lord's prayer and sang *Kreste yo o Galalelang* as petitions, Psalm 23 was the assurance of my answered prayers. It stood as the answered prayer.

But above all, the three pieces presented God in and through images and metaphors of nature: green pastures, still waters, valleys, dawn, shining rays, clouds, night, day, morning star – so much so that, for me, the Earth constituted the house of God. The divine travelled with me, provided, and manifested in the natural world that surrounded me (Dube 2015). Given that I lived on this farm, in a rather flat landscape, with a wide blue sky that rimmed with the ground at the furthest horizon, it was God's magnificent house, lit by an unfailing daily sunlight. At night, God's house transformed itself into another amazing beauty, as the stars populated the massive sky and painted breathtaking galaxies. Morning broke with awesome golden dawn and evening arrived with the same wonder – accompanied by singing birds, cooing doves, clucking Guinea fowls, croaking frogs, crowing corks, mooing cows, bleating goats and sheep among others. Dwelling in the house of God was the most luxurious mansion I ever inhabited. Psalm 23, the Lord's Prayer and *Kreste yo o Galalelang* thus were the core of my early spirituality. They were not grounded in the literary context of their specific books. They circulated orally and were understood contextually within my natural world. They were apparently in a perfect harmony with my natural world, where they were seamlessly grafted.

Conclusion: The Musical Afterlives of Psalm 23

The popularity of Psalm 23 in Botswana is evident in the number of songs it has inspired. Some of the songs are almost the exact text of the psalm, while others indicate additions, omissions, rearrangements, and repetitions. While space does not allow me to exegete the journeys of Psalm 23 into the Botswana hymnal landscape, the following short chorus is notable.

Johafa Ke Modisa//The Lord is the Shepherd

Setswana Version	English Version
Jehofa ke Modisa, Ka Metlha 2x	The Lord is my shepherd, all the time 2x
Ka metlha 4x	All the time 4x
Jehofa Ke modisa Ka metlha 2x	He is my Shepherd all the time 2x
Ka metlha 4x	All the time 4x

This short chorus is normally sung in both Setswana and English (so the translation is not mine). It is sung with a fast tempo, much joy, clapping and dancing. In this short chorus, only the first part of the opening sentence of Psalm 23 is cited verbatim, 'The Lord is my shepherd'. The rest of the psalm is summarized in the phrase 'all the time,' which is repeated up to eight times. The phrase '*ka metlha*/all the time' is thus the interpretative commentary on the meaning of the rest of the psalm. It underlines the presence of God as the shepherd for all needs (pasture, water, peace, etc.) and for all circumstances (danger, fear, sadness, insecurity, etc.). Lastly, Psalm 23 is also powerful for its ethical implications. In other words, beyond the individual assurance that a believer receives, there is also a powerful ethical message in Psalm 23. The message asserts that God cares about every person, so much so that God assumes the role of being a shepherd and a provider to each person – ensuring that all their needs are met. Second, since a shepherd cares for both the flock and the pastures, the psalm depicts God as a shepherd to the whole creation. This image bids us to value all members of the creation community and to be wary where the Earth's pastures are no longer green, where our waters are not still; and where many members of the Earth Community lack everything.

Now, if given a choice, what would be my second favorite psalm? It would have to be Psalm 150. It invites us to praise God on Earth and in heaven (all creation, v. 1); it invites human beings to pick every instrument and praise God, to dance (vv. 3-5). It invites everything that has breath (all creation) to praise God (v. 6). It gives the reason for praising God; namely, for God's 'mighty acts' and 'excellent greatness' (as creator of the universe, v. 2). I find this psalm consistent with my reading of Psalm 23.

Professor Musa W. Dube, the William Ragsdale Cannon Distinguished Professor of New Testament, is a biblical scholar based at Candler School of Theology, Emory University. She studied New Testament at the University of Durham (UK, 1990) and Vanderbilt University (USA, 1997). Her research interests include African literature, religion, gender, postcolonialism, translation, HIV&AIDS, *Botho/Ubuntu* and Earth studies. Professor Dube is the author of *Postcolonial Feminist Interpretation of the Bible* (2000) and co-editor (with Paul Leshota) *of Breaking the Master's S.H.I.T Holes: Doing Theology in the Context of Global Migration* (2021).

References and Further Reading

Asumang, Annang (2010), 'The Presence of the Shepherd: A Rhetographic Exegesis of Psalm 23', Conspectus: *The Journal of South Africa Theological Seminary* 9 (3): 1–24.
Dube, Musa W. (1997), 'Praying the Lord's Prayer in the Global Economic Era', *Ecumenical Review* 49 (4): 439–50.
Dube, Musa W. (2013), 'Decolonizing the Darkness', 40–55 in *Soundings in Cultural Criticism: Perspectives and Methods in Culture: Power and Identity* in the New Testament. Edited by F. Lozada and G. Carey; Minneapolis: Fortress.
Dube, Musa W. (2015), 'And God Saw that it was Good! An Earth-Friendly Theatrical Reading of Genesis 1', *Black Theology* 13 (3): 1–17.
Gilbert, W.B., '*Kreste yo o Galalelang*', Hymn 346, *UCCSA Dihela*.
Masenya, Mmadipoane (2022), 'Ecological Hermeneutics and Postcolonialism', 49–62 in *The Bible and Ecology*. Edited by Hilary Marlow and Mark Harris; Oxford: Oxford University Press.

PSALM 37
LIVING FAITHFULLY

D.N. Premnath

Psalm 37 has intrigued me for quite some time. I was fourteen years old when I learned that my paternal grandmother used to recite (in Tamil) her favorite Psalm 37 many times in her life and even recited it in its entirety on her death bed. Although I was not there in person to witness this, her twelve children talked about this amazing feat at family gatherings through the years. Now, fifty-eight years later, I have an opportunity to reflect on the meaning of the psalm in general and its appeal to my grandmother in particular. Better late than never, I suppose.

As a context, a brief family background may be in order. My grandmother, Mrs. Maragatham Joseph, came from a humble background. She went into vocational training as college education was beyond her reach. She excelled at sewing, so much so that she taught this skill to others at a training facility. She also did volunteer work as a 'Bible Woman'. This was the designation given to folks who would go around various villages to teach the Bible through storytelling to mostly poor folks who didn't have any formal education. My grandfather, Mr. Rayan Joseph, worked as a teacher and catechist. Both my grandparents were second-generation Christians. Their parents were converts to Christianity through the missionary work of the Reformed Church in America in South India, which began in 1839, lasting over a hundred years (David 1986). A discussion of the merits and drastic effects of the colonial missions of the past is beyond the scope of this essay. But I would like to highlight one aspect which might be of relevance in providing a context for my family history. While critics highlight the appeal of material things such as food, education, and medical aid for the mass conversions from lower castes, socially this conversion came at a high cost. The converts had to live and interact with a majority of people who were Hindus. In a cultural sense, embracing Christianity entailed adopting a Western way of life reflected through attire, food, and style of worship. Clearly, this was a discernible biproduct of the colonial missions which created resentment and, in some instances, hostility towards the converts. One such case was my other (maternal) grandmother, Mrs.

Hepzibah Samuel. At a young age, attracted to the teachings of Jesus, she became a Christian much to the alarm and anger of not just her family but the whole village. My mother often recounted the horrific incident of how the missionary (who was a woman) had to rescue my grandmother in a horse-drawn carriage with the villagers chasing behind, pelting stones and sticks. The missionary raised my grandmother, gave her education, and married her to my maternal grandfather who was a teacher. Even though my paternal grandmother didn't seem to have faced overt hostility and persecution, I wonder now if part of the appeal of Psalm 37 was the contrast between the 'righteous' and the 'wicked'. It is hard to ignore the ubiquitous presence of the 'wicked' (14 times) in the psalm. I believe the consolation of living faithfully was probably the greater message for her than the preoccupation with the wicked. To the task of unpacking the deceptively simple psalm we now turn. The translation used here is from the NRSV unless otherwise noted.

Literary Type

It is customary to designate this psalm as a Wisdom psalm. However, in more recent times, there have been some fundamental questions raised in connection with the origin, scope, content, and intent of categories such as 'Wisdom Literature' or 'Wisdom Tradition'. Will Kynes has forcefully argued that '…reliance on a vague, abstract, ill-defined, circularly justified, modernly developed, and extrinsically imposed definition of the category has enabled scholars to extend the boundaries of Wisdom Literature indefinitely, leading to a pan-sapiential pandemic in biblical scholarship' (Kynes 2019: 2). Mark Sneed also questions the appropriateness of classifying Wisdom Tradition as a distinct literary tradition (Sneed 2011: 50). For the purposes of this essay, it is sufficient to note that the meaning and relevance of the psalm depends less on its designation than the actual insights conveyed by the psalmist. I am sure a non-technical reader like my grandmother would concur.

Structure

The psalm lacks a discernible pattern of thought and movement. Brueggemann and Bellinger see a four-part structure: vv. 1-11 contain instructions in the imperative mode; 12-20 contain observations about life; 21-29 contrast the lifestyles of the righteous and the wicked; and 30-40 present a combination of instructions and observations (Brueggemann and Bellinger 2014: location 4990-5012).[1] I would modify the structure slightly differently. Verses 1-8 contain a series of imperatives intended as instruction; vv. 9-22 present the juxtaposition of the righteous and the wicked, followed by insights more on a personal note in vv. 23-26; vv. 27-34 offer

---

1. The Kindle edition lacks traditional page numbers. Hence the location numbers are provided.

words of encouragement, framed by imperatives at the beginning and the end; further personal reflections follow in vv. 35-36, concluding with words of encouragement in 37-40. Seeing through the eyes of my grandmother, the personal reflections in vv. 23-26 and 35-36 would have provided key intersecting points for internalizing the spirit and meaning of the psalm. The lack of a discernible structure might partially be due to a preoccupation with finding appropriate words to fit the acrostic pattern based on the Hebrew alphabet.

Key Ideas

Inter-textual Connections

Psalm 37 echoes some key aspects of Psalm 1, which is now recognized as the introduction to the Psalter and, as such, setting the tone and theological perspective for the entire collection (Wilson 1985: 207). Of particular importance are the overarching theme of the contrast between the righteous and the wicked, *Torah* meditation (Ps. 1.2 = Ps. 37.30-31) and the tree imagery (1.3 = 37.35-36). We will explore the first two aspects in more detail below.

In Psalm 1, the righteous are compared to a firmly rooted and fruit-yielding tree. But in Psalm 37, the tree imagery is turned on its head to not only represent the powerful wicked but also as something that will vanish. The Hebrew text is unclear as to which specific tree is intended here. Also, the idea of the meek inheriting the earth (Mt. 5.5) clearly echoes Ps. 37.11, where the idea is repeated several times (vv. 9, 11, 22, 29, and 34).

Torah Meditation

One of the key links between Psalms 37 and 1 is the verb הגה, *hāgāh*. While in 1.2 it is 'on His Torah they *meditate* day and night', in 37.30 it is 'the mouth of the righteous *utter* wisdom' (emphasis mine). In current English the usage 'meditate' has the connotation of reflecting or contemplating; focusing one's thoughts; or engaging in mental exercise for the purpose of reaching heightened level of spiritual awareness (Merriam-Webster's Dictionary). In Hebrew, *hāgāh* means to moan, growl, utter, speak or muse BDB: 211). As Michael LeFebvre (2005: 219) points out, two important aspects are worth noting. First, *hāgāh* is a vocal activity not just mental. Second, it is a whole-hearted articulation of something the speaker embraces. In 37.30-31, the psalmist reinforces this thought by the references to 'mouth', 'tongue', 'heart', and 'steps', indicating that the righteous enunciate what they have embraced with their whole being, including walking the talk. This resonates with what I know about my grandmother. Family was important to her. Raising her kids with care, discipline and compassion was important to her. To that end, she dedicated her life. She was truly the cog that held the family together. Though diminutive in stature and humble in disposition, she commanded much respect from her children and grandchildren because there was an authenticity that could only come from the correlation of testimony (talk) and witness (walk).

It is interesting to note that the psalm refers to 'speaking *ḥokmāh* (wisdom)' (v. 30) in the sense of conveying a perspective gained through a lifetime. As someone who valued learning, one of my grandmother's wisdom legacy was her insistence that her children and grandchildren should receive a good education. She always made sure of encouraging our academic endeavors. Even though we had our own residences, some of us grandchildren would gather at her house after school to do homework. During summer months, she taught us the practical skill of gathering, processing and preserving fleshy tamarind skins (used in Indian cooking), a process which lasted over several weeks.

Righteous versus Wicked

The teaching concerning choices in life and the consequent results are presented with some nuanced perspectives. Good conduct leading to good outcome and bad conduct leading to bad outcome have been traditionally associated with Wisdom teaching. But a serious student of the Hebrew Bible might recognize that grappling with such teaching is not confined to the so-called Wisdom books. I will highlight three nuanced perspectives presented in Psalm 37. First, implicit in the psalmist's approach is the recognition that good conduct does not always lead to good result, as borne out by the reality that the wicked continue to prosper. This might be indicative of the social context in which the wicked were in power (vv. 12, 14, 21, 32, 33 and 35). The righteous fret (vv. 1, 7) and are angry (v. 8) because the wicked do not face the consequences of their actions. Verse 21 suggests an intriguing context, where the wicked borrow and do not pay back and the righteous keep giving. 'Wicked' may be a blanket term for not only those in power but also for those who are short-changing the righteous. On the converse, 'righteous' may include not just the poor but also those with some means who are able to lend but powerless to enforce the repayment. Second, in the face of powerlessness, how are the righteous supposed to live without worry, anger, and anxiety? That is a tough predicament that many have experienced across the centuries, irrespective of time and place. As I write this, it is hard to ignore the plight of millions of Ukrainian civilians – men, women, and children – subjected to unspeakable atrocities, suffering, and annihilation by a murderous dictator as the world watches. Many similar happenings can be cited around the globe. How does one make sense of these chilling realities? For the psalmist, it is the trust in YHWH that generates hope (vv. 3-4, 33, 34, 39-40). Living faithfully with this hope leads one to find purpose in life. The strength derived from this outlook counteracts the anxiety, threat, and anger caused by the prospering of the wicked (Brueggemann and Bellinger 2014: 4990). Third, there is an honest acknowledgment in this psalm that the righteous may stumble, although YHWH prevents a head-long fall (v. 24).

Inherit the Land

The phrase 'inherit the land' appears five times in the psalm (vv. 9, 11, 22, 29 and 34), coupled with the idea of living in the land securely (v. 3) and in prosperity (v. 11b). It is possible to interpret this as an agrarian dream of living a self-sufficient and fear-free existence, as envisioned by the prophet Micah (Mic. 4.4). The choice of the translation 'meek' in v. 11 represents a generalizing tendency in place of a more a specific group that is intended here. For highlighting this point, Psalm 37 needs to be placed in the larger context of the collection in which it appears. There are certain key emphases reinforced by a cluster of words that suggest an unmistakable theology of the poor.

Theology of the Poor

Johannes Bremer (2017: 102) makes an important point that the first Davidic collection (Pss. 3–41) incorporates a theology of the poor. This can be illustrated through certain key elements. First, each of the four groups of psalms in the above collection (Pss. 3–14; 15–24; 25–34 and 35–41) concludes with a psalm that incorporates a theology of the poor. Additionally, the last two groups are framed by psalms of the poor on both ends (Bremer 2017: 102–103). Second, in the fourth group (Pss. 35–41), the combination of עָנִי, *ānî* ('poor', 'afflicted', 'humble'), and אֶבְיוֹן, *ʾebyôn* ('needy', 'poor') appears also in Pss. 35.1, 37.14, and 40.18. The term דל, *dal* ('weak', 'poor'), also occurs in 41.2 (Bremer 2017: 104). In the context of an agrarian society, the genus to which ancient Israel belonged, each of the terms listed above refers to a segment of the vast majority of the peasant population. The various terms used here signal their condition of being poor, afflicted, oppressed or in need. Third, the use of the *Hiphil* forms of the verbs נצל, *nṣl* (literally 'snatch away', 'rescue' or 'deliver') and/or ישע, *yšʿ* ('deliver' or 'save') in Psalms 34, 35, 37, and 40–41 reinforces the idea of God delivering the poor from their oppression or suffering (Bremer 2017: 104). Fourth, if one were to look at the use of the terms צדיק, *ṣaddîq* ('righteous') and רשע, *rāšāʿ* ('wicked') through the lens of the eighth-century BCE prophets, the specific legal connotations of the terms become relevant. The oppressed are called 'righteous' because they are innocent in the eye of the law. Conversely, the oppressors are called 'wicked' because they are guilty in the eye of the law. In light of this perspective, the concept of the poor inheriting the land takes on a whole different meaning of subverting the existing unjust social order.

Why was Psalm 37 so important to my grandmother? What particular aspects of the text made it come alive for her? In asking these questions, I would have to put myself in the shoes of a casual, non-technical reader who may not approach the texts the same way as a trained reader does. Identifying the overarching themes, patterns of thought and key ideas may be the delight of a technical reader. But for a casual reader meaning happens at points where the insights of the psalmist align with the human condition of a faith-filled reader. The basis of that interface is the underlying human situation. Four such points of contact might have drawn my grandmother to the psalm. The two interconnected ideas of the LORD as refuge in times of trouble (v. 39b) and trusting in the LORD and doing good (v. 3a) would have been important elements for a faithful living. Third, the idea that the steps of the righteous do not falter (v. 31b) because the *Torah* of the LORD is in their hearts (v. 31a) would have resonated with her as someone who lived by the witness of Scripture and taught it to many women in the rural areas. Finally, for someone who raised twelve children with meagre resources, a great source of comfort would have been the observation that 'better is a little the righteous person has than the abundance of many wicked' (37.16).

D.N. Premnath is an Indian Bible (OT) scholar and pastor. He lives and works in Rochester, New York.

References

Bremer, Johannes (2017), 'The Theology of the Poor in the Psalter', in W.D. Tucker, Jr, and W.H. Bellinger, Jr (eds), *The Psalter as Witness: Theology, Poetry and Genre*, 101–16, Waco: Baylor University Press.

Brueggemann, Walter and William Bellinger, Jr (2014), *Psalms*, New Cambridge Bible Commentary, New York: Cambridge University Press, Kindle edn.

David, Immanuel (1986), *Reformed Church in America Missionaries in South India, 1839-1938: An Analytical Study*, Bangalore: Phoenix Printing.

Kynes, Will (2019), *An Obituary for 'Wisdom Literature': The Birth, Death and Intertextual Reintegration of a Biblical Corpus*, Oxford: Oxford University Press.

LeFebvre, Michael (2005), 'Torah-Meditation and the Psalm: The Invitation of Psalm 1', in D. Firth and P.S. Johnston (eds), *Interpreting the Psalms: Issues and Approaches*, 213–25, Downers Grove: InterVarsity.

Sneed, Mark (2011), 'Is the "Wisdom Tradition" a Tradition?', *CBQ* 73: 50–71.

Wilson, Gerald (1985), *The Editing of the Hebrew Psalter*, SBLDS 76, Chico: Scholars Press.

PSALM 39
SILENCE THAT SPEAKS

Mercedes L. García Bachmann

I once met a woman working in the Amazon with indigenous groups. As we introduced ourselves, she started by saying that she had decided on a call to silence, and then proceeded to speak for ten minutes about her reasons. I could not help but wonder what would have happened had she decided to speak up instead of being still! The psalm of my choice reminded me of her. Like the psalmist, she was torn between a self-imposed silence and an anguished cry, and both required a commitment to YHWH, courage, and wisdom. Let us first shortly describe the psalm's contents, then return to the silence that lurks beneath its vocality.

In terms of its text, this psalm is well preserved. There are four *hapax legomena*,[1] a few terms not otherwise attested in the Psalter, and a couple of very usual terms, whose meaning here is unclear (for example, טוב, *ṭôb*, 'good').[2] Although comprehensible, true to its links to wisdom, the psalm is a real *māšāl*, an enigma. A short sample of some of its interpretations will show this point.

Regarding its literary genre, some common interpretations among scholars see it as a thanksgiving song, 'report[ing] a past crisis and also quot[ing] a bit of the prayer that the sufferer had cried out during the crisis' (Jacobson 2014: 364); as an individual lament, with wisdom characteristics (Forti 2015); as an elegy: 'A resolution to repress complaint for suffering in the presence of the wicked, which can only partly be carried out because of internal excitement, and which therefore takes the form of prayer that YHWH may make him [*sic*] know the brevity of life (vv. 2-6a)' (Briggs and Briggs 2004: 344); and as a 'meditative prayer', in which the individual complaint overture has been replaced 'by a rather strange meditation', thus producing 'an enigmatic piece' (Gerstenberger 1988: 165).[3]

---

1. Briggs and Briggs 2004: 345: מחסום, *maḥsôm*, in v. 2, נעכר, *neʻkār*, in v. 3, מדת ימי, *middat yāmay*, in v. 5, and חרפת נבל, *ḥerpat nābāl*, in v. 9.

2. In v. 3. Usually טוב, *ṭôb*, means 'good' or 'proper'. However, in this verse this meaning is not suitable, and the lexeme is mostly translated as 'very', as in Hos. 10.1 or היטב (from the same Heb. root, meaning 'very', 'well'), as in Jon. 4.4.

3. Similarly, Hossfeld (1993: 245) calls it 'a meditative lament about sickness and life's transience'.

Regarding the psalm's structure, there are several markers. First, there is the heading attributing it to David, important in terms of the Psalter and Davidic theology in the Bible. Then there are two *selah* indications at the ends of vv. 6 and 12, after the realization that every human is vanity, הבל *hebel*. This would establish three strophes (vv. 2-6, 7-12, 13-14). On the other hand, and not easily fitting into this structure, there are three vocatives: in vv. 5 (YHWH), 8 (*Adonai*), and 13 (YHWH or God-YHWH), which might also indicate strophes.[4] Beyond the fact that each section includes one of these vocatives, it is hard to fit together both kinds of markers.[5] Scholars wonder whether the tone of the psalm is pessimistic or optimistic, prayerful or meditative, and call for the one or the other choice; we may read this diversity of scholarly opinion, however, as an invitation to wonder at the text's polysemy.[6]

The psalm's speaker starts in the first person (vv. 2-4), then turns to YHWH: 'Let me know' (v. 5). It could be said that the rest of the psalm is an address to YHWH, from this 'teach me' to the 'turn away your gaze from me' of the last verse. I find it challenging that even when the addressee from v. 5 onwards is YHWH, the psalmist is always self-referential. Already in v. 5, when asking YHWH to disclose his/her end-term, the prayer continues: 'I will know how transient I am'.[7] And at the very end of the psalm, the request is, again, that YHWH gazes away: 'and I will smile, before I walk and I am no more'.

The more I read the psalm, the more I get the sense that the speaker's suffering determines the focus so much that other issues, even YHWH or the general

---

4. Dahood 1965: 242, breaking up the compound divine name.

5. Furthermore, the internal logic within each strophe is unclear. For instance, there are several repetitions of the same word: שמר, *šmr*, 'watch' (v. 1); לשון, *lāšôn*, 'tongue' (vv. 2, 4); [נ]אלם, [*n*]*'lm*, 'make oneself mute' (vv. 3, 10); אין, *ĕn* (the particle indicating non-existence, vv. 6, 14); הלך, *hlk*, 'go / walk' (vv. 7, 14); the nouns אדם, *ādām*, 'human being, person' (vv. 6, 12) and איש, *'îš* (vv. 7, 12), usually translated 'man, male'; and also the pronoun אנ[כ]י, *ān[ōk]î*, 'I' (once in the longer and once in the shorter forms, vv. 5 and 13). For further examples and a short discussion of possible origins of the different pieces, see Crenshaw 2012: 181–82.

6. Briggs and Briggs (2004: 345, 347) speak of a first strophe 'composed of a syn[onymous] couplet, a synth[etic] couplet, a syn[onymous] triplet, and a monostich or refrain'; and a second one of 'two synth[etic] couplets, a synth[etic] triplet, and a monostich or Refrain'. Hossfeld (1993: 246) detects a (personal) introduction (vv. 2-4) and the prayer (vv. 5-14), subdivided into the lament on human transience (vv. 5-7), prayer over sickness (vv. 8-12), and a closing prayer (vv. 13-14). Jacobson (2014: 360–61) sees five strophes related to the psalmist's silence (vv. 2-4b), speech (vv. 4-6), meditation (vv. 7-9), new speech (vv. 10-12), and prayer (vv. 13-14).

7. Clifford (2000: 60–61) states that מדת ימי, (*my*) *middat yāmay*, 'is simply a set period of time, not an undetermined period'; and חדל, *ḥādal*, indicates the end time of a situation, not fragility.

human condition, get focused on only briefly – only as long as a breath.[8] I am borrowing here one of the key images of this psalm, lifespan's brevity or breath, הבל *hebel* (vv. 6, 7, and 12). The word is identical in Hebrew with the personal name of the murdered Abel (Gen. 4). Alonso Schökel too plays with the possible allusion to Abel in Psalm 39, reminding us that 'every Adam is Abel'.[9] The psalmist seems torn between spending the little breath remaining in her/him in silence or in clamor – or in a silence that speaks. I can see the psalmist in the woman I met years ago, wanting to speak volumes by sealing her lips and yet, being unable to keep her resolve when this silence does not seem to help her either.

My last point in this short contribution is a more general reminder. Silence plays different roles for powerful and for vulnerable groups. Speaking up may mean death for a woman in an abusive relationship. At the same time, silence on the part of society as a response to her cries may mean death for that abused person as well.[10] Verse 1 ascribes this piece to David. Imagining his voice speaking of silence in Psalm 39 plays a different tune in my ears than Bathsheba's and Uriah's silence (2 Sam. 11), or David's concubines' silence (2 Sam. 15.16; 16.20-22) at their fates in David's hands. Silence is not neutral!

Regarding myself: I am an ordained Pastor and Director of the Institute for Pastoral Contextual Studies of the United Evangelical Lutheran Church of Argentina and Uruguay. My immediate context is that of a female religious leader in a nominally Christian society, with many more churches that, because of their patriarchal mindset, do not recognize female ministries than those that do recognize them. Our struggle is not to keep silent, but to make our voices heard, both as institutions and as persons, both within and without the ecclesial institutions. Women and other underprivileged groups are often explicitly or covertly silenced. My broader context involves engagement with vulnerable groups in the region (and elsewhere, whenever possible). Among these vulnerable groups, women are my foremost commitment. Aware of my privileges compared to other women in terms of class, education, gender identity, and other factors, I try to consider a

---

8. Several intertextual references are worthy of further meditation, such as Job's and Qoheleth's cries, and YHWH's commands to and actions towards a person to be mute(d) in Jeremiah and Ezekiel. Also relevant is Zechariah's silence in Lk. 1, and the word play on *hebel*, 'breath', and *hebel*, Abel, the name in Gen. 4. I would also argue for an intertextual reading of Ps. 39 with the rebuke of Lemuel's mother (Prov. 31.1-9) concerning the good use of one's assets for the sake of justice, especially when to open one's mouth in this service (vv. 8-9).

9. Alonso Schökel 1988: 269–82.

10. Although vaguely identified, the mere fact that the psalmist mentions wicked ones, death, reproach by fools, and sojourners and nomads, together with YHWH's punishment of evildoers and YHWH's unwelcome gaze, hint at the psalmist's experience of life's hardships. Usually, vulnerable people such as women, the elderly, and children suffer these hardships the most.

text's impact on vulnerable women and people who do not conform to a patriarchal heteronormative model. Such people find themselves constrained to silence instead of showing pride and thankfulness to God for their identity, their gender, and their daily experiences.[11] Theirs are also silences that speak.

My second choice would have been Psalm 117, because I long for a time of quietness in which we can focus only on praising God: no complaints, no longings, no enemies, no requests, just praise.

Dr Mercedes García Bachmann is an ordained pastor of the United Evangelical Lutheran Church (Argentina-Uruguay). From 1999 to 2015, she taught at the ecumenical seminary in Buenos Aires, ISEDET in the field of Old Testament / Hebrew Bible. Since 2015 she is director of the Institute for Contextual Pastoral Studies of her church. She is also Distinguished Affiliate faculty of the Lutheran School of Theology at Chicago. Her home base is Buenos Aires but she travels a lot, particularly in the region.

References

Alonso Schökel, L. (1988), 'Todo Adán es Abel: Salmo 39', *Estudios Bíblicos* 46: 269–82.
Briggs, C.A. and E. Briggs (2004), *Psalms: Volume 1: 1–50*, London: Bloomsbury T&T Clark.
Clifford, R.J. (2000), 'What Does the Psalmist Ask for in Psalms 39:5 And 90:12?', *JBL* 119: 59–66.
Crenshaw, J.L. (2012), 'The Journey from Voluntary to Obligatory Silence (Reflections on Psalm 39 and Qoheleth)', in J.L. Berquist and A. Hunt (eds), *Focusing Biblical Studies: The Crucial Nature of the Persian and Hellenistic Periods: Essays in Honor of Douglas A. Knight*, 177–91, London: T & T Clark.
Dahood, M. (1965), *Psalms, I: 1–50. Introduction, Translation, and Notes*, New Haven: The Anchor Yale Bible.
DeClaissé-Walford, N.L. (2012), 'Psalms', in C.A. Newsom, S.H. Ringe and J.E. Lapsley (eds), *The Women's Bible Commentary*, 221–31, Louisville: Westminster John Knox, 3rd edn, revised and updated.
Efthimiadis-Keith, H. (2004), 'Is there a Place for Women in the Theology of the Psalms? Part II: Self-Expression and the "I" in the Ancient Hebrew Psalter', *OTE* 17 (2): 190–207.
Forti, T. (2015), '*Gattung* and *Sitz im Leben*: Methodological Vagueness in Defining Wisdom Psalms', in M. R. Sneed (ed.), *Was There a Wisdom Tradition? New Prospects in Israelite Wisdom Studies*, 205–20, Ancient Israel and Its Literature, 23, Atlanta: SBL Press.
Gerstenberger, E.S. (1988), *Psalms. Part 1, With an Introduction to Cultic Poetry*, FOTL 14, Grand Rapids: Eerdmans.
Hossfeld, F.-L. (1993), 'Psalm 39: Meditative Klage über Krankheit und Vergänglichkeit des Menschen', in F.-L. Hossfeld and E. Zenger (eds), *Die Psalmen I, Psalm 1–50*, 245–51, Die Neue Echter Bibel, Würzburg: Echter.

11. See Kamionkowsky (2006: 405–406) on queer commentaries; Efthimiadis-Keith 2004; DeClaissé-Walford 2012.

Jacobson, R.A. (2014), 'Psalm 39: From Silence to Speech to Silence', in N.L. DeClaissé-Walford, R.A. Jacobson and B.L. Tanner (eds), *The Book of Psalms*, 360–72, NICOT, Grand Rapids: Eerdmans.

Kamionkowski, S.T. (2006), 'Psalms', in D. Guest *et al.* (eds), *The Queer Bible Commentary*, 401–27, London: SCM.

PSALM 46
PRESENCE, WAR-LANGUAGE, AND FEMINIST DIRECTION

Beth LaNeel Tanner

My first published article was a feminist reading of the Psalms many years ago. Since then, I remained a scholar of the Psalms and often get lost in the poetic beauty of it all. I have also become more of a feminist as I see the rights of women making few strides and, in some countries, like the United States, going in reverse. Psalm 46 has always been one of the ones I return to again and again. I found it a comfort during the pandemic. I also find it a psalm of motivation and support as a woman in the United States where the weight of patriarchy is ever-present. It is comforting and fierce and full of war imagery, and it has a clear hierarchy – 'Be still and know that I am God'. So why would a feminist choose this psalm?

I think I am drawn to the first stanza. It became a mantra for me during the pandemic. I live right outside of New York City, and my community was hit hard. In the seminary community, there were days with multiple deaths. Days were hard and grim, and it looked as if the world was coming apart at the seams. Like everyone else, I had to learn to live with the trauma, uncertainty, and fear. And these words were like a balm:

> God is our refuge and strength,
>   an ever-present help in trouble.
> Therefore we will not fear, though the earth give way,
>   and the mountains fall into the heart of the sea,
> though its waters roar and foam
>   and the mountains quake with their surging. (vv. 2-4, NRSVue)

The metaphors hit the right spot because it did feel like everything was falling away. And for the first time in my life, the whole world was experiencing the same thing – not equally, but we were all fighting the same demon. We saw our vulnerability, and we realized that despite all our advances, we were fragile creatures. Of course, we knew all this deep down somewhere in our souls, but we humans, especially in the first world, could usually ignore those truths before the pandemic.

The comfort comes in the first words, 'God is our refuge and strength, an ever-present help in trouble'. It is even more powerful in Hebrew,

אלהים לנו מחסה ועז עזרה בצרות נמצא מאד

> God to us is a refuge and strength, a helper in distress [he] is found exceedingly. (v. 2, my own translation)

Of course, for me, the word 'helper' takes me back to the narrative of Mother Eve. She is also named a 'helper,' and it is this and several other psalms that vindicate her title in Gen. 2.18. Eve is a helper, just as God is a helper who is ever present in distress. She is much more than the afterthought she has been cast as in our patriarchal world.

Remaining with this line a bit longer, in the ancient world, people gave gifts and sacrifices to the gods to receive good things like fertility and prevent the gods from doing bad things like storms or famines. It was the ancient equivalent of *quid pro quo*. Gods were associated with kings and kingdoms and wars. Psalm 46 describes God differently as a 'helper in distress, God is found exceedingly'. It is a line easy to overlook, but it defines the heart of the God of the Hebrews. This God hears the cry of the Israelites in Egypt and acts. This God saves God's people repeatedly from their troubles. This God does not turn God's back on the bad, the suffering, or the sinful. God stays in Jerusalem during the siege by the Babylonians even as God wishes to leave,

> 'Oh, that my head were a spring of water,
> and my eyes a fountain of tears,
> for then I would cry day and night for those
>   of my people who have been killed.
> ² Oh, that I had a lodging place for travelers in the desert,
>   so that I could leave my people
>   and go away from them.
> For all of them are adulterers,
> a band of traitors. (Jer. 9.1-2, NRSVue)

The God of the Hebrews is different from the gods that support regimes and the powerful. This God rescues those in distress. God's power is not used for the powerful but the powerless.

The next stanza describes the refuge from the previous verse. The roar of the waters and the quaking of the mountains (vv. 3-4) transform into a life-giving stream in the peaceful city of God. For a moment, we can rest reassured in the city of God where God dwells. But like the first stanza, this is a psalm of contrasts. Here is peace, but right outside we are reminded that 'the nations are in an uproar, and kingdoms fall' (v. 6), but without a breath or space in the Hebrew text, the God in the city lifts God's voice, and the earth sways. The nations and kingdoms are contrasted with God's stable peaceful city. Here we are reminded that the nations can rage, but God will quiet the world with God's voice. God's quiet is more powerful than all the nations' noise. God's action is followed by the refrain (v. 7). The refrain declares God's power over all others and God's protective role for God's people. The language is militaristic and hierarchical declaring God above all others.

After the refrain, the scene changes. We are invited to a heavenly realm overlooking the whole earth. We are lifted from our distress into the heavens, and this gives a new perspective. The next line is the height of our change in perspective,

לכו חזו מפעלות ה׳ אשר שם שמות בארץ

> Come behold the works of the Lord; see the desolations he has brought on the earth. (v. 9, NRSVue)

The Hebrew word שמות, according to *HALOT*, always refers to the destruction following the execution of God's justice. The psalm appears to say God has become fed up and destroyed those nations and kingdoms. But the next verse (v. 10) pushes our change of perspective further, for God's 'desolation' is the cessation of human war as God breaks the bow and shatters the spear and burns the shields with fire. God's destruction is to end human destruction. God's 'desolations' are not human ones. We should never mistake them for such.

The psalm also condemns the nations and kingdoms and names us for who we are. The truth is that for those in power, peace would be a 'desolation' to their thinking and way of life. God's world would bring peace with no instruments of war to craft, people to capture, or women to control. The machines built on power and privilege would cease. Isaiah's vision of a peaceable kingdom (65.17-25) would replace our competition and striving to win.

Humans without privilege are hard to imagine. The contrast between human-created chaos and God-created *shalom* is clear. Psalm 46 deconstructs the ways we have built this patriarchal world. The ways we have divided ourselves into nations and kingdoms that wage war and kill. As I traveled with this psalm during the pandemic, its words helped soothe the fear and the longing to get back to my life. Then, it reminded me that, maybe, getting back to the way it was might not be the best thing. We could reset our perspective and decrease the contrast between the holy and the human. We could, but we will probably not because the psalms also know human nature and how we often choose what is right in our own eyes.

הרפו ודעו כי אנכי אלהים ארום בגוים ארום בארץ
ה' צבאות עמנו משגב לנו אלהי יעקב

> Be still and know that I am God! I am exalted among the nations;
> I am exalted in the earth. The Lord of hosts is with us; the God of Jacob our refuge [fortress]. (vv. 11-12, NRSVue)

This phrase is full of military language: 'the God of the armies' and 'God as our fortress'. Can the language of war here be redeemed? Does it need to be? Like all poetry, it is all a matter of how we understand the metaphors.

So, how can a feminist understand this language? First, one must ask why we think that war language is not feminist. The question implies binary thinking – a poem is either this or that. The psalm does display a binary contrast in the first two stanzas, but the third (vv. 8-10) offers a way past the impasse and into another perspective. It is this different perspective that feminists seek in their work to see old worlds in a new way that offers openness to something beyond patriarchy.

The psalm also calls out the powers and kingdoms that have created the binary thinking and colonialism of patriarchy. Indeed, the psalm turns their words against them. Their definition of power will be desolated by the voice of God. God will take their machines of war and destroy them. Any psalm that upends power and privilege can be seen as a feminist psalm.

Feminists cannot get wrapped up in the cosmetics of this battle. In my circle, I work with both white women, or those considered white in European circles, and with women of color. In my experience, white women focus more on the cosmetics of our power struggle, preferring terms like kin-dom instead of kingdom, and believing we can leave behind the patriarchy of the past without stomping it out of existence. Women of color know they are in the fight of their lives and often, for them, there is much more at stake. They cry to the God of Jacob as a fortress against the harsh power and privilege and racism of the world. They see the need for God of the armies to fight for them. I think we need to listen to them and let them lead us or at the very least get out of their way. They know these powers will not take a seat politely at the back of the bus.

Sadly, in today's world, we cannot leave behind the language of war. Women are fighting and dying in wars all over the world. Women in my country are waging a war to reclaim our reproductive rights. Until the patriarchal privilege is dead, we have no other options. We need a God who has the power and might to fight with us and provide shelter when we need to rest or hide. Psalm 46 knows that the fight is real and while God is with us in our distress, the distress is still there, and it seems in no hurry to be going anywhere. The psalm is one of confidence in God's vindication of those in distress. The psalm proclaims a world that is not yet, while calling on us to change the one we have. I do not know anything more feminist than that.

My students tell me that my favorite psalm is the one we are doing in class that day. I have to admit they are right. My central focus has always been the laments because of the relationship between God and the human represented in the harsh words. The psalms narrative real life lived in a blessed and broken world. I remain in awe of a God who is 'ever present in distress'.

Beth LaNeel Tanner is the Academic Dean and Kansfield Chair of Old Testament at New Brunswick Theological Seminary, USA. She has published several articles and books on the Psalms and is currently working on a commentary for the Wisdom Commentary series. She is an ordained pastor in the PCUSA (Presbyterian Church [USA]).

PSALM 49
TWO UNSOLVED RIDDLES AND ONE NEW PROVERB

Klaas Spronk

Forty years ago I started working on my dissertation. Following the advice of my promotor, Johannes de Moor, I abandoned my own vague ideas of studying something about animals or something about sexuality in the Old Testament and chose as my topic the rise of positive ideas about life after death in ancient Israel. That was a hotly debated subject in that period, due among other things to the assertion by Mitchell Dahood in his Anchor Bible commentary on the book of Psalms (1970) that many psalms and also proverbs express the belief in resurrection of the dead and of immortal heavenly afterlife. Dahood's ideas in this matter fitted well to the Christian belief in life after death, but went against the common scholarly views. Dahood based his ideas on the comparison with ancient Ugaritic texts. De Moor had criticized Dahood's methodology in a number of review articles, calling it 'pan-Ugaritism' (de Moor and van der Lugt 1974). Nevertheless, according to my Doktorvater, a comparison with the Ugaritic conceptions of the afterlife, especially concerning the cult of the dead, would help me get a better view on related – be it clearly related, but clearly distinguished – expectations in ancient Israel with regard to the afterlife (de Moor and van der Meer 1988).

When dealing with the Psalms, I had to position myself in my dissertation also in another much-discussed field of research, namely the study of poetic structures. Here, de Moor had developed some firm convictions. With a number of colleagues he had established the 'Kampen school' (named after the location of our university), propagating in many publications a method based on the idea that poetry and poetic prose in the Hebrew Bible was built up of strophes in well-balanced bigger structures. So, it was obvious that I would start my discussion of the relevant psalms for my research of ancient Israelite ideas about life and death with a formal analysis according to the 'Kampen' rules.

Although I did not mention this in my dissertation (Spronk 1986: 327–34), here some first doubts about the concepts handed to me by my supervisor crept in. It started with the structural analysis of Psalm 49. With every new attempt to find a regular structure I ended with different results. This should have come as no surprise, because an overview of recent research on the structure of the psalm shows that consensus in this matter is not in sight. When I returned thirty years later to Psalm 49 in my contribution to the Festschrift for Oswalt Loretz, I added to the increasing number of proposed structures no fewer than two possible new reconstructions (Spronk 2016).

Then why is this psalm among my favourites? It is, because I managed to solve its riddle – not the riddle of its structure, but the riddle that is explicitly mentioned in the poem itself. Looking for the former I found the latter or – to be more precise – the proverb solving the riddle. This started with my focus on the repetition of words. This is an important element for the analysis of the structure, because it yields hard formal evidence of the way the poet may have related different parts of the poem to each other. Among the many repetitions in Psalm 49 was the one based on the Hebrew root משל, connecting vv. 5, 13 and 21. Verse 5 is part of the rather bombastic announcement of the riddle in vv. 2-5 as something all people should know and as something wise. It speaks in v. 5 of a riddle which shall be solved in a proverb:

> I will incline my ear to a proverb;
> I will solve my riddle with the lyre.[1]

The riddle is indicated by the question in the following verse, 'Why do I have to be afraid in the days of evil?', and is further described as the fact that everyone has to die and that death makes no distinction between rich and poor. The emphasis is on the fact that you cannot buy your way out. Death also stops the boasting of the rich. So it can be concluded in v. 13:

> Yea, a man with wealth does not abide;
> he is like the beasts that are destroyed.

This does not look like a convincing solution to the riddle. It is just another description of the problem. Nevertheless, it seems to point to the proverb announced in the introduction. In Hebrew the verb נמשל (*nimshal*), which is translated here as 'he is like', is closely related to the noun משל (*mashal*), which stands in parallelism to 'riddle' in v. 5 and is translated as 'proverb'. The fact that the riddle is not solved yet is also indicated by the fact that in vv. 14-21 another description of inescapable death follows, which leaves no hope for the rich, contrary to those who trust in God. The concluding v. 21 repeats v. 13, but with a slight difference:

> A man with wealth, but who does not understand,
> is like the beasts that are destroyed.

---

1. Translation mine.

The difference concerns the verb at the end of the first line: בין (*bin*, *Hiphil*), 'to understand', instead of לין (*lin*, *Qal*), 'to abide'. Also another negative particle is used: לא, *loʾ*, instead of בל, *bal*. Taken together one notices that in both cases the same letters are used, but that the order has changed: from בל ילין (*bal-yalin*) to לא יבין (*lo yabin*). With Hermann Gunkel, the godfather of modern scholarly Psalms studies, it is often suggested that the text should be corrected and that we should also read *yabin*, 'he understands', in v. 13 (Gunkel 1929: 212). Others assume that it should be the other way around, and correct v. 21 on the basis of v. 13. This is found, for instance, in the NRSV, which reads in both verses (in the NRSV vv. 12 and 20) 'Mortals cannot abide in their pomp'. It is far more attractive, however, to trust the accuracy of the transmission of the Hebrew text and assume a deliberate wordplay. One can go even a step further – this was my *aha!* moment: the wordplay contains the announced proverb as the solution to the riddle. The riddle is that there seems to be no difference between humans and beasts. The solution is that what does make a difference between humans and beasts is whether or not one has understanding. Put next to each other the related lines form a nice proverb:

אם לא יבין כי בל ילין (*ʾim loʿ yabin ki bal yalin*),
'If you do not have insight, surely you shall not stay'.

This can be compared to the famous saying in Isa. 7.9, with a wordplay with the Hebrew verb אמן, *ʾaman*, first in the *Hiphil* (*taʾaminu*, 'will believe') and then in the *Nif.* (*teʾamenu*, 'be confirmed'):

אם לא תאמינו כי לא תאמנו (*ʾim lo taʾaminu ki lo teʾamenu*),
'If you do not believe, surely you shall not be confirmed'.

In Psalm 49 the verb בין, *bin*, *Hiphil*, 'to understand', refers back to the word תבונות, *tebunot*, 'insight', used in the announcement in v. 4. What then is this insight? It is what is described after v. 13 and culminates in v. 16:

Truly, God will ransom my life;
He will surely take me from the hand of Sheol.

The poet underlined these words by introducing them with an exclamation (אך, 'truly'), further emphasized by adding *selah* at the end of the line, possibly indicating that a later editor of the poem advises the reader to take some time to consider what is said here.

I have not solved the riddle of the regular structure of this psalm, at least not along the lines of my supervisor. It had put me on track, however, to better understand the literary style of the poet. The same goes for the other riddle I was facing: why does the Hebrew Bible contain hardly any indication of hope for the afterlife? I realized that I may have posed – again – the wrong question. Just as I had been looking for a literary structure which was more in my head than in the text, so I ran the risk of finding a conception of the afterlife which was more inspired by later Christian traditions than by ancient Israelite ideas on this matter. The fact is that whereas v. 16 touches upon this subject, the text continues with advice about coping with the boasting of rich people in this life. What was meant exactly in v. 16 when it is said that God 'will ransom my life' remains a riddle. Perhaps it is better to leave it this way. History shows that as soon as people start speculating about it, they tend to try manipulating it and, in this way, take the role of God. There are many examples of how this can go terribly wrong.

In my dissertation I emphasized the reluctance of the Hebrew Bible with regard to everything related to the afterlife. Apparently, I was not clear enough, as can be divulged from the fact that, in a recent survey of scholarly research on this issue, I am mentioned next to Mitchell Dahood as someone assuming ancient Israelite belief in a blissful afterlife (Wyatt 2021: 155–56). For me this is a case of *bien étonné de se trouver ensemble*.

Be that as it may, as I see it now, in the end the two riddles remain: one about the structure of the psalms, and the other about the afterlife. I am comforted, however, with the find of an unexpected proverb.

My second choice would have been Psalm 73. More explicitly than Psalm 49, it discusses the problem of bad things happening to good people; but, from a literary point of view, it is less exciting.

Klaas Spronk is professor of Old Testament at the Protestant Theological University, Amsterdam.

References

Dahood, Mitchell (1970), *Psalms III. 101–150*, AB 17A, Garden City: Doubleday.
Gunkel, H. (1929), *Die Psalmen übersetzt und erklärt*. 4. Auflage, Göttingen: Vandenhoeck & Ruprecht.
de Moor, Johannes C. and Pieter van der Lugt (1974), 'The Spectre of Pan-Ugaritism', *Bibliotheca Orientalis* 31: 3–26.
de Moor, Johannes C. and Willem van der Meer, eds (1988), *The Structural Analysis of Biblical and Canaanite Poetry*, JSOTSup 74, Sheffield: JSOT Press.
Spronk, K. (1986), *Beatific Afterlife in Ancient Israel and in the Ancient Near East*. AOAT 219, Neukirchen-Vluyn: Neukirchener Verlag.
Spronk, K. (2016), 'The Unsolved Riddle of the Structure of Psalm 49', in L. Hiepel and M.-T. Wacker (eds), *Zwischen Zion und Zaphon: Studien im Gedenken an den Theologen Oswald Loretz (14.01.1928–12.04.2014)*, 243–58, AOAT 438, Münster: Ugarit Verlag.
Wyatt, N. (2021), 'Immortality and the Rise of Resurrection', in F. Stavrakopoulou (ed.), *Life and Death: Social Perspectives on Biblical Bodies*, 141–69, London: Bloomsbury.

PSALM 51
A MAN RENEGOTIATING HEROISM

Mikael Larsson

What makes a 12-year-old boy from the pietistic north of Sweden identify so strongly with words attributed to King David's confession after the rape of Bathsheba and the killing of her husband (Ps. 51.1-2)? And how come the psalm maintains its pull decades later, as the young adult questions his theology and attempts to negotiate a more egalitarian fatherhood? It came as a bit of a surprise to me that my choice of Psalm 51 was so immediate. Reading about its reception, I realize this is no coincidence. After a brief presentation of the psalm, I reflect on how my experiences in two formative contexts, evangelical Christianity and feminism, have affected my engagement with the psalm and the figure of David.

Scholars generally categorize Psalm 51 as an individual song of lament, with the important adaptation that a confession of sin replaces the complaint element. The psalm lacks a description of the actual situation of distress, it features no external enemies and the petitioner refrains from claims to innocence. Disagreement has revolved around the precise situation of the petitioner. Is it a prayer for healing or for forgiveness (which could amount to the same)? A majority goes for the latter, consigning the song to the subcategory of penitential psalms.

In terms of dating, three main components constitute the psalm. The core of the psalm (vv. 3-19) is the oldest and contains a number of linguistic echoes from 2 Samuel 11–12, for example through the verbs 'to be merciful' (חנן *Qal*) and 'to sin' (חטא *Qal*). The language of this section of the psalm, furthermore, shows affinities with exilic and postexilic prophetic texts, in particular through its conception of sin and forgiveness (e.g. Jer. 2.22; 4.14; Isa. 1.18), its call for new beginnings (e.g. Isa. 65; Jer. 31; Ezek. 36) and its critique of sacrifice (Jer. 6.20; 7.22; Isa. 1.11-13). The latter also echoes pre-exilic texts like Amos 5.21-22 and Hos. 6.6. The final two verses (vv. 20-21) are a later addition, which refers to YHWH's rebuilding (תבנה, jussive or indicative of בנה *Qal*) of the walls of Jerusalem. Celebrating the prospect of sacrifice, the ending appears to be at odds with the preceding critique of sacrifice (v. 18). As a 'liturgical appendix', the ending reshapes an earlier individual lament to serve the community and to offer eschatological hope (Zenger 2000: 22–23). Building on a core of post-exilic traditions, the psalm may have found its final form as late as mid-fifth century BCE.

The heading (v. 1) and the biographical superscription (v. 2) are part of the reception of the psalm and invite us to read it through King David's life. The placement of the psalm, opening the Second Davidic Psalter, points in the same direction. Psalms 51 and 72 thematically frame the collection, by featuring Bathsheba and her son Solomon, and by addressing the issue of the monarch's compliance to the law (Gillingham 2018: 302–304). The main body of the psalm divides into two distinct parts. The call to 'blot out' (מחה *Qal*) transgression frames the first one (vv. 3-11). The repetition of Elohim, 'heart' (לב) and 'spirit' (רוח) serves as *inclusio* for the other (vv. 12-19). Focus in the first part lies on seeking deliverance in the present for past sins. The train of thought goes from appeal and initial petition (vv. 3-4) to confession of sin (vv. 5-8), prayer for forgiveness (vv. 9, 11) and renewal (v. 10). The second part looks to the future, with pleas for ongoing support and transformation that lasts. This comes to expression through prayer for restoration (vv. 12-14), a vow to teach sinners (v. 15) and a prayer for the ability to praise (vv. 16-19).

The central ideas of the psalm concern sin and forgiveness. Three different concepts cover the range of human wrongdoing: 'transgression' (פשע, vv. 3b, 5a, 15a) emphasizes the aspect of crime and rejection of authority; 'iniquity' (עון, vv. 4a, 7a, 11b) that of destruction and injury; and 'sin' (חטא, vv. 4b, 5b, 6a, 7b, 9a, 11a, 15b) that of deviation and missing one's goal. The terminology for forgiveness likewise invokes three images, all belonging to the cultic sphere. 'Blot out' (מחה, vv. 3b, 11b) can refer to the erasing of writing from a tablet or to the cleansing of a dish. 'Wash' (כבס *Piel*, vv. 4a, 9b) normally relates to clothing. 'Cleansing' (טהר *Piel*, vv. 4b, 9a) is what the priests do when they declare something as pure, but the term can also refer to the refinement of metal.

The most contested passage of the psalm is v. 7 and the issue revolves around the origin and nature of sin. What does it mean to be 'brought forth' and 'conceived' in sin? Whereas the first verb (חיל *Polal*) relates to birth pangs, the second (יחם *Piel*) invokes being in heat, i.e., desire. Scholars generally agree that the passage does not imply that sin is rooted in genetics or sexuality, while it attests to the idea of humankind's over-individual orientation towards sin. Another dispute concerns the meaning of sinning 'only' against the deity (לבדך, v. 6). The idea here is not to exclude transgressions against fellow humans, but that sin, ultimately, always counts as an offense against YHWH (Kraus 1993: 501–502). Finally, the somewhat puzzling request in v. 16 to be delivered 'from bloods' (מדמים) may either refer to threats of violence directed at the petitioner (blood vengeance) or to acts of violence committed by the petitioner (bloodguilt).

The impact of the psalm for theology and liturgy is considerable. Jewish interpretative tradition upholds David as a model of repentance, stressing his remorse, and deals with the relationship between forgiveness and sacrifice. The psalm significantly features at Yom Kippur and at the Sabbath of the Passover. In Christian tradition, the psalm has been instrumental for the concept of original sin (Origen) and the notion of justification by faith (Luther). As the preeminent penitential psalm, it appears in particular at Advent, Lent and Easter. Its influence is evident in the monastic prayer. Supersessionist tendencies surface in twentieth-century commentaries, by scholars who celebrate the high 'spiritualization' of sin in the psalm (Gese 1974: 23) or denounce the rehabilitation of sacrifice in the last two verses.

Re-reading the psalm from the point of view of the present, the struggle with masculinity and power stands out as the theme that links the psalm to the narrative of my past. Such a struggle centers around two main ideas, self-control and complicity, of which I will offer a few examples. Whereas the claim to know what one has broken (vv. 5-6a) expresses the notion of the fully transparent subject, the prayer for a new creation (v. 12) implies that total transformation of the subject is possible. Although the psalmist expresses these dreams in starkly individual terms (36 first person pronouns or verbs in this psalm!), self-mastery assumes submission under YHWH and comes with the offer of disciplining others (v. 15). The desire for closeness permeates the psalm (vv. 6, 8, 13a, 18); the turn to the agent of violence (vv. 10, 19) for protection from violence and shame (vv. 16, 19) suggests complicity; and the superscription (v. 2) connects David and Nathan in a similar way by describing both crime and judgement as a 'coming in' (בוא): Nathan the prophet 'came' to David when he, David, 'came' to Bathsheba.

I grew up in one of Sweden's 'bible belts', Västerbotten. I was the short chubby guy with thick glasses, who played table-tennis and the flute and who took his religious commitment very seriously. Being raised in a small Baptist parish meant inhabiting an outsider position, both in relation to the Lutheran state church and to normative secularism. With the counter-cultural confidence of a tween radical, I found my parents spiritually 'lukewarm', despite their decision to leave Sweden for Congo-Kinshasa (then Zaïre) with three kids and serve as missionaries.

My years in Africa involved moving between worlds, where being a foreigner meant very different things. The American school of Kinshasa was a cosmopolitan milieu; I found myself in a setting where everyone identified as religious and where respectful co-habitation was the norm. As a missionary kid, I belonged to a 'working class' majority. As a European, I seemed to represent something more ambiguous, exciting but not entirely kosher, whether licentious sexuality (Bergmanesque 'Swedish sin') or effeminate masculinity (politically engineered gender equality?). Although cultural differences could be confusing, they were surmountable. I felt less like an outsider in the Congolese capital than in the Swedish north.

Rural Mimia, where my parents worked, brought more contradictory experiences. On the one hand, village life literally meant vacation to me. On the other hand, I became acutely aware of my privileges, in particular my whiteness. Life at the missionary station translated into being part of a strictly bilateral patron–client system, where I represented the ruling class and constituted a link in a long chain of history. This fact constituted a source of alienation and discomfort that I could not grasp. An undeniable outsider, my guilt was vague, and coupled with a sense of adventure. Whereas I cherished doing 'boyish' things (climbing trees, hunting), I freaked out at some of the assumed prerogatives ('sharing' my friend's girlfriend). Relating these experiences to the psalm's reception of the David figure, one point of contact lies in clinging to the identity of the select underdog/outsider, even when all the evidence points to the contrary.

With regard to the Bible, life in the village made me aware of a different canon in the canon along with different reading strategies. A reoccurring favorite was the parable of the rich man and Lazarus (Lk. 16.19-31), with divine justice rather than compassion with sinners as the ethical outcome. Encountering Congolese reading practices meant a sort of decentering; I was now at the receiving end of oracles of doom. The experience made me somewhat suspicious of my own traditions, sensing their limitations and specificities. At the same time, I felt at home in an environment where religious fervor was the norm. Possibly, I was even relieved to be 'outmanned' in terms of piety; it allowed me to think of myself as still a child. In retrospect, my experience seems to mirror the situation that the psalm assumes, Nathan's confrontation of David (2 Sam. 12); exposure meant a combination of shock and relief, condemnation was not absolute and served both to affirm the authority of the Law and to blur accountability.

The return to Sweden initiated a phase of religious re-orientation, which eventually led me to the majority Lutheran Church and to theology studies in Uppsala. The university provided a space for intellectual playfulness and for coming to terms with my heritage. Encountering academic feminism, I found a language for the experience that something was very wrong with the world (and not only with me), along with a vision for making it better. I can see that I embraced feminism with a passion that I had previously reserved for God. To me, the shift was seamless; the call for justice, the identification of the world as corrupt, the sense of urgency and the significance of interpretation (with a spark of literalism) had been there all along. The missing element was of course grace. With Butler (1990), the hope for radical change had grown bleaker. If there was no escape from the matrix, the small alterations became a matter of life and death. If we are socialized into a system of oppression, then subjectivity is compromised and I can trust neither my desires nor my good intentions.

Whereas exposing power seemed somewhat easy (at first), actually living the alternative presented a more formidable task. The challenge manifested concretely in personal–political issues, like whether it was possible to become a father without repeating the sins of the fathers or whether I had the right to take up (a woman's) space in the academy and in feminism. I scrutinized my practices as a partner and later parent, reading dissertations of sociology as if they were scripture (Holmberg 1993; Elvin-Nowak 2001). In retrospect, one can discard such attitudes as gallantry or as a sign of a superiority/inferiority complex (Larsson 2021: 137). With Connell (2005: 130–34), I recognize that I opted for a tactic of individual life style renunciation for political structural problems. However misguided, these struggles constituted an attempt to address my own complicity with power. As in Congo, I found myself entangled in a system I wanted to counter-act, balancing the position of simultaneous insider–outsider. Guilt remained vague in some ways (belonging to the wrong group), yet it also appeared as more immediate and personal (in daily life).

Relating these endeavors to Psalm 51, it strikes me how confession can serve as a means of evasion, denial, and self-obsession; but also how masculinity manifests as lack, defect and competition. The implied David claims to see his responsibility (v. 5), while simultaneously lamenting his birth into sin (v. 7). His confession is abstract and immaterial, a settlement between men (v. 6). Kelly Murphy (2019a and b) has recently demonstrated how biblical traditions re-assess and re-fashion an earlier warrior-ideal. In my reading, Psalm 51 attests to such a process, subjecting even the Ur-alpha-male David to adaptation. When killing and collecting trophy wives no longer are feasible, the reconstructed hero rather excels at repentance. In war and piety, excess seems to be the common denominator; although the forms may vary, grandiosity remains the goal.

I recognize the big gestures of my younger self (Sjöberg 2006: 15–17). Denouncing the hegemony of the past as toxic, the one attachment I could not let go of was guilt. Unable to see how it bolstered narcissism in the name of the struggle and served as a sneaky way to counter-cultural greatness, I was oblivious of my co-dependence on power in the very act of opposing it. The attraction was to be an agent for change, a bigger cause, a new covenant. Yet there was grace in that practice after all. The necessary shift of focus somehow happened through the humbling, decades-long experience of raising my children, thereby providing a relief from lofty ideals or intimidating norms. I continue to struggle with the inner/structural drama queen that I share with King David. On good days, she serves as a soothing reminder of the contradictoriness and volatility of inhabiting masculinity.

My second choice would be Psalm 139, which in my reading offers the prospect of infinite embrace, of relinquishing pretense and achievement. Evoking a respite from competitive masculinity, I perceive it as a corrective counterpart to Psalm 51.

Dr. Mikael Larsson is currently associate professor in Hebrew Bible at the faculty of theology, Uppsala University.

References

Butler, J. (1990), *Gender Trouble: Feminism and the Subversion of Identity*, New York: Routledge.
Connell, R.W. (2005), *Masculinities*, Berkeley: University of California Press.
Elvin-Nowak, Y. (2001), *I sällskap med skulden: om den moderna mammans vardag*, Stockholm: Bonnier.
Gese, H. (1974), *Von Sinai zum Zion: Alttestamentliche Beiträge zur biblischen Theologie*, EvTh 64. Munich: Kaiser.
Gillingham, S. (2018), *Psalms through the Centuries: A Reception History Commentary on Psalms 1–72*, Vol. 2, Blackwell Bible Commentaries, Hoboken: Wiley-Blackwell.

Holmberg, C. (1993), *Det kallas kärlek: en socialpsykologisk studie om kvinnors underordning och mäns överordning bland unga jämställda par*, Göteborg: Anamma.

Kraus, H.-J. (1993), *Psalms 1–59: A Continental Commentary*, Minneapolis: Fortress.

Larsson, M. (2021), 'Reinventing the Wheel? – or Imagining Collaborative Spaces at the Intersection of Masculinity Studies and Feminism', *Advances in Ancient, Biblical and Near Eastern Research* 1 (2): 109–44.

Murphy, K. (2019a), *Rewriting Masculinity: Gideon, Men, and Might*, Oxford: Oxford University Press.

Murphy, K. (2019b), 'Wisdom Is Better Than Gold: Masculinity and Money in the Book of Proverbs', in O. Creangă (ed.), *Hebrew Masculinities Anew*, 274–89, Sheffield: Sheffield Phoenix.

Sjöberg (Larsson), M. (2006), *Wrestling With Textual Violence: The Jephthah Narrative in Antiquity and Modernity*, Bible in the Modern World 4, Sheffield: Sheffield Phoenix.

Zenger, E. (2000), *Psalms 2: A Commentary on Psalms 51–100*, Minneapolis: Fortress.

PSALM 68
FURTHER HARMOLODIC MUSINGS

Hugh R. Page, Jr

Introduction

As a seminarian in the late 1970s and graduate student in the 1980s, I was fascinated and intrigued by the metanarratives about the ancient Near East and/or scholarship thereon that were considered the bedrock for critical and theologically informed Bible reading. Such metanarratives appeared to have an internal logic and coherence, even in those instances when there were differing views about material artifacts, various readings of texts, or competing theories regarding daily life in antiquity. Most were based on presuppositions many historians and social scientists might not deem credible. Nonetheless, they were advanced in classes and informal conversations as near certainties – facts whose reliability was unassailable. We were invited, indeed required at times, to suspend disbelief and embrace an intellectual *Weltanschauung* within which these 'stories' were held to be canonical and only certain methodologies for engaging them were considered to have merit.

The Psalms were an interesting case in point, given the implicit difficulties with reference to date, authorship, and provenance and the extraordinary range of opinion about how to interpret so many of them. Abundant were the musings about: the spirit animating Israel's ancient poets; form, redaction, and rhetorical criticism; the value of superscriptions; whether there was at some point an annual enthronement festival for YHWH; what the building blocks of Hebrew poetry were; the extent to which Ugaritic literature could shed light on Hebrew grammar and myth; or the value of Russian formalist and other approaches to poetics in deciphering the mysteries of Hebrew parallelism. These discussions were informed by the work of a select group of notables: e.g., Gunkel (1928); Muilenburg (1969); Childs (1971); Mowinckel (1966); Cross and Freedman (1997); Kugel (1998); Berlin (2007); Dahood (1965); Cross (1983); and Jakobson (1966). Absent were references to the work or worldview of scholars from Africa or the African Diaspora, even in such instances where cross-cultural or transdisciplinary research could have been potentially illuminating.

Such is part of the backdrop for my abiding interest in Psalm 68. For my part, I enjoy pondering conundrums, especially those that are longstanding, difficult, and known to have elicited passionate debate. This is exactly why it happens to be one of my favorites. Its peculiarities became of personal interest when I discovered that this psalm was thought to be by some – particularly those who were part of the cohort of students trained by William F. Albright – part of the Hebrew Bible's earliest corpus of poems. Albright himself noted its strangeness in an intriguing article published in the *Hebrew Union College Annual*, in which he posits that it consists of thirty *incipits* from ancient Hebrew poems (1950/1951: 8). Several major commentaries from the early twentieth century to the present have noted its peculiar structure, mused about the resonances of its imagery with ancient Canaanite texts, and wrestled with critical issues such as its genre, setting, date, significance, and life applications. These include volumes in the International Critical Commentary (Briggs and Briggs 2004), Old Testament Library (Weiser 1962), and Hermeneia (Hossfeld and Zenger 2005) series; as well as entries in *The Global Bible Commentary* (Adamo 2004), *The Africana Bible* (Murrell, Shannon, and Adamo 2010), and *The Fortress Commentary on the Bible* (Suderman 2014).

Harmolodics and the Weirdness of Psalm 68

Nonetheless, Psalm 68 remains an intractable mystery, though one amenable to the testing of new hermeneutical paradigms, particularly those heretofore ignored. One such model is that of Ornette Coleman's harmolodic theory – a way of approaching jazz and blues composition that places harmony, melody, and rhythm on equal footing – which I utilized in an earlier exploratory treatment (Page 2013: 81–110). Then, I posed the following questions:

> Are symmetry, regularity, repetition, and structure inhibitors of freedom? Is an implicit harmolodic poetics the stimulus for the deformation of structures of oppression and the development of lifeways oriented toward unfettered individual expression? Is Psalm 68 the one composition in early Hebrew poetry that enshrines a notion somewhat akin to this in ancient Israel? Is it the center of gravity for the entire assemblage of Israel's earliest verse? (Page 2013: 107)

At this point, I continue to wonder how the democratizing of harmony, melody, and rhythm in musical composition might be appropriated to understand at least three elements within Psalm 68.

The first is the presence of topics, themes, and allusions reminiscent of Canaanite myth. These include reference to God as 'cloud rider' (68.4) and storm deity (v. 33); divine warrior imagery akin to that found in Ugaritic lore (vv. 7-10, 14); allusion to the so-called olden gods (vv. 15-16);[1] and veiled or perhaps concretized allusions to the deities *Mot*/Death (v. 17) and *Yamm*/Sea (v. 22).

---

1. On the olden gods, see Cross 1976: 329–38.

The second is a focus on the self-disclosure and actions of Israel's deity. For example, theophanic language is prominent in 68.1-2, 7, 11-14, 17-18, and 28. References to YHWH's action on behalf of those in need (vv. 2, 5-6, 10, 22-23); certain groups within the tribal confederation (v. 27); the temple and cult in Jerusalem (vv. 24-25, 29, 35); the subjugation of neighboring peoples (v. 25); and overcoming of adversaries (vv. 14, 30) – are also found in this psalm.

The third is the literary structure of the psalm, which consists of numerous short units that offer disparate 'snapshots' of religious ideas and scenes.[2] The following is a plausible breakdown:

vv. 1-3	Rubric and invocation
vv. 4-6	Praise for God as cosmic and earthly protector
vv. 7-10	Theophany in the wilderness and at Sinai
vv. 11-14	God's victory over earthly adversaries
vv. 15-18	God's self-disclosure at Sinai
vv. 19-23	Praise to God as savior
vv. 24-35	A triumphal temple liturgy

As a result, instead of spending most of my time 'thumbing through' older Psalms scholarship, I ponder the implications of Coleman's theory while listening to his music; practicing the note and chord progressions foundational to harmolodic composition on my piano;[3] and wondering whether harmolodic theory opens a door for understanding what Psalm 68 may reveal about community formation and the quest for freedom in early Israel.[4] From those musings, it seems reasonable to posit that the 'melodic' core of this psalm consists of a series of divine self-disclosures, specifically referring to YHWH. Its 'harmonic' complement is composed of tropes, allusions, and lexical items drawn from what appears to be a larger *matrix* of Canaanite lore. The 'tempo' or rhythm of the text is asymmetrical and set by the sequential juxtaposition of brief 'scenes', akin to the musical 'phrasing' one encounters in Jazz or Blues improvisational performance. These features lead me to think of Psalm 68 as 'weird', in the Old

---

2. Here, one is reminded of what the late Frank Cross termed 'impressionistic paralalelism' (Cross and Freedman 1997: viii). In my earlier treatment, I also use the 'snapshot' image, along with those of 'collage' and 'strip quilt' (Page 2013: 108).

3. See the note and chord progression in Litweiler's biography on Coleman (1992: 149).

4. 'The Harmolodic Manifesto' (2013) has a strange textual history. I first discovered it on Coleman's personal website (http://www.ornettecoleman.com/course.swf) almost a decade ago. Its exact date of composition is difficult to pinpoint, and it is no longer available *via* this URL. What appear to be the same, or similar, versions of this document are currently available on two different websites. The first is http://preparedguitar.blogspot.com/2014/11/the-harmolodic-manifesto-by-ornette.html (accessed on 22 December 2022). The second is https://professorscosco.wordpress.com/ornette-coleman-the-harmolodic-manifesto/ (accessed 22 December 2022). In some respects, Coleman's manifesto can now be considered part of the 'shadow book' genre described by Kevin Young (2012: 11).

English sense – i.e., an entity possessing unearthly or numinous power. Consistent with this notion, I would classify it as a poem that seeks to conjure and reify an early Israelite communal identity that is hybrid, fluid, and resistant to oppressive external control. It is an interesting heuristic exercise to consider how it might have been received as part of the corpus of early poems hailing from the period of 'Monarchic Syncretism' identified by the late David Noel Freedman (1980: 79). Otherwise, I find it a useful conversation partner in thinking about how poetry and other artforms, ancient and modern, often serve as implements of power capable of generating social transformation.

It is for these reasons that Psalm 68 is a crucial literary artifact for me as an *Africana* philologist and Episcopal cleric seeking both to understand and apply the Blues aesthetic and harmolodic theory to research, teaching, academic administration, ecclesial service, and the fraught enterprise of promoting BIPOC (Black, Indigenous, and People of Color). A second key poetic touchstone in such efforts – not within the Psalter, but critical nonetheless – is 1 Sam. 2.1-10, the 'Song of Hannah'.

Were I to choose a second favorite text specifically from the Psalter, it would be Psalm 49, in which a sage uses their[5] 'harp' (49.4) to ponder the mysteries of abundance, poverty, life, death, human thriving, and the surety of divine rescue.

Hugh R. Page. Jr. is Professor of Theology and Africana Studies at the University of Notre Dame, USA, where he also serves as Vice President for Institutional Transformation and Advisor to the President. A philologist, Hebrew Bible Scholar, and priest in The Episcopal Church, his work seeks to mainstream BIPOC (Black, Indigenous, and People of Color) epistemologies and critical theories in scholarship on the Bible and the ancient Near East.

References

Adamo, David T. (2004), 'Psalms', in Daniel Patte (ed.), *Global Bible Commentary*, 151–62, Nashville: Abingdon.
Albright, William F. (1950/1951), 'A Catalogue of Early Hebrew Lyric Poems (Psalm 68)', *Hebrew Union College Annual* 23 (1): 1–39.
Berlin, Adele (2007), *The Dynamics of Biblical Parallelism*, Grand Rapids: Eerdmans, 2nd edn.
Briggs, Charles Augustus and Emilie Grace Briggs (2004), *The Book of Psalms, in 2 Volumes*, S. R. Driver, A. Plummer and C. A. Briggs. Reprint of 1921 (Vol. 1) and 1907 (Vol. 2) ed, *The International Critical Commentary on the Holy Scriptures of the Old and New Testaments*, London: T & T Clark International.
Childs, Brevard (1971), 'Psalm Titles and Midrashic Exegesis', *Journal of Semitic Studies* 16 (2): 137–50.

---

5. The author uses 'their' here as a gender-neutral pronoun.

Coleman, Ornette (2013), 'The Harmolodic Manifesto', available online at https://harmolodicprogrammes.files.wordpress.com/2012/03/the-harmolodic-manifesto-vol-2006.pdf (accessed 8 August 2023).

Cross, Frank Moore (1976), 'The "Olden Gods" in Ancient Near Eastern Creation Myths', in Frank Moore Cross, Werner E. Lemke and Patrick D. Miller (eds), *Magnalia Dei, The Mighty Acts of God: Essays on the Bible and Archaeology in Memory of G. Ernest Wright*, 329–38, Garden City: Doubleday.

Cross, Frank Moore (1983), 'Studies in the Structure of Hebrew Verse: The Prosody of Lamentations 1:1-22', in C.L. Meyers and M. O'Connor (eds), *The Word of the Lord Shall Go Forth: Essays in Honor of David Noel Freedman*, 129–55, Winona Lake: Eisenbrauns.

Cross, Frank Moore and David Noel Freedman (1997), *Studies in Ancient Yahwistic Poetry*, The Biblical Resource Series, Grand Rapids: Eerdmans, 2nd edn. Reprint, Reprint of 1975.

Dahood, Mitchell (1965), *Ugaritic–Hebrew Philology: Marginal Notes on Recent Publications*, Biblica et Orientalia, Rome: Pontifical Biblical Institute.

Freedman, David Noel (1980), 'Divine Names and Titles in Early Hebrew Poetry', in David Noel Freedman (ed.), *Pottery, Poetry, and Prophecy: Studies in Early Hebrew Poetry*, 77–129, Winona Lake: Eisenbrauns.

Gunkel, Hermann (1928), *What Remains of the Old Testament and Other Essays*, trans. A.K. Dallas, New York: Macmillan.

Hossfeld, Frank-Lothar and Erich Zenger (2005), *Psalms 2: A Commentary on Psalms 51-100*, trans. Linda M. Maloney, ed. Peter Machinist *et al.*, 3 vols, Hermeneia – A Critical and Historical Commentary on the Bible. Minneapolis: Fortress.

Jakobson, R. (1966), 'Grammatical Parallelism and its Russian Facet', *Language* 40: 399–429.

Kugel, James (1998), *The Idea of Biblical Poetry*, Baltimore: The Johns Hopkins University Press, reprint of 1981.

Litweiler, John (1992), *Ornette Coleman: A Harmolodic Life*, New York: William Morrow & Co.

Mowinckel, Sigmund (1966), *Psalmenstudien: 1921–1924*. Amsterdam: B.R. Grüner – Imprint of John Benjamins Publishing Co.

Muilenburg, James (1969), 'Form Criticism and Beyond', *JBL* 88: 1–18.

Murrell, Nathaniel Samuel, David T. Shannon and David T. Adamo (2010), 'Psalms', in Hugh R. Page, Jr. et al. (ed.), *The Africana Bible: Reading Israel's Scriptures from Africa and the African Diaspora*, 220–36, Minneapolis: Fortress.

Page, Hugh R., Jr (2013), *Israel's Poetry of Resistance: Africana Perspectives on Early Hebrew Verse*, Minneapolis: Fortress.

Suderman, W. Derek (2014), 'Psalms', in Gale A. Yee, Hugh R. Page Jr and Matthew J.M. Coomber (eds), *Fortress Commentary on the Bible: The Old Testament and Apocrypha*, 547–99, Minneapolis: Fortress.

Weiser, Artur (1962), *The Psalms: A Commentary*, trans. Herbert Hartwell, ed. Peter Ackroyd *et al.*, The Old Testament Library, Philadelphia: Westminster.

Young, Kevin (2012), *The Grey Album*, Minneapolis: Graywolf.

PSALM 71
DO NOT DUMP ME IN TIME OF OLD AGE

Athalya Brenner-Idan

Do not cast me off in old age;
when my strength fails, do not forsake me!…
and even in hoary old age do not forsake me, God
(Ps. 71.9, 18a; JPS)

When I get older losing my hair
Many years from now
Will you still be sending me a Valentine
Birthday greetings, bottle of wine
If I'd been out till quarter to three
Would you lock the door
Will you still need me, will you still feed me
When I'm sixty-four
(P. McCartney, 'When I'm Sixty-Four', on The Beatles' 1967 album, *Sgt. Pepper's Lonely Hearts Club Band*)

When I [re]read Psalm 71, my eyes migrate immediately to v. 9. No mystery there: with the advance of old age, it is difficult to ignore the fearful anxiety of being left alone, especially in times of illness and infirmity, before the end. So, passages such as this one, as well as the superb description of the ageing body's deterioration in Qoh. 12.1-7 (when 'the days of trouble come, and the years draw near when you will say, "I have no pleasure in them"'), are of morbid interest to me.

And then, almost at the same time, a tune runs in my head, whose lyrics are the text of vv. 8-9, with a soundtrack composed by the Israeli Avihu Medina who also performs it, on his own[1] or together with Shimi Tavori for instance,[2] although there are many more presentations for this tune, which is played constantly on

1. https://www.youtube.com/watch?v=cN8BjWxI_N0 (accessed 1 January 2023).
2. https://www.youtube.com/watch?v=SakT8sbMNP0 (accessed 1 January 2023).

Israeli radio and television, not to mention privately in Spotify etc. and of course, there are other tunes, Chassidic[3] and non-Chassidic alike.

And my second quick association, as my vision travels to v. 18, is the Beatles' 'When I'm Sixty-Four', the lyrics of whose first stanza are reproduced above.

First, some information about Avihu Medina, his music and place in Israeli contemporary, popular culture. Avihu Medina (born 1948 in Tel Aviv, of Jewish oriental descent) is an Israeli singer, songwriter, composer, producer and music copyrights activist who is central in transforming so-called Mizrahi ('oriental'), that is, Mediterranean popular music, into a successful mainstream genre in the Israeli scene.[4] In 2016 he received the Ministry of Education prize for Jewish culture in the music domain, and in 2022 the Israel prize in the Hebrew music domain.[5]

Many contemporary Israeli composers, of Mizrahi (Eastern) as well as Ashkenazi (Western) descent, have set biblical verses to music that became popular outside the realm of bible recitation and prayer, especially texts that feature in religious practice or incorporated into the Jewish prayer book.[6] Such biblical verses processed into songs may become pop successes, as happened to Avihu Medina's musical rendering of Ps. 71.8-9; so much so that for me – and for my Israeli students past and present, of any background (checked many times!) – when we read those verses, we actually sing them, at least internally. One reason for that is, probably, the song's popularity; and it must be stated that in this song the biblical phrases were reproduced accurately, without change. Another, less obvious, may be an even unconscious realization that such Eastern music, with its typical elaborations and cadences, may represent well some similarity to a lost, original musical performance of a psalm; or to the original performance of later *piyyutim*,[7] whose texts, again, have received much musical rendering in Jewish/ Israeli culture.

---

3. As in the Motty Steimentz's takeoff, available at https://www.youtube.com/watch?v= AxcNHU5dt68 (accessed 1 January 2023).

4. For Medina's discography, see https://www.discogs.com/artist/4289761-%D7%90 %D7%91%D7%99%D7%94%D7%95-%D7%9E%D7%93%D7%99%D7%A0%D7%94.

5. https://www.ynet.co.il/entertainment/article/byudow1g5 (Heb.), https://www.haaretz.com/israel-news/culture/2022-03-15/ty-article/.premium/singer-avihu-medina-awarded-israel-prize-for-music/00000180-5bb7-d615-a9bf-dff75e760000 (Eng.) (accessed 1 January 2023).

6. Within the Jewish practice of personal recitation of psalms (considered apotropaic and protective at all times) during the week, Ps. 71 is traditionally assigned to Fridays (or according to the believer's need).

7. '*piyyut*, also spelled *piyut*, plural *piyyutim*, or *piyutim*, Hebrew *piyūṭ* ("liturgical poem"), one of several types of liturgical compositions or religious poems, some of which have been incorporated into Jewish liturgy and have become virtually indistinguishable from the mandatory service, especially on the Sabbath and on Jewish religious festivals' (https://www.britannica.com/topic/piyyut, and see further there [accessed 1 January 2023]).

And then, the association with the Beatles' 'When I'm Sixty-Four' hardly requires explanation, I think.[8] Suffice be it to add here that,

> The song is sung by a young man to his lover, and is about his plans of growing old together with her. Although the theme is ageing, it was one of the first songs McCartney wrote, when he was 16… McCartney may have thought of the song when recording began for Sgt. Pepper in December 1966 because his father turned 64 earlier that year.[9]

Apart from a small smile about 'sixty-four' defined as old age, I reflect to myself that experiencing both associations almost simultaneously upon reading the biblical text is indicative of many aspects, among which is the automatic blending – even for a secularist of my ilk – of biblical and other Jewish religious texts and popular culture, often with no knowledge of the lyrics' base or origin.

To return to old age and old people in the Hebrew Bible in general, and in Psalm 71 in particular. The term זקן, *zāqēn*, and its derivatives are often translated simply as 'old'. It may mean that, as in the inclusive expression מנער עד זקן, literally 'from boy to *zāqēn*' (Gen. 19.4). However, no simple equivalence of *zāqēn* = 'old' covers all occurrences. Often a person dies not only as *zāqēn* but also 'full', 'full of/ replete with days/years', 'with good *śēḇāh*' (grey hairs, a metonym for 'old age');[10] the translations wrestle with such texts, preferring to understand those repetitions as dual or triple indications of 'old age', as synonyms in poetic texts. But this is not necessarily so: given the low life expectancy for humans in ancient worlds, *zāqēn* may be understood as a relative term, our 'older', with a qualifier such as the actual age, or 'full of days', necessary. Furthermore, if *zāqēn*, as it seems, is derived from the Hebrew *zāqān*, 'beard', it would mean 'a [male] adult', one who is marked by his facial hair as suitable to serve as a community leader, even if not 'full of years'. And indeed, *ziqnê*[11] Israel, זקני ישראל, is usually and rightly translated as '*elders*

---

8. Recordings of the song and the full lyrics are readily available on the internet.

9. https://www.the-paulmccartney-project.com/song/when-im-sixty-four/ (accessed 1 January 2023).

10. For instance, Abraham in Gen. 25.8, Isaac in Gen. 35.29. Cf. also the seemingly antithetical pair of King Rehoboam's advisers, the ילדים and זקנים (1 Kgs 12 = 2 Chron. 10). Since King Rehoboam is registered as forty-one years old upon succeeding to the throne (2 Chron. 12.13), the ילדים (usually 'children') who advised him were not necessarily 'young' but 'novices', in as much as the זקנים were not necessarily 'old' but 'veterans' in their occupation as advisers. In this and other contexts, therefore, a functional social status rather than age is at stake.

11. The 'elders' as well as 'the aged' in the Hebrew Bible are somehow always (grammatically!) masculine/male, apart from in one instance, Zech. 8.4, where both 'old men' and 'old women' are defined by using a cane: עוד ישבו זקנים וזקנות ברחבת ירושלים ואיש משענתו בידו מרב ימים. 'Old men and old women shall again sit in the streets of Jerusalem, each with staff in hand because of their great age'. (NRSVue).

of Israel', with the plural of *zāqēn* as a social, titular designation not a biological one (Brenner 2002).

In *Pirqe Avoth* 5.21 we read:

בן חמש שנים למקרא, בן עשר למשנה, בן שלש עשרה למצות, בן חמש עשרה לתלמוד, בן שמונה עשרה לחופה, בן עשרים לרדוף, בן שלשים לכח, בן ארבעים לבינה, בן חמשים לעצה, בן ששים לזקנה, בן שבעים לשיבה, בן שמונים לגבורה, בן תשעים לשוח, בן מאה כאילו מת ועבר ובטל מן העולם.[12]

However, in spite of the great ages assigned in the Hebrew Bible to many biblical figures, a great age is perhaps an ideal and idyllic age assignment for postbiblical Judaism,[13] but it is certainly not applicable to the facts regarding life expectancy throughout the second and first millennium BCE, as they are known to us.[14]

So, what are the biblical attitudes to human old age, when indicated by the word and narrative context? The value of human life is a guiding principle; longevity, a divine blessing if limited. The location of the mythological Tree of Life in the Garden (Gen. 2–3); the descending order of longevity in the ten antediluvian generations (Gen. 5); the divinely ordained upper human age limit of the 120 living years (Gen. 6.3); and longevity of the Genesis Patriarchs, the Matriarchs, and other personages of Israel's beginnings, not to mention other instances, all point in this direction. To grow old (and to be a parent, preferably of sons) is to be desired and demonstrates divine favor. The dual signification of *zāqēn* (and its derivatives) as biological ('old[er] in age') and social ('elder', leader, adviser) amount to an association of wisdom with long life, in ancient Israelite as in other cultures ancient and newer. In theory old[er] has a lot to teach the young and is to be respected – this is a divine commandment:

---

12. In translation (https://www.chabad.org/library/article_cdo/aid/2099/jewish/Chapter-Five.htm#:~:text=Five%20years%20is,from%20the%20world): 'Five years is the age for the study of Scripture. Ten, for the study of Mishnah. Thirteen, for the obligation to observe the mitzvot. Fifteen, for the study of Talmud. Eighteen, for marriage. Twenty, to pursue [a livelihood]. Thirty, for strength. Forty, for understanding. Fifty, for counsel. Sixty, for sagacity. Seventy, for elderliness. Eighty, for power. Ninety, to stoop. A hundred-year-old is as one who has died and passed away and has been negated from the world'.

13. For Judaism's attitudes to old age and the aged see Cohen, She'ar Yashuv (n.d.), 'Old Age in Judaism', https://www.medethics.org.il/book/%d7%a1%d7%a4%d7%a8-%d7%90%d7%a1%d7%99%d7%90-%d7%95/ [Heb.]. (accessed 1 January 2023).

14. For life expectancy and the subject in general cf. the two comprehensive essays by Douglas A. Knight: Knight 2014 and forthcoming. My thanks to Professor Knight who gave me access to the latter essay pre-publication.

לפני שיבה תקום והדרת פני זקן

You shall rise before the aged and show deference to the old (Lev. 19.32, JPS);

or

Stand up in the presence of the aged, show respect for the elderly (NIV).

And yet, this is not the whole picture. Not only is ethical respect required. What happens to the old[er] when they become physically, maybe mentally, incapacitated and cannot look after themselves? Biologically and socially, this duty falls to the young[er] in society. They must cherish the older, typically cast as 'parents':

כבד את אביך ואת אמך למען יארכון ימיך על האדמה אשר ה' אלהיך נתן לך
(Exod. 20.5)

Honor your father and your mother, that you may long endure on the land that the LORD your God is assigning to you (JPS).[15]

As is clear from this text, as well as from others, such as the case of the 'wayward and defiant son' (Deut. 21.18-21), the 'honoring' of parents is a basic tenet for the continuation of society: take care of its old[er] members if you want to get the same treatment when your time comes. Doing this, whatever your stage in life, carries rewards. Even Yhwh is promised a reward (v. 18b) if he looks after the aged petitioner. To return to our psalm –

וגם עד זקנה ושיבה אלהים אל תעזבני עד אגיד זרועך לדור לכל יבוא גבורתך
(Ps. 71.18)

Even when I am old and gray, do not forsake me, my God, till I declare your power to the next generation, your mighty acts to all who are to come. (NIV)[16]

And yet, despite these wise words, anxiety remains, especially for old[er] or ill people, as it must. What will happen to you, or to me, or to them when we are old and infirm (Qoh. 12 returns to mind here)? Will anybody look after us? With luck, a social grid will be put into place; will it be enough? Will it counter

---

15. And a longer parallel version in Deut. 5.16: 'Honor your father and your mother, as the LORD your God has commanded you, that you may long endure, and that you may fare well, in the land that the LORD your God is assigning to you.'

16. Similarly, the psalmist promises Yhwh 'praise' and tales of his 'glory' 'the whole day' if not discarded in old age.

successfully the deterioration of our existing faculties? Will it supply food, solace, physical comfort, a roof? Or will you, she, I be forgotten in our old age and left to die on our own?

In our Western culture, attitudes to old[er] age are ambivalent and ambiguous. On the one hand, youth and youth culture are glorified, and ageism dictates that older ages and their physical and mental and health manifestations are vilified, especially for women. Wrinkles, y'all. On the other hand, political leaders tend to be seventy-something males (2022: Joe Biden and Donald Trump in the USA, Netanyahu in Israel…); old men keep sending young males to their death in military situations. Women, young and old, and children suffer because of their decisions. Diverse societies in East and West define the constitutional fulfilment of senior citizens' needs, and help toward those differently. Even when you have a pension, and devoted family members, and your faculties are for the time being intact, if weakened, being a senior citizen is no joke. The psalmist's cry in v. 9 –

אל תשליכני לעת זקנה ככלות כחי אל תעזבני

> Do not dump me in time of old age, when my strength ends, do not leave me (my translation) –

reverberates with me. In the form of Avihu Medina's song. Many, many times during waking hours. As does the Beatles' 'When I'm Sixty-Four'. I'm aged. I'm anxious.

My second choice would have been Psalm 150. It calls for praising the Lord with musical instruments, without specific text. Such a delicious irony: the psalm verbally deconstructs the previous 149 psalms, all containing short or lengthy prayers or hymns in words, by calling for a non-verbal praise of the divine, emphasizing musical but wordless supplication, supplication that is open to the non-literary as well as to the more educated. And of course, although the psalm is recited in the morning prayer every day, most Israelis will recognize it immediately as a popular song rather than part of a regularly repeated prayer, or biblical text. The beginning of v. 1, as well as vv. 5-6, are set to a tune whose provenance is often defined as 'Chassidic' and anonymous, and lyrics as 'from the sources' [sic]. Would you like to listen to it? Here's a link.[17]

Dr. Athalya Brenner-Idan is professor of Hebrew Bible/Old Testament (emerita) at the Universiteit van Amsterdam (The Netherlands). She also taught at Tel Aviv University, in Hong Kong and in the USA. She defines herself as a born-Jewish secularist. She lives in Haifa, Israel and Amsterdam, The Netherlands.

---

17. https://www.youtube.com/watch?v=lCnK3xMcxt4 (accessed 1 January 2023).

References

Brenner, Athalya (2002), 'Age and Ageism in the Hebrew Bible in an Autobiographical Perspective', in A.G. Hunter and P.R. Davies (eds), *Sense and Sensitivity: Essays on Reading the Bible in Memory of Robert Carroll*, 302–10, Sheffield: SAP/Continuum.

Cohen, She'ar Yashuv (n.d.), 'Old Age in Judaism', https://www.medethics.org.il/book/%d7%a1%d7%a4%d7%a8-%d7%90%d7%a1%d7%99%d7%90-%d7%95/ [Heb.]. (accessed 1st January 2023).

Knight, Douglas A. (2014), 'Perspectives on Aging and the Elderly in the Hebrew Bible', *Interpretation* 68 (2): 136–49, http://int.sagepub.com/content/68/2/136.

Knight, Douglas A. (forthcoming), 'Seniors in Ancient Israel', in John T. Fitzgerald, Carol Meyers, Eric M. Meyers, Chris L. de Wet (eds), *The [Oxford] Handbook of Households in the Biblical World*, New York: Oxford University Press USA.

PSALM 73
BUT I... (*WA'ĂNÎ*)

Ekaputra Tupamahu

After finishing my master's degree at Claremont School of Theology, I did Optional Practical Training (OPT) for one year working as a pastor of an Indonesian immigrant church in Redlands, California. It was one of the most difficult times of our lives for me and my family as we lived on only a few hundred dollars every month. Life was tough. My wife was pregnant with our second son. As a pastor, I had to stand in front of the church and preach every Sunday. It was a hard and dissonant experience because while I declared the goodness of God from the pulpit on Sundays, my everyday life was filled with pain. But not only my own life: also that of some of the many other immigrants who live on the fringes of US life with little to no socio-political capital. Psalm 73 resonates particularly well with this experience thanks to its honest words about the reality of human struggle.

The psalm begins with a theological declaration, with a creed: 'Truly God is good to the upright, and to those who are pure heart'.[1] Everyone knows this. This is a declaration of communal belief, widely held knowledge about who God is, namely, that God is good. If it is true that 'The psalms are scripted to be sung and recited repeatedly', as Walter Brueggemann puts it,[2] then the opening words of this psalm might be a communal song sung in a cultic setting. As a pastor of this immigrant church, I declared this same sentiment to the congregation every week with words that sound encouraging, hopeful, and reassuring.

Thankfully, the psalmist does not stop at the theological declaration. The reality of life often looks quite different from the theological declaration of who God is. Why? Because life is messy, chaotic, unpredictable, difficult, and often unjust. Verse 2 brings this messiness of life to the surface:

---

1. English translations of the Hebrew text are from the NRSV.
2. Walter Brueggemann, 'Psalms in Israel's Worship', n.p. [cited 2 December 2022]. Online: https://www.bibleodyssey.org:443/en/passages/related-articles/psalms-in-israels-worship.

> But as for me, my feet had almost stumbled;
> my steps had nearly slipped.
> For I was envious of the arrogant;
> I saw the prosperity of the wicked.

The expression 'but as for me…' is written as merely one compounded word in the Hebrew: *waănî* (the word *wa* usually means 'and,' as well as 'but'). I am interpreting *waănî* here as 'but I'. This 'but I' (*waănî*) expression signifies two things: First, the disjunction 'but' marks a shift in the narrative, and the beginning of a contending narrative. It is used to introduce a contrasting statement from what has already been said. This 'but' reflects and reminds us that life is often more complex, more complicated, more tangled, than the simple theological slogans that people proclaim or sing in public worship. As the renowned Swiss theologian Karl Barth once stated: 'Life is neither simple, nor straightforward, nor obvious. Things are simple and straightforward and obvious only when they are detached from their context and then treated superficially' (Barth 1968: 425). The 'but' is a critical moment in this psalm that introduces the complexity of life to the larger theological abstraction.

Second, the 'I' (the first-person pronoun) signifies the particularity of one's individual story. The 'I' is someone with a story. Anybody can insert their name at this point in the psalm. The 'I' signifies that each person has a unique story, that no two persons' stories are the same! Yes, we find here a theological belief or conviction about God. But we also find a personal and individual story. My story is different from someone else's story. I am an immigrant. I was not born in the US. I speak a different language, a minoritized language. As a first-generation immigrant in the United States, what drives me every day is not a desire to thrive, but rather to survive. That is my story. The collective theological narrative should not be an erasure of each particular story. Communal identity ought to respect each individual story, each narrative. Community has to affirm one's particular story rather than erase it.

What comes after the 'but I…' is a series of laments, complaints, and objections. What we see in vv. 2-14 is a struggle with the painful reality of injustice. If God is good to the upright, why in the world do the wicked prosper while good people endure poverty and suffering? People who oppress and exploit others are often more prosperous, healthier, and happier than those who live uprightly. Why do those who oppress and exploit seem to live with no pain, no troubles, no plagues (vv. 4-9)? Why do people turn and praise them (v. 10)? Why do their riches increase (v. 12)?

The 'I' expression appears again in vv. 13-14, where it compares the prosperity of the wicked with the lived struggle of the 'I'. The psalmist says:

> All in vain I have kept my heart clean
> and washed my hands in innocence.
> For all day long I have been plagued,
> and am punished every morning.

These words are so raw, intense, and honest. There's no sugarcoating reality here! These words can be read as an expression of sadness, disappointment, or anger, in so doing making space for human struggle with God. In effect, the psalm gives humans permission to complain, to challenge, to be angry at God. It also reminds readers that we don't have to pretend that we have everything figured out. God, life, and we ourselves are full of mysteries that are often unfathomable. This is precisely what this psalm tries to capture in the following words:

> But when I thought how to understand this,
> it seemed to me a wearisome task… (v. 16)

> When my soul was embittered,
> when I was pricked in heart,
> I was stupid and ignorant;
> I was like a brute beast toward you. (vv. 21-22)

But notice something: in vv. 23-26, the expression 'but I' (*wa'ănî*) returns:

> Nevertheless I (*wa'ănî*) am continually with you;
> you hold my right hand.
> You guide me with your counsel,
> and afterward you will receive me with honor.
> Whom have I in heaven but you?
> And there is nothing on earth that I desire other than you.
> My flesh and my heart may fail,
> but God is the strength of my heart and my portion forever.

This is the climax of the psalm. It is a declaration that 'I' will continue to be with God in spite of my inability to understand the disparities in life. Trusting in God means that one has to live with mystery, with the unknown, with uncertainty. To thrive, one does not need to identify or understand the 'meaning' (the transcendental signified) behind human suffering.[3]

The last part of the argument is in vv. 27-28. It reads like a closing remark. And notice that once again there's the 'but I' (or in the English translation, 'but for me') that is another 'hinge' in the declaration:

> Indeed, those who are far from you will perish;
> you put an end to those who are false to you.
> But for me (*wa'ănî*) it is good to be near God;
> I have made the Lord GOD my refuge,
> to tell of all your works.

---

3. See Barbara Meyer's fascinating discussion on 'against redemptive suffering' in Meyer 2020: Chapter 5.

This section follows the same pattern as in vv. 1 and 2. Here in v. 27, there is a theological declaration that those who are far from God will perish. It is the vision of the end-times damnation of the wicked. In v. 28, however, the psalmist uses the same expression again: 'but I' (*wa'ănî*). Although the psalmist agrees with the theological vision of the end, or the telos, of the wicked, the 'I' declares that for now, 'it is good to be near God'. Again, being near God does not mean that everything gets completely figured out. It refers to a willingness to live with mystery.

Let me circle back to my opening story. When I was smack dab in the middle of the toughness of life in Southern California, things felt so uncertain, unclear, confusing, and puzzling. At many moments I felt like giving up because life was so arduous. This psalm reminds me that although I believe in God, I do not need to sugarcoat my life's experiences. I'm permitted to struggle, to wrestle with the painful reality of life. I'm permitted to complain, to be angry, to be upset. And I don't have to have the final answer to that struggle. Amidst life's real complexity, messiness, and cacophony, I am nonetheless near to God. And that in itself is good.

My psalm of second choice is Psalm 10. Just like Psalm 73, this psalm is also full of bitter struggles with God and honest expressions of disappointment, anger, and annoyance in the face of the difficult and unjust reality.

Ekaputra Tupamahu is Assistant Professor of New Testament and Director of Masters Programs at Portland Seminary. He received his Ph.D. in New Testament and Early Christianity from Vanderbilt University.

References

Barth, Karl (1968), *The Epistle to the Romans*, Oxford: Oxford University Press.
Brueggemann, Walter, 'Psalms in Israel's Worship', n.p. [cited 2 December 2022]. Online: https://www.bibleodyssey.org:443/en/passages/related-articles/psalms-in-israels-worship.
Meyer, Barbara U. (2020), *Jesus the Jew in Christian Memory: Theological and Philosophical Explorations*, Cambridge: Cambridge University Press.

PSALM 78.67-72
KING DAVID AND THE CHINESE 'MANDATE OF HEAVEN'

Archie C.C. Lee

For many years now, I've been working on cross-cultural, cross-textual readings of the Hebrew Bible together with literary and theological readings from my own Chinese culture, with the intention to demonstrate how these two disparate cultures can illuminate and elucidate each other, even without assuming any direct or indirect contact between them. Following this line of thought and investigation, Psalm 78, and especially vv. 67-72, seem to me highly adequate to exemplify this quest.

But there is also another personal and contextual dimension to my choice. In my context in Hong Kong, I encounter the same unsolved dilemma between different communities of ethnic Chinese who have fled to Hong Kong after the waves of persecutions in China in the 1950s and 1960s, and those who are legal immigrants from China in recent years. People with differences in background, education, political orientation, and economic condition tend to interpret Chinese history in amazingly diverse ways. This context of mine further prompts my interest in Chinese recitations of the past, and its comparison to recitation of the past in the Hebrew Bible, such as in Psalm 78.

* * *

Psalm 78 is highly politicized: it presents the perplexing problem of Israelite history as a paradigmatic lesson. Strikingly, at its end, the election of King David as God's servant, the choice of the tribe of Judah and designation of Mount Zion where God's temple stands, are presented in drastic contrast with the utter rejection of Ephraim, the disfavor of the tribe of Joseph/Ephraim and the desertion of God's former dwelling in Shiloh. This short essay revisits the psalm from the cross-cultural perspective of the ancient Chinese conception of Heaven's choice or abandonment of an emperor. I propose to look at a retelling of the past in *The Book of Poetry (Shijing)*, with its notion of the 'Mandate of Heaven', to understand the process of how God/Heaven is coopted and politicized to legitimize a sovereign power. This Mandate of Heaven depends on the morality and ethical behavior of the king in power and may thus change over time. These insights will contribute to the discussion of the ideology of an everlasting kingship in the divine promise to David and its subsequent development in the historical fact of devastation. Since the kings in Judah are repeatedly designated as Yahweh's chosen ones via David and his dynasty[1] and as Yahweh's anointed,[2] the fall of Davidic dynasty and the destruction of God's Temple on Mt. Zion in 586 BCE called for a theological revision of the eternal validity of the Davidic kingship.[3]

The Moral Dimension of the 'Mandate of Heaven' in the Zhou Dynasty

When defeating the Shang Dynasty (1600–1046 BCE), the new (1046–256 BCE) Zhou leadership under King Wu (武王) had to legitimize its power and explain the fall of the former in its own rise to power and to unite the two peoples into one country under *Tian*, the Sovereign Ruler in heaven. *The Book of Poetry* contains the poem 'King Wen' (文王), which is assumed to be composed by the Duke of Zhou (周公) in praise and honor of the virtuous King Wen in the Zhou Dynasty. The local rulers and princes of the vassal states of the confederation were invited to assemble to celebrate the illuminous achievement of the Zhou emperor (Chen 2001: 909–10). The hymn constitutes the important political epic of King Wen, the ancestor who was believed to receive the Mandate of Heaven to rule as the Son of Heaven (天子). The repeated use of the word 命 ('mandate'), eight times in a short poem of seven stanzas, illustrates the importance of the theme not only for the divine legitimization of the human sovereign embodied in King Wen and his successors based on his moral and ethical behaviors (Chen 2001: 912), but also the rejection of the Shang Dynasty which has been formerly endowed with a similar Mandate of Heaven. This poem also states that the defeat and therefore rejection of the Shang rule in the east would serve as a warning for the current powerful generation of the Zhou people in the west. The last emperor of the Shang was portrayed as conducting a brutal and tyrannical regime (无道) that justified the revolt by the Zhou people. In Chinese the term for revolution (革命) literally means revoking the Mandate. The complete hymn is translated into English[4] as follows:

1. King Wen is on high (文王在上), Oh! bright is he in heaven (於昭于天). Although Zhou is an old state (周雖舊邦), Its Mandate is still new (其命維新).

---

1. In Pss. 78.70-72; 89.3, 20, 35; 132.1, 10, 17; 144.10.
2. Pss. 2.2; 20.7; 84.8; 89.38, 51; 132.1.
3. On the king in the Psalms, see the chapter on 'The King' in Kraus 1986: 107–23.
4. There are several English translations of *Shijing*: Waley 1996; Xu Yuanchong (许渊冲) 1993; An Zengcai (安增才) 1999. See also Yao Jiheng 1994, Vol. 1, for his comments on the *Book of Poetry*.

Illustrious is the House of Zhou (有周不顯), The Mandate of *Di* endowed timely (帝命不時).
King Wen ascends and descends[5] (文王陟降), At *Di*'s left and the right (在帝左右).

2. Earnest and dedicated was King Wen (亹亹文王), And his fame is without end (令聞不已).
The gifts to Zhou (陳錫哉周), Extend to the descendants of King Wen (侯文王孫子),
To the descendants of King Wen (文王孫子), The direct line and branches in hundred generations (本支百世),
All the officers of Zhou (凡周之士), Shall be illustrious from age to age (不顯亦世)

3. Being illustrious from age to age (世之不顯), Zealously and reverently pursuing their tasks (厥猶翼翼)
Brilliant are the many officers (思皇多士), Born in this royal kingdom (生此王國).
The royal kingdom is able to produce them (王國克生), The backbones of Zhou (維周之楨).
Numerous is the array of officers (濟濟多士), King Wen enjoys his repose (文王以寧).

4. How dignified is King Wen (穆穆文王); Oh! Reverence to him will be extended without end (於緝熙敬止),
Great is the Mandate of Heaven (假哉天命)! There the descendants of former Shang (有商孫子);
The descendants of Shang (商之孫子), Are numerous in hundreds of thousands (其麗不億);
But when Di gave the Mandate (上帝既命), They are to submit to Zhou (侯于周服)

5. Submitted to Zhou they did (侯服于周), The Mandate of Heaven is not permanent (天命靡常)
The officers of Yin, admirable and alert (殷士膚敏), Assist at the libations in the (Zhou) capital (祼將于京).
They assist and serve at those libations (厥作祼將), Always wearing their Shang style cap and garment (常服黼冔)
O you loyal ministers of the king (王之藎臣), Ever remember your ancestor (無念爾祖)!

6. Ever remember your ancestor (無念爾祖), Cultivating your virtue (聿脩厥德).
Should always accord with the Mandate (永言配命), Seeking to secure for abundant blessing (自求多福)
Before Yin lost the multitudes (殷之未喪師), [Its kings] were in accord with *Shangdi* (克配上帝)

---

5. Some exegetes assume that this refers to the spirit of King Wen, see Ma Chiying (马持盈) 1972: 398.

You should take lesson from Yin (宜鑒于殷), The great Mandate is not easily kept (駿命不易)

7. The Mandate is not easily kept (命之不易), Do not bring about your own extinction (無遏爾躬).
Display and radiate your righteousness and fame (宣昭義問), And take warnings from Heaven for Yin (有虞殷自天).
The doings of High Heaven (上天之載), Have no sound nor smell (無聲無臭)
Take your model from King Wen (儀刑文王), and all the states will have confidence in you (萬邦作孚).

Due to the limited scope of this study only a few aspects of the Chinese dynastic hymn, relevant to the discussion of Psalm 78, will be elaborated here. King Wen is at the outset thought as a benevolent and brilliant ancestor who has ascended to the left and right side of *Di*, the Sovereign Lord of the Zhou people in heaven. He is in possession of the Mandate which is considered as being still new for the old state and is applicable to the present generation of King Wu who is the son of King Wen. Indeed, the Mandate is believed to be extended to hundreds of generations to come. King Wen is both in heaven and at the same time present on earth as he ascends and descends between heaven and earth. In drawing lessons from the revocation of the Mandate of Heaven, the Shang people are being invited to submit to the Zhou.

At this point the important aspect of the Mandate of Heaven is introduced: its changing and transient character as expressed in 'The Mandate of Heaven' is not permanent (天命靡常) (Stanza 4). This is one of the stages of the development of the notion of the Mandate of Heaven from Shang's idea of constancy (天命恒常) to the new understanding of inconstancy (天命靡常) (Stanza 5) with a conception of it being able to be transferred (天命转移) from one dynasty to another, depending on the virtue of the person concerned. It is also admitted that the Mandate of Heaven is not easy to keep (Stanzas 6-7). The poem goes on to invite the Shang leaders to assemble in the Zhou capital to participate in the cultic ritual of the Zhou: 'Assist at the libations in the (Zhou) capital (祼將于京)' (Stanza 5). The Shang people are allowed to wear their Shang ritual costumes (Stanza 5) but they are to identify themselves with the Zhou ancestors. It is further claimed that whereas the Shang ancestors once had the Mandate and were once in accord with the will of *Shangdi*, they have subsequently gone astray. Their fall has become a warning given by *Tian* to the present generation which is advised to cultivate its virtue (聿脩厥德) in order to be 'in accord with the Mandate [of Heaven] (永言配命)' (Stanza 6). The example of King Wen is then lifted up as a model to be followed at the end of the hymn: 'Take your model from King Wen (儀刑文王)'.

What is presented in this hymn is also supported by a rich collection of archaeological finds in China, especially the inscriptions on bronze vessels uncovered from excavation sites of the Zhou period (Schwartz 1985, esp. Chapter 2). The Dai Yu Tripot (大盂鼎) is one of the major representations of the bronze corpus known to us:

In the ninth month, King Kang, at the temple of the Zhou royal family, issued an order to his minister, Yu. Thus said the King, 'Oh Yu, the most illustrious King Wen has received the Great Mandate possessed by Heaven (*Tian*)'. And King Wu, succeeding King Wen, has established the national boundary, eradicated the enemies, and pacified the people. (modified from Chiu 1984: 96)

Contextual Reconstruction from Cross-Textual Insights

Scholars widely agree that this Chinese dynastic ritual hymn reveals a certain degree of discontinuity from the Shang to the Zhou Dynasty, a transformation of the idea of divine–human relationship. Although the Zhou people developed and formulated the idea of the Mandate of Heaven, which emphasized the emperor's morality and virtue, there remains the belief in *Shangdi* as commanding the submission of the Shang to the Zhou in Stanza 4: 'But when *Shangdi* gave the Mandate (上帝既命)' and 'They are to submit to Zhou (侯于周服)'. Heaven is assumed to work mysteriously in human history, 'the doings of High Heaven' (上天之載) have no 'sound and smell' (無聲無臭).

A similar approach to the transfer of power is seen in Psalm 78. According to R.P. Carroll the psalm is a vestige of a tribal polemic, 'a polemic directed against the holders of the older faith in favor of the more recent claimants' (Carroll 1971: 144). Carroll proposes that the occurrence of בחר ('choose') in the negative form לא בחר ('not choose', v. 67) suggests a polemical intent (Carroll 1971: 136). It is, however, very unlikely that the intention of the psalmist was to alienate the people of Israel or to promote hostility among the Judahite community against the Northern Kingdom. Taking a more positive view on 'not choose' does not mean undermining the tension and controversy between Israel and Judah. Furthermore, the address in the introduction (78.1-8) points to 'our ancestors' as the rebellious generation of the wilderness (v. 8; cf. vv. 17-31, 40-41) and the stubborn generation of the conquest (vv. 9-11, 56-58). The 'rebellious' and 'stubborn' generations are referred to and identified as the audience's ancestors. Similar tensions are expressed in the Chinese poem, between the Shang people of the East and the Zhou people of the West. With a cross-textual reading of Psalm 78 in the Hebrew Bible with 'King Wen' in *Shijing*, we can argue that alienation of the former dynasty and polemical opposition against the defeated people may not be the major concern of a new ruling power. There is no indication of historical influence and interaction between the two texts; however, comparing the literary production of two states (Shang-Zhou and Israel-Judah) in contest for legitimacy may give some insights from the relatively well-established Chinese tradition (and see further Schwartz 1985: 41–46) for the comprehension of Psalm 78, whose context and setting are open to dispute.

The basis of Zhou's Mandate is established on the ideal kingship demonstrated by King Wen, the virtuous ruler remembered by the subsequent generations. Similar claims are found in the climax of Psalm 78 (vv. 68-72), in which the election of Judah and God's choice of David are confirmed and the rejection of Israel is declared. In the psalm, the use of בחר (vv. 68, 70) and לא בחר (v. 67) clearly indicates an election theme, a tradition formulated clearly in deuteronomic terminology in the Hebrew Bible.

Reading the Chinese text of 'King Wen' with Psalm 78, we immediately spot the difference in the latter having Zion as the site of the Temple (vv. 68-70), against the absence in the former of a cultic site where the name of God is to rest. Though there is no mention of any rejection of former temple site for the service to the Tian in the Chinese hymn, such as that of the rejection of the former cultic place of God at Shiloh (v. 60) and the choice of the Temple on Zion, the context of inviting the defeated Shang remnants to come to the Zhou capital to participate in the ritual of reverence to the ancestors (with the aim to unite the two peoples as one) is clearly expressed. This may also be plausible for Psalm 78, a call to exchange Northern cultic centers after the fall of Samaria in 722 BCE, such as Shiloh, for Zion.

According to Finkelstein's archaeological surveys, the fall of the kingdom of Israel after 722 BCE brought about dramatic growth in terms of total built-up area in Judea. The doubling, if not trebling, in the number of settlements and increase of population of Judah in just a couple of decades in the second half of the eighth century may well be explained by the influx of a large number of Israelite refugees (Finkelstein 2013: 154).

Further, on the notion of the changing character of the Mandate of Heaven in the Chinese hymn ('The Mandate of Heaven is not always permanent', 天命靡常), it is worth noting that the human dimension of virtuous behavior in Zhou time has superseded Shang's idea of the Heavenly Mandate's constancy (天命恒常). Heaven's Mandate being inconstant (天命靡常), and not unconditionally eternal, has facilitated dynastic changes with its transfer (天命转移) from one dynasty to another. This aspect leads us to a consideration of conditional and unconditional dynastic promise to David in the Bible.

There are at least two forms of the promise articulated in the Psalms: the unconditional (Ps. 89.30-34) and the conditional (Ps. 132.12; and see Johnson 1979: 83, 166).

> If his children forsake my law and do not walk according to my ordinances, if they violate my statutes and do not keep my commandments, then I will punish their transgression with the rod and their iniquity with scourges; but I will not remove from him my steadfast love, or be false to my faithfulness. I will not violate my covenant, or alter the word that went forth from my lips. (Ps. 89.30-34, NRSV)

> If your sons keep my covenant and my decrees that I shall teach them, their sons also forever shall sit upon your throne. (Ps. 132.12, NRSV)

God's unconditional promise to David may go back to Nathan's formulation in 2 Sam. 7.14-15, understood as the original unconditional formulation, to which Psalm 89 is a return (Mettinger 1976: 276). Whichever is the case, the biblical traditions did undergo a change through problematizing the promise's continued validity in the view of human behavior, although never to the anthropocentric extent shown by the Chinese poems.

In addition to the issue of conditional/unconditional promise, there is the belief in the supremacy of Judah and certain degree of inviolability of Zion and the Temple. This reflects a biased position as expressed in 2 Kings 17. When at the tragic devastation of the destruction of Jerusalem and its Temple, the deportation of the leadership and the population of Judah and the fall of the dynasty, the excessive confidence in the choice of David was confronted by the hard historical experience of disorientation, there developed another stage of the relationship between the North and the South. Later, in the times of Jeremiah and Ezekiel,

> (T)he fall of the Northern Kingdom was a great temptation to Judah to see itself as alone the chosen of God. The impending, and then actual, fall of the South evened the score, as it were, so that neither side could vaunt itself. (Scobie 1976: 92)

Concluding Remarks

Psalm 78 may well be a didactic psalm composed in Jerusalem after the fall of the Northern Kingdom. The rejection of Ephraim-Joseph became a historical reality in the catastrophe of Samaria's defeat. Past history is remembered and interpreted to illustrate a puzzling historical problem of the present situation of the North's fall, and the desire to unite the North with the South. The Mosaic traditions of the Exodus and wilderness period are attached to royal theology to form a whole piece of historical recitation for didactic purpose. If the historical, prophetic, sapiential and royal traditions were blended together in the time of Hezekiah, Psalm 78 reflects a similar context and may play a role in such a stage of development.

Divine rejection of humans can be understood properly in connection with human rejection of God. Such divine rejection is almost always understood in the Bible as a response to human abomination. The reaction of Yahweh to having been first rejected by humans is illustrated in the case of the Northern Kingdom. The Chinese notion of Heaven's Mandate being withdrawn from the ill-behaved Shang Dynasty and newly endowed on the virtuous king of the Zhou well elaborates the human dimension of rejection and election. The invitation of Zhou leadership to the former officials to participate in the ritual celebration for the unification of the two states may provide some insights for our reading of the divine election of Judah, Zion and David in Psalm 78.

My second choice is Psalm 1, a wisdom-Torah poem, which defines the sapiential character of the book of the Psalms as a whole. Psalms 1–2 should be considered together as a pair of twins, introducing what follows and integrating the themes of wisdom, Torah, kingship, ritual, oracle and many more that characterize the richness and profundity of the book and, for that matter, the Hebrew Bible as a whole.

Professor Archie C.C. Lee (PhD in HB, University of Edinburgh) served as Professor of Hebrew Bible in the Department of Cultural and Religious Studies of the Chinese University of Hong Kong, also as Dean of Arts and Director of the Institute of Chinese Studies before his retirement in 2014; and then Distinguished University Professor of Humanities and Social Sciences, Center for Judaic and Inter-Religious Studies and Director, Jao Tsung-I Institute of Religion and Chinese Studies, Shandong University, China. He is the Founding President of the Society of Asian Biblical Studies (SABS). His research interest is in cross-textual interpretation of the Bible and Asian culture.

References

An, Zengcai (安增才) (1999), *The Book of Songs Translated into Modern Chinese*, Shandong: Shandong Friendship Press.
Carroll, Robert (1971), 'Psalm 78: Vestiges of a Tribal Polemic', VT 21: 133–50.
Chen, Zizhan (陳子展) (2001), *Commentary on the Three-Hundred Songs* (《诗三百解题》), Shanghai: Fudan University Press.
Chiu, Milton M. (1984), *The Tao of Chinese Religion*, Lanham: University Press of America.
Finkelstein, Israel (2013), *The Forgotten Kingdom: The Archaeology and History of Northern Israel*, Atlanta: SBL.
Johnson, A.R. (1979), *The Cultic Prophet and Israel's Psalmody*, Cardiff: University of Wales Press.
Kraus, Hans-Joachim (1986), *Theology of the Psalms*, Minneapolis: Augsburg Fortress.
Ma Chiying (马持盈) (1972), *Modern Commentary and Translation of Shijing* (诗经今注今译), Taipei: Taiwan Shangwu Publishing Co.
Mettinger, T.N.D. (1976), *Kingship and Messiah: The Civil and Sacral Legitimation of the Israelite Kings*, Lund: C.W.L. Cleerup.
Schwartz, Benjamin I. (1985), *The World of thought in Ancient China*, Cambridge: The Belknap Press of Harvard University Press.
Scobie, Charles H.H. (1976), 'North and South: Tension and Reconciliation in Biblical History', in R. Johnston et al. (ed.), *Biblical Studies: Essays in Honour of William Barclay*, 87–98, London: Collins.
Waley, Arthur (1996), *The Book of Songs: The Ancient Chinese Classic of Poetry*, New York: Grove Press.
Xu Yuanchong (许渊冲) (1993), *Book of Poetry* (The Chinese-English Bilingual Series of Chinese Classics), Peking: Hunan Publishing.
Yao Jiheng (姚际恒) (1994), *Collection of Yao Jiheng Writings* (姚际恒著作集), Vol 1, General Comments on the Book of Poetry (诗经通论), Taipei: Institute of Literature and Philosophy, Academia Sinica.

PSALM 84
WHERE IS HOME?

Meira Polliack

Throughout the ages writers and thinkers, as well as ordinary people from all walks of life, have asked themselves the apparently simple yet challenging question: 'Where is home'? Some may elide this question with a similar, perhaps more philosophical line of inquiry: 'What is (a) home'? Yet the psalm I have chosen, as I see it, concentrates on the 'Where?' The poet's answer seems, at first glance, to be the more-or-less-expected 'God's Temple'. The psalm's circular structure reiterates the opening verse, 'How lovely is your *dwelling place*, O Lord Almighty!' (v. 2 NIV, 1 MT), with one of its three closing verses, emphasizing God's physical shrine:

> Better is one day in your *courts* than a thousand elsewhere; I would rather be a *doorkeeper* in the *house* of my God than dwell in the *tents* of the wicked. (v. 10 NIV, 11 MT)

Nevertheless, the last two verses make it clear that the physical shrine is but an extension or representation of a wider sense of home/house, apparently expressing a notion of one's 'home is with God' in the spiritual sense:

> For the Lord God is a sun and shield; the Lord bestows favor and honor; no good thing does he withhold from those whose walk is blameless.
>
> O Lord Almighty, blessed is the one who trusts in you. (vv. 11-12 NIV, 12-13 MT)

Biblical critics are apt to hear a dissonance between the physical and spiritual senses, and sometimes allocate the final two verses to a postexilic editor who was alive during or after the destruction of the First Temple, thus inserting a metaphysical ending into the final version of the psalm (Wallace 2013; Wilson 1985; Cole 2000: 115–25). Yet, the bulk of the psalm as we have it is indeed more bound to a tangible place, articulating the speaker's almost physical yearning for God's home on earth, a yearning that reflects the Hebrew Bible's perspective on the Jerusalem Temple edifice, especially in the Psalms collection.

Personally, I am not convinced that the question of spiritual versus physical reading was of such paramount concern to the psalmist as to generate tension between the two readings. Is 'home' the physical place in which we were born and grew up, or where we have chosen to live or 'make our home'? Or is it a mental place, as in 'home is where your heart is', especially in our relationships with other people? Or is it in both the mental and physical senses of the place where we 'feel most at home', as the English expression puts it so finely, rather than the location of our actual home? Psalm 84 certainly offers a mixed answer, and more than one type of answer, in the metaphorical and literal senses, through its wonderful Hebrew poetic parallelism:

גם צפור מצאה בית
ודרור קן לה

> Even the sparrow has found a home,
> and the swallow a nest for herself. (v. 3 NIV, v. 4 MT)

This sweetly evocative stanza has always rung a special bell with me regarding the notion of 'home'. For it rightly expresses, in an image from nature rather than philosophy, what we all know intuitively so well: home is where one finds a sense of peace and rest from life's physical and mental 'wanderings', where one can shelter from hardship and feel safe.

The question of an inner-home, or an inner sense of peace, is part of the wider symbolism of 'home' in the psalm, as it is in our minds and our languages. The ancient and modern Hebrew and Arabic lexemes for 'home' (בית, *bayit*; *beyt*) are often used in the sense of 'family' (wife, children), and at times in the Bible too.[1] The stark opening with the preposition 'even'/גם (in v. 3/4) draws attention to the speaker's restless tone. Why start with a disclaimer, as it were? 'Even' is a rather good translation of the Biblical Hebrew's ambiguous גם, *gam*, which can likewise be rendered 'even so' and 'also'.[2] It stresses, I think, the speaker's extreme yearning for a home: if such migrating birds as the דרור, *dror* (the lexeme also used for 'freedom' in the HB)[3] can find a home in God's Temple, to the point where they

---

1. See the illuminating semantic and cultural discussion of the term בית, *bayit*, and other related terms by Chapman 2016: 20–74. For an important global and environmental perspective on this issue see Boer 2008: 81–108 (Chapter 4: 'Home is Always Elsewhere: Exodus, Exile, and the Howling Wilderness Waste').

2. גם (*gam*) appears 371 times in the HB. Cf. for instance Gen. 3.6 ('also'); 27.33; 30.8 ('even so').

3. דרור (*dror*) appears six times in the HB in the sense of 'freedom'; cf. Lev. 5.10; Isa. 61.1. The bird is identified with the 'swallow' species in various translations, probably due to its speed of flight and migratory patterns, which have also made it a symbol of the changing

choose to bring up their next generation in its precincts, then what about us poor humans? The next line of the same verse continues, therefore:

> …where she places her young near Your altars, O LORD of Hosts, my King and my God,

to be reinforced yet again in v. 4/5:

> Blessed are those who dwell in your house
> They are ever praising you. *Sela.*

The imagined answer to the speaker's yearning is evident: surely we, who can come to God's Temple whenever we want and live with it in our midst, have found a secure home. Yet still there is a perceptible tension in the speaker's line of thought, a nuance and ambivalence that lingers in the striking image of the navigating birds sheltering in the crevices of the Temple's walls and the nooks of its altar.

To my mind at least, the pull is between the free-flying birds and the so-called permanence of home. In fact, the wider 'notion of a home' is what underlies this beautiful imagery. Birds can come and go whereas humans, even in the age of airplanes, are less able to pick up and fly. Birds can navigate home, sometimes every year (as the ancients knew very well), but can humans navigate back to the very place they have left? Can they find their way home after they have left it or, more likely, were forced to leave? Yes, even before the invention of a compass, humans had ways to navigate; yet still, knowing exactly how to get home, especially after a long migratory journey, was no simple matter – not to mention surviving hazards on the way (cf. Clackson 2020; Trinka 2022). The suggestive opening גם, 'even', encourages identification with the human voice in the psalm. If migrating birds can find a home, what about the psalm's speaker? Can a human truly find a home, or a place that feels like home? Migration, forced and voluntary, has always been part of the human story, as has the quest for a secure identity. Is this why this verse (84.3/4) has always chimed, in my mind, with a sense of loss and longing? Do I have a home? And if so, where is it?

Mine is the *third* consecutive generation of transposition in my family. I know from personal experience that even when certain houses are abandoned, emptied, or left behind they can continue to feel like homes, no less than being remembered as homes and sometimes, mysteriously, even more so. In the same manner, paradoxically, even when certain houses are still functioning as homes, they have ceased to feel like homes, or perhaps that sense was never there in the first place.

---

seasons in many cultures, in particular the coming of spring. See, as an illustration, 'More than just a bird' (Korea.net: The official website of the Republic of Korea; https://www.korea.net/NewsFocus/Culture/view?articleId=121330). It appears only one more time in the HB in the sense of 'bird', in Prov. 26.2: 'Like a fluttering *sparrow* [Heb. צפור, 'bird'] or a darting *swallow* [Heb. דרור], an undeserved curse does not come to rest' (NIV).

Let me illustrate this paradox with a far-fetched example and then come back to my own experience, closer to home, as it were.

In a rare BBC recording of Sigmund Freud, which I happened to hear recently through the earphones of a hop-on hop-off bus tour while visiting Vienna, the father of modern psychology describes, with a frail voice in fine German, how he was forced to leave '*mein Heim in Wien*', and the loss of freedom he experienced. I was struck by the poignancy of that phrase *mein Heim in Wien* and Freud's attachment to the city.[4] Later, roaming through Freud's famous apartment and clinic on Berggasse 19 (now the Freud Museum) – where Freud lived with his family for over four decades, wrote his most important works, and analyzed his famous patients – I think I understood what he meant.[5] The rooms are mostly bare – original furniture and items were transferred in 1938, and now furnish his final residence, the Freud Museum in 20 Maresfield Gardens in Hampstead, London.[6] Yet the lush green trees through the windows, the front street and the backyard, the staircase leading to the flat and, more than anything, the sense of intimate space, remain as they must have been in the late nineteenth and early twentieth centuries. The angle through which a patient lying on the famous couch would have seen the trees through the window, the peaceful view from the bedroom balcony with its patterned tiles, seem to be just as they were. One can almost feel the former residents and guests (including Freud's wife, six children, sister-in-law, and maid!) still inhabiting the rooms with relative ease and cheerfulness. What would Freud have answered, I wonder, to the two questions I began with? Without presumptuousness, I suppose his answer to 'Where is home?' would have been 'Vienna'; and his answer to 'What is home?' would have been 'Berggasse 19' – in the sense of what was created over time in that flat. In this, as in many other aspects, Freud was a most fortunate man, having escaped by a hair's breadth the death camps that were the final destination of scores of thousands of genteel Viennese Jews of his generation. With his family fully intact and spared these horrors, he never really 'lost' his home.[7] All that he and his family achieved in Vienna managed somehow to keep them miraculously safe, and the city can celebrate his heritage in relative comfort.

---

4. When a child, the family of Sigmund Freud (b. 1856 in Moravia, d. 1939 in London) moved to Vienna, where he studied medicine and would spend most of his life. For the recording (in German and English), visit: https://www.mediathek.at/katalogsuche/suche/detail/?uid=014F3D71-123-001E6-00000D5C-014E5066.

5. For details see https://www.freud-museum.at/en/. That so many modern museums celebrating the lives of great thinkers and artists are active in their former places of residence, drawing thousands of visitors every year in a type of modern pilgrimage, is certainly worthy of consideration.

6. This is where Freud spent the last year of his life, as described in the London home website of Freud and his daughter Anna: https://www.freud.org.uk/.

7. Sophie Freud (1893–1920) died in the inter-war influenza epidemic. Freud's other children and grandchildren were unscathed by the Holocaust. Further on the history and fate of the Jews of Austria and Vienna see https://www.yadvashem.org/righteous/

Yet if another active son of the very same city at roughly the same time – Theodor Herzl, the father of modern political Zionism, who sensed the approaching Holocaust with every fiber in his body and pleaded with every European leader and diplomat he could get access to for the establishment of a Jewish state as a haven for persecuted Jews – were asked the same questions, I very much doubt that he would have called Vienna '*mein Heim*'. An acclaimed journalist and writer who lost his wife's family fortune in pursuit of the Zionist cause, Herzl died at the age of 44, leaving his wife Julia and their three children to a virtually penniless and otherwise tragic ending.[8] Vienna honored him by naming a staircase after him, yet it has not turned any of his or his family residences in the city into museums.[9] Why would it, if Herzl spent all his energy devising how to leave that enchanted city? In the *Altneuland* of which he dreamed, now embodied in the modern State of Israel, there is a Herzl Street or Boulevard in every village, town, and minor or major city.[10] Yet, would Herzl have called any version of modern Israel *his* home? And would he have been able to describe 'what is (a) home?' Somehow, I doubt it.

Let's return to our opening questions: Is home the physical place in which we were born and grew up, or have chosen to live or 'make our home'? Or is it a mental place, as in 'home is where your heart is', especially in our relationships with other people? Or is it the place where we 'feel most at home', rather than where our home is physically located? As I noted earlier, mine is the *third* consecutive generation of transposition in my family. I am the first of my family to be designated a native Israeli, born in Jerusalem of Zionist parents who emigrated there from Cape Town, South Africa in the early 1960s, out of their own free will

stories/vienna.html; https://www.claimscon.org/our-work/negotiations/austria/history-of-the-austrian-jewish-community/; https://www.wien.gv.at/english/culture/jewishvienna/. For a vivid portrayal of this epoch of cultural life in Vienna see Beller 1989.

8. The family of Theodor Herzl (b. 1860 in Budapest, then part of the Austro-Hungarian Empire; d. 1904 in Edlach in lower Austria, first buried in Vienna, and in 1949 reburied in Israel according to his wish), moved to Vienna in 1878, where, like Freud, he studied at the University of Vienna (Law). See further on his life, works and family history: Elon 1975; Falk 1993; Avineri 2013. His younger daughter, Margarethe Gertrude Herzl (known as Trude), was the only one to survive her parents and siblings, yet along with other Jewish patients she was transferred from a public mental hospital in Vienna in September 1942 to Theresienstadt concentration camp, where she died in the camp hospital. Trude's son (Herzl's only surviving grandson), Stefan Theodor, committed suicide upon hearing of the loss of both his parents in the Holocaust (1946). On the fascinating relationship between Freud and Herzl (including the question of whether they met in person in Vienna or only knew of each other), see Falk 1978: 357–78.

9. https://www.viennaitineraries.com/Theodor_Herzl_Stiege.html.

10. Herzl's utopian novel (in German), *Altneuland* (1902), describing his vision of a Jewish return to the land of Israel, was translated into English as *The Old New Land*, and into Hebrew as *Tel Aviv* (literally, 'Mount of Spring'; a name then adopted for the newly founded city) by Nahum Sokolow (Warsaw 1902). It appeared six years after Herzl's political pamphlet, *Der Judenstaat* (*The Jewish State*, 1896).

and ideological accord. I often wonder whether I ever really felt at home in my native city, towards which I feel growingly estranged over time; or in the relatively young State of Israel to which my parents set their idealistic wings from the southern tip of Africa. This question resonated with me during my recent week in Vienna. I suppose that culturally, and in other ways, I feel relatively at home in a democratic, free-thinking Europe. I have a strong emotional attachment to the traditions of Western Europe, including its Jewish heritage, and physically too, I confess, the weather suits me better. When I reach the Baltic areas of the continent, especially by the grey sea, I experience a sense of calm that I rarely feel elsewhere. If I were a bird, would I navigate towards the Baltic, with the help of a GPS system encoded in my genes? Because although my young parents voluntarily emigrated, or made *aliyah* (in Hebrew 'came up/rose') to Israel (then barely 15 years from its Independence) from South Africa, their parents, my grandparents, emigrated to South Africa from Lithuania, from which they fled (like Freud) in the 1930s. Yet as attracted as I am to watery Baltic hues, I have no wish to visit Lithuania, where so many close relatives of my grandparents – parents, brothers and sisters, and their children –were murdered and buried in mass graves during the Holocaust. Lithuania was most probably 'home' to my grandparents and their forefathers, in the deepest physical and spiritual sense, but for me it is unalterably defiled. My grandparents chose to flee to one of the few countries that still took in Jewish refugees at the time, just a while before it too shut its doors to Europe's Jews. This choice saved their lives and brought about my existence, in yet another continent shift from Southern Africa to the Asia of the Middle East, where I, my family's first-generation native Israeli, live with my husband, born in another Middle Eastern country, and our two Israeli-born daughters. Do my daughters feel at home in Israel, as I rarely feel? I think they do, as does their father, despite the fact he was forced to emigrate to Israel, aged eight, from Beirut, Lebanon. Although Lebanese Jews remained relatively comfortable in their native land even after the establishment of the State of Israel (1948), they had to leave when Beirut became a major Palestinian Liberation Organization (PLO) stronghold after the 1967 war between Israel and its Arab neighbors. How, in years to come, will our daughters answer the question 'Where is home?' More importantly, will they and their children need to take flight again due to political or environmental upheaval? I sincerely hope that they will always have a home, and feel at home, in Israel; but I will settle for their being safe and secure anywhere on God's planet, His 'sun and shield' (84.12 MT).

* * *

My choice of Psalm 84 was inspired by a painting admired by my late mother, Lily. Its amateur painter named it 'Psalm 84.4', and it depicts a flock of birds flying to the Temple through a series of kabbalistic symbols in red, white, and blue. Therefore, my siblings and I chose to inscribe v. 4 MT of the psalm (in English v. 3, 'even a bird') on our mother's tombstone, ending the inscription with *our* own words: 'A pioneer from Table Mountain to the Mountains of Jerusalem' (all in Hebrew). Many birds pass over Israel during their annual migration from Africa to the Baltic region; and this verse seemed to bring together our family history.

My second choice would have been Psalm 23, beginning with the immortal

ה' רעי לא אחסר

the Lord is my Shepherd, I shall not want (23.1, NRSV and other translations).

In Biblical Hebrew, this verse is but four words, eight syllables, long: *'adonay ro'i lo' 'eḥsar*. For me, it's the most beautiful line of Hebrew poetry ever written.

Meira Polliack is Professor of Bible and the Joseph and Ceil Mazer Chair in Jewish Culture in Muslim Lands and Cairo Geniza Studies at Tel-Aviv University, where she has been teaching biblical literature and medieval exegesis since 1995. She specialized in medieval Arabic Bible manuscripts and Geniza sources, including Karaite literature, during her graduate and post-graduate years at Cambridge University (1988–95), and was one of the Principle Investigators of the international research project *Biblia Arabica - The Bible in Arabic among Jews, Christians and Muslims* (2012–18).

References

Avineri, Shlomo (2013), *Herzl: Theodor Herzl and the Foundation of the Jewish State*, London: Weidenfeld & Nicolson.
Beller, Steven (1989), *Vienna and the Jews, 1867-1938: A Cultural History*, Cambridge: Cambridge University Press.
Boer, Roland (2008), *Last Stop before Antarctica: The Bible and Postcolonialism in Australia*, Atlanta: Society of Biblical Literature.
Chapman Cynthia R. (2016), *The House of the Mother: The Social Roles of Maternal Kin in Biblical Hebrew Narrative and Poetry*, New Haven: Yale University Press.
Clackson, James (2020), *Migration, Mobility and Language Contact in and around the Ancient Mediterranean*, Cambridge: Cambridge University Press.
Cole, Robert Luther (2000), *The Shape and Message of Book III (Psalms 73–89)*, Sheffield: Sheffield Academic Press.
Elon, Amos (1975), *Herzl*, New York: Holt, Rinehart & Winston.
Falk, Avner (1978), 'Freud and Herzl', *Contemporary Psychoanalysis* 14: 357–87.
Falk, Avner (1993). *Herzl, King of the Jews: A Psychoanalytic Biography of Theodor Herzl*, Washington: University Press of America.
Herzl, Theodor (1896), *Der Judenstaat (The Jewish State)*, Leipzig: M. Breitenstein's Verlags-Buchhandlung.
Herzl, Theodor (1902), *Altneuland*; Eng. *The Old New Land*. Heb. *Tel Aviv*, trans. Nahum Sokolow (Warsaw, also in 1902).
Trinka, Eric M. (2022), *Cultures of Mobility, Migration, and Religion in Ancient Israel and its World*, London: Routledge.
Wallace, Robert E. (2013), 'The Narrative Effect of Psalms 84–89', in Ehud Ben Zvi (ed.), *Perspectives on Hebrew Scriptures VIII*, 283–97, Piscataway: Gorgias.
Wilson, G.H (1985), *The Editing of the Hebrew Psalter*, SBLDS 76, Chico: Scholars Press.

PSALM 90
IT SOON BECOMES EMPTY –
MY CHINESE READING OF THE PSALM

Yanjing Qu

Psalm 90 contains a complaint that is full of poetic beauty:

> The days of our years are threescore years and ten; and if by reason of strength they be fourscore years yet is their strength labour and sorrow; for it is soon cut off, and we fly away. (v. 10, KJV)

This complaint approaches human reality from the temporal dimension, along with the rest of the poem, which perceives time in two different perspectives: the transient lifecycle of human beings, and the infinite continuation of God. This poem, through the contrast between the temporal nature of human existence and the perpetuity of God, highlights a theological conviction that the cycle of human life and death is under God's control (vv. 1-2). With this conviction, the psalm recognizes the ephemerality of human life (vv. 5-6) and appeals to God to grant humanity more of this finite life (vv. 12-17).

As part of the biblical corpus, Psalm 90 was composed in a cultural context that had certain, widely recognized standards defining a fulfilled life. These standards include aspects of a person's material life and his or her social relations. For example, old age is one of the criteria of the blessed life of Abraham, who sets a precedent in the generations to follow. He lived to a good old age, was rewarded with affluence, and was surrounded by his children and grandchildren when he was catching his last breath in his own land (Gen. 25.1-10). Abraham represents the happy ending that anyone would have wished for themselves. In fact, in the book of Genesis old age even becomes a metonymy, an epithet, for the blessed patriarchs, i.e., Abraham, Isaac, and Jacob.[1] Hence, long life is an important condition for a well-lived life in the culture of ancient Israelites. In this regard, Psalm 90's regretful tone over old age, seventy and eighty years old, is contra-cultural.

---

1. Isaac and Jacob's stories deviate from Abraham's precedent in some respects. See Sternberg 1987: 349–54.

It challenges the meaning of a human being's long life, which is ephemeral comparing to God's presence, if one cannot live a good life.

I fell in love with Psalm 90 when I first encountered it in my early twenties. However, I must admit it was the Chinese Union Version (CUV) that I fell in love with. First, the metaphor of transient grass in vv. 5-6 resonates with a classical Chinese saying, 'Man has but one life, grass but one spring'.[2] Humans are like grass and their life is like the season of spring, which is beautiful but short. In comparison, the biblical metaphorical expression is more extended: human life 'flourishes' (יָצִיץ, from צוּץ, ṣwṣ Qal), 'grows' (חָלַף, from חלף, ḥlp Qal),[3] 'is cut off' (יְמוֹלֵל, from מלל, mll Poel) and 'withers' (יָבֵשׁ, from יבש, ybš Qal). The biblical text describes the unending process of flourishing and withering of the grass and juxtaposes it with the violence of death (v. 3).[4] This image brings out the idea that human life is not only transient, but also trivial. It is but an insignificant fleeting moment of the unending cycle of nature's regeneration. Furthermore, the CUV's translation of v. 10 is my favourite part of this poem. The linguistic sophistication of this translated line is incredible. It recalls the spirit of Zen through its rendering. CUV translates גָז ('cut off', from גוז Qal) as 轉眼成空 /zhuǎn yǎn chéng kōng/ ('soon becomes empty'), thus achieving one of the important aims of Zen meditation: 見性 /jiànxìng/ ('to see the nature of things'), perceiving the true nature of being through penetrating the disguises of the human world. CUV uses the word 空 /kōng/ ('void', 'empty'), to grasp the futility of human toil and trouble. This word is loaded with rich meanings in Chinese culture, partly because it has its root in Chinese Buddhism. 'Emptiness' is often used to express the futility of suffering that results from pursuing worldly gains such as fame and wealth. These highly regarded human desires are mere vanity because they will eventually vanish and become empty.[5] The CUV's translation highlights the futility of the unnecessary suffering of a long life, and it presents this insight as philosophical

---

2. This verse is from the 《增广贤文》 /zēng guāng xián wén/, which was first translated into English in 2021: see Kuang et al. 2021.

3. The translation of חָלַף is disputed. Tate (1990: 434) translates both occurrences as 'pass on, change, disappear'. Booji (1987: 396) renders a similar translation by taking 'in the morning' from v. 5. Tsevat (1985) understands the occurrence in v. 5 as 'pass by, pass away', while the other one in v. 6 as 'sprout, grow'. This translation needs to include a textual emendation to delete the adverbial 'in the morning' in v. 5.

4. Verse 3 implies a link with Gen. 3.19, but the choice of words is different in either source: דַּכָּא ('dust') in Ps. 90.3 and עָפָר ('dust') in Gen. 3. דַּכָּא is a *hapax legomenon* that shares the same root, דכא (mostly *Piel* and *Pual*, 'to crush'). Hence it has 'an uncertain meaning that indicates a violent, unnatural event that is laid directly at God's feet'. See DeClaissé-Walford et al. 2014: 694.

5. In the translation of the *Prajna Paramita Heart Sutra* by Xuanzang (602–664 CE), there is a famous proverb: 色即是空，空即是色 ('Form is emptiness, and emptiness is form'). This means that sense is emptiness, and human beings should see the truth underneath the appearance of the world.

knowledge of the nature of human existence. This translation can instantly attract a Chinese mind.

Because of the blunt statement about the emptiness of human toils, Psalm 90 provides a resource for resisting the materialist tendency of contemporary life. For a Chinese reader, the lifespan of seventy and eighty years (v. 10) recalls a Confucian proverb in the *Analects*:

> The Master said:
> At fifteen, I had my mind bent on learning.
> At thirty, I stood firm.
> At forty, I had no doubts.
> At fifty, I knew the decrees of Heaven.
> At sixty, my ear was an obedient organ for the reception of truth.
> At seventy, I could follow what my heart desired, without transgressing what was right.[6]

This proverb is by far the most influential teaching of the lifecycle in Chinese culture.[7] It pushes Chinese readers to comply with the social expectation to achieve these life criteria at the right time. Otherwise, their life is considered a failure.

In contemporary Chinese society there is an emphasis on 'standing firm' at the age of thirty. This social expectation puts enormous pressure on young Chinese. Before turning forty, young Chinese are expected to reach a 'good place', which means to have a decent job which supports a family #with children; and, more importantly, to own a property to live in and to show their value. However, this criterion for 'standing firm' is not attainable for everybody. It is not even possible for most people who are struggling to keep their jobs with the declining economic growth. In fact, the rising housing prices, decreasing birth rate and increasing cost of health and education have made the situation even worse for the younger generation. Compounded with the thirty-year history of the one-child-per-family policy, the social expectation of 'standing firm' at the age of thirty is intensified, because an only child holds the entire aspirations of a family. Hence, the younger generation of Chinese lives under enormous pressure, which limits their choices of life. The reason for this horrendous situation is so complicated that it is impossible for any individual to tackle the structural issues behind it. Psalm 90 does not offer a quick solution to this problem, but it provides a contra-cultural idea that could shake the unshakable expectations of each life stage. For the fleeting seventy or eighty years of our life, the ambition to have it all at the cost of freedom and enjoyment is mere toil and trouble. However long a life is, death will eventually come and erase all the human effort. The ultimate hope of human suffering is from God.

---

6. Confucius 2005: Book II, Chapter IV, http://ebookcentral.proquest.com/lib/cam/detail.action?docID=4697581. And cf. the Hebrew saying from *Pirqe Avoth* 5.21 and its translation, in Brenner-Idan, p. 93 and n. 12 there.

7. Sultantepe Tablet no. 400 and *m. Ab.* 5.21 contain teachings on lifecycle. See Weinfeld 1992: 182, 186.

Psalm 90 acknowledges that God, who gave birth to the earth and world (v. 2), has authority over the human experience of a lifecycle. It also recognizes that the iniquities and sins of human beings may cause their death in God's anger (vv. 7-9) and their life was spent only in trouble and toil (v. 10). The sins in our world weave a snare that confines, at the same time, every individual who sins and is being sinned against. These problems contain complex cultural, socio-economic, and political dimensions. The sufferings induced by sins are too huge for any individual to relieve. To appeal to God to alleviate suffering is the last resort for an ordinary person, because suffering is structural. Suffering may feel personal but to relieve it is the collective responsibility of our society. As Psalm 90 suggests, we should stand together in God-fearing ways (v. 11), and then gain wisdom from God (v. 12) to alleviate suffering.

In conclusion, the CUV's translation of Psalm 90 is deeply rooted in Chinese religio-philosophical traditions. For me, it corresponds to the Buddhist quest of perceiving truth, responds to the Confucian expectations of life stages, and provides resources for alleviating the cultural bondages discussed. As a Chinese, I inevitably read this psalm in a Chinese cultural context and, consciously and subconsciously, search for insights to tackle my community's problems. I resonate with the psalmist's commitment to the faith in God: when individuals feel disempowered in the face of structural suffering, God can give us hope for a better future.

My second choice would be Psalm 137. It suggests that cruelty, 'dashing the little ones against the stone' (137.9, after the KJV), is an important means to justice. The differences between the biblical world and our contemporary world give me insights into how to evaluate culture and history.

Yanjing Qu was born and raised in mainland China. She is a PhD candidate at the Faculty of Divinity, University of Cambridge, UK.

References

Booij, Thijs (1987), 'Psalm 90:5-6: Junction of Two Traditional Motifs', *Biblica* 68 (3): 393–96.
Confucius (2005), *The Analects*. Newburyport, US: Open Road Integrated Media, Inc., http://ebookcentral.proquest.com/lib/cam/detail.action?docID=4697581.
DeClaissé-Walford, Nancy, Rolf A. Jacobson and Beth LaNeel Tanner (2014), *The Book of Psalms*, New International Commentary on the Old Testament, Grand Rapids: Eerdmans.
Kuang, Ken, Runyu Ye, Yanjun Cheng and Jenny Tripp (2021), *Chinese Wisdom and Philosophy through the Ages: Proverbs from the Ming Dynasty*, Torrey Hills Technologies.
Sternberg, Meir (1987), *The Poetics of Biblical Narrative: Ideological Literature and the Drama of Reading*, Bloomington: Indiana University Press.
Tate, Marvin E. (1990), *Psalms 51–100*, WBC 20, Nashville: Thomas Nelson.
Tsevat, Matitiahu (1985), 'Psalm 90:5-6', *VT* 35 (1): 115–17.
Weinfeld, Moshe (1992), 'The Phases of Human Life in Mesopotamia and Jewish Sources', in Eugene Ulrich, John Wright, Robert P. Carroll and Philip R. Davies (eds), *Priests, Prophets and Scribes: Essays on the Formation and Heritage of Second Temple Judaism in Honour of Joseph Blenkinsopp*, 182–89, Sheffield: JSOT Press.

PSALM 90
IN PRAISE OF PSALM 90

Jonathan Magonet

When I announce to my rabbinic students that we are about to study one of my favourite psalms, and name it as Psalm 90, it tends to produce an expression of surprise, if not shock. If I ask why there seems to be a problem, those who have some knowledge of the psalm will usually point to vv. 7-9:

> For we are consumed by Your anger,
> dismayed by Your wrath.
> You lay bare our iniquities before You,
> our hidden sins in the light of Your presence.
> Our days pass away in Your wrath,
> so we end our years like a sigh.[1]

I can understand their surprise, or even chagrin. Is not this depiction of an angry and vengeful God precisely the kind of sentiment that sends people fleeing from anything to do with religion? However, I hope that by contextualizing these verses within the psalm as a whole, it may become clear that the psalmist also had an opinion about them.

Setting aside the superscription, the contextualization begins with vv. 2-3:

> Lord You have been our refuge from generation to generation.
> Before the mountains were born,
> before You brought the earth and world to birth,
> from eternity to eternity You are God.

These verses effectively provide two different 'time signatures' for understanding two perspectives within the psalm. Verse 2 uses the language of 'generation

---

1. The translation of biblical verses here is a hybrid, the author's own and borrowings from various translations.

to generation', that is to say, a way of denoting history in purely human terms, the succession of generations. A biblical individual contemplates the past in terms of three generations of ancestors – the God of Abraham, of Isaac and of Jacob. Similarly, adults can experience in their own lifetime three generations into the future – children, grandchildren and great-grandchildren – the probable meaning of the troubling 'unto the third and fourth generation' (Exod. 20.5; 34.7).[2] Thus we are invited to consider human existence and all that pertains to it in these highly personal terms, the nature and limits of our individual lives.

However, the next sentence tries to imagine the kind of perspective God must have on 'history', a God who pre-existed the very creation of the physical earth, ארץ ('eretz), and the inhabited world, תבל (tevel, Ps. 24.1), and who will continue to exist long after they might cease to be. How must such a God view these short-lived creatures, transient and insignificant, from this divine perspective?

This distinction in perspective is reinforced by the use of two different designations of God. The intimate God experienced in the lifetime of human beings as a refuge, who can be addressed and known, is expressed with the word 'adonai, conventionally translated as 'Lord', the name in the same consonantal form that will return in v. 17. Conversely the transcendent, distant, unknowable God is characterized by the word 'el. Just as the opening word of v. 1b is the divine name 'adonai, the God who is our refuge and home, so the near-final word of v. 2c that closes this defining framework of the psalm is the distant, remote 'el.

Having established these two perspectives, the psalmist sets about trying to understand how our brief human existence might be viewed by the timeless, cosmic God, for whom a thousand years must seem as insignificant as a single night, not even an entire night but only the length of a watchman's duty (v. 4). It is an extraordinary act of imagination, as if the psalmist has contemplated the sky at night and tried to take a position beyond its vastness, seeing it and our world from without (cf. Ps. 19.1)

Since we are distinguishing the nature of human and divine time, the next step of the psalmist is to focus on a moment at which they most directly meet one another:

> You turn human beings back to dust,
> and You say, 'Return you children of Adam'. (v. 3)

An immediate association is the story of the creation of the first human being out of the 'dust of the ground' (Gen. 2.7). Such is the brevity of human life that after a short span humans return to the dust from which they were created. But the psalmist makes a small adjustment to this scenario, one which I came to recognize following a visit many years ago to an organic farm. The farmer turned

---

2. Both of these texts are addressed directly to the adult Israelite patriarch to whom 'belong' wife and offspring. So, in effect, this is a warning that the patriarch's wrongdoing will also impact directly on all those, living in that moment in time, for whom he bears responsibility.

out to be a scholarly, Christian reader of the Bible. In the course of our conversation, he pointed out that the 'dust' of Gen. 2.7 is a wrong translation of the Hebrew word עפר (*'aphar*). Rather, he insisted, it should be translated as 'humus', that is to say, a handful of earth is not made up of inanimate but of organic matter, the source of life (Shewell-Cooper 1977: 188). With that in mind it is necessary to pay more attention to the term for 'dust' to which the psalmist suggests we return. דכא (*dakka'*) denotes crushed, pulverised stone, truly inorganic matter, out of which nothing can grow or flourish. We return to nothing. However, the apparent finality of this ending is either reinforced by God's closing words: 'return to that dust!', or possibly, given the ambiguity of the verb שוב (*shuv*) Qal, a hint at a different kind of return. What the reader cannot 'know' at this stage in the psalm is how the psalmist will use the same verb later. In v. 13, the psalmist will appeal to God to 'return' to a relationship with 'us', which will allow the reader, retrospectively, to reconsider God's apparent dismissal as itself a potential offer to return to God on the very brink of death.

The psalmist has established this brevity of human existence from the divine perspective and reinforces it in vv. 5 and 6. We are like 'grass that springs up and flourishes in the morning but by evening withers and dies'. And this ushers in the verses already noted that effectively dismiss our entire human existence as a kind of perpetual disappointment to the all-powerful cosmic God, here viewed as eternally angry at our failures and wrongdoing.

Yet the following verse, v. 10, begins what will be a consistent challenge to this characterization of both divine displeasure and the inevitability of our human failures. What has gone before may well be a way of imagining how God perceives human existence in the contemporary religious world of the psalmist, but based on what authority? Given the dual time signatures available to us, what might be our human perspective on the duration and nature of our life? Surely, we are not to be dismissed as merely grass that speedily flourishes and withers, leaving nothing behind. Each of our seventy or possibly eighty years is made up of entire days, each unique, and within which we struggle against trouble and sorrow (v. 10). Indeed, they pass quickly and then we 'fly away'. But we are entitled to ask with the psalmist:

> Who knows the power of Your wrath[3]
> or the extent of Your anger on those who fear You? (v. 11)

Perhaps the tension between the two perceptions of God, the distant and the near, the unknowable and the intimate, can be addressed by seeking a kind of collaboration. That questioning of the assumption that someone can *know* God's intentions in v. 11 may provide the key that can build a bridge. The same root verb, *yada'*, reappears:

---

3. 'Who knows' can be a rhetorical question, or a direct challenge to those who claim to know exactly what God is doing and thinking.

למנות ימינו כן הודע... (*limnot yameinu kein hoda'...*)
So *teach us to know* how to count our days
so that we gain a heart of wisdom. (v. 12)

On the basis of this willingness to learn, the psalmist is emboldened to ask God to return to a relationship that seems to have been temporarily lost, though the psalm offers no direct evidence of what historical context, if any, might have triggered the sense of distance.

Turn/Return, O Lord![4] How long?
Show mercy on your servants.

Now the psalmist can revisit the same domains where previously we cowered in fear, oppressed by God's anger. In the 'morning' (v. 6) in which we sprouted like grass, only to wither away by evening, we may now be sated with God's faithful love (v. 14); and the entire day can be alive with rejoicing. Days that we have experienced as punishment, years we saw misfortune, are replaced by days of joy. God's deeds will now become evident to 'Your servants', and Your glory to their children (v. 16).

With this verse we have returned thematically to the intimate relationship with God, attested to in the opening verse. Whereas past 'generations' experienced God as a place of refuge and shelter, now we feel able to project this expectation into the lives of future generations, beginning with our children (v. 16). Thus v. 17 rounds out the psalm by reintroducing the same *'adonai* of v. 2, now designated as אלהינו (*'eloheinu*), our God. Moreover, an extraordinary word play directly evokes that earlier, ideal state. Whereas at the beginning we existed within the מעון (*ma'on*), the shelter, of *'adonai*, we now ask that the נעם (*no'am*), 'pleasantness', of *'adonai* be upon us. I had often thought that, delightful as this wordplay was, *ma'on* being replaced by the identical letters in reverse as *no'am*, it was too much of a poetic conceit. It seemed a clever pun, but surely 'pleasantness' was too weak a promise for the conclusion. But after the terror-inspiring divine anger trumpeted in the first half of the psalm, and the memory of days of oppression and years of misfortune recorded in the second part focusing on real human suffering, perhaps a time of pleasantness and comfort may indeed be the kind of experience to be hoped for.

The twofold implications of this restored state are spelled out:

ומעשה ידינו כוננה עלינו (*uma'aseh yadeinu konena 'aleinu*)
ומעשה ידינו כוננהו (*uma'aseh yadeinu koneneihu*)

to support us in the work we do
and support the work we do.

---

4. The use of the tetragrammaton here, rather than the consonantal form in vv. 2 and 17, suggests a conscious echo of this phrase as, for example, in Num. 10.36.

This wished-for state is characterized as one in which a unity exists between us, the community of the psalmist, and God, such that God will underpin and sustain *us* in what we undertake, and the *undertakings* themselves. This is no casual request. The root כון (*kun*) carries considerable weight, from its first appearance, almost unnoticed, in anchoring the stages of creation (ויהי כן, *vayehi khen*, Gen. 1.7, 9, 11, 15, 24, 30), and as guaranteeing the eternal stability of the earth itself under God's rule (Ps. 93.1-2). The psalmist has taken us a long way in this view of the ideal relationship possible between us transient creatures and the God who is utterly other and yet intimately near.

What is it about this psalm that makes it among my favourites?

Firstly: the elegance and sophistication of the composition, the designation of the dual perspectives on time, divine and human, and the way in which the two, seemingly incompatible, might come together.

Secondly: the internal dialectic, acknowledging the conventional image of a raging punitive God, and then challenging it in detail and offering another possible relationship.

Thirdly: offering an important critique, within the tradition itself, of a tendency of religions to use the vision of a powerful, threatening God as a way of exerting control over a dependent community. Instead, this humanist psalmist emphasizes the real challenges of daily life and encourages our individual and collective journey to acquire a heart of wisdom.

All of the above feed into two roles I play: as emeritus Professor of Bible at Leo Baeck College, and as the co-editor of a number of Shabbat and Festival prayerbooks of the UK Movement for Reform Judaism. The former leads me to seek as far as possible the 'plain meaning' of a psalm to satisfy my own intellectual curiosity and that of my students; the latter, to help weave psalms into the consciousness and prayer-life of countless unknown individuals and even generations.

I had problems regarding choosing a second-favourite psalm, but here is my choice: Psalm 115, because in the guise of mocking idols it challenges all kinds of hubris – spiritual, intellectual and artistic.

Rabbi Professor Jonathan Magonet is the Emeritus Professor of Bible at Leo Baeck College and visiting lecturer at Seinan Gakuin University, Japan. He has co-edited several generations of prayerbooks of the UK Movement for Reform Judaism and is editor of the journal *European Judaism*. His most recent book is *How Did Moses Know he was a Hebrew? Reading Bible stories from within* (Hakodesh Press, 2021)

References

Shewell-Cooper, W.E. (1977), *God Planted a Garden: Horticulture in the Bible*, Worcsester: Arthur James.

PSALM 91
LIFE IN THE SHELTER OF THE 'MOST HIGH'

Susan Gillingham

How to decide a 'favourite psalm'? I have several criteria. Given that not all psalms display the same literary quality, a preferred psalm has to be skilfully brought together, both in sound and sense, drawing from a rich store of metaphors in its poetic appeal.

Another criterion is that it should have a rich history of interpretation, both Jewish and Christian, thus offering insights about the readers as well as the text. A third related criterion is that there should be an abundant artistic and musical reception history, feeding the imagination as well as the intellect. Finally, it has to have an ongoing impact for life today, both for the faithful and appealing to those with no particular faith.

Psalm 91 fulfils all these criteria by a long way.[1] Its context is the second of a trio of psalms, all of which concern the transitory nature of humanity and the importance of refuge in God (see Pss. 90.1; 91.1-2, 9-10; and 92.12-13). It stands as a psalm of promise between the lament in Psalm 90 and the thanksgiving in Psalm 92.

1. *A Compelling Literary Artifact*

It might seem odd to emphasize literary merits when Psalm 91 may initially have been used in Temple worship: its threefold structure and changes of speakers, its use of metaphors associated with the Temple (such as shelter and refuge) and its concluding oracle all suggest liturgical influence. To imagine the performance of a psalm in worship can also enhance our literary appreciation: later readers become participants, rather like reading prayers and hymns today.

Verses 1-2 offer a striking introduction, exhorting trust in a God known by four different names. He is *El Elyon* (the Most High God of other nations, now

---

[1]. Works on Ps. 91 include Breed 2014; Gillingham 2015; 2022: 87–93; Jenkins 2023; and Hunziker-Rodewald 2012.

embraced by Israel), *El Shaddai* (the God of Abraham [Gen. 17.1]), *Adonai* (the God revealed to Moses [Exod. 3.14]), and *Elohay* ('my God', placing the God of history in a personal sphere). Verses 3-13 offer practical encouragement as to how this trust in God might work out, especially when encountering different forms of evil. The second-person address, perhaps initially offered by a priest, refers to both personal attacks (vv. 3-6) and those of an unknown enemy (vv. 7-13). In vv. 14-16 the speaker changes: the 'I' here imitates the voice of God, mediated through some cultic figure who addresses the community in the third person, using eight short blessings. These different liturgical settings, to my mind, enhance the literary dynamic.

The 'iconography of consumption' which we experience today contrasts starkly with the metaphorical world of Psalm 91, whose images invite us to turn to a transcendent reality.[2] God is described anthropomorphically as a 'refuge' (vv. 1, 9), 'fortress' (v. 2), and 'dwelling place' (v. 9) and, more vividly, as in other ancient Near Eastern cultures, as a protective bird (v. 4).[3] Metaphors personifying evil encourage resistance: 'the terror of the night' and 'the arrow that flies by day' (v. 5) and the 'pestilence that stalks in darkness' and 'the destruction that wastes at midday' (v. 6) cannot match the constancy of God (vv. 1-2). These images of demonic forces are countered by images of protective angels (v. 11) whose 'hands' bear us up to protect our 'feet' from being dashed against a stone (v. 12). The imagery is continued in our 'treading on' and 'trampling under' evil, now personified as 'lion and adder' and 'young lion and serpent' (v. 13). A cluster of verbal metaphors completes the psalm through the offer of God's blessings (vv. 14-16), encouraging calm trust in the face of evil: 'I will deliver' / 'I will protect' / 'I will answer' / 'I will be with them'/ 'I will rescue'/ 'I will honour' / 'I will satisfy' / 'I will show my salvation'.

In evoking both a liturgical and literary appreciation, Psalm 91 is, for me, a compelling psalm.

2. *A Rich History of Jewish and Christian Interpretation*

Psalm 91 has many apotropaic readings. As early as the first century BCE, at Qumran, in 4QPs[b] (vv. 5-8 and 12-15), and again in the big Qumran Psalter, 11QPsAp[a] (vv. 1-4 and 16), Psalm 91 is included alongside three other non-canonical psalms as the 'Fourth Exorcism Psalm'.[4] The Septuagint translation emphasizes the demonic aspects: for example, the difficult phrase in v. 6, 'the destruction that wastes at noonday' (מקטב ישוד צהרים, *miqqeteb yashud ṣohorayim*) is personified as 'the noonday demon' (*daimoniov mesēmbrinos*). The *Talmud's* heading for Psalm 91 is 'A Song referring to Evil Demons' (*b. Shavu'ot* 15b) and *Midrash*

---

2. See Brown 2002: 13.
3. Translations from the Hebrew text follow the NRSV.
4. Van der Ploeg 1965; Eissfeldt 1968; Beckwith 1984: 512; Evans 2011: 541–45, citing Josephus, *Ant.* 8.45-47.

Tehillim explains how Moses composed this psalm while ascending to heaven in order to defend himself against some demonic attack, a point on which Rashi also agrees.[5] The Aramaic *Targum* paraphrase of vv. 5-6 is explicit: 'Be not afraid of the terror of demons that go about in the night, nor of the arrow of the angel of death that he shoots in the daytime, nor of the death that goes about in the darkness, nor of the company of demons that destroys at noon'.[6] In *Shimmush Tehillim*, a medieval text on the magical use of the psalms, Psalms 90 and 91 are to be recited over a person tormented by an evil spirit. Parts of Psalm 91 are also found on several incantation bowls, written in Aramaic – in this instance the bowls were turned upside down, supposedly to trap the evil spirits.[7] There is also evidence that v. 16 of this psalm (ארך ימים אשביעהו, 'with long life I will satisfy him') served as a medical amulet in Hebrew.[8]

The psalm is referred to on two occasions in the Gospels. The first concerns an ironic citation by Satan: 'For he will give his angels charge of you… On their hands they will bear you up' (Ps. 91.11-12), as in Mt. 4.6 and Lk. 4.11, as part of Satan's second challenge (in Matthew) and third challenge (in Luke) to Jesus to throw himself from the pinnacle of the Temple. Christ's response seems to reject the magical use of this psalm: 'Do not put the Lord your God to the test', citing Deut. 6.16 (Mt. 4.7 and Lk. 4.12). Nevertheless, the magical associations of this psalm are implicitly affirmed in Lk. 10.19, which cites 91.13 ('you will tread on the lion and the adder…').

Through the Latin translation of the Greek in the *Gallican Psalter*, Psalm 91 was also known by the church fathers as an 'exorcism text'. By the Middle Ages, in the *Glossa Ordinaria*, the marginal comment reads 'a hymn against demons'. In the medieval monastic tradition this 'midday demon' was popularized as one of the four vexations of the church, each assigned to a specific devil: this particular demon, disguised as an angel of light, plagued the monks with lethargy at noontime.[9] Parts of this psalm are found on door lintels in Syria, Cyprus and in two Byzantine churches in Ravenna where again they point to its apotropaic quality. Most tellingly, at least twenty-five examples of vv. 4-5 and v. 11 have been found on Byzantine amulets and rings from the sixth to twelfth centuries CE.[10]

The history of interpretation of many psalms reveals conflicting readings between Jews and Christians.[11] Psalm 91 is quite different. Each faith tradition shares a similar dependency in facing the personification of evil in spiritual and human forms: this is what makes this psalm so significant.

5. Braude 1959: 101 and Gruber 2004: 583.
6. Stec 2004: 174–75.
7. Breed 2014: 298–303.
8. Davis 1992: 174–75.
9. Kaulbach 2008.
10. Breed 2014: 301–302.
11. See, for example, Gillingham 2018: 13–25 (Ps. 1), 25–43 (Ps. 2), 267–76 (Ps. 45), and 386–94 (Ps. 72); also Gillingham 2022: 72–78 (Ps. 89), 182–92 (Ps. 110) and 353–70 (Ps. 137).

3. *An Abundant Reception History, especially in Art and Music*

Verses 11–13, centring on trampling underfoot the 'lion and adder', are a frequent image in Christian illuminated Psalters. The subject is often Christ, as in the ninth-century *Utrecht Psalter*, adapted more clearly in the twelfth-century *Eadwine Psalter*.[12] Another striking example is found in the twelfth-century *St Albans Psalter*, where the illuminated initial 'Q' (for '**Q**ui habitat' in Latin, the first words of the psalm) depicts Christ stamping on the basilisk, asp, lion and dragon, prodding them with his crozier shaped as a 'tau' and clasping a book with v. 13 written on the cover.[13] One example from a Byzantine Psalter is a marginal illustration: the eleventh-century *Theodore Psalter* (fol. 123v) also selects v. 12, but here this depicts Jesus' temptations. He stands, resolute, on the roof of the Temple.[14]

In other images the subject is a soldier, by implication trampling over a physical enemy. In the ninth-century *Stuttgart Psalter* (fol. 157v) a soldier combats a lion and adder, and here the inference is about military might not spiritual evil.[15] A more subtle example is found in another ninth-century Carolingian Manuscript, made in Aachen at the court of Charlemagne. Known as *The Douce Ivory*, the ivory plaque on the cover depicts Christ in majesty, bearing a cross-staff over his shoulder, trampling on a lion and a serpent-dragon. He carries an open book inscribed 'HIS XPS' ('Iesus Christus') and 'SVP[er] ASP[idem]' ('*super aspidem*', from 91.13). However, given the associations between Charlemagne as king and Christ as king, the military connotations of this victory over evil forces are obvious.[16] The imagery of God as 'Shield and Buckler' (v. 4) further contributes to more military readings: these themes have often been used in heraldry.[17]

Musical representations reflect more an engagement with personal evil. Mendelssohn's 'He shall give his angels charge over thee' in his *Elijah* (first performed in 1846) uses 91.11 in Part One, Movement 7, when Elijah raises from the dead a widow's son, set as a double quartet sung by angels.[18] Another example is the more recent composition by Alon Wallach, for the Frankfurt 'Tehillim Project', which uses a 5/4 time to indicate the vicissitudes found within this psalm.[19] The Irish singer Sinead O'Connor chose 'The Lion and the Cobra' as the title of her

---

12. https://bit.ly/2QaBDDn (accessed 5 April 2023).

13. https://www.albani-psalter.de/stalbanspsalter/english/commentary/page256.shtml (accessed 5.4.2023).

14. http://www.bl.uk/manuscripts/Viewer.aspx?ref=add_ms_19352_f207v (accessed 5 April 2023).

15. https://bit.ly/3xalSzn (accessed 5 April 2023).

16. Hebron 2014: 174–75.

17. Huxley 1949, citing 91.4 and 11 as popular mottos.

18. Verse 7 ('A thousand may fall at our side') is also used in Part Two, after Elijah has faced Jezebel. See 'Eljiah' in Stern 2011: 259–79; also Dowling Long and Sawyer 2015: 75.

19. http://www.bettina-struebel.de/wp-content/uploads/Vorank%C3%BCndigung.pdf (accessed 5 April 2023).

debut album (1987), based on 91.13. O'Connor produced another version of this psalm as 'Whomsoever dwells'. Her lyrics reflect on its quasi-magical qualities:

> Whomsoever dwells
> In the shelter
> Of the most high
> Lives under the protection of the Shaddai…[20]

Psalm 91 challenges our imaginations, and for that reason it is a memorable psalm.

5. *The Contemporary Impact for All Faiths and None*

Psalm 91 still has an important role in Jewish and Christian liturgy. In some Jewish traditions it is read, along with Psalm 90, at funerals: as the coffin is carried to its grave, these two psalms are chanted between three and seven times along the way. It is also read with Psalm 90 as one of the additional 'Verses of Song' in the morning services of Sabbaths and feast days.[21] In Christian liturgy, Psalm 91 became one of the most frequently prayed psalms at Compline, along with Psalms 4 and 134, as found in the Benedictine Rule from the sixth century onwards.[22] Here the association is of Christ's protection over the night-time demons through the night hours of the *Opus Dei*. For similar theological reasons Psalm 91 is an important psalm in Good Friday Liturgy in the Western churches, when it is often used with John 3, also with the motif of the serpent, whereby the crucifixion is understood as the means whereby Christ trampled underfoot (see Ps. 91.13) the demonic forces.[23]

Myles Coverdale's Bible (1535) translated v. 5 as 'Thou shalt not need to be afrayde for any bugges by nyghte', so that the entire publication was known as *The Bug Bible*. In an untitled poem attributed to C.S. Lewis, which adapts several verses from Psalm 91, one line, in part using Coverdale, stands out: "Bogies will not scare her in the dark; bullets will not frighten her in the day".[24] This line encapsulates the different universal uses of this psalm. Throughout history it has been repeatedly used to address both plague and warfare – two issues which, at the time of writing in 2022, have a profound contemporary ring.[25]

---

20. https://www.youtube.com/watch?v=5_CoCepMu7k (accessed 5.4.2023).
21. Hertz 1942: 61–83.
22. Neale and Littledale 1874–79: 3:162–63.
23. Breed 2014: 303–307.
24. Lewis 1945: 134.
25. In what follows, see Gillingham 2022: 87–93; Breed 2014: 297–310; and Jenkins 2023: Chapters 2, 7, 9, and 10 (on Ps. 91 as a 'Plague Psalm') and Chapters 5 and 6 (as a 'Soldiers' Psalm').

'The Soldier's Psalm' uses phrases such as 'A thousand may fall at your side, ten thousand at your right hand, but evil will not come near you' (v. 7) and 'the young lion and the serpent you will trample under foot' (v. 13). Section 3 above noted how v. 13 has been used for military purposes. It has been cited not only during the times of Constantine and Charlemagne but also throughout the Crusades, the Napoleonic Wars, the American Civil War, and the First and Second World Wars. In more recent times, Chuck Norris cited this psalm in the context of Islamic Fascism: 'Remember the God of 911, Psalm 91.1, that is'.[26] 91.5 is one of the verses found on the telescopic sights of Accupin rifles made by the American firm Trijicon: 'Thou shalt not be afraid of the terror by night, nor of the arrow that flieth by day'. Furthermore, the camouflage bandana for the US Marines has part of Psalm 91 printed on it, with the slogan: 'Someone is watching over you'.[27] More recently still, the psalm has been used as a defiant worship song by songwriters in Ukraine.[28]

As a 'Plague Psalm' this depends on phrases such as 'he will deliver you from the snare of the fowler and from the deadly pestilence' (v. 3). We have already noted (Section 2) its use as a medical amulet to ward off evil assaults of death and disease, and it was repeatedly used throughout the centuries of the Black Death. In African countries today – in Nigeria, Rwanda, Ghana, or Malawi – it is frequently used as an incantation against evil spirits causing diseases.[29] Its prominence during the Covid pandemic was enhanced by the symmetry between Covid 19 and Psalm 91 – often cited to persuade people to get vaccinated. There was a brisk trade in facemasks quoting the psalm as a prayer of protection and perhaps a kind of talisman.[30]

Before 2022 it would have been incongruous to associate this psalm with both a bandana and a facemask. It now not only addresses the horrors of human suffering in countering a global pandemic, but also the threat on world peace because of the atrocities in Ukraine. A psalm of faith – about renouncing all forms of evil and finding shelter in our Most High God – has become a psalm of universal significance. This is why Psalm 91 is one of my favourite psalms.

Sue Gillingham is Emeritus Professor of the Hebrew Bible, University of Oxford; Emeritus Fellow of Worcester College, Oxford; and Research Associate at the Faculty of Theology and Religion, University of Pretoria, South Africa.

26. Cited in Breed 2014: 306–307.

27. On Ps. 91 on Christian rifles, see https://en.wikipedia.org/wiki/Trijicon_biblical_verses_controversy. On the citation of this psalm on bandanas, see, for example, http://www.operationbandanas.org/.

28. https://globalworship.tumblr.com/post/678732580659576832/psalm-91-modern-song-ukraine/.

29. Jenkins 2023: Chapter 10; also Welshman 1974.

30. https://journal.cjgh.org/index.php/cjgh/article/view/461/869

References

Beckwith, R.T. (1984), 'The Courses of the Levites and the Eccentric Psalm Scrolls from Qumran', *Révue de Qumran* 11 (4): 499–524.

Braude, W.G. (1959), trans. *The Midrash on Psalms*, Vols. 1 & 2. YJS XIII, New Haven: Yale University Press.

Breed, B. (2014), 'Reception of the Psalms: The Example of Psalm 91', in *The Oxford Handbook of The Psalms*, 297-310, Oxford: Oxford University Press.

Brown, W.P. (2002), *Seeing the Psalms: A Theology of Metaphor*, Louisville: Westminster John Knox.

Davis, E. (1992), 'Psalms in Hebrew Medical Amulets', *VT* 42: 173–78.

Dowling Long, S. and J.F.A. Sawyer (2015), *The Bible in Music: A Dictionary of Songs, Works, and More*, Lanham: Rowman & Littlefield.

Eissfeldt, O. (1968), 'Eine Qumran-Texfform des 91 Psalms', in S. Wagner (ED.), *Bibel und Qumran, Beiträge zur Erforschung der Beziehungen zwischen Bibel und Qumranwissenschaft. Festschrift Bardtke zum 22. 9. 1966*, 82–85, Berlin: Evangelische HauptBibelgesellschaft.

Evans, C.A. (2011), 'Jesus and Psalm 91 in Light of the Exorcism Scrolls', in P.W. Flint, J. Duhaime and K.S. Back (eds), *Celebrating the Dead Sea Scrolls: A Canadian Collection*, 541–55, Atlanta: SBL.

Gillingham, S.E. (2015), 'Psalms 90–92: Text, Images, Music', *Revue des Sciences Religieuses* 89 (3): *Le Psautier: poésie et théologie*: 255–76.

Gillingham, S.E. (2018), *Psalms through the Centuries: A Reception History Commentary on Psalms 1–72*, Vol. 2, Blackwell Bible Commentaries, Oxford: Wiley-Blackwell.

Gillingham, S.E. (2022), *Psalms through the Centuries: A Reception History Commentary on Psalms 73–151*, Vol. 3, Blackwell Bible Commentaries, Oxford: Wiley-Blackwell.

Gruber, M.I. (2004), *Rashi's Commentary on Psalms*, Leiden: Brill.

Hebron, S., ed. (2014), *Marks of Genius: Masterpieces from the Collections of the Bodleian Libraries*, Oxford: Bodleian.

Hertz, J.H. (1942), *The Authorised Daily Prayer Book: Hebrew Text, English Translation, with Commentary and Notes*, New York: Bloch.

Hunziker-Rodewald, R. (2012), 'Image et Parole en dialogue avec Dieu. Le dynamisme communicatif du Psaume 91', in J. Cottin, W. Gräb and B. Schaller (eds), *Spiritualité contemporine de l'art. Approches théologique, philosophique et pratique*, 79–100, Labor et Fides: Geneva.

Huxley, W. (1949), 'The Psalms in Heraldry', *Evangelical Quarterly* 21: 297–305.

Horkheimer, M. (2006), 'Psalm 91', in W. Goldstein (ed.), *Marx, Critical Theory and Religion: A Critique of Rational Choice*, 115-120, trans. M. Ott, Leiden: Brill.

Jenkins, P. (2023), *'He Will Save You from the Deadly Pestilence': The Many Lives of Psalm 91*, Oxford: Oxford University Press.

Kaulbach, E.N. (2008), 'Noonday Demon', in D.L. Jeffrey (ed.), *A Dictionary of Biblical Tradition in English Literature*, 553–54, Grand Rapids: Eerdmans.

Kraus, T.J. (2011), ' "He That Dwelleth in the Help of the Highest": Septuagint Psalm 90 and the Iconographic Program on Byzantine Armbands', in C.A. Evans and H.D. Zacharias (eds), *Jewish and Christian Scripture as Artifact and Canon*, 137–47, London: T&T Clark.

Lewis, C.S. (1945), *The Great Divorce*, London: Geoffrey Bles; repr. London: Collins, 2012.

Neale, J.M. and R.F. Littledale, eds. (1874–79), *A Commentary on the Psalms: From Primitive and Mediaeval Writers*, 4 vols, London: Masters, 2nd edn.

van der Ploeg, J.P.M. (1965), 'Le Psaume XCI dans une recension de Qumran', *Révue Biblique* 72: 210–19.

Ruth, P.J. (2012), *Psalm 91 Military Edition: God's Shield of Protection*, Lake Mary: Charisma House.

Stec, D.M. (2004), *The Targum of Psalms, Translated, with a Critical Introduction, Apparatus, and Notes*, The Aramaic Bible 16, Collegeville: Liturgical Press.

Stern, M. (2011), *Bible & Music: Influences of the Old Testament on Western Music*, Jersey City: KTAV.

Welshman, F.H. (1974), 'Psalm 91 in Relation to a Malawian Cultural Background', *Journal of Theology of South* Africa 8: 24–30.

PSALM 100
'WORSHIP THE LORD WITH ROUSING ACCLAMATION!'

Vanessa Lovelace

Psalm 100 is recognized as a thanksgiving psalm according to the superscription. Its superscription or title מזמור לתודה, *mizmor le-todah*, is translated 'Psalm of Thanksgiving' (NRSV), 'A Psalm of praise' (KJV), 'A psalm for praise' or 'a psalm for the thanksgiving offering' (JPS), referring either to its genre, thanksgiving, or perhaps its cultic function as the psalm recited over the thanksgiving offerings brought to the temple in Jerusalem (cf. Lev. 7.12).[1] Scholars continue to debate the liturgical use of *todah* in Psalm 100. Does it refer to the thanksgiving offering or sacrifice (Tate 1990), the accompanying praise, or both (Schaefer 2001)? While some scholars argue determinedly that the superscription indicates the use of the psalm in the framework of bringing a thanksgiving offering to the temple, the psalm does not offer enough information to conclude its liturgical use by the ancient Israelite community.

While the superscription is generally considered a heading separate from the psalm and perhaps added later by someone other than the author, medieval Jewish rabbi and scholar Rashi's commentary on Psalm 100 does not distinguish the superscription from the psalm. Psalm 100.1, as commented on by Rashi, begins with 'A song for a thanksgiving offering' with instructions to recite Psalm 100 over the thanksgiving offerings (Cohen 1945). The Hebrew word *todah* ('thanksgiving') does not appear in any superscription in the Psalter other than Psalm 100.

Structured along two hymn parts or strophes – vv. 1-3, and vv. 4-5 – the psalmist beckons the people to praise the Lord with a string of plural imperative verbs. While some scholars place Psalm 100 among the kingship hymns (Ps. 96 to Ps. 99), others contend that the psalm is distinct from the kingship psalms collection, given the omission of the kingship of God in it (Berlin and Brettler 2014).

---

1. The NRSV Bible translation is used unless otherwise noted. Several other English translations are consulted and noted throughout.

Psalm 100.1-3: Serve the Lord with Gladness

The first strophe, with its successive imperatives, begins with an exhortation to 'shout' to the Lord (v. 1). Some translations add the adjective 'joy' as in 'shout for joy' (NIV) or 'joyful' as in 'Make a joyful noise' (ESV, NRSV) to the original text that perhaps reflects the interpreter's need to distinguish shouts of delight from a cacophonous sound. However, the distinction seems unnecessary given that this is clearly a psalm of praise. The Hebrew verb רוע, *ru'a* Hiphil (BDB s.v.) can be translated 'raise a shout' or 'give a blast with clarion or horn' (cf. Ps. 98.4-6). The implication is that this is no request for a modest, subdued clamor, but rather a command for a full-throated shout along the lines of a battle cry or shout of triumph from one who anticipates a victory. Not only are the people of Israel commanded to make a noise to the Lord, but also the whole earth should participate.

The second imperative is 'serve' (v. 2) the Lord. The Hebrew root עבד, *'abad* Qal (BDB s.v.) means 'to work' or 'serve', as translated by the ESV, JPS, and KJV; but it is translated 'worship' in the NIV and recently the NRSV. However, the updated edition of the NRSV, the NRSVue (2022), has replaced 'worship' with 'serve'. In one sense, 'to serve' is to work or labor for another forcibly or with remuneration; in another sense, it means to be in the service of an official or military. The idea that the Israelites went from being servants of Pharaoh to servants of the Lord, and received instructions in how to serve the Lord, is not lost on the psalmist. Thus, to serve the Lord has broader implications than simply worship. But not only are the people summoned to serve the Lord, they are also to do so with בשמחה, with joy or gladness, from the Hebrew root שמח, *samaḥ*. To serve the Lord with joy is to acknowledge the saving act of being freed from slavery in Egypt (Exod. 13.14) to being servants of the Lord, to include worshiping the Lord.

The third imperative is באו, 'come' (v. 2). The invocation is to 'Come before him' (NIV), 'Come into his presence' (ESV, JPS, NRSV), or 'Come before his presence' (KJV) with רננה. Various translations of רננה, *renanah* (BDB s.v.) – 'joy', 'exultation', 'jubilation', 'song', 'singing' (*HALOT* s.v.) – include 'singing' (NRSV), 'shouts of joy' (JPS), and 'joyful songs' (NIV). At least twice, using two different terms (three times in the NRSV), the psalmist entreats the people to worship the Lord in a posture of joy or gladness. Clinton Arnold states that the 'Experience of deliverance and the anticipation of salvation provide the most significant occasions for rejoicing among the people of God in the OT' is the meaning of this joy (Arnold 1992: 1022). This statement reflects the psalmist's view that serving the Lord brings joy and thus should be done uproariously.

Rounding out the first strophe is the command to 'know', דעו (v. 3a). If v. 2 offered how one should serve the Lord, v. 3 includes motivations for serving the Lord. First, because worshipers are called to acknowledge that the Lord is God, understood to mean Israel's patron deity, perhaps with the view that the Lord alone is God. The psalmist declares that such knowledge extends to the awareness that the Lord created humanity and thus humanity belongs to the Lord: 'It is he who made us, and we are his' (v. 3b), as if the people needed reminding. The

KJV translates the verse, 'it is he that hath made us, and not (לא) we ourselves', following the MT. This translation reflects the only significant textual variant in Psalm 100. Two words that sound the same (לא, 'not', and לו, 'to him') frequently appear written differently in the MT. Such is the case with the 'written' form (*Ketiv*) of Ps. 100.3b, which in the MT is לא *lo*, 'not', and the 'called out' form (*Qere*) לו *lo*, 'his, to him'. Theologically, either interpretation can be supported by the text. Both reflect the divine–human relationship of the creation as the work of the creator. This is expressed metaphorically as the shepherd caring for her or his sheep.

Psalm 100.4-5: Worship with Thanks and Praise

The second strophe continues with three more imperative verbs in the plural. The people are first entreated to 'enter' the Lord's temple gates with thanksgiving (v. 4a) or with a thanksgiving offering (JPS) and the temple courts with praise, reflecting the theme of the psalm. As mentioned above, some argue that *todah* is the thanksgiving offering and v. 4 is offered in support: 'In this verse, the reference is certainly to a thanksgiving-offering, or to a procession of those bringing such a sacrifice, as we are dealing with entry into the Temple gates and courtyards' (Samet 2016).

The final two imperatives are to 'give thanks' to the Lord or more directly 'thank him' and 'bless' the name of the Lord (v. 4b). As if anyone needed further motivation to give thanks and praise to the Lord, the psalmist declares: 'For the Lord is good' or, literally, 'For good is the Lord' (v. 5a). Added is the liturgical refrain, 'his steadfast love endures forever' (v. 5b; cf. Ps. 106), which perhaps the congregation sang responsively (cf. Ezra 3.11). The psalmist and worshipers together affirm that the Lord's mercy is forever to generation after generation (v. 5c).

Psalm 100 is a brief but skillfully written hymn that interweaves invocations of praise with motivations for why one should praise the Lord. It beckons all the earth to give thanks and praise with a loud voice to the Lord and serve the Lord with gladness, because we belong to the Lord. Although we do not know the original use of Psalm 100 in the cultic liturgy rites, it enjoys a place of honor in Jewish and Christian worship today.

Why Psalm 100?

I selected Psalm 100 because of its significance in Black church worship experience. While Psalm 100 is well attested in Christian worship, it is usually recited with a solemnity that betrays the words of the psalm. However, the appropriation of Psalm 100 by Black Christians as a call to worship on Sunday mornings is delivered with the exuberance called for by the psalmist. The King James Version is often used; and therefore, the worship leader shouts enthusiastically that 'it is he that hath made us, and not we ourselves'. Verse 5 has come to include a call and response reminiscent of the congregational response in the ancient context. When the worship leader proclaims, 'The Lord is good', instead of the response, 'his steadfast love endures forever', the worshipers often respond, 'All the time!' Although this is a more recent theological practice that arguably conflicts with the biblical witness, the praise of the worshipers matches the enthusiasm of the psalm.

My second choice would be Ps. 30.1-12, because 30.5 is a favorite of mine when times are dark.

Vanessa Lovelace is associate dean and associate professor of Hebrew Bible/Old Testament at Lancaster Theological Seminary in Lancaster, Pennsylvania.

References

Arnold, C. (1992), 'Joy', in D.N. Freedman (ed.), *Anchor Bible Dictionary. Vol. 3*, 1022–23, New York: Doubleday.

Berlin, A. and M.Z. Brettler (2014), 'Psalms', in A. Berlin and M.Z. Brettler (eds), *The Jewish Study Bible: Jewish Publication Society Tanakh Translation*, 1265–435, Oxford: Oxford University Press, 2nd edn.

Cohen, A. (1945), 'The Psalms, English Translation', in *Sefaria* (accessed 30 June 2022), https://www.sefaria.org/Rashi_on_Psalms.100.1.1?lang=bi.

Samet, R.E. (2016), *Tehillim 100: 'A Psalm of Thanksgiving' – The Psalm's Heading and Its Place in the Liturgy (Appendix)*, 11 November 2016, https://etzion.org.il/en/tanakh/ketuvim/sefer-tehillim/tehillim-100-%E2%80%93-psalm-thanksgiving-psalm%E2%80%99s-heading-and-its-place (accessed 30 June 2022).

Schaefer, K. (2001), *Psalms*, Berit Olam, Collegeville: Liturgical Press.

Tate, M. (1990), *Psalms 51–100*, WBC 20, Nashville: Thomas Nelson

PSALM 104
A DISCOMFORTABLE READING BY AN IMPLICATED SUBJECT

Gerrie Snyman

Our house has an abundant intuitive garden. It is halfway up a hill, and the terrain is very rocky. One cannot really make a typical suburban garden with lawns and flowerbeds. Our flowers grow in pots, and the garden is full of trees and bushes. It attracts a lot of birds; I have counted fifteen different kinds. Thirteen of them are from the region, one kind is migratory, and one is alien, and has been classified as an invasive species. The invasive species is aggressive and chases away the other birds from the fruit and seeds we put out on the birdfeeder. My husband and I take turns to drive the non-native birds off, as we are protective of our native species. Interestingly, the birds that are from the region only scatter a little distance off, looking on as the two humans chase away the aliens. When the coast is clear, our local birds promptly return to feed.

Here in South Africa the Indian mynah is listed in the Limpopo Environmental Act (by the Limpopo Provincial Government 2003, published 2004) as an aggressively invasive alien species. Legend has it that the ancestral couple escaped from a cage in Durban, the harbor that received the migrant workers from India, in 1902. The urban environment made it easy for them to thrive and raise four or five chicks a year. According to the act, an invasive animal is 'an alien wild animal [birds included] whose establishment and spread' not only threatens 'ecosystems, habitats or other species or has demonstrable potential to threaten ecosystems, habitats or other species', but may also result in 'economic or environmental harm' (Limpopo Provincial Government 2004: 4). The term 'alien' refers to 'any live vertebrate' or egg of such vertebrate (including birds and reptiles but excluding fish) that belong to a species or subspecies that is not a recognized domestic species and the natural habitat of which is not in the Republic of South Africa (Limpopo Provincial Government 2004: 1).

The Indian mynah, and the Environmental Act of 2003, makes a reading of Psalm 104 rather problematic. As part of creation, the mynah feeds on what creation provides: seeds and trees in which to make nests (Ps. 104.14 and 17).

However, one can argue their presence in Southern Africa is not according to the rules of nature. Psalm 104.6-9 implies the chaotic waters before creation. When it fails to remain in its allocated space, it threatens earth. Invasive species, like the Indian mynah, did not stay in its allocated space and now threatens the ecology of a different place. A human law was constructed to deny them any real protection.

Yet I have an unsettling empathy for them (Krondorfer 2020), engendered by a hermeneutic of vulnerability (Gilson 2016; Snyman 2021), as I find myself in a similar position. The great and wild seas, with ships faring on them through storms (Ps. 104.25-26) and wicked piracy (v. 35a) brought my ancestors from their designated places in Western Europe and southern Asia to procreate in Africa. My presence at the southern tip of Africa is thanks to colonialism and the benefit accrued with it. And with colonialism came conquest to enforce settlement.

What kind of deity are we dealing with here? It is an active creating and punishing deity. I am always reminded of the central problem Robert Warrior (1989: 264) confronts me with in the reading of any text of the Bible: 'As long as people believe in the Yahweh of deliverance, the world will not be safe from Yahweh the conqueror'. Psalm 104 is a hymn in praise of the deity behind creation. Most commentators simply gush here over the beauty and the functionality of nature. It is a sensation of perfect harmony that can be echoed by the psalm (Lioy 2017; Brown 2006). I have an uneasiness which Ellen van Wolde shares (2017: 644): within a hymn of praise, there are also emotions of fright and dread. The creator evokes admiration as well as awe as creation depends on its creator: the creator provides, but also withdraws (vv. 24-27 vs. 28-30).

The hymn starts with the creation of heaven (vv. 1-4), followed by the creation of the earth (vv. 5-9). Verses 10-18 praise the way the deity sustains the earth by providing water, a chaotic entity the deity succeeded in taming. God designates a place not only for the water, but for the living beings (domestic animals grazing on grass, the earth producing food for humankind, even wine to warm the heart), the mountains where the goats find refuge, the trees in which the birds nestle. Verses 19-23 accentuate the point that the deity created a specific order: seasons to live by, and day and night for humankind and animals to go about. The following verses proclaim the huge variety of what had been created and its possibilities (vv. 24-26). Humankind constructed ships to move around and explore and even the mythic sea monster, the Leviathan, has been tamed. In vv. 27-31 the dependence of creation on the deity is again appreciated and highlighted. Nothing would have existed were it not for the deity. In the conclusion of the psalm, the joy and the enjoyment of creation is palpable: the poet wants to sing and rejoice in the deity. But then the spoilsports are mentioned in v. 35: sinners and the wicked, for whom there is thought to be no place in creation.

Psalm 104 portrays a perfect world where there is no place for sinners and the wicked (v. 35). It spells out a belief in line with what happens to perpetrators, or what I would call 'implicated subjects', in the Old Testament. I follow Michael Rothberg's definition (2019: 1) of this term, which suggests someone who is not a direct agent of harm but nonetheless aligned to power and privilege, thus contributing to domination and benefitting from it. An implicated subject does not have a clear-cut role of either perpetrator or victim but participates and is involved in some way in the situation.

Cain as perpetrator had to move away from Adam and Eve after he murdered Abel. His progeny is implicated by his murderous act, although they are named the founders of art, science, and technology (Gen. 4.17-22). Ishmael and Hagar, implicated subjects via Abraham, were sent into the desert (Gen. 21). This separation denied Ishmael a life with a father and a brother. The story cycle of Jacob and Esau makes Esau the culprit, whereas the real perpetrators are Rebekah and Jacob, and Esau a mere implicated subject (Gen. 27-28). After Jacob's fraud against Esau, he fled to Laban. When he and Esau reconciled, Esau decided not to trek with Jacob (Gen. 32-33). The people that are said to have developed out of Jacob and Esau, the Israelites and Edomites, could never live peacefully next to each other. Edom even became the focus of some prophecies that condemned them (for instance Hos. 12.3b-4; Amos 1.11-12; Josh. 4.19; Mal. 1.1-5).

Perpetrators, or implicated subjects, are removed. Revolutions are bloody because the identified enemy must be removed from power. The removal from power usually results in a violent overthrow of power structures. It did not happen in South Africa. There was no ethnic cleansing but a relatively peaceful transfer of power, although it did not mean we never teetered on the brink of civil war. As a white male South African who benefitted from apartheid, but who also was conscripted to defend the apartheid regime in the 1970s, I now must look into black eyes and experience the embarrassment of having been found out. Some of my compatriots have emigrated and removed themselves from the black scrutinizing gaze. For those who stay behind, there is a feeling of an unsettling or difficult empathy whereby opposing identities are forged into one, reframed in a new political community in which everyone received a second chance (Mamdani 2020: 195). Psalm 104 provides one then with a glimpse of what creation can become in a process of decolonization. As survivors of racism which has its roots in the Western Enlightenment, looking into each other's eyes becomes a process of looking for answers to do good with what creation has entrusted us with.

I have no illusion that many a black eye had a silent wish, quite like Ps. 104.35, during colonization and apartheid. There was an armed struggle from 1962 to 1993 (Lissoni 2021). Before that, between 1659 and 1902, there were twenty colonial wars (Mellet 2020). The last one affected the entire population in South Africa due to imperial Britain's introduction of concentration camps and a scorched earth policy (Lewis 2016). Whereas water in Psalm 104 is attributed to the possibility of causing chaos and therefore designated to specific places like the clouds, rivers, and seas, in the war of 1899-1902 fire did the trick in destroying homesteads and livelihoods (Saunders 2008; Packenham 1986). In the struggle, fire found a similar expression. And in each of these violent conflicts the perpetrating other, the sinner and the wicked, were wished away as they are in v. 35. But it never happened. Each time afterwards, the conqueror stayed with conquered, the implicated subject, the bystander with the victim.

Now the tables have yet again been turned, and the progeny of the conqueror experiences an unsettling empathy in a new reality. As Perkinson (2004: 3) formulates succinctly, this is a position from which one can become conscious of oneself as white by 'daring to look into black eyes and not deny the reflection…hearing and internalizing black critiques [confronting] the embarrassment of having been "found out" by one's most frightening other'.

As the kind of reader suggested in vv. 27-30 and v. 35a, the psalm provides the possibility of embracing an epistemic vulnerability which allows for openness towards the Other and a willingness to change and participate in a non-hierarchical relationship which Hennie Viviers (2017: 7, with reference to vv. 14-23) describes as harmonious living of each without any custodianship.

Will I leave the Indian mynah alone? On the one hand, I am part of a larger ecosphere and have no role as a custodian, with each part of creation having its own intrinsic value. On the other hand, the presence of the mynah in my garden is the result of a disharmony incurred by colonial human action in undermining the harmonious natural order. But then, ironically, apartheid was theologically justified on the notion of a harmonious natural order.

The next psalm I would read is Psalm 8, which praises creation, its creator, and human dignity. My understanding of Psalm 8 is the cornerstone of my hermeneutic of vulnerability and its relationship to Chapter 2 of the South African Constitution.

Gerrie Snyman is retired and currently a Professor Extra-Ordinarius and Research Fellow in the Department of Biblical and Ancient Studies at the University of South Africa (UNISA) in Pretoria, South Africa.

References

Brown, W.P. (2006), 'Joy and the Art of Cosmic Maintenance: An Ecology of Play in Psalm 104', *Word & World Supplement Series* 5: 23-32.

Gilson, E. (2016), *The Ethics of Vulnerability: A Feminist Analysis of Social Life and Practice*, London: Routledge.

Krondorfer, B. (2020), *Unsettling Empathy: Working with Groups in Conflict*, Lanham: Rowman & Littlefield Publishers.

Lewis, H.O. (2016), *Apartheid: Britain's Bastard Child*, Wandsbeck: Reach Publishers.

Limpopo Provincial Government (2004), 'Limpopo Environmental Management Act, 2003', *Limpopo Provincial Gazette* 996: Polokwane.

Lioy, D. (2017), 'Part Two: Affirming God's Majesty in Creation: A Literary and Descriptive Analysis of Psalm 104', *Conspectus: The Journal of the South African Theological Seminary* 24 (1): 325–58.

Lissoni, A. (2021), 'Umkhonto We Sizwe (Mk): The ANC's Armed Wing, 1961–1993', *Oxford Research Encyclopedia on African History*, https://doi.org/10.1093/acrefore/9780190277734.013.1098 (accessed 19 December 2022).

Mamdani, M. (2020), *Neither Settler nor Native*, Boston: Harvard University Press.

Mellet, P.T. (2020), *The Lie of 1652: A Decolonised History of Land*, Cape Town: Tafelberg.

Packenham, T. (1986), 'The Anglo-Boer War', in T. Cameron (ed.) *An Illustrated History of South Africa*, 200–218, Cape Town: Jonathan Ball.

Perkinson, J.W. (2004), *White Theology: Outing Supremacy in Modernity*, Black Religion/Womanist Thought/Social Justice, New York: Palgrave.

Rothberg, M. (2019), *The Implicated Subject: Beyond Victims and Perpetrators*, Stanford: Stanford University Press.

Saunders, C. (2008), 'South African War', in *The Oxford Encyclopedia of the Modern World*, Oxford: Oxford University Press, https://0-www-oxfordreference-com.oasis.unisa.ac.za/view/10.1093/acref/9780195176322.001.0001/acref-9780195176322-e-1479 (accessed 19 December 2022).

Snyman, G.F. (2021), 'A Hermeneutic of Vulnerability: Difficult Empathy in Response to Moral Injury within Whiteness', *Koers: Bulletin for Christian Scholarship / Koers: Bulletin vir Christelike Wetenskap* 86 (1): 1–17.

Van Wolde, E. (2017), 'Separation and Creation in Genesis 1 and Psalm 104: A Continuation of the Discussion of the Verb ברא', *VT* 67 (4): 611–47.

Viviers, H. (2017), 'Is Psalm 104 an Expression (also) of Dark Green Religion?', *HTS Teologiese Studies/Theological Studies* 73 (3): a3829, https://doi.org/10.4102/hts.v73i3.3829.

Warrior, R.A. (1989), 'Canaanites, Cowboys, and Indians: Deliverance, Conquest and Liberation Theology Today', *Christianity in Crisis* 49 (12): 261–65.

PSALM 104
HUMANITY'S FIRM GROUNDING

Nancy L. DeClaissé-Walford

Psalm 104 is located near the end of Book Four of the Psalter. For those who read the Psalms as the story of ancient Israel's relationship with God from the time of David to the time of the return from exile in Babylon, Book Four's focus or setting is the exilic period, in which the people are in Babylon and have no king, temple, or royal administration. Throughout the book, with its frequent references to Moses (Pss. 90.1; 99.6; 103.7; 105.26; 106.16, 23, 32), the psalmists celebrate God as sovereign over all creation (Pss. 93–98, in particular), reminding the people that during the Exodus from Egypt and the Wilderness Wanderings, Israel did not have a king, a temple, or a royal administration; rather, God provided for the people, just as God will provide for the people in exile in Babylon.

Psalm 104 is characterized variously as an 'exuberant poetic reflection' (McCann 1996: 1096), a 'cosmic hymn of praise' (Brown 2002: 158), and a 'sapiential creation hymn' (Zenger 1991: 77). This writer sees it as a magnificent poetic account of God's sovereignty over all creation. The psalm's 'exuberance' and 'magnificence' makes finding a structure for its 35 verses difficult, however, and scholars have proposed many options.[1] J. Clinton McCann points out shifting foci in the psalm's first 24 verses, which move fluidly back and forth as the psalmist sings: the heavens in vv. 2-4, the earth in vv. 5-6, waters in vv. 7-10, wild animals in v. 11, birds in v. 12, the earth again in v. 13, plants to feed the animals and the people in vv. 14-15, the trees in v. 16, birds again in v. 17, back to wild animals in v. 18, the heavenly bodies in vv. 19-20, a return to the wild animals in vv. 20-22, and a focus on humanity in v. 23 (McCann 1996: 1097). The psalm singer concludes in v. 24 that, by wisdom, God made God's 'manifold works'.[2]

In vv. 25-26, the psalm singer offers another exuberant outburst, this time with a focus on the sea and leviathan and, according to William P. Brown, God

---

1. See, for example, Allen 2002: 44; Mays 1994: 331-37; Hossfeld and Zenger 2011: 48.
2. Scripture references are taken from the NRSV. See Prov. 8.22-31 for words about Woman Wisdom's role in creation.

'sporting' or 'playing' with leviathan (Brown 2006: 16). The psalm closes with the reminder that all of creation depends on God, and God alone, for sustenance and for life itself, and that the only proper response by creation is praise and rejoicing (vv. 33-34).

The singer of Psalm 104 reflects on the myriad elements of God's creation – the light, the heavens, the waters, the clouds, the wind, the fire and flame, the mountains, the valleys, the springs of water, the grass and plants, the wild asses, the birds, the cattle, the plants, the wine and oil and bread, the trees, the storks, the goats and the rock-badgers, the moon and the sun, the young lions, and humans going forth to work. Interestingly, in the narrative framework of Psalm 104 humanity plays a 'bit part', appearing only in vv. 14, 15 and 23.[3] In v. 15, God provides plants for the cattle and people to use (notice that the cattle are mentioned first); God gives wine to 'gladden the human heart', oil 'to make the face shine', and bread 'to strengthen the human heart'. And in v. 23, humanity is granted the daylight hours to 'go out to their work and to their labor until evening', at which time, in the cover of darkness, 'all the animals of the forest come creeping out' (v. 20).

Humankind has too often over the millennia considered itself the pinnacle of creation, given permission by the creator God to 'subdue' and 'have dominion' over it (Gen. 1.28). Psalm 104 reminds us that humanity is just one part of God's vast created order; and that we, like the animals, have our place in that order. Richard Bauckham, in a book titled *The Bible and Ecology*, sums up best the message of Psalm 104. He writes.

> All God's creatures are first and foremost creatures, ourselves included. All earthly creatures share the same Earth; and all participate in an interrelated and interdependent community… Cosmic humility is a much needed ecological virtue. We need the humility 'to walk more lightly upon the Earth, with more regard for the life around us'… We need the humility to know ourselves as creatures within creation, not gods over creation, the humility of knowing that only God is God. (Bauckham 2010: 64, 46)

I was born into a farming family in southwestern Indiana in the 1950s. My great grandfather bought a 100-acre farm in the 1800s and my grandfather inherited it, passed it along to my father and aunt, and now my sister and I own it. In 1960, however, my father determined that he did not want to be a farmer and so he and my mother moved our family of six to the western United States. But I and my siblings were the only grandchildren, so my grandparents and aunt made it possible for us children to spend every summer, all summer on the farm. That is where I found my love for the land and came to a beginning of my understanding of my place in this created world. That farm is now where I live and work and find my 'firm grounding' after spending years in city environments.

---

3. Many scholars have noted the similar sentiments of Ps. 104 with Job 38–41. While Job 38–41, though, are the words of God's challenge to Job, the singer of Ps. 104 celebrates creation and humanity's place within it without challenging God.

But I would be remiss if I did not add that for centuries before my great-grandfather bought the land, it was occupied by the Shawnee Native American Tribe. In an 1804 treaty, the United States government 'purchased' the land from the Shawnee and resettled them further west in the United States. Thus, long before I came to this farmland, it was someone else's firm grounding. While much of the land here in southwestern Indiana was cleared to make room for crops, every farmer left a stand of woods on their property – home to deer, coyotes, racoons, owls, snakes, wild turkeys, and other wildlife. It is not a perfect system, but it far surpasses the various urban environments in which I have lived during most of my life.

Indeed, this land has humanity's indelible 'footprints'. We have cleared the forest, tilled the ground, built roads and houses, and developed the infrastructures 'necessary' for modern life. But as I observed my grandparents during those magical summers here on the farm, I realized how magnificently 'in tune' with nature they lived their lives. They rose with the sun each morning; they fed the cattle and the poultry; they, like their ancestors, painstakingly tended the ground to produce their food. And their life followed the seasons – blackberries and plums and peaches in the spring; tomatoes and squash and strawberries in the summer; pecans in the fall; and quilting and embroidery and repairing the farm equipment in the dark winters.

Today I observe (and am learning the rhythm of) the planting, tending, and harvesting the cash crops with each turn of the seasons. I watch and listen as the farmers 'walk the fields' to see if the crops are doing well, so that they can sing with the psalmist, 'You cause the grass to grow for the cattle, and plants for people to use, to bring forth food from the earth' (v. 14). I listen as they discuss the rain or the lack thereof, so that they can sing again with the psalmist, 'From your lofty abode you water the mountains; the earth is satisfied with the fruit of your work' (v. 13). But most of all, I hear in their words reverberations of vv. 27 and 28 of Psalm 104: 'These all look to you to give their food in due season; when you give it to them, they gather it up; when you open your hand, they are filled with good things'.

Yes, it is the twenty-first century with all of its so-called modern conveniences, but living on a farm a thirty-minute drive from the nearest grocery store; sitting outside at the night looking at the night sky 'wrapped in light as with a garment' (v. 2); and contemplating the tremendous legacy that I have been privileged to safeguard, the words of Psalm 104 remind me daily of my very precarious place in this created world and of my tremendous responsibility for the care of the small part of the world that has been entrusted to me.

A final note is in order. The last verse of Psalm 104 addresses 'sinners' and 'the wicked'. As with Ps. 139.21-22, these words seem incongruent with the rest of Psalm 104: 'Let sinners be consumed from the earth, and let the wicked be no more'. Why do these words appear at the end of a psalm that celebrates the wonders of creation? 'Sinners' and 'the wicked' are common actors in the Psalms, those who act in defiance of the good, created order. Their inclusion at the end of Psalm 104 may be seen as a reference to those who disregard the God who set the earth on its foundations (v. 5); who causes grass to grow for the cattle (v. 14); who established the high mountains for the wild goats and the rocks for the coneys (v. 18); and who gives food to all in due season (v. 27) and who pursue their own interests in 'subduing' the land and its inhabitants.

My life growing up on the farm as a child, and now my life as an adult caring for this farm that my great-grandfather purchased and that once belonged to the Shawnee Native Americans, has taught me the sacredness of the land and the importance of preserving it. Perhaps, then, those who come after me can, in the words of Richard Bauckham, 'walk more lightly upon the Earth, with more regard for the life around us' (2010: 64). If we can do so, then we will be able indeed to celebrate with the psalmist, 'O LORD, how manifold are your works! In wisdom you have made them all; the earth is full of your creatures' (v. 24).

As a second favorite, I would choose Psalm 92, a joyous 'song of the sabbath'. In vv. 12 and 13, the psalm singer states that the righteous will flourish and grow like the palm tree and a cedar in Lebanon. The palm tree (*tamar*) is associated with the feminine and fertility, while the cedar of Lebanon conveys a more masculine image. And both, the feminine and the masculine, will be planted and flourish in the 'house of the LORD'.

Dr. Nancy L. DeClaissé-Walford is Emeritus Professor of Old Testament and Biblical Languages at the Mercer University School of Theology in Atlanta, Georgia, US; and Research Associate in the Department of Old Testament at the University of Pretoria in South Africa. She is the Old Testament Editor of the *Word Biblical Commentary* Series, and ordained minister in the Baptist tradition, currently serving as a lay leader in a United Churches of Christ congregation.

References

Allen, L.C. (2002), *Psalms 101–150*, WBC 21, Nashville: Thomas Nelson.
Bauckham, R. (2010), *The Bible and Ecology*, Waco, TX: Baylor University Press.
Brown, W.P. (2002), *Seeing the Psalms: A Theology of Metaphor*, Louisville: Westminster John Knox.
Hossfeld, H.-L. and E. Zenger (2011), *Psalms 3*, Hermeneia, Minneapolis: Fortress Press.
Mays, J.L. (1994), *Psalms*, Interpretation Bible Commentary, Louisville: Westminster John Knox.
McCann, J.C. (1996), 'The Book of Psalms', 639–1280 in L. Keck (ed.), *The New Interpreter's Bible*. Nashville: Abingdon Press.
Zenger, E. (1991), '"Du kannst das Angesicht der Erde erneuern" (Ps 104,30): Das Schöpeferlob des 104. Psalms als Ruf zur ökologischen Umkehr', *Bibel und Liturgie* 64: 75–86.

PSALM 104
THE SIGNIFICANCE OF ITS ENDING

Yairah Amit

This is written from the viewpoint of a Jewish, Israeli, secular Bible scholar/critic with literary and historical interests. A literary device – 'reversal' or 'reverse ending' – is first analyzed, and then I move – in accordance with my place- and time-conditioned personal views – into present 'non-scholarly', political concerns.

1. Introduction

The view of literature as an art of time progression caused literary research to focus on the sequence of the text: namely, its linear nature, in which the elements follow one another in sequence, with a beginning and an end. Consequently, the artist, who is aware of this, devotes much thought to the starting point and the conclusion of the process – that is, the beginning and end of the work – which constitute its framework and are thus of special significance. While the opening introduces the reader to the world of the work, presents its background and directs the attention to particular features, the ending represents a finality, directing the reader to consider the sequence of the text in light of the concluding information and to evaluate the work as a whole.

In this short article I shall focus on a particular kind of ending, which I propose to call 'reverse ending'.[1]

2. What is 'Reversal' or 'Reverse Ending'?

There are biblical texts whose endings are of especial significance to the understanding of the work as a whole, because they cast the texts in a new or different light. The reverse ending bears a unique contribution to the meaning of the entire text. The reader recognizes a reverse ending when there is tension or some

---

1. I am following Menachem Perry's studies (1968; 1969; 1977 [Heb.]), which deal with the semantic structure of Ch.N. Bialik's poems, and discuss the phenomenon of the 'reversing' poem.

inconsistency between it and the preceding text. The discovery of the tension leads back to renewed examination of the whole text and its significance. Thus, in Psalm 104 we can see how the ending contributes to the different meaning of the whole text.

3. *Psalm 104: An Example for Reverse Ending*

Psalm 104 is a hymn of praise to God for the creation.[2] The poet jubilantly describes the diverse elements of the creation, each of which has its place and boundary, while the whole world is controlled by harmony. Seeking to glorify the divine act of creation, the poet ignores its darker aspects. Thus, human labor is not sorrowful, nor is bread won by the sweat of the brow (Gen. 3.17-19). Rather, bread is said to strengthen humans' heart and wine makes it glad (Ps. 104.14-15). Likewise, the relations between humans and wild animals is equally benign, as the young lions hunt by night and when the sun rises they retire to their dens, just when humans go out to work: thus, predators and laborers are kept safely apart (vv. 20-23).[3] Moreover, even the roaring of the young lions is described as entreating God for their prey; and if that were not enough, the whale (Leviathan) is said to be a plaything for God's leisure (v. 26). Finally, even death is transient and therefore unthreatening: 'send back Your breath, they are created, and You renew the face of the earth' (v. 30).[4] The reader naturally expects the hymn to conclude with the same exultation as the earlier exclamation, 'How many are the things You have made, O Lord; You have made them all with wisdom; the earth is full of Your creations' (v. 24).

However, the final verse appears to dent this perfect picture: 'May sinners disappear from the earth and the wicked be no more' (v. 35a). Suddenly it seems there is something in the world that disturbs its harmony and must be removed, namely, the sinners and the wicked. The second part of this verse, which is the hymn's ending, uses the opening phrase, 'Bless the Lord, O my soul' (v. 35b). In any case, the ending shows that the creation is not entirely perfect and even needs rectifying, and calls on God to do so.

This circular ending directs the reader back to the beginning of the hymn, forming an *inclusio*; but nevertheless, this casts a different light on the opening and the sequence as a whole which – up to the ending – is totally laudatory. Thus, the ending implies that 'the presence of sins in this world detracts from the perfection of the divine glory as revealed in the creation, and that while the wicked continue to exist in the world, joy in the Lord is incomplete'.[5] Now it becomes

---

2. According to the Gunkel and Begrich (1998: 22) categorization of the Psalms. See Hoffman 1992: *13-*14 and n. 3 there, and also Allen 2002: 39.

3. A different view is found in the Hymn to the Aten, see Lichtheim 1997: 44–46. Noted also by Hoffman 1992: *17-*19, as well as other interpreters of this hymn, see for example Allen 2002: 40–41.

4. All translations from the Hebrew texts are from the JPS.

5. Hakham 1990: 262 [Heb.].

evident that all those praises, at times utopian and prelapsarian and hardly a reflection of real life, are essentially an introduction to what troubles the poet most: social injustice. The detailed list of the marvels of creation in fact points out to the deity that, in view of the marvels He has made, there is but one more act that will enable the speaker to bless Him and rejoice in Him wholeheartedly, and which he begs to witness with his own eyes (v. 33).[6]

The existence of v. 35a creates a sharp dissonance, after the sweet harmony of the entire hymn. To me it seems that the appearance of this verse is a jarring note right at the end of the hymn, giving it the quality of a powerful chord that counterbalances the preceding text. This ending, acknowledging the existence of a problem, disrupts the perfect harmony presented to the reader up to that point, and reveals that the speaker knows perfectly well what is wrong in our world and what to criticize about the creation.

As I see it, a closer look at the entire hymn in light of the reverse ending leads one to conclude that the speaker is less naive or optimistic than was previously thought.[7] The circling back to the opening of the hymn, the appreciation that it opens with a prompting to bless rather than with praise, the recognition that the praise is purposeful and unrealistic – all these reveal the hymn to be not only a celebration of creation, but a palliative in the run-up to the main point, which is a precise and unequivocal statement on what must be done for cosmic harmony to be truly all-inclusive.

4. *Summary*

Readers of biblical literature, encountering a text ending that introduces new and different information, will realize that it directs them to re-read the text from the beginning and to see to what extent the new material integrates into the preceding semantic pattern, or whether it is necessary to find a new semantic structure appropriate to all of the text's components, including the ending with its added information. In this way it will be discovered that Psalm 104, more than it exalts the creation, calls for its amelioration. The knowledge that sometimes the ending directs readers to re-examine and consider the whole sequence in the light of its concluding information contributes to our interpretations and may even lead to novel and possibly contradictory understandings.

Finally, I would like to propose that my interpretation fits our chaotic times, because a military/political crisis has now emerged. Russia is now performing a devastating attack on Ukraine, a democracy of more than 40 million people. Although the Russian President Vladimir Putin has denied for months that he would invade his western neighbor Ukraine, this is exactly what he is doing now (February–March 2022). Putin's false excuse for attacking Ukraine is the seeming threat to Russia from modern Ukraine; and now Russian forces attack Ukraine by

---

6. Despite the foregoing praise, 'send back Your breath, they are created' (v. 30a).

7. As for example see the interpretations of Weiss 1984: 88–90; 1987; Hoffman 1992: *23; 1995: 128.

air, land, and sea. A nuclear threat has been pronounced; and threats of a third world war are in the air, together with grave economic hardships for Ukrainians, Russians, other European countries and the world at large. The Russians are bombing the Ukrainian capital Kyiv and many other city centers, thus prompting a mass exodus of refugees who are looking for shelter in other eastern and western countries. Justifiably, as the number of dead climbs, Russia's ruler is accused of shattering peace in Europe and the world.

As we read in Psalm 104, the creation may be viewed as ideal and perfect – until we get to the reverse ending of the text, and to human society. We nevertheless allow ourselves to entertain hopes that this crisis too would end soon and peace and harmony will be part of life in the world, in Ukraine, and in our small country, Israel, as well.

Had I not chosen Psalm 104 for this short study, I would have chosen Psalm 78 – for its historical allusions, which at times are different from other biblical descriptions of the events depicted, and require further thoughts.

Yairah Amit is Professor emerita of biblical studies at the department of biblical studies, School of Jewish Studies and Archaeology, Tel Aviv University, Israel.

References

Allen, L.C. (2002), *Psalms 101–50, Revised*, WBC 21, Nashville: Thomas Nelson.
Gunkel, H. and J. Begrich (1998), *Introduction to Psalms: The Genres of the Religious Lyric of Israel*, trans. J.D. Nogalski, Macon: Mercer University Press.
Hakham, A. (1990), *Psalms 73–150: Books 3-5*, Da'at Miqra, Jerusalem: Harav Kook [Heb.].
Hoffman, Y. (1992), 'Psalm 104: A Literary Examination', in M. Fishbane and E. Tov (eds), with the assistance of W.W. Fields, *Sha'arei Talmon: Studies in the Bible, Qumran, and the Ancient Near East Presented to Shemaryahu Talmon*, 13*–24*, Winona Lake: Eisenbrauns [Heb.].
Hoffman, Y. (1995), 'Psalm 104', in *Psalms, Part 2, Olam HaTaNaKh*, 124–8, Tel-Aviv: Davidson-Ittai Publishers [Heb.].
Lichtheim, M. (1997), 'The Great Hymn to the Aten', in W.W. Hallo (ed.), *The Context of Scripture, Volume One: Canonical Compositions from the Biblical World*, 44–6, Leiden: Brill.
Perry, M. (1968/9), 'The Inverted Poem: On a Principle of Semantic Composition in Bialik's Poems', *Hasifrut/Literature* 1: 607–31 [Heb.].
Perry, M. (1969/71), 'Thematic Structures in Bialik's Poetry: The Inverted Poem and Related kinds', *Hasifrut/Literature* 2: 40–90 [Heb.].
Perry, M. (1977), *Semantic Dynamics in Poetry: The Theory of Semantic Change in the Text Continuum of a Poem, Especially in the Hebrew Poetry of Ch. N. Bialik*, Hebrew, Literature, Meaning, Culture 3, Publication of the Porter Institute for Poetics & Semiotics, Tel-Aviv: Tel Aviv University [Heb.]
Weiss, M. (1984), *The Bible From Within: The Method of Total Interpretation*, trans. R. Levy and B. Schwartz, Jerusalem: Magnes, The Hebrew University, [Heb. 1962].
Weiss, M. (1987), '"Bless the Lord, O my soul" – Psalm 104', in *Scriptures in Their Own Light: Collected Essays*, 15–412, Jerusalem: Bialik Institute [Heb.].

PSALM 106
BLESSED LIVING AS A MIXED-RACE DESCENDANT

Lisa J. Cleath

I have chosen to reflect on Psalm 106 during a time when I have been thinking intensively about what it means to live as a mixed-race individual in the US. I have always looked for ways to understand myself as a whole person while claiming both of my heritages: fifth-generation Chinese American on my mother's side, and fifth-generation Scandinavian American on my father's side. Even as a child I took pride in having both lines of ancestry, amidst frequent, unsolicited, and confusing comments from others: How Asian are you? You don't look Asian! You don't look American. You are exotic. Do you speak Chinese?

Since I was raised in a Protestant tradition that views the Bible as deeply relevant to every individual, I have a drive to ask how the text might be in conversation with my own life, including my racialized experiences. However, living as mixed race in the US is complicated, especially as I continue to learn about the ramifications of my white ancestors' settlement of indigenous lands and my Asian ancestors' impulses to acculturate to whiteness. Grappling with how I came to be a woman with this particular ancestry in this particular place has come to mean holding love of my cultural traditions along with grief over ancestral wrongdoing and compromises. How can I live a blessed, thriving life with this complicated ancestry?

Psalm 106 speaks to this personal pursuit through its emphasis on a profound connection to and responsibility for one's ancestors: 'We have committed misdeeds *with* our ancestors, we have offended, we have done evil'[1] (v. 6). Jewish traditions today still practice such ancestral prayers of repentance, even though most Christian traditions do not. It has taken time for me to wrap my Protestant mind around this concept of liturgically taking responsibility for generations past, but

---

1. All Hebrew translation is my own. Like Alter, I have shifted away from terms for 'sin' that arise from Protestant 'salvation history' and Latinate terms like 'iniquity' and 'transgression', to avoid imposing Christian theology upon distinct concepts in the Hebrew Bible (Alter 2007: xxxi–xxxii).

this opens up a possibility for me to communally respond to my own ancestors. As I now see it, none of us lives outside of the choices of our elders, but all of us have the opportunity to shape how we individually and collectively engage with their legacies.

Most form-critical scholars classify Psalm 106 as a historical psalm, due to its lengthy body of vignettes from Israel's past. Its placement after Psalm 105, which is also considered a historical psalm, emphasizes the difference between these two historical psalms: while Psalm 105 responds to the past by emphasizing God's covenant faithfulness, Psalm 106 focuses on Israel's past offenses (Gärtner 2015: 373). Some have suggested that this could be a communal lament psalm. Brueggemann brings this up but prefers the historical genre (Brueggemann and Bellinger 2014: 458). However, I see no reason to choose between these two genres, as the psalm has characteristics of both: it laments through its rehearsal of Israel's history.

In the Masoretic text, Psalm 106 serves as the final psalm of book 4 of the Psalter, thus concluding the sub-collection with a focus upon communal repentance (Gosse 2010: 185). There is scholarly consensus that books 4 and 5 of the Psalter came together as collections in the eras following the Babylonian exile. This means that Jewish communities were utilizing and transmitting the psalms in these collections in the context of multigenerational colonization and dispersion. This minoritized and disempowered perspective draws me to reflect on my lifetime of being othered as a mixed-race Asian in America.

Part of what intrigues me about the final form of this psalm are its shifts in rhetoric, which guide the reader through the liturgy. Scholars have especially debated the relationship between the praise-oriented frame and the repentant body of the poem, most finding tension between the two (Brueggemann and Bellinger 2014: 458, Hossfeld and Zenger 2011: 82–84). Most have divided the psalm so that the introductory frame is vv. 1-5, the body is composed of vv. 6-46, and the closing frame is vv. 47-48. The language used in the framing is common to many psalms of thanksgiving and praise, including Psalms 105 and 107. However, the body starts with communal repentance and proceeds into historical selections from the Pentateuch. So, the question for me is: How might praise and gratitude frame repentance?

Further exploration of the psalm's framing might help us answer this question. Verse 1 begins with 'Hallelujah', which is also the final word of the whole psalm, creating an *inclusio* of praise. Next, there is a formula that is common to other imperative hymns of thanksgiving, including Psalm 105: 'Give thanks to the LORD' (הודו ליהוה). The whole of this verse also appears in Ps. 107.1 and 1 Chron. 16.34: 'Give thanks to the LORD, for the LORD is good, and the LORD's covenant faithfulness is forever' (Weber 2016: 14).

Verses 2-3 set up a question-and-answer structure: 'Who will tell of the LORD's great deeds, make heard all of the LORD's praise?' The answer is a beatitude about a 'blessed' or 'happy' person (אשרי), a formula from wisdom literature: 'Blessed are the keepers of justice, the doer of righteousness at all times'. Verses 4-5 tie up the introduction with a call to God to be remembered among the chosen community, as the righteous ones of the beatitude. In other words, this psalm's framing evokes familiar language of praise and thanksgiving that would have been known in Hebrew liturgy throughout post-exilic communities.

I would argue that the potential tension between the framing and the body of the psalm serves a purpose in the overall structure. If that beatitude sets up a structure in which 'only the righteous person may praise God' (Hossfeld and Zenger 2011: 87), and the body of the poem then proceeds through a confession of the ancestors' misdeeds, the implication is that a righteous person's praise includes and requires repentance that takes responsibility for the community's past. We do not need to find contradiction here, as there is no ideal of justice or righteousness in the Hebrew Bible that exists without acknowledging wrongdoing. The restorative concept of justice throughout the Hebrew Bible further supports this interpretation, as 'keepers of justice' should be those who seek to bring about wholeness and healing in creation.

The beatitude sets up the idea of justice, and the body of the psalm delves into the kinds of lived experiences that need to be made whole again: the experiences of hostility, hunger, egotism, dehumanizing violence. So, the communal repentance in v. 6 is not in tension with the beatitude, but rather is enacting it by seeking healing through restoration. The recounting of past offenses in the psalm's body in fact illustrates one element of restoration: forthright, recorded memory of wrongdoing. The hope for salvation in the end provides a hope for wholeness and healing at the hands of the divine. Although no generation will fulfill the ideal of the beatitude, remembering and repenting is the way of justice.

When it comes to the body of the psalm, I am struck by the alternation between third-person plural verbs, with all Israel as the subject, and first-person singular verbs, with God as the subject. Long sections focused on what 'they did' are punctuated by short statements of what 'God did'. Because the body begins in the first-person plural 'we did with our ancestors', the recitation of the third-person plurals articulates what 'we' have done 'with them'. The past experiences, whose negotiation ended in offenses, are so relatable that they remind *us* of what we have in common with *them* (Stinson 2021: 588). This sense of empathy with and responsibility for consequences of the past should pervade our reading of what 'they did'. While on the one hand this may speak to a social function of shame which could permit a community to have a sense of agency over its oppression (Smith-Christopher 2002: 120), I also see a reaffirmation of the necessity for a just community to humbly repent at all stages of its empowerment and disempowerment: as enslaved, as colonizers, as colonized, as exiles.

As a descendant of colonizers of North America and of immigrants who were at the mercy of the colonizing machine, I resonate with the idea that an individual reciter of this psalm could identify with all of these stages, and with the need to explore the consequences of each of them. My European ancestors displaced others, an action which still produces privilege for me. My Chinese ancestors have fought against a marginalized status in the same colonizing system, and yet five generations later I am regularly treated as 'other' by people who simply see my face as Asian.

If living justly means remembering honestly one's ancestral legacies, I can and should remember both sides of my family ancestry. I can use my scholarly training to address my ignorance of relevant history and try to continue to grow and learn (Cleath 2023: 1). I also am empowered to ask questions about the way each side of the family narrates their legacy: Why does the white side construct a triumphant narrative of hard work? What socio-political forces were at play that influenced their separation of Native Americans from their story, even though they immigrated to North America in order to settle Native American land? Why does the Chinese side value acculturation to white American ways? What socio-political forces were at play that made acculturation challenging yet desirable? Who benefits and who hurts as a result of these narratives?

Perhaps my family's version of Psalm 106 is the family records we have kept and rehearse regularly. My father's mother (Scandinavian American) set down her and my great-grandmother's life story before she passed away, and gifted copies to all of the family members. My mother's uncle is a filmmaker and has created a documentary of my great-grandfather's (Chinese American) legacy. Psalm 106 reminds me to not take these records solely as sources of facts, but also as sources that illustrate familial narrative shaping. I do not have to rely on my memory alone to access how my family tells its stories, but I can look to this shared documentation and analyze it critically. My identity as a biblical scholar thus pervades my engagement with my racial identities, aiding my parsing of the past and hopefully my repentance for ongoing consequences.

I personally find this freeing – the value of honesty, the externalization and context for wrongdoing and its consequences, and the role this can play in doing justice. It is important to me that *sin* is not primarily about internal guilt or shame, but rather is a holistic sense of something that has the potential to be healed. As I move forward from my Protestant roots, I am learning that sin operates socially and structurally, even when individuals bear responsibility within those systems. Remember the praise and thanksgiving framing of Psalm 106: this psalm illustrates that historical repentance can be approached with joy. Such a holistic model opens up the possibility to not operate out of fear, but rather to simultaneously make space for tensions, disagreements, and joy in ancestry. This is blessed living, to honestly seek restorative justice while finding pleasure and belonging in ancestral identity.

My second choice of a psalm would have been Psalm 65, because of its powerful creation imagery.

Dr. Lisa Cleath spent five years on faculty at George Fox University in Newberg, Oregon, US; and is now on faculty at Princeton Theological Seminary as Assistant Professor of Old Testament. She has strong ties to Californian cultures, especially Californian Asian American cultures.

References

Alter, R. (2007), *The Book of Psalms*, New York: W.W. Norton.
Brueggemann, W. and W.H. Bellinger, Jr (2014), *Psalms*, Cambridge: Cambridge University Press.
Cleath, L. (2023) 'Rebuilding Jerusalem: Ezra-Nehemiah as Narrative Resilience', *Jewish Studies Quarterly* 30 (1): 1–27.
Gärtner, J. (2015), 'The Historical Psalms: A Study of Psalms 78; 105; 106; 135, and 136 as Key Hermeneutical Texts in the Psalter', *HeBAI* 4: 373–99.
Gosse, Bernard (2010), 'Le parallélisme synonymique *hsd 'mwnh*, le Ps 89 et les réponses du quatrième livre du Psautier, Ps 90–106', *ZAW* 122 (2): 185–98.
Hossfeld, F.L. and E. Zenger (2011), *Psalms 3*, Hermeneia, Minneapolis: Fortress.
Smith-Christopher, D. (2002), *A Biblical Theology of Exile*, Minneapolis: Fortress.
Stinson, M.A. (2021), 'Turning Tables in Israel's History: Food Language and Reversals in Psalms 105 and 106', *CBQ* 83 (4): 588–98.
Weber, B. (2016), 'Die doppelte Verknotung des Psalters: Psalm 18//2 Samuel 22 und Psalm 105; 106//1 Chronik 16', *Biblische Zeitschrift* 60 (1): 14–27.

PSALM 114
A BEAUTIFUL COUNTER-CULTURAL PSALM

Marc Zvi Brettler

I have long loved Psalm 114, which is part of the collection of *Hallel*, comprised of Psalms 113–118, which I, as an observant Jew, recite on several Jewish festivals.[1] The tune to which it is traditionally sung is very upbeat and easy to sing,[2] even for people like me who are tone-deaf. This nice and short psalm sounds straightforward at first, but a close reading belies its simplicity.

Its apparent simplicity starts with its clear and obvious structure. At only eight verses long, it is composed of four couplets, with the middle two couplets mirroring each other in question-and-answer form. I have labelled these A, B, C, D:

A

בית יעקב מעם לעז	בצאת ישראל ממצרים	114.1
ישראל ממשלותיו	היתה יהודה לקדשו	114.2

¹ When Israel went forth from Egypt, the house of Jacob from a people of strange speech,

² Judah became His holy one, Israel, His dominion.[3]

B

הירדן יסב לאחור	הים ראה וינס	114.3
גבעות כבני צאן	ההרים רקדו כאילים	114.4

³ The sea saw them and fled, Jordan ran backward,
⁴ mountains skipped like rams, hills like sheep.

---

1. I would like to thank Matthew Arakaky for his assistance with this article. For a more complete treatment of Ps. 114, see Brettler 2016 and 2020.
2. See, e.g., https://www.youtube.com/watch?v=8kMu0U5Ped4 (accessed: 5 April 2023)
3. I am using the NJPS translation throughout.

		C
הירדן תסב לאחור	מה לך הים כי תנוס	114.5
גבעות כבני צאן	ההרים תרקדו כאילים	114.6

⁵ What alarmed you, O sea, that you fled,   Jordan, that you ran backward,
⁶ mountains, that you skipped like rams,   hills, like sheep?

		D
מלפני אלוה יעקב	מלפני אדון חולי ארץ	114.7
חלמיש למעינו מים	ההפכי הצור אגם מים	114.8

⁷ Tremble, O earth,
at the presence of the Lord,   at the presence of the God of Jacob,
⁸ who turned the rock into a pool of water,   the flinty rock into a fountain.

Each verse neatly divides in half – I have overemphasized this by putting in extra spaces between the halves. Each half is approximately the same size; that is what makes it so easy to set to music. Scholars continue to debate if biblical poetry, including psalms, had rhythm or meter,[4] but many have verses and even half-verses of approximately the same length or syllable number; this makes sense especially for the many psalms that were set to music, where regularity might be expected.

Each couplet is tightly constructed, albeit in different ways. Couplet A begins in v. 1 with a preposition and infinitive, which connect to the beginning of v. 2 (בצאת ישראל…היתה, 'When Israel went forth…became'). Geographical entities tie together B and C (ים, 'sea'; ירדן, 'Jordan'; הרים, 'mountains'; and גבעות 'hills'). This fourfold repetition can become monotonous, and that is why, as often happens in biblical poetry, the author introduces slight variation, visible only in the Hebrew: The first three geographical bodies are preceded with the definite article (הים, 'the sea'; הירדן, 'the Jordan'; and ההרים, 'the mountains'), while this is lacking before the final noun (גבעות, 'hills'). Couplet D is unified by the opening of v. 8, which uses the definite article to connect back to the previous verse.[5]

An unusual feature ties the entire psalm together: The first couplet uses the pronoun 'his', but the referent of this 'his' is only clarified in the very last couplet: it is אדון, the Lord. In addition, different epithets of Israel, geographical terms, and water imagery unify the psalm. Clearly, the poet of the psalm was unusually skilled.

---

4. See most recently Martin 2021: 523–29.
5. In Biblical Hebrew, before participles, 'the definite article essentially stands in place of a relative pronoun'. See further Rubin 2013. Waltke and O'Connor 1990: §19.7c notes that this usage is typically late, which comports with other evidence for the dating of this psalm.

Poetic skill goes beyond technical features such as verse-length or structuring. The imagery of the psalm's center, couplets B and C, is extremely vivid: the sea and Jordan are fleeing backward, while mountains and hills skip like rams or sheep. It is possible that the first image goes back to ancient Syro-Palestinian depictions of vanquishing the river-deity, but the second image has no comparable ancient Near Eastern parallel. In any case, the two images work together to create a highly dynamic picture – just close your eyes and imagine the scene!

The poet's skill is also seen in the choice of words and grammatical forms. Good poetry is characterized by some, but not too many, fancy words. It is hard for us, now, to know which words were considered fancy in the biblical period, but it is likely that words that appear only once in our biblical corpus, words that scholars call *hapax legomena*, had an ornamental function in poetry. The final word of v. 1, לעז, is a *hapax legomenon*; Biblical Hebrew has other more common words for 'foreign' (זר and נכרי). In addition, the grammatical form that begins the final verse is unusual and ornate. Translated 'who turned', it reads ההפכי, 'who turns', instead of the more expected, plain form ההפך. The poet added the final morpheme *-i* to fancify the poem.

But it is the content of the psalm that attracts me, content that I labelled 'counter-cultural' in the title. On the surface, this psalm looks like it is retelling the story of the Torah, but read carefully, it does not. The first couplet suggests that Israel became YHWH's nation at the time of the exodus; in contrast, most Torah sources suggest that this happened at Mount Sinai, when Israel entered into a covenant with YHWH. This is explicit in Exod. 19.5-6:

ועתה אם שמוע תשמעו בקלי ושמרתם את בריתי והייתם לי סגלה מכל העמים כי לי כל הארץ
ואתם תהיו לי ממלכת כהנים וגוי קדוש אלה הדברים אשר תדבר אל בני ישראל

[5] 'Now then, if you will obey Me faithfully and keep My covenant, you shall be My treasured possession among all the peoples. Indeed, all the earth is Mine,

[6] but you shall be to Me a kingdom of priests and a holy nation'. These are the words that you shall speak to the children of Israel.

This psalm, however, declaims that Israel became YHWH's nation earlier, in a manner unconnected to law or covenant. This has important theological consequences: here, Israel's relationship with its deity is unconditional and independent of observing the law. This fits the general optimistic tenor of this psalm, which focuses on YHWH's miraculous help and salvation of Israel.

The central imagery of the psalm, highlighted above, is also counter-cultural, or better yet, counter-Torah. Nowhere in the Torah does the Jordan River join the Reed Sea at the time of the exodus, and nowhere do mountains dance then. Yes – according to Exod. 19.18, Mount Sinai shakes during the revelation – but that was Mount Sinai alone, and this happened after the exodus, and it shook rather than danced. If a person reads the Psalter with the assumption that it must comport to an authoritative Torah, that person might somehow make these images agree – but they really are quite distinct.

That same person might also make the final verse, with the image of the flinty rock turning into water, correspond with the stories where Moses hits a rock to make water emerge (Exod. 17.1-7; Num. 20.1-13). But that is not what these verses say. In the psalm, it is YHWH who is the actor, not Moses; Moses is completely absent in this psalm that highlights YHWH's power – no intermediaries are necessary here. That too is a remarkable divergence from the Torah's story, which has Moses as the protagonist in most of its final four books. (But this absence of Moses makes sense in a late psalm, where Israel is looking for assistance directly from YHWH.) In contrast to the Torah story, where water emerges from the struck rock, in this psalm, the rock turns into water; the Hebrew is quite clear and unambiguous about this. Some attribute this difference to a poetic retelling of the Torah's story, but given that elsewhere the psalm does not agree with the Torah, why should we reconcile the two traditions here?

I love this psalm for several reasons. It is upbeat and picturesque. In its likely exilic or post-exilic setting, it could offer hope for a quick and miraculous return from Babylonia to the land of Israel, and this message of sudden restoration is comforting, especially for a people suffering under great duress. But what I love most about this psalm is that while its form is symmetrical and tame, its content is not, creating tension between form and content. Its language, and its placement in the fourth book of the Psalter, suggest that it is from the very time when the Torah, close to a form we know it, was becoming the guidebook for the Jewish community in the exilic or post-exilic period. Yet, this psalm does not give in, and disagrees with Torah traditions on three points: when Israel became YHWH's people, which geographical bodies did what at the time of the exodus, and exactly how the Israelites were provided with water in the wilderness. I think it is intentionally resisting the stories that the Torah tells.

Although scholars have developed different theories for when and how the Torah came together as the central text in the ([post]-exilic) period, these are little more than guesswork. It is likely that this was a contested process, for surely more laws and stories than those now incorporated in the Torah were circulating, and their exclusion must have bothered some groups.[6] The author of Psalm 114 belonged to one such group, and wrote this psalm, his story of the events connected with the establishment of Israel as YHWH's people, as protest literature.

But what is the best way to protest? At times we must stand up tall and yell and scream, but sometimes it is more effective to protest quietly, and that is what this psalm does. It hides its radical ideas in a very staid and symmetrical structure, and only by reading it carefully, independently of the Torah, is its protest evident.

6. For example, aside from the two creation stories in Gen. 1–3, a creation tradition where the world is created through YHWH's vanquishing of a sea-deity is depicted in Isa. 51.9 and Job 26.12-13, among other texts. See also Ballentine 2015.

I love the quiet but effective manner that it disputes tradition, which may serve as a model for us, even today.

And my second favorite is Psalm 113, the very first psalm in the *Hallel* collection.[7] As with Psalm 114, I like its traditional melodies, and I appreciate its structure, somewhat similar to Psalm 114. As a Hebraist, I especially appreciate how hard the author tried, without succeeding, to mimic ancient classical Hebrew diction[8] – I give him an 'A' for effort.

Marc Zvi Brettler is Bernice and Morton Lerner Distinguished Professor of Jewish Studies in the Department of Religious Studies at Duke University, and the co-founder of TheTorah.com.

References

Ballentine, Debra S. (2015), *The Conflict Myth and the Biblical Tradition*, Oxford: Oxford University Press.

Brettler, Marc Zvi (2016), 'A Jewish Historical-Critical Commentary on Psalms: Psalms 114 as an Example', *HeBAI* 4 (5): 401–34.

Brettler, Marc Zvi (2019), 'A Women's Voice in the Psalter: A New Understanding of Psalm 113', https://www.thetorah.com/article/a-womens-voice-in-the-psalter-a-new-understanding-of-psalm-113 (accessed 5th April 2023).

Brettler, Marc Zvi (2020), 'Encouraging Babylonian Jews to Return, Psalm 114 Tells a Unique Exodus Story', https://www.thetorah.com/article/encouraging-babylonian-jews-to-return-psalm-114-tells-a-unique-exodus-story.

Hurvitz, Avi (1985), 'Originals and Imitations in Biblical Poetry: A Comparative Examination of 1 Sam 2:1-10 and Ps 113:5-9', in Ann Kort and Scott Morschauser (eds), *Biblical and Related Studies Presented to Samuel Iwry*, 115–21, Winona Lake: Eisenbrauns.

Martin, Michael Wade (2021), 'Does Ancient Hebrew Poetry Have Meter?', *JBL* 140 (3): 503–29.

Rubin, Aaron D. (2013), 'Definite Article: Pre-Modern Hebrew', in G. Khan *et al.* (eds), *Encyclopedia of Hebrew Language and Linguistics*, Leiden: Brill, http://dx.doi.org.proxy.lib.duke.edu/10.1163/2212-4241_ehll_EHLL_COM_00000853 (accessed 14 May 2022).

Waltke, Bruce K. and Michael P. O'Connor (1990), *An Introduction to Biblical Hebrew Syntax*, Winona Lake: Eisenbrauns.

---

7. For my understanding of this psalm, see Brettler 2019.
8. See the discussion of the *-i* suffixes in Hurvitz 1985.

PSALM 117
A HYMN OF STEADFAST LOVE

Barbara E. Reid

In 1980, when I was preparing to take life-long vows as a Dominican Sister, I saw this quote on a greeting card: 'All I have seen teaches me to trust God for all I have not seen'. It spoke to me of how to trust God in a time of great uncertainty about the road ahead for us, all of us, in religious life. I put it on the cover of the worship aid for the liturgy of my final vows. I was sure the quote must have been from Scripture, but at that time I knew very little about the Bible. It wasn't until years later – after the internet was invented – that I Googled the phrase and found out that it was really from Ralph Waldo Emerson! I later discovered that the place in Scripture where the same sentiment is found is Psalm 117.

> Praise God, all you nations!
>   Extol God, all you peoples!
> For great is God's steadfast love toward us,
>   and God's faithfulness endures forever.
> Praise God![1]

This hymn of praise is the shortest psalm in the Psalter. Like other hymns, it begins with a call to praise God, gives reasons for this praise, and concludes with a recapitulation of the call to praise. Like other hymns, it can only be expressed by an assembly of believers; 'a lone singer could never proclaim enough praise' (Nowell 1993: 150). In this hymn, not only the assembly of Israel, but all peoples (גוים, *goyim*, 'gentiles', 117.1a and האמים, *ha'ummim*, 'peoples, tribes', 117.1b) are called to praise God.

The reason for praise, introduced with כי, *ki*,[2] is because God's steadfast love (חסד, *hesed*) 'towers over us' (117.2a, translation by Allen 1983: 116) and divine faithful mercy (אמת, *'emet*) lasts forever (117:2b). Steadfast love and faithfulness

---

1. Author's adaptation of the NRSV translation.
2. As also Pss. 33.4; 135.4, 5, 14; 136.1.

are the two divine attributes that characterize God's fulfillment of the covenantal promises. There is a strong echo in Psalm 117 of the revelation to Moses on Mount Sinai in Exodus 34, where God passes before Moses and proclaims,

> The LORD, THE LORD,
> a God merciful [רחום, *raḥum*] and gracious,
> slow to anger,
> and abounding in steadfast love and faithfulness [חסד ואמת, *ḥesed we'emet*],
> keeping steadfast love [חסד, *ḥesed*] for the thousandth generation. (Exod. 34.6-7, NRSV)

The image evoked in Exod. 34.6 is 'womb compassion' (רחום, *raḥum*, 'mercy', is from the root רחם, *reḥem*, 'womb'), the tenderness of a mother who can never forget her child (Isa. 49.16). Just so, all that Israel had experienced of God's love and faithfulness in the past and present gave them the assurance that the divine promise would endure into the future.

Biblical scholars speculate that the original setting for the psalm was cultic (Allen 1983: 117). Because of its brevity and because some Hebrew manuscripts attach it to Psalm 116, some scholars think it may have been used as a concluding doxology to a collection of psalms of praise, Psalms 111–116. But the textual evidence points more strongly toward Psalm 117 as a discrete psalm 'with a simple yet powerful statement about the relationship between a believing community and its God' (DeClaissé-Walford 2020: 142). Its resonances with Second Isaiah suggest a post-exilic date (Allen 1983: 117).

The final words of the psalm, הללו־יה, *Hallelu-ya* (NRSV: 'Praise the Lord!'), occur in the Egyptian Hallel psalms (Pss. 113–118), sung in connection with the Jewish Passover meal and other festivals that celebrate God's redemption of Israel from bondage in Egypt (הללו־יה occurs in 113.1, 9; 115.18; 116.19; 117.2).

For me, Psalm 117 has served as a mantra that anchors me in steadfast trust that when all else changes, disturbs, disorients us, God's steadfast and enduring love continues to embrace us. I was fortunate to have a mother such as this, who put a human face for me on this kind of ability to trust in love and mercy that never fail. Likewise, the sisters in my religious congregation have been daily companions in living together over the past forty-eight years in this stance of reliance on God in times of great unknowing.

Living from the stance that Psalm 117 invites has made me open to a shift in my understanding of my call to serve God. In my younger years, I thought of myself as trying to make myself constantly available to God's people to do God's work. Interiorizing the call of Psalm 117 to continually praise God for God's steadfast love and faithfulness has helped me shift toward a stance of making myself constantly available to God for the sake of God's people. It may sound like a subtle difference, but it's actually a crucial change in what is at the center: the starting point and the anchor for everything is not me and my desire to serve God, nor is it the needs of God's people that face me, but God's steadfast love and mercy. Everything else flows from that.

As I read the scriptures, I see a key aspect of how divine steadfast loving mercy is revealed through God's care for those who are poorest and most in need. I am moved not simply to appreciate this dimension of divine love, but I hear the call to emulate God's boundless womb-compassion in the way that I live and minister. I recognize that I have lived a fairly privileged life as a lower-middle-class white North American woman with advanced education, and that I have the means by which to extend womb-compassion to those in need. I see myself doing this primarily through my teaching, preaching, and scholarship. While I may not often minister directly to those who are most marginalized, I influence those who are on the front lines in such ministry.

The older I get and the more I pray with Psalm 117, the more willing I am to go out on a limb. This is particularly true of my work in feminist biblical interpretation. I have learned to pay attention to the inequities toward women and other disadvantaged persons, to name these inequities, to analyze why they are so, and to engage the Bible as an ally in creating a more equitable world. As a younger scholar, I was afraid that I could ruin my career or my standing in the Roman Catholic Church if I wrote about and taught feminist biblical interpretation. Now in my mature years, my experience is that God's steadfast love and compassion have never failed me. This emboldens me to make riskier choices.

The uncertainties now in every arena of life are far more than when I was younger. The whole world has changed and is still changing in dramatic ways since the world-wide pandemic. Challenges that were already emerging before the pandemic have become more pronounced. As a Catholic, I watch as the number of Catholics who leave the church continues to grow, as does the number of young people with no institutional religious affiliation. As a vowed woman religious, I have watched the total number of Sisters in the US decline from over 181,000 in 1966 to approximately 45,000 today, with the vast majority of our members over 70 years old. As one who has spent thirty-five years in theological education and is now entrusted with leading a Roman Catholic School of Theology and Ministry, I know that the models that worked in the past no longer function to form ministers for what the Church and the world need from us now. What Psalm 117 offers to me now is the reassurance that although we do not see the future to which God is drawing us, we can move forward with confidence in divine enduring love and faithfulness. It also provides a beacon when I have difficult decisions to make, as the central question for me is: What is the faithful thing to do? We know that God is doing something new in us (Isa. 42.1). Although we do not yet know all of what that is, unshakeable faith in God's steadfast love and faithfulness, based on all the ways we have experienced it in the past, enables us to be faithful to God's ways into a future full of hope.

I am grateful for this opportunity to reflect on Psalm 117 from my context. My second choice would have been Psalm 150, which invites not only all people, but all creation, 'everything that breathes' (v. 6), to join in exuberant praise of God. It reminds me to sing God's praise with every breath I take.

Barbara E. Reid, O.P., Ph.D is the president of the Catholic Theological Union in Chicago; the Carroll Stuhlmueller, C.P., Distinguished Professor of New Testament Studies; a member of the Dominican Sisters of Grand Rapids, Michigan; and the general editor of the Wisdom Commentary series (Liturgical Press).

References

Allen, Leslie C. (1983), *Psalms 101–150*, WBC 21, Waco: Word.
DeClaissé-Walford, Nancy L. (2020), *Psalms. Books 4-5,* WCS 22, Collegeville: Liturgical Press.
Nowell, Irene (1993), *Sing A New Song: The Psalms in the Sunday Lectionary*, Collegeville: Liturgical Press.

PSALM 118
POETRY AND POETICS THROUGH A PAST IN SCIENCE

Kevin D. Chau

Psalm 118 is deeply meaningful because it reminds me that my earlier training in science is a fundamental element of who I am as a HB (Hebrew Bible) poetry scholar. But before sharing this earlier life, I survey the psalm as it eventually relates to my experiences.

Psalm 118 (postexilic)[1] opens with a burst of thanksgiving, praising God multiple times: 'his faithfulness is for eternity' (vv. 1-3).[2] Thankful praise resounds throughout the psalm, emerging prominently also in the second half's opening and conclusion. The psalm's first half (vv. 1-18) recounts the plea and deliverance that leads to thanksgiving, and the second half (vv. 19-29) portrays entry into the temple for a thanksgiving offering. Psalm 118 is conventionally designated as a psalm of thanksgiving for God's good faithfulness. But equating its thanksgiving elements with its ultimate purpose robs the psalm of its richness. The performance (uttering) of thanksgiving is merely an instrument for the ultimate goal of inducing a stouter faith in God. This psalm was constructed for people who indeed doubt God's faithfulness at some point or level. If God's faithful love is undeniably experienced as eternally present, then there would be no need for such a psalm. Culler explains how lyrical poetry (to which the Psalms belong) can be considered as 'thought writing': poetry composed for us to utter such that 'we are trying on a thought as much as expressing it, projecting and perhaps above all intensifying a mood' (Culler 2015: 119–20). Thus, when this psalm's readers utter its poetry of thanksgiving and praise, they cannot help but be enraptured by the poetry (language of heart, of power) that magnifies moods and emotions, namely their love for God and love felt from God. They 'try on' God's faithful love, feel it out in its poetic expression, and decide if it is for them. Thus, with filled hearts readers may truly embrace 'indeed God's faithfulness is for eternity', ultimately strengthening faith.

---

1. Hossfeld and Zenger (2011: 236) take for certain its postexilic dating. Gerstenberger (2001: 307–8) hedges, with an exilic or postexilic origin.

2. Translations of the Hebrew text throughout are the author's.

The theme of God's faithful goodness as eternal is further expressed through the numerous allusions to the Reed Sea deliverance (Exod. 14–15; cf. Hossfeld and Zenger 2011: 234–35), ranging from direct quotations from the Song of the Sea (Exod. 15.1-19) to subtler allusions veiled in the poetry (e.g., v. 18; vv. 15c-16). Although these allusions certainly re-contextualize the psalm's portrayed plight, how the allusions align with the psalm's purpose (emboldening faith) has not been seriously considered. Similar to how lyrical poetry can offer thoughts and emotions that the reader tries on like clothing, Culler (2015: 226) also explains lyrical poetry as creating a 'lyric present' where a past event may be summoned into an utterer's presence. The Reed Sea deliverance allusions bring the victory at the Reed Sea into the utterer's lyric present, so that they may both feel and experience the triumph and power that comes through faith in YHWH in one of the community's most powerful collective memories.

Psalm 118 has a special place in my heart because the psalm's poetics (i.e., how poetry is put together) in particular lends itself well to remind me that, although I am a HB poetry scholar utilizing linguistic and literary approaches, my STEM (Science, Technology, Engineering, Math) training still deeply influences how I read poetic texts. The psalm reminds me that I never lost that first love and that this STEM 'voice' still informs how I think, observe, sense, communicate, feel, etc. poetry (as I illustrate later in this essay). As an undergraduate, I studied chemistry and biology; and upon graduation, I pursued my Masters of Divinity and eventually a PhD in Hebrew and Semitic Studies. Because I knew during undergraduate studies that my science degree was not to be continued, I took additional chemistry courses at the graduate level to glimpse what another life would have entailed. During my PhD, I was also afforded the serendipitous opportunity to continue in science as a teaching assistant for undergraduate chemistry, nurturing me in science in new ways. Now as a specialist in poetry, I often hear comments on how my presentations are 'science-y', or how one can see my previous science training. Initially, I did not know how to react to these remarks: Were they just oblique criticisms? But now I embrace them because I realized that my science training forms a major part of my identity by affording me the analogies, idioms, and analytical paradigms for studying and communicating poetry.

As a second-generation Chinese-American born in the 1970s, my undergraduate study in STEM is common among other Chinese-Americans (and Asian-Americans). Although Asian-Americans formed just one-third of my undergraduate colleagues, my STEM major classes were overwhelmingly Asian-American. I believe that I find a special affinity with other Asian-American HB scholars because of our shared academic training that is intertwined with our ethnicities. Many Asian-Americans likely entered science because of the influence of our parents who, as immigrants, necessarily entered STEM fields. They did not have the English language skills to flourish in non-STEM majors, and in Asia the premium on mathematics undoubtedly encouraged them to study and practice STEM. For others, STEM was a means to citizenship: my father took an engineering degree solely because it guaranteed a US green card. Thus, in Asian-American cultures STEM was the road to 'success' because that road was well-trodden.

I share this experience because many of us Asian-American scholars are outliers in our field not only because of our ethnicities, but also because of our STEM training. I believe that many in this specific context may fundamentally differ in how we approach texts, precisely because of our STEM training. Whereas for some time it has been fashionable for medical students to have undergraduate classes in humanities to become well-rounded professionals, I think that among HB scholars with prior STEM training this balance is much less celebrated. When I come to know other Asian-American scholars, sheepish amusement inevitably arises upon our sharing information about our science degrees, often characterized as a 'misspent youth'. However, I hope that others with similar backgrounds, especially those in Asian-American contexts, find similar celebration and gratitude for our past training, which I suspect still deeply influences us as scholars whether we realize it or not.

I conclude with two examples from Psalm 118's poetics to illustrate how science enters my thinking about poetry. While explaining poetry through STEM is neither efficient nor accessible for most, I ask for indulgence since I am only sharing how my STEM training has shaped how my mind wraps itself around poetry. This is neither a defense nor endorsement, but merely a description for how my ruminations on poetry are inspired, impacted, and developed. I offer a view into my thought life in the hope that others see what thoughts may also be haunting them, yearning to be loved again.

Psalm 118 provides its utterers a lyric present in which they can battle their enemies 'in the name of YHWH' (i.e., both for God's honor and by God's power; vv. 10-12). Verses 10-12 present the utterer three instances in which they may confront and prevail over their opponents in God's name, despite the opponents' more powerful success each time. The succeeding vv. 13-14, with their explicit allusions to the Reed Sea deliverance, further categorizes the lyric present of this battle as possessing the same level of power and significance. But the allusion in the triplet of vv. 15c-16 concerning YHWH's powerful right-hand prevailing is significantly different.[3] Whereas the previous allusions were direct quotations or were derived with minimal, yet understandable poetic manipulations from the source material, the source *couplet* from the Song of the Sea (Exod. 15.6) has become the *triplet* in vv. 15c-16, begging the question: Why the change?

Here my chemistry training in two teaching mantras – 'different/similar structures – different/similar properties' and the related 'like dissolves (attracts) like' – spark my thinking on this question.[4] Our source couplet has become a triplet in vv. 15c-16, exclaiming the power of God's right hand, in order to attract itself to vv. 10-12's own abundant 'three-ness'. Verses 10-12 unfold as three poetic

---

3. I translate vv. 15c-16 as: 'The right hand of God acts in valor. // The right hand of YHWH exalts. // The right hand of YHWH acts in valor'.

4. For example: volatile compounds easily become gaseous because they are small molecules (similar structures). Oil does not dissolve into water ('like attracts like') because each is fundamentally different in how the former evenly distributes electrons (nonpolar) and the latter does not (polar).

movements (two couplets and triplet). The three movements each begin with 'they have surrounded me' and conclude with 'indeed in the name of the LORD I cut them off'. And perhaps, most significantly, the last poetic movement is a climaxing triplet where even when the enemies burst powerfully like a sudden fire, the utterer still prevails. As a result of this abundant repetition of threes at different levels, the triplet of vv. 15c-16 creates a felt connection for its readers.[5] This triplet becomes a heard word addressing the utterer's own battle in vv. 10-12, allowing the utterer to share in God's glorious victory, how God's powerful right hand has been expressed through their faith and valor in God's name. While many non-STEM-trained scholars may indeed see these same patterns of attraction, I am grateful for my science training, which has afforded me, at a minimum, the imagination and metaphors for thinking about how poetry works.

My final rumination concerns structure: What does the psalm accomplish by employing another allusion from the Song of the Sea (v. 28; cf. Exod. 15.2) immediately before the psalm's concluding couplet (v. 29)? Such allusions prevail in the psalm's first half but in the second half appears just once here, in v. 28. Is the allusion mere poetic ornamentation, or does its position at the end have a purpose? Similarly, in chemistry I spent countless hours analyzing chemical structures. I believe that time spent thinking about structures has contributed significantly to my present fascination with poetic structure – how, like in chemistry, structure and function go hand-in-hand. Returning to our question, v. 28 certainly recalls its specific source of Exod. 15.2 and consequently the Song of the Sea as a whole, but it also frames v. 29 to recall the Song of the Sea's climactic concluding singlet line: 'YHWH reigns for *eternity* (*'ōlām*) and ever' (Exod. 15.18).[6] Because Psalm 118 has been so explicitly drawing upon the Song of the Sea throughout the poem, and v. 28 operates as a *Wiederaufnahm* to the Song of the Sea, when v. 29 concludes the poem as an envelope refrain with v. 1, the verse not only signals the poem's closure (i.e., completion) but also highlights the significance of that refrain (particularly 'his faithfulness is for *eternity*') to the Song of the Sea. Thus, the highlighting of the refrain at the *position* of the poem's closing allows the psalm's oft-repeated 'eternity' to resound with the 'eternity' at the closing position of the Song of the Sea. The melding of these two endings reminds the post-exilic community that whereas their foreign sovereigns allow them no king, this YHWH of old who proved himself as king of creation at the Reed Sea is indeed still working as their good and faithful king. This reminder comes as subtle as a whisper through the poetry, but once heard it is a whisper piercing in the darkness of foreign imperialism for those desperate to hear and to sense their god. Similarly, Psalm 118 also reminds me to be thankful for those voices from my own past, to remember that they have formed a huge part of who I am and how I work.

My second choice from the Psalms would be Psalm 1, because it tells me who I must be.

---

5. Not coincidentally in the psalm's first half (vv. 1-18), v. 12 and vv. 15c-16 are the only two triplets in a sea of couplets.

6. On the significance and rarity of singlet lines, see Dobbs-Allsopp (2015: 84–9).

Kevin Chau is a Senior Lecturer at The University of the Free State (South Africa) in the department of Hebrew. He teaches post-graduates in Hebrew language and linguistics and supervises MA and PhD students specializing in biblical Hebrew Poetry.

References

Culler, Jonathan (2015), *Theory of the Lyric*, Cambridge, MA: Harvard University Press.
Dobbs-Allsopp, F.W. (2015), *On Biblical Poetry*, Oxford: Oxford University Press.
Gerstenberger, Erhard S. (2001), *Psalms, Part 2, and Lamentations*, Forms of the Old Testament Literature 15, Grand Rapids: Eerdmans.
Hossfeld, F.L. and E. Zenger (2011), *Psalms 3*, Hermeneia, Minneapolis: Fortress..

PSALM 121
IN THREE RECEPTIONS

Gerald West

Introduction

Psalm 121 has had three quite distinct receptions in my life, first in the chapel of my Anglican boarding hostel, second as I attempted as a young Hebrew Bible scholar to read any and every biblical text from an economic perspective, and third as I embraced African understandings of the Psalms as performative speech. My reflections are located within a series of intersected contextual sites.

The Cadence of the Psalm

In the mid-1960s I travelled by train from Botswana to South Africa to attend school. These were different worlds, a world of racial integration and a world of racial segregation, a world in which my friends were mostly black and a world in which my friends were entirely white. Even as a young boy, in my early teenage years, as I travelled on the train, back and forth, four times a year, I was aware of the dissonance. A distinct memory from that time was being encouraged by our Anglican boarding hostel chaplain to attend a political anti-apartheid protest demonstration in Kimberley, the city where I went to school, on the stairs of the Catholic cathedral. I remember vividly sitting on the steps of the cathedral in my school uniform and hostel blazer, surrounded by anti-apartheid activists, singing protest songs, having white passers-by throw things at us, and having the white police photograph us. Though I understood little, I knew this was the right place to be.

Our hostel chaplain tried hard to connect us to the wider world, inviting us to listen to classical music, arranging for us to listen to the music of 'Jesus Christ Superstar', which was banned by the South African government, and prompting us to attend anti-apartheid protests. He also tried hard to draw us into participating in the daily chapel service at the hostel. Christianity did not make much sense to me at the time, partly because I was interested in the array of other religions and partly because apartheid was so publicly linked to Christianity. Yet when the chaplain invited me to read a lesson in chapel, I agreed. He asked me to read Psalm 121.

I was apprehensive. I had a slight stutter and was very self-conscious among my peers. A public reading generated the kind of anxiety that would bring on my stutter. I had been taught by the school speech therapist to prepare, silently in my mind, for the first phrase I was about to speak before speaking. This I did, practising and practising. 'I will lift up mine eyes unto the hills...' Something quite profound happened as I read this psalm. The cadence of the language, in King James English, soothed my stutter. I allowed the language of this psalm to take control of my tongue, and in the process discovered that biblical text was literature, was poetry.

I did not engage at all deeply with the theological content of the psalm and I did no overt analysis of its structure. But the cadence of the poetic language touched me, and I would return to this psalm again and again. Indeed, reading this psalm aloud contributed to my love for literature and language, which became my life's work, first as a linguist and then as a biblical scholar.

The Economy of the Psalm

When I made the move from lecturing within Linguistics and Applied Language Studies at Rhodes University in South Africa to furthering my studies within Biblical Studies at the University of Sheffield in England, I carried the South African context with me, leaving the country to avoid detention under the 1985 State of Emergency. The major reason for my shift from linguistics to Biblical Studies was that the Bible was so clearly a site of struggle in South Africa, serving political apartheid (Vosloo 2015) and also a weapon (Mofokeng 1988: 40) in the hands of those who resisted apartheid. The Sheffield Department of Biblical Studies at the time, 1985, offered me an appropriate location, within the literary and linguistic emphasis that was being pioneered there and within proximity of the Urban Theology Unit (UTU), with strong links to the anti-apartheid struggle in South Africa and a place where Norman Gottwald taught through formal ties with New York Theological Seminary. It was here that I first met Gottwald, forging a friendship through his mentorship of me, which endured until his death in March 2022.

Though my biblical interpretive interests were, and remain, primarily literary, I was deeply influenced by the kind of socio-historical work Gottwald was doing at the UTU and in *The Tribes of Yahweh* (Gottwald 1979). The conjunction of my literary textual orientation and Gottwald's argument in *The Tribes of Yahweh* led me to revisit Psalm 121. Gottwald's Marxist orientation in *The Tribes of Yahweh* resonated with South African Black Theology's understanding of apartheid as a form of 'racial capitalism' (Sebidi 1986: 31–32). More specifically, Gottwald's understanding of 'Yahwism' as the ideological and theological 'symbolic side' of 'early Israel as an egalitarian social-action system' (Gottwald 1999: 642-49, 618–21) resonated with my own yearnings for a politically relevant form of Christianity in South Africa. On my return to South Africa in 1987, I engaged with and was embraced by South Africa's two interrelated liberation theologies, South African Black Theology (Mosala and Tlhagale 1986) and South African Contextual Theology (Kairos 1985).

Immersed once again in the struggle against settler-colonialism and apartheid, I re-read Psalm 121 with the Hebrew Bible in my left hand and *The Tribes of Yahweh* in my right hand. What if, I reflected, there was an interdependent or reciprocal relationship (Gottwald 1999: 618) between vv. 1 and 2, between 'the hill-country' (1) and 'Yahweh' (2), with the hill-country representing the socio-historical site (Gottwald 1999: 580–83) of the early Israelite social revolutionary project? Psalm 121 could then be read as an affirmation of the people's revolution (vv. 3-4), with Yahwism as the facilitator (v. 2) (Gottwald 1999: 646) of the social revolution's vigilant care (vv. 3-4), enduring protection (vv. 5-6), commitment to resist injustice (v. 7a) and affirmation of dignity (v. 7b), guiding the social revolution unto its end (v. 8).

I recognize that then, and now, my interpretations are ideologically driven. Given that biblical texts are the products of sites of economic contestation (Mosala 1989: 20), Itumeleng Mosala, from within Black Theology, urges us to persist in our liberation-oriented attempts to detect 'glimpses of liberation and of a determinate social movement galvanized by a powerful religious ideology in the biblical text' (Mosala 1989: 40). Could Psalm 121 reflect, in symbolic form, I asked, just such a glimpse?

The Psalm as Performative

With the political and juridical (but not yet economic) liberation of South Africa in 1994, South Africa's connections with the African continent became more accessible, as anti-apartheid academic boycotts were lifted and movement across the continent increased. African biblical scholarship flourished as South Africa reconnected with West, East, Southern, and North Africa. Among the distinctive features of West African biblical scholarship I became more familiar with was its work analyzing local post-missionary understandings of biblical text as performative, particularly as regarding the Psalms (Adamo 2000).

Through my linguistics training I was familiar with speech-act theory. Indeed, Anthony Thiselton's work on linguistics in general and speech-act theory in particular, within the Department of Biblical Studies at the University of Sheffield (Thiselton 1980), was one of the reasons I chose Sheffield as my destination in 1985. Though not as prevalent as in West Africa, the appropriation of biblical text as performative was common in South Africa. While Thiselton was cautious about attempts to harness the performative 'power' of biblical texts (Thiselton 1974), my West African biblical colleagues embraced this postcolonial neo-indigenous form of African biblical appropriation.

Kwabena Asamoah-Gyadu, a scholar of Ghanaian African Christianity, recognizes that 'African Christians are generally in love with the Old Testament precisely because several parts of it, particularly the Psalms, resonate with the primal imagination that associate the divine realm with salvation, strength and healing' (Asamoah-Gyadu 2012: 49). He then goes on to refer to Psalm 121 directly: 'The opening verse of Psalm 121 is a much loved example: I will lift up my eyes to the hills – where does my help come from? My help comes from the Lord, the Maker of heaven and earth' (121.1). He goes on to explain: 'The "hills", where Yahweh dwells, is that unseen supernatural realm from where power and salvation emanate'. Within West African indigenous African Religion, he explains further, '[t]he seen or natural realm occupied by humans is crowded with all kinds of benevolent and malevolent spirit powers including the ancestors. Unlike the supernatural realm, the natural one is characterized by various limitations and enfeeblements – confusion, ill health, fear, weakness, resistance to success and prosperity, and ultimately, death'. 'What is natural or human therefore', he continues, 'constantly stands in need of supernatural power for survival and salvation' (p. 49).

The Nigerian biblical scholar David Tuesday Adamo situates his exegetical work on Psalm 121 within this kind of African performative context, where reciting Psalm 121 has performative power (Adamo 2017). He concludes his analysis by stating that '[i]t is the habit of most Nigerian churches, especially the indigenous churches, to inscribe either a portion or the entire Psalm 121 in a cloth on their doorposts or motor vehicles for protection, because they believe', he continues, 'that if Psalm 121 or other psalms are inscribed or chanted repeatedly, God's protection from witches and wizards is guaranteed' (Adamo 2017: 6; see also Adamo 2015). In sum, says Adamo of Psalm 121: 'It is often used as a talisman for protection, for healing and success' (Adamo 2017: 6).

South African anti-apartheid theologian Johannes (Klippies) Kritzinger offers a similar, though more political, performative-type liturgical version of Psalm 121 for the Melodi ya Tshwane congregation of the Uniting Reformed Church in Southern Africa (URCSA) in the inner city of Pretoria, set within a post-apartheid South Africa yearning for a fuller freedom.

> Leader: We lift up our eyes to the hills,
> to the high places in and around Pretoria;
> Where does our help come from? Does our help come from Meintjieskop,
> from the Union Buildings, centre of political power?
>
> Congregation: Our help comes from the LORD,
> who made heaven and earth. (Kritzinger 2008: 337)

The liturgical leader continues, asking a series of poetic questions about where power resides in the new South Africa, scanning the hills of the political capital city of South Africa, Pretoria. And in each case the congregation responds, rejecting these politically ambiguous forms of help, saying: 'Our help comes from the LORD, who made heaven and earth' (121.2).

Does our help come from Thaba Tshwane,
the National Defence Force, centre of military power?
…

Does our help come from Monumentkoppie,
from the Voortrekker Monument, reminder of the power of the past?
…

Does our help come from the high building
of the Reserve Bank, centre of economic power?
…

Does our help come from the high buildings of Unisa or the University of Pretoria, centres of intellectual power?
…

Finally, the congregation concludes the liturgy:

Our help comes from the LORD,
who made heaven and earth;
who is the same yesterday, today and forever;
who remains faithful to his promises,
who never forsakes the work of his hands. Amen. (Kritzinger 2008: 337–38)

Though more political in its imagery, I worry that performative appropriations like this, as with this form of biblical appropriation more generally, are not political enough. Can Psalm 121 bear the weight of a political reading, along the lines of my early economic-oriented attempt?

Gerald West is Professor Emeritus in the School of Religion, Philosophy, and Classics & Ujamaa Centre, University of KwaZulu-Natal, South Africa

References

Adamo, David Tuesday (2000), 'The Use of Psalms in African Indigenous Churches in Nigeria', in Gerald O. West and Musa Dube (eds), *The Bible in Africa: Transactions, Trajectories and Trends*, 336–49. Leiden: Brill.

Adamo, David Tuesday (2015), 'Semiotic Interpretation of Selected Psalms Inscriptions (23, 35, 121) on Motor Vehicles in Nigeria', *Scriptura: Journal for Contextual Hermeneutics in Southern Africa* 114 (1): 1–13.

Adamo, David Tuesday (2017), 'The Significance of Psalm 121 in an African Context', *Journal for Semitics* 26 (1): 33–46.

Asamoah-Gyadu, Kwabena (2012), 'Mediating Power and Salvation: Pentecostalism and Religious Mediation in an African Context', *Journal of World Christianity* 5 (1): 43–61.

Gottwald, Norman K. (1979), *The Tribes of Yahweh: A Sociology of the Religion of Liberated Israel, 1250–1050 B.C.E.*, Maryknoll: Orbis.

Gottwald, Norman K. (1999) *The Tribes of Yahweh: A Sociology of the Religion of Liberated Israel, 1250–1050 BCE*, Sheffield: Sheffield Academic. Maryknoll: Orbis.

Kairos Theologians (1985), *Challenge to the Church: A Theological Comment on the Political Crisis in South Africa: The Kairos Document*, Braamfontein: The Kairos Theologians.

Kritzinger, J.N.J. (Klippies) (2008), 'Where Does Our Help come from? Psalm 121 in Tshwane', *Missionalia* 36 (2/3): 337–38.

Mofokeng, Takatso (1988), 'Black Christians, the Bible and Liberation', *Journal of Black Theology* 2 (1): 34–42.

Mosala, Itumeleng J. (1989), *Biblical Hermeneutics and Black Theology in South Africa*, Grand Rapids: Eerdmans.

Mosala, Itumeleng J. and Buti Tlhagale (1986), *The Unquestionable Right to Be Free: Essays in Black Theology*, Johannesburg: Skotaville.

Sebidi, Lebamang (1986), 'The Dynamics of the Black Struggle and its Implications for Black Theology', in Itumeleng J. Mosala and Buti Tlhagale (eds), *The Unquestionable Right to Be Free: Essays in Black Theology*, 1–36, Johannesburg: Skotaville.

Thiselton, Anthony C. (1974), 'The Supposed Power of Words in the Biblical Writings', *Journal of Theological Studies* 25 (2): 283–99.

Thiselton, Anthony C. (1980), *The Two Horizons: The New Testament Hermeneutics and Philosophical Description with Special Reference to Heidegger, Bultman, Gadamer, and Wittgenstein*, Grand Rapids: Eerdmans.

Vosloo, Robert (2015), 'The Bible and the Justification of Apartheid in Reformed Circles in the 1940s in South Africa: Some Historical, Hermeneutical and Theological Remarks', *Stellenbosch Theological Journal* 1 (2): 195–215.

PSALM 121
ASCENDING TO THE HOLY WITH THE PSALM

Marvin A. Sweeney

Psalm 121 is a classic example of the Psalms of Ascent, here labelled in Hebrew as שיר למעלות, *šîr lammaʻălôt*, 'a song for the ascents', in v. 1a. The songs of ascent were sung as Jews ascended the Temple Mount in antiquity to take part in the worship services at the Jerusalem Temple. Gerstenberger identifies Psalm 121 as a 'Pilgrimage Song' with 'Words of Assurance', and lays out a formal structure which includes the superscription in v. 1a; the 'Affirmation of Confidence (in YHWH)' in vv. 1bc-2 expressed through a question and answer schema; and 'Consolation, words of assurance' in vv. 3-8, which provide the basis for the confidence expressed in vv. 1bc-2 (Gerstenberger 2001: 322–26). Hossfeld and Zenger provide extensive discussion concerning the roles of the gods in protecting people in ancient Near Eastern and Greco-Roman culture (Hossfeld and Zenger 2011: 315–31). And Brueggemann and Bellinger pay close attention to YHWH's vigilance and the role of the L-rd, who 'will bless you and keep you' (Brueggemann and Bellinger 2014: 525–27). All of these commentators provide valuable and astute analyses of Psalm 121. But two important dimensions are missing, viz., (1) how does one understand Psalm 121 as a song that is sung? and (2) how does one read Psalm 121 as a Jew?

I am Jewish, born to a Jewish Mother from Springfield, Illinois, and a nominally Christian Father from Pax, West Virginia. I was raised Jewish in Decatur, Illinois, and went to synagogue at Temple *B'nai Abraham*, where I became *Bar Mitzvah* on Friday night, August 5, 1966, in the classic Midwestern Reform tradition, under the tutelage of Rabbi Dr J. Jerome Pine, *z"l*. I learned Hebrew, first in Ashkenazi and later in Sefardi pronunciation, from the 'Rocket Ship to Mars' series, in which Jewish children travel to Mars, where the people speak Hebrew, which is actually English written in Hebrew consonants and vowels. I learned the basic prayers of the Jewish worship service, a few dozen Hebrew words, and songs, such as *Zum Gali, Gali*, and *David Melech Yisrael*. Some might be surprised to learn that I do believe in G-d, and I served as the Chaplain and later Vice President of the Temple Youth Group (National Federation of Temple Youth) during my high school years.

By 1980–83, I was a PhD student in Hebrew Bible at Claremont Graduate School, now Claremont Graduate University, working on quals and later a dissertation on Isaiah 1–4, which was especially inspired by my Reform Jewish interest in the vision of Isa. 2.1-4, in which the nations ascend to Mount Zion to learn Torah from YHWH, and bring an end to war (Sweeney 1988). During this period, I was member of Congregation Emanuel in San Bernardino, California, where I taught Hebrew to sixth- and seventh-grade students.

Congregation Emanuel was where I learned to understand Psalm 121 as music, based on the performances of Cantor Gregory Yaroslow z"l, then the congregation's Cantor. Cantor Yaroslow's renditions of Psalm 121 made it come to life for me, both as music and as spoken Hebrew. My scholarly training, under the direction of Professor Rolf Knierim z"l, was superb in that I gained the analytical tools to think critically and theologically about the Bible. But it did not enable me to understand Psalm 121 as music or as an expression of Jewish identity. I had not yet learned to understand Hebrew as the living language of the Jewish people.

I had never been to Israel, and I was only just beginning to understand my future role as a Jewish biblical theologian. I also began to understand the role of suffering during this period, both personal and collective. My Mother died of cancer on the day prior to what would have been her fiftieth birthday while I was still studying for quals. And I began to understand the role of Jewish identity through the influence of Professor Zev Garber, who taught a course at UC Riverside which I audited. Although Psalm 121 provides assurance of G-d's support, what does one do when G-d doesn't act, as demonstrated in the experience of the Shoah during World War II? And what responsibility do we human beings have as partners with G-d in ensuring the sanctity and righteousness of G-d's creation when the Shoah and other human experience demonstrate that our world can go so badly wrong?

My first academic appointment was at the University of Miami, where I served as Assistant and Associate Professor of Religious Studies and taught in the Judaic Studies program for eleven years. I taught undergraduate courses in Bible, Jewish history and thought, Jewish mysticism, and Asian religions. I was heavily involved in the University of Miami Hillel Jewish Student Center, initially directed by Rabbi Mark Kram, who became a close friend and colleague. My time at the University of Miami provided opportunities to put issues raised by Psalm 121 into action.

The first was a mission to the Soviet Union, sponsored by the South Florida Conference on Soviet Jewry, to make contact with Jewish Refuseniks, Jews who had been refused permission to leave the Soviet Union and were subsequently persecuted by the Soviet government. I travelled to Moscow and Leningrad (St. Petersburg) with a UM student, Marc Slotnick, now an attorney in Charleston, West Virginia, in March 1987. We met with many Refuseniks in both cities and brought in medical supplies, study materials, kosher food, and other items. Most importantly, we brought back reports on the status and needs of Soviet Jews in both cities. When I contacted people by phone one morning, a Soviet agent immediately stationed himself outside the phone booth and recorded everything I said in my broken Biblical Hebrew. Later in the day, we were stopped and questioned by the Soviet Militia, who let us know that they were watching us. And we were followed and watched all the way to Leningrad – and presumably, before that – until we left after making our contacts there. Mikhail Beizer, then one of the leaders of Leningrad Refusenik community, guided us, and he remains a friend (in Jerusalem!) to this day. All of our contacts were able to go to Israel or elsewhere following the collapse of the Soviet Union in 1991. I was also involved in support for Operation Moses, which enabled Ethiopian Jews to come to Israel, where they could live freely as Jews.

The second was the opportunity to travel to Israel. My first visit was in the summer of 1987 when I was a fellow at the W.F. Albright Institute, pursuing research on the book of Habakkuk. As a result of this visit, I undertook modern Hebrew ulpan studies in 1988–90, which gave me a far better understanding of Hebrew as a living language – and not simply as the classical language in which I had been trained. I had a year-long sabbatical in 1989–90 as a Yad ha-Nadiv Barecha Foundation visiting scholar in Jewish studies at the Hebrew University of Jerusalem, which enabled me to work with Professor Moshe Greenberg z"l on Targumic Aramaic and Jewish Biblical Exegesis and to begin work on my Forms of the Old Testament Literature Commentary on Isaiah 1–39 (Sweeney 1996). In 1993–94, I had another year-long sabbatical as the Dorot Research Professor at the W.F. Albright Institute in Jerusalem, where I began work on my 2001 monograph on King Josiah of Judah, which laid the foundations for my research through the present (Sweeney 2001).

In 1994, I accepted an offer to serve as Professor of Hebrew Bible at the Claremont School of Theology (CST). The appointment enabled me to address directly theological questions in the interpretation of the Bible, in training a combination of ministerial and academic students at both the master's and doctoral levels. During my first year of teaching the introductory course in Hebrew Bible at CST, my lecture on the book of Isaiah sparked a very interesting discussion of YHWH's commission to Isaiah in Isaiah 6, particularly the instruction to render the people blind, deaf, and undiscerning (Isa. 6.9-10), to enable YHWH to punish generations of Jews so that YHWH's divine sovereignty could be recognized throughout the world. That discussion sparked my work in post-Shoah Jewish biblical theology and my 2008 monograph, *Reading the Hebrew Bible after the Shoah* (Sweeney 2008). The book was also inspired by my reflection on Psalm 121 and the recognition that YHWH's assurances of protection as articulated in the psalm do not always materialize. While recognizing the threat posed by the Shoah and the long history of persecution of Jews, the book argues that we humans have the responsibility to act in the world to complete YHWH's creation of a holy and just world of creation.

I was later also appointed as Professor of Tanakh at the Academy for Jewish Religion California (AJRCA), a trans-denominational rabbinical and cantorial school, where I served for nineteen years training rabbis, cantors, and other Jewish professionals. Together with my Claremont appointment, AJRCA provided the foundations for thinking about the Jewish character of the Bible. Although I had already begun this process while still at Miami, my work at CST and AJRCA enabled me to conceptualize and write my 2012 work about the Tanakh as a Jewish biblical theology, an introduction to the Bible (Sweeney 2012). The work argues that the three-part canonical structure of the Tanakh differs markedly from the four-part canonical structure of the Christian Old Testament. Whereas the Tanakh presents a model of the Torah as an ideal expression of Jewish life; the Prophets as an expression of the disruption of that ideal; and the Writings as an expression of the restoration of that ideal, the Christian Old Testament presents a linear progression of early human history in the Pentateuch; later history in the Historical Books, contemporary concerns in the Wisdom and Poetic Books; and future concerns in the Prophets, which leads to the New Testament and its own analogous structure. The book also argues that the books of the Bible do not represent a single, consistent message; but, like the model of the talmudic Babylonian rabbis' *Kallah* meetings,[1] they present a variety of viewpoints that contribute to the variety of theological perspectives of the Bible as a whole. Such a work then provides instruction on how the ideals expressed in the Torah might be understood, developed, and implemented in the world.

I have also written other books – commentaries on the Prophets, studies on the Torah, and a volume on Jewish mysticism – which points to the continuity between the Bible and later Jewish mysticism, particularly in efforts to discern and implement the presence of the divine in the world (Sweeney 2020). I am currently working on commentaries on Samuel and Jeremiah, and I project commentaries on Exodus and Leviticus as well. All of these works have been stimulated by my early encounter with Psalm 121 and the perception of the psalm as an expression of Hebrew as a living language and Jewish identity, and the issues that arise when the ideals of the psalm are not realized.

Marvin A. Sweeney is Professor of Hebrew Bible at the Claremont School of Theology. He is the author of some seventeen volumes in Prophetic Literature, Narrative Literature, Jewish Mysticism, and other topics. He has previously taught at the Academy for Jewish Religion California; Hebrew Union College–Jewish Institute of Religion, Los Angeles; the University of Miami; Yonsei University; and elsewhere. Dr. Sweeney is Jewish, having become Bar Mitzvah and Confirmed at Temple B'nai Abraham, Decatur, IL. He is a member of Temple Beth Sholom, Salem, OR.

---

1. The rabbinic *Kallah* was the semiannual meeting of the Babylonian Rabbis during the latter talmudic Amoraic period to discuss their understandings of halakhah. They were known for recording multiple opinions, including both the majority and the minority opinions on points of halakhah, in case the minority proved eventually to be correct. Consequently, they were known for recording a variety of opinions that were often in conflict. See Bacher in *The Jewish Encyclopedia*, original edition 1905-6, 7:423; Gilat in *Encyclopedia Judaica*, originally 1972: 10:709–12; Goodblatt 2006: 4:821–39 (esp. 835–6, 837).

References

Bacher, W. (original edition 1905–6), 'Kallah', in I. Singer (ed.), *The Jewish Encyclopedia*, 7:423, New York: KTAV.

Brueggemann, W. and W.H. Bellinger, Jr (2014), *Psalms*, NCBC, Cambridge: Cambridge University Press.

Gilat, Yitzhak Dov (original edition 1972), 'Kallah, Months of', in C. Roth (ed.), *Encyclopedia Judaica*, 10:709–12, Jerusalem: Keter.

Gerstenberger, E.S. (2001), *Psalms, Part 2, and Lamentations*, FOTL 15, Grand Rapids: Eerdmans.

Goodblatt, David (2006), 'The History of the Babylonian Academies', in S.T. Katz (ed.), *The Cambridge HIstory of Judaism, Vol. 4: The Late Roman-Rabbinic Period*, 4:821–39, Cambridge: Cambridge University Press.

Hossfeld, F.L. and E. Zenger (2011), *Psalms 3*, Hermeneia, Minneapolis: Fortress.

Sweeney, M.A. (1988), *Isaiah 1–4 and the Post-Exilic Understanding of the Isaianic Tradition*, BZAW 171, Berlin: W. de Gruyter.

Sweeney, M. A. (1996), *Isaiah 1–39: With an Introduction to Prophetic Literature*, FOTL 16, Grand Rapids: Eerdmans.

Sweeney, M.A. (2001), *King Josiah of Judah: The Lost Messiah of Israel*, Oxford: Oxford University Press.

Sweeney, M.A. (2008), *Reading the Hebrew Bible after the Shoah: Engaging Holocaust Theology*, Minneapolis: Fortress.

Sweeney, M.A. (2012), *Tanak: A Theological and Critical Introduction to the Jewish Bible*, Minneapolis: Fortress.

Sweeney, M.A. (2020), *Jewish Mysticism: From Ancient Times Until Today*, Grand Rapids: Eerdmans.

PSALM 121 AND SYNAGOGUE MUSIC: HOPE IN A MINOR KEY

Helen Leneman

I became a cantor in the 1970s, having been trained as a classical singer (and pianist) and having loved cantorial music since my early childhood. When I was growing up, no one thought a woman could be a cantor, but that changed with the feminist movement. One of my cantorial duties was training children for their *Bar Mitzvah* ceremonies. In the process, I became increasingly intrigued with the biblical narratives I was teaching. I decided to put my love of vocal music and of Bible together and open up a new field within interdisciplinary studies: musical interpretations of biblical narratives. I spent months in the Library of Congress exploring music based on biblical stories, particularly music I could sing. And when I did, I realized how alive these texts became, through the power of music.

This eventually led to a PhD and a succession of books (six to date) on this topic. I occasionally discuss individual song settings in these books, which is what I'm doing here. My goal is always to explain and demonstrate how music can enhance or alter the listener's perception of the sung texts.

It is appropriate to discuss psalms together with music, since the word 'psalm' derives from the Greek *psalmos* meaning 'song sung to a harp'. Its root, *psallein*, means 'to play a stringed instrument'. Psalms today are not often accompanied by a harp, but they are frequently sung with musical accompaniment in synagogues and churches. The great Israeli musicologist and music historian A.Z. Idelsohn wrote that 'the song is the tonal expression of ideas and sentiments' (Idelsohn 1975: 318). Psalms in Hebrew is *Tehillim* (תהילים), which means 'praises', based on the Hebrew root הלל (*hll*), 'praise' (linked to the word Hallelujah, 'praise God').[1]

I will focus on Psalm 121, אשא עיני, *'essa' 'enay* ('I [will] lift up my eyes'), which is often sung in synagogues. Two popular musical renditions pop immediately into my head (by Shlomo Carlebach and Gershon Ephros), particularly the strong contrast in mood between the two settings. Carlebach's tune is upbeat and

---

1. Transliteration of Hebrew words in this article is in the General Purpose (popular) transliteration method.

folklike, while Ephros's version is more pleading and meditative. Yet, both are set in a minor key: it would take a lot of searching to find a cantorial or synagogue melody in a bright major key! Very early in my cantorial career I was studying voice in Los Angeles. My teacher was not Jewish, but I asked her for help with my cantorial music, which poses vocal challenges that are different than opera or art song. After hearing a few melodies, she asked: 'Is *all* Jewish music in the minor key?' I will come back to this point.

This essay is more personal than academic. Nonetheless, a few brief comments from Robert Alter bring out highlights of this psalm. He points out the description of God in v. 2 as maker of heaven and earth. All the subsequent verses specify what God's help means: he is the guardian of Israel, your shade to protect you, day and night, from evil. Alter points out that the somewhat formulaic ending, 'The Lord will guard your going and coming now and forevermore' (v. 8)[2] actually traces an arc back to v. 2, 'maker of heaven and earth', tying together the eternity that has passed since creation and the eternity that lies ahead. Alter comments that the psalm suggests 'a kind of luminous immediacy in the apprehension of the world through the eyes of faith' (Alter 1990: 254-55).

It has generally been assumed that the 'lifting of the eyes' that opens this psalm refers to looking up to the sanctuary, as sanctuaries were usually built on hills. At the same time, the poet was raising his eyes to the God of Israel for whom the temple on Mount Zion was built. In v. 5 God is referred to as 'your guardian…and protector at your right hand'.

י-הוה שמרך י-הוה צלך על יד ימינך.

This alludes to a trial, in which the accused's advocate or defender would stand at his or her right hand. The root שמר *Qal* (*shmr*), meaning 'to guard', or the noun derived from the root ('guardian'), is repeated six times in the short psalm, clearly indicating the poet's confidence in God as the people's guardian.

The Music

One of the most known and popular musical versions of Psalm 121, a congregational tune, is by Shlomo Carlebach (1925-1994).[3] His setting of *'essaʽ 'enay* was one of his earliest hits, though he apparently did not intend it for worship services. Many of Carlebach's songs were winners in the Chassidic Song Festival, which originated in Israel and was introduced in the US in 1971.[4] Carlebach was one of the first Orthodox singer-songwriters to have this kind of success. In musicologist

---

2. Translations of the Hebrew text are from the JPS, with some adaptations.

3. For Carlebach's life and work see for instance https://www.jewage.org/wiki/ru/Article:Shlomo%20Carlebach%20-%20Biography?embedded=true&textonly=1.

4. Some information about the festival at https://www.latimes.com/archives/la-xpm-1986-12-08-ca-1798-story.html.

Marsha Edelman's words, his songs were popular for 'their short melodies and easy lyrics'.[5] These catchy tunes appealed to synagogues that wanted more congregational participation.

Carlebach's version of *'essa' 'enay* is very short, including only the first two verses of the psalm. The tempo is marked 'Lively' and the tune has a catchy rhythm. In spite of these features, the tune begins in the minor key. Verse 2 has a more flowing melody and could be sung in a major key. Since the song is written for guitar accompaniment, only chords are indicated in the music. If the interpreter were to alter the chords of the second half, the entire tune could be sung in a minor key. But even if it were, the musical message remains one of affirmation and triumph.

The message of the psalm seems hopeful: the psalmist turns his eyes to the mountains, expecting to find help from God. A positive message would normally be supported by upbeat music, in a major key. But Jewish music does not follow that formula. For those familiar with synagogue services: think about the *Etz Chaim* ('Tree of Life') song, which the Ashkenazi congregation sings as the Torah is returned to the ark.[6] The most commonly sung melody is in the minor key, while we are singing about the Torah being the tree of life – not a sad concept. This apparent contradiction is found everywhere in Jewish music.

The second song I'm discussing is by Gershon Ephros (1890–1978) and is unabashedly a pleading melody from the start, in a minor key. It is not meant as a sing-along, but could be either a cantorial solo, a solo alternating with choir, or choral. The full text of Psalm 121 is set.

Ephros was born in Poland. His father died when he was ten, and he moved to live with his grandfather, a cantor. He received his first musical training in his grandfather's choir, traveling and performing in the countryside. In 1909, he immigrated to Palestine, where he studied *chazzanut* (cantorial music) and harmony with Idelsohn while working as Idelsohn's choir director. In 1911, he moved to the US, where he continued his studies. He served as cantor of several congregations over his lifetime, as well as composing and researching cantorial music. He was a founder and faculty member of the Hebrew Union College School of Cantorial Music.[7]

---

5. https://www.myjewishlearning.com/article/shlomo-carlebach/; accessed 10 May 2022. In the years after Carlebach's death in 1994, numerous women came forward to allege that he sexually assaulted them. These allegations first appeared in a 1998 article in *Lilith*, the Jewish feminist magazine (Blustain in the 9 March 1998 issue), and have continued to surface. Many synagogues no longer include his music.

6. See, for instance, https://www.zemirotdatabase.org/view_song.php?id=206.

7. Ephros's main publication is his *Cantorial Anthology* in five volumes (1929–57), a practical collection of older and more recent works (in 1957) for all the synagogue services of the year (The Jewish Music Center, https://jewish-music.huji.ac.il/content/gershon-ephros#:~:text=Cantor%20and%20composer.,and%20performing%20in%20the%20countryside; (accessed May 2022).

Ephros's version of *'essa' 'enay* differs in every way from Carlebach's and is one of my favorite versions. Cantorial music, though found in published anthologies, is traditionally often handed on from one cantor to another. These are usually copied or photocopied pages (today, it's all digital), sometimes with scribbled remarks indicating whether the piece is to be sung by a soloist or a choir. Keys are never fixed, since much of this music is sung unaccompanied.

The version of Ephros's *'essa' 'enay* handed down to me many decades ago is an 'arrangement', by an anonymous arranger (lost in the back and forth between cantors). No chords are indicated, except those written in by the accompanist; they are not necessarily the harmonies Ephros intended. The arranger has turned the song into a very effective 'conversation' between the cantor and choir. The opening rising and falling melody (v. 1) is sung by the cantor:

אשא עיני אל ההרים מאין יבוא עזרי

I lift up my eyes to the hills – from where will my help come?

The choir, almost as if responding to the question (in 1b), sings v. 2 in a kind of musical mirror image, beginning with a descent before ascending:

עזרי מעם י-הוה עשה שמים וארץ

My Help comes from the Lord, maker of heaven and earth

The last note of their response, *wa-'aretz* ('and earth'), is sustained.

The cantor continues with vv. 3 and 4, in variations of the original opening melody. There are subtle changes, though: on the word *raglecha* ('your foot') in v. 3a (אל יתן למוט רגלך, 'He will not let your foot be moved') the key abruptly shifts into major and remains in a major key through the first half of v. 4. After the words *velo' yishan* ('nor sleeps'):

הנה לא ינום ולא יישן שומר ישראל

The guardian of Israel neither slumbers nor sleeps

there is a rest – as if the poet is catching his breath – before the verse is concluded in the original minor key. The choir re-enters singing vv. 5 and 6 to the opening melody. A rest appears again as before, this time after *lo' yakekha* ('will not strike you') in v. 6.

יומם השמש לא יככך וירח בלילה

By day the sun shall not strike you nor the moon by night

As earlier, the choir's final note, on *ba-laylah* ('by night') is sustained.

The cantor sings v. 7 to the same melody as v. 3, including the shift to a major key in the middle. The closing line of the psalm, 'now and forever', is sung in unison by the cantor and choir.

י-הוה ישמר צאתך ובואך מעתה ועד עולם

The Lord will guard your going and coming now and forever

Musically, this is a strong affirmation of the text's message of faith.

The musical setting, with its rising and falling phrases, enhances the expression of hope shadowed by fear and uncertainty expressed in the psalm text. There is always an element of these mixed feelings in Jewish music, because of the experience of the Jewish people over thousands of years. This may be why the major key never triumphs completely over the minor.

A Different Example

And now for a completely different interpretation of Psalm 121, from the world of classical music. Antonin Dvořák's (1841–1904) version is part of his set of *Biblical Songs*. He wrote these settings of ten psalms for voice and piano in 1894, then orchestrated the first five the next year. They were written in Czech, English and German. The manuscript was lost until 1914, when a Czech conductor orchestrated the rest of the songs.[8] The singer is German baritone Christian Gerhaher, who sings in Czech. (There is a recording [2004] of the Royal Concertgebouw Orchestra of Christian Gerhaher singing the psalm, conducted by Nikolaus Harnoncourt; I translated a few of these songs into Hebrew for a recital that I gave.)

This fascinating setting of Psalm 121 (only vv. 1-4 in this case) opens with a few quick chords. The first verse is sung *a capella* and predominantly in intervals of open fifths, a mysterious and modal sound (keys that differ from the basic major and minor). The same orchestral chords are heard again, very softly. Verse 2 is sung to a strumming harp accompaniment – very appropriate for a psalm. The key switches suddenly to minor at v. 3, followed by several modulations leading to a bright, major closing section with a triumphant, though very soft conclusion.

My second favorite psalm would be, for musical reasons, Psalm 23. This is because I have heard and sung many beautiful, moving, heartbreaking renditions of this psalm in synagogue services all my life. Such settings are a prime example of music's ability to transcend text and move the listener to experience greater depths of emotion than words alone ever elicit. The use of the minor key to express – and elicit – both hope and grief in Jewish music is found in these, and other psalm settings.

---

8. See also https://www.antonin-dvorak.cz/en/work/biblical-songs/.

Dr. Helen Leneman is a Bible scholar and cantor, and combines her two professional loves – music and Bible – in her scholarly work. Originally from the US, she currently lives in London, UK.

References

Alter, Robert (1990), *The Literary Guide to the Bible*, Cambridge, MA: Harvard University Press.

Blustain, Sarah (1998), 'Rabbi Shlomo Caelebach's Shadow Side', https://lilith.org/articles/rabbi-shlomo-carlebachs-shadow-side/.

Ephros, Gershon (1929–57 and later editions), *Cantorial Anthology of Traditional and Modern Synagogue Music*. 5 volumes (The Jewish Music Center, https://jewish-music.huji.ac.il/content/gershon-ephros#:~:text=Cantor%20and%20composer.,and%20performing%20in%20the%20countryside, accessed May 2022).

Idelsohn, A.Z. (1975), *Jewish Music*, New York: Magnes.

PSALM 121
WHY THIS PSALM IS POPULAR IN CONTEMPORARY ISRAEL*

Ora Brison

1. Introduction

In the last decades, we have witnessed a significant increase of 'old-new' Jewish cultural-social-spiritual trends among the traditional (*masoretic*) and non-religious majority of the population in contemporary Israel. Among them are various 'Return to Judaism' or the 'Return to the Religious Fold', the חזרה בתשובה (*chazarah be-teshuvah*) movements.[1] The designation 'Return to Judaism' means the transition from a secular/non-religious lifestyle to a Jewish orthodox-conservative religious lifestyle. Such widespread trends also include the revival of hagiolatry worship, pilgrimages to holy men's graves, and visits to sanctuaries of 'ancient forefathers' (Bilu 1991). There is also a growing interest in and popularity of consulting Kabbalah specialists, mediums, healers, astrologers, and spiritual gurus. Additional trends are expressed in the renewal of traditional rituals such as the ḥenna dye (pre-wedding ceremonies)[2] and the 'dough (*challah*) offering'[3] ceremonies (a ritualistic process of baking bread).[4] The tendency toward mysticism and traditional rituals is understandable in the times of uncertainty and danger we live in. The instability in the lives of individuals and communities has

---

* This essay is expanded from a paper presented at the SBL International Meeting in Berlin in July 2017. Special appreciation and thanks to my mentor Athalya Brenner-Idan for her inspiration, guidance and friendship.

1. Beit-Hallahmi 1992: 55.

2. http://www.myjewishlearning.com/jewish-and/embracing-a-jewish-henna-wedding-tradition/.

3. The name חלה, *challah* comes from the commandment known as הפרשת חלה, *hafrashat challah* – 'separation of a loaf' [of dough] as a cultic donation based on the commandment in Num. 15.20.

4. Brison 2018.

a major effect on people's need to seek divine guardianship and protection: this occurs not only in Israel but is a worldwide phenomenon.

The most noticeable phenomenon of these spiritual trends is that of individuals quietly reciting psalms in public places. This pervasive trend is practiced in Israel by men and women, young and old, healthy and sick, non-religious, traditional and ultraorthodox, in liturgical and religious contexts, and even more in non-religious circumstances. The reciting of psalms as part of the daily routine has become a significant occurrence for many people in Israel. We witness this in public transportation, municipal offices, hospitals, gardens, almost everywhere. Psalm 121, אשא עיני אל ההרים, 'I lift up my eyes to the hills',[5] is one of the most frequently recited psalms in Israel and possibly the most popular. My aim here is to understand its particular appeal, popularity, and *Sitz im Leben* in the context of the current non-religious Israeli spiritual culture.

2. *The Popular Status of the Psalms*

The universal themes/motifs of hope, protection, compassion, redemption, and peace the book of Psalms presents appeal to most people around the world.[6] The psalms have significance and liturgical standing for various Christian denominations; and references to certain psalms are also found in the Qur'an and are well-known in the Islamic world. In Israel, the reciting of psalms has acquired the special status of unique spiritual standing and significance, drawing non-religious people to regard this practice as a spiritual, cultural alternative to full observance. Notably, the apotropaic qualities attributed to various psalms and the book of Psalms have attained the status of a sacred object; hence, carrying, holding, and touching the printed book is believed to bring divine blessings and protection. This popularity explains why the book sells in a compact, even mini, format as a volume separate from the rest of the Hebrew Bible at most bookstores.

3. *Psalm 121 – 'I lift up my eyes to the hills'*

Psalm 121 is one of the fifteen-psalm 'Songs of Ascents' collection, interpreted as a pilgrimage song, a blessing hymn, or a farewell liturgy (Westermann 1980: 102; Limburg 1985: 183–84).[7] The hymn describes the setting out on a dangerous, unsafe journey (either actual or metaphorical). Three participants are referred to in the text: the psalmist, the speaker, and God. The hymn is short, intense, and consists of eight verses divided into three parts: vv. 1-2; vv. 3-6; and vv. 7-8. The first part is constructed as a monologue between the psalmist and his inner voice. The psalmist describes his distress and dire situation: 'I lift up my eyes to

---

5. English Bible quotations are from the NRSV.

6. On the book of Psalms in general see Dahood 1966–70; Westermann 1980; Day 1990; Brueggemann 1995; Allen 2002.

7. And cf. also Barker 1995: 163–81; Willems 1998: 24–33, 427–37.

the hills…' This dramatic expression emphasizes his loneliness and anxiety. But it also reminds him of where his help and support would come from. Hence, he makes a rhetorical request for help: 'from where will my help come?' to which he replies: 'My help comes from the Lord.' The second part of the psalm is a dialogue between the psalmist and the speaker-in-the-text. It could be a dialogue between an individual and a choir, between a voice that poses questions and a voice that responds. The speaker tries to calm the psalmist's fears and convince him of divine assistance. He then introduces the main themes/motifs of the Psalms in general and the Songs of Ascents in particular. The first theme is the greatness of God, manifest in the Creation and His control over the cosmos and time: 'The Lord, who made heaven and earth (v. 2); The sun shall not strike you by day, nor the moon by night (v. 6); …from this time on and forevermore (v. 8).'

Next comes the second theme, one of the most central motifs of the book: God's providence and his continuous divine protection and guardianship. This theme is expressed in a series of short, rhythmic expressions repeating the root שמר *Qal*, 'keep, guard'. The multiple repetitions make these verses sound like an apotropaic formula or mantra: 'He who *keeps* you (v. 3); He who *keeps* Israel (v. 4); The Lord is your *keeper* (v. 5); The Lord will *keep* you; he will *keep* your life (v. 7); The Lord will *keep* your going (v. 8).' The speaker assures the psalmist of God's protection in threatening situations. The third theme is the message of faith: 'My help comes from the Lord…' The last part (vv. 7-8) is an assurance of blessing for the individual believer and the community (Leibreich 1955: 33–36; Weiner 2020: 1–8). The dominant motif throughout the psalm is the proximity and personal relations between God and the psalmist. This is expressed by the first person singular that the psalmist uses to address God, and by the second person singular the speaker describes these relations. Weiss summarizes this motif thus: 'The uniqueness of the book of Psalms is that while many biblical books transmit theological and religious messages through human historiography, with a view from God to man, the Book of Psalms expresses man's relationship to God' (Weiss 2001: 14).

The emphasis on the motif of God's protection and the multiple repetitions of the key verb 'keep/guard' (שמר) echoes the Priestly Blessing (Num. 6.24-26). Liebreich (1955: 33–36) argues that the fifteen Songs of Ascents were intentionally chosen to accord with the fifteen words of the priestly blessing. He suggests that the four expressions used in the Blessing, namely that God,

יברכך
Will bless you
וישמרך
Will keep you
יאר…פניו אליך ויחנך
Will be gracious to you
וישם לך שלום
And will give you peace

occur throughout the Songs of Ascents and that these psalms are, in fact, commentaries on these words. The similarity in concept and at times terms (God's care and guardship) contributes to the psalm's sacred status and its universal appeal. Psalm 121 is one of the most recurrent psalms in Jewish liturgy, recited every weekday in the afternoon prayers, in the Shabbat (Saturday) and Holy Days prayers. Some of its verses are frequently recited on religious cultic occasions accompanying the Jewish individual from cradle to death.[8]

4. *Psalm 121 in Contemporary Israeli Poetry and Music*

Psalm 121 has been set to liturgical music and sung by well-known cantors and singers.[9] However, as noted, its presence reaches far beyond liturgy into the collective culture and daily life. Many Israeli poets wrote poems inspired by it.[10] It has also been set to different tunes and performed by trendy pop singers.[11] It is played regularly on all radio and television stations, and is part of the songs constantly performed at private concerts and huge shows.[12]

5. *Concluding Remarks*

Psalm 121 offers an example presenting, illuminating, and explaining the tremendous magical appeal and universal popularity retained by the book of Psalms in modern times worldwide, particularly in contemporary Israel. Reciting psalms could be part of any individual or community's routine and might apply to every context of their lives.

Psalm 121 is a plea and prayer of an individual embarking on an unknown journey. Its main appeal is the motif of God as the keeper and guardian of humanity. The meta-message that individual and community alike can rely on God for protection and guidance is a common thread through the psalm. The needs of the psalmist are unclear and add to the appeal of the psalm. Those reciting or singing it can interpret the psalmist's journey as a metaphor for their own life's journey, beyond a specific time and place. The verbal repetitions of words and expressions that promise God's protection support individuals in finding answers to their existential questions and meaning. The positive feelings

---

8. On psalms in the Jewish Prayer Book see Steinzaltz 2002; Wieder 1998: 352–57.

9. See Helen Leneman's essay in this volume, pp. 180–85.

10. A sample, for readers of contemporary Hebrew, is to be found at Shaked 2005: 315–33.

11. A sample is available for listening on https://shirlamaalot.wixsite.com/maalot.

12. A collection of Ps. 121 performances in contemporary Israel can be found and listened to on https://jewishstandard.timesofisrael.com/watch-the-ancient-psalm-that-became-an-israeli-classic/ (accessed January 2023). Other, mostly older recordings and including traditional, at the National Library of Israel site, https://www.nli.org.il/he/items/NNL_MUSIC_AL003977394/NLI (accessed January 2023).

and thoughts resulting from repeating Psalm 121 enable a process of consciousness transformation: a transition from anxiety, distress, and despair to positive thinking, courage, and hope. The psalm's messages are relevant to and suitable for the life of the individual and society today as when it was written/composed, contributing to its popularity in today's Israel and Judaism, especially during these strange and difficult times. A ray of hope – maybe.

My second option would have been Psalm 45: a royal wedding psalm no doubt, in which the bride is called upon to remain more or less cloistered (Heb. v. 14a; Eng. 13a) and obedient to her husband.[13] Much can be said about the wedding envisaged here, and the woman's status in the marriage this psalm celebrates.

Dr. Ora Brison is an independent scholar living in Tel Aviv. Her main fields of interest are biblical studies and Ancient Near Eastern Literature, to which she came from general Religion.

References

Allen, Leslie C. (2002), *Psalms 101–150*, WBC 21, Nashville: Thomas Nelson, rev. edn.
Barker, David G. (1995), '"The Lord Watches over You": A Pilgrimage Reading of Psalm 121', *Bibliotheca Sacra* 152: 163–81.
Beit-Hallahmi, Benjamin (1992), *Despair and Deliverance: Private Salvation in Contemporary Israel*, Albany: State University of New York Press.
Bilu, Yoram (1991), 'Personal Motivation and Social Meaning in the Revival of Hagiolatric Tradition among Moroccan Jews in Israel', in Z. Sobel and B. Bei-Hallahmi (eds), *Tradition, Innovation, Conflict: Jewishness and Judaism in Contemporary Israel*, 47–69, SUNY Series in Israeli Studies, Albany: State University of New York Press.
Brison, Ora (2018), 'Women's Banquets and Gatherings in Text and Context: The Queens-Banquets in Esther and Contemporary Women-Only Israeli/Jewish Ceremonies', in A. Brenner-Idan *et al.* (eds.), *The Five Scrolls*, 189–209, Texts@Contexts 6, London: Bloomsbury T&T Clark.
Brueggemann, Walter (1995), *The Psalms: The Life of Faith*, Minneapolis: Fortress.
Crow, Loren D. (1996), *The Songs of Ascents (Psalms 120–134): Their Place in Israelite History and Religion*, Atlanta: Scholars Press.
Dahood, Mitchell, SJ (1966–70), *Psalms III, 101–150*, AB 17A, Garden City: Doubleday.
Day, John (1990), *Psalms*, Sheffield: Sheffield Academic.
Liebreich, Leon J. (1955), 'The Songs of Ascents and the Priestly Blessing', *JBL* 74: 33–36.
Limburg, James (1985), 'Psalm 121: A Psalm of Sojourners', *Word & World* 5: 180–87.
Morgenstern, Julius, (1939), 'Psalm 121', *JBL* 58: 311–23.
Shaked, Malka (2005), לנצח אנגנך – *I'll Play You Forever: The Bible in Modern Hebrew Poetry, An Anthology*, Tel Aviv: Miskal [Heb.].

---

13. The Hebrew text here is difficult grammatically, and modern translations (such as the JPS and NRSV) sidestep the issue and meaning. However, the KJV ('The King's daughter is glorious within') and NIV ('All glorious is the princess within her chamber') capture the sense of the Hebrew text.

Simon, Uriel (1991), *Four Approaches to the Book of Psalms: From Saadiah Gaon to Abraham Ibn Ezra*, trans. from the Hebrew by Lenn J. Schramm, Albany: State University of New York Press.
Steinsaltz, Adin (2002), *A Guide to Jewish Prayer*, Tel Aviv: Schocken.
Weiss, Meir (2001), *Ideas and Beliefs in the Book of Psalms*, Jerusalem: Bialik Institute [Heb.].
Weiner, Michael (2020), 'Psalm 121: Of Pilgrims, Perils, and a Personal God', https://thelehrhaus.com/scholarship/psalm-121-of-pilgrims-perils-and-a-personal-god/
Westermann, Claus (1980), *The Psalms: Structure, Content and Message*, trans. Ralph D. Gehrke, Minneapolis: Augsburg Publishing House.
Wieder, Naphtali (1998), 'The Fifteen "Songs of the Ascents" and Psalm 119: The Division of Their Reading for the Seven Days of the Week (in the Prayer Customs of the Karaites and in Rabbinic Judaism)', in *The Formation of Jewish Liturgy in the East and the West: A Collection of Essays*, Vol. 1, 352–57, Jerusalem: Ben-Zvi Institute [Heb.].
Willems, Bernd (1998), *Jahwe: ein schlummernder Beschützer? Zur Exegese und zum theologischen Verständnis von Psalm 121*, Biblisch-theologische Studien 35, Neukirchen-Vluyn: Neukirchener Verlag.

PSALM 123
THE 'FLOW' OF SEEING

Monica Jyotsna Melanchton

This short psalm and its significance came to my notice quite recently when it appeared as a lectionary reading. Identified as a prayer in the sequence of the Songs of Ascent (Ps. 120–134), the many references to eyes and the power of seeing captured my attention and reminded me of the many allusions to divine 'eyes' and 'seeing' within the Hindu and Dalit traditions and religious iconography. Equally significant within these traditions is the practice of pilgrimage. In what follows, I look at this Hebrew psalm considering the significance of 'eyes' and 'seeing' or '*darshan*' (the auspicious sight of the deity) in the faith of these communities.

The eyes are a 'mirror to the soul' of an individual and we learn how to gauge an individual's response to us by watching the eyes. Eyes are needed for effective communication. The inability to look at another in the eyes signals a breach in the relationship. The Deity has eyes too. Eyes animate the image/idol; if the Divine is present, the Divine sees. Hence eyes are a distinct feature of both Hindu and Dalit gods, demonstrated in the names of several goddesses – composite with the Sanskrit *akshi*, meaning 'eyes'. *Meenakshi* (fish-eyed), *Kamakshi* (Loving eyes), *Visalakshi* (large eyed), *Neelayathakshi* (blue eyed), *Rudrakshi* (eyes of Lord Shiva), *Indrakshi* (beautiful eyes) are some, to name a few. Male gods in Hindu iconography are also represented with large eyes, often disproportionate to the size of the icon, representing the all-seeing Supreme Truth, the one who is all seeing, the 'eternal witness', who can see all that the devotee says and does. The eyes of the deity are meant to evoke both consolation and fear,[1] and the glance of the deity can be beneficent or destructive. A deity, male or female, is therefore understood to favor a devotee with their eyes; they can pass on their blessings and powers through the eyes, even if by a sidewards glance, known as *Nayana* (eyes) *Deeksha* (looking). The Hindu epics witness to ardent devotees being blessed with

1. Rajendran 2017 (https://www.hindu-blog.com/2017/09/why-do-idols-of-certain-hindu-gods-have.html) (accessed 26 August 2022)

the vision/eyes or *darshan* of the Deity.² Divine sight 'involves aesthetic and moral appreciation, a transfer of authority, an acknowledgement of moral uprightness, and a judgment fitting the crime' (Howell 2013: 174).

'Eyes' are mentioned four times in the first two verses of this psalm. They all refer to the eyes of the psalmist who is looking directly at God –

To you, I raise my eyes, You, who are enthroned in the heavens (v. 1).³

Voiced in the first person singular, this line acknowledges the sovereignty and majesty of YWHW enthroned in the heavens to whom the worshipper is looking as he/she ascends the hill to the temple, the abode of the presence of God. Embedded in this declaration of action is also the belief that YHWH has eyes and is looking down and seeing. The psalm does not explicitly declare that God has eyes or sees. But there are numerous texts within the Hebrew Bible that testify to YHWH as a God with eyes and who sees,⁴ the most familiar being Gen. 16.13:

And she called the name of YHWH, the One Who spoke to her, 'You are a God Who Sees', for she said, 'Indeed here, I have truly seen, just as the One Who sees me'.⁵

Human sight, but also Divine seeing, is central to our understanding of this psalm.

The psalmist is spurred on by the faith that one is benefitted by going on a pilgrimage, to see the deity but also to be seen by the deity. What the psalmist is therefore seeking is a visual interaction with the deity based on an understanding of 'seeing' as an effusive, continuous 'flow',⁶ a coherent experience of God that brings the one seeing and the one being seen (both the worshipper and God are both seeing and being seen) into genuine, meaningful and intimate contact

---

2. For example, in one of the variations of the *Ramayana* there is the story of Shabari, of a disadvantaged caste group, an ardent and faithful devotee who is blessed by a *darshan* of Lord Rama. She prepares over days and awaits the arrival of Lord Rama along with many others. She decides to host Rama with an offering of berries. She would pick the berries and taste each of them to keep the best tasting ones for the Deity. When Lord Rama does come, he chooses to visit Shabari who offers hospitality and acknowledges that she has been blessed by his compassionate regard. Rama blesses her with his *darshan* (the auspicious sight of the deity). See Raman 2020, https://www.thehindubusinessline.com/blink/explore/shabari-of-ramayana-the-woman-who-broke-norms/article32810973.ece (accessed 28 August 2022).

3. My translation, inspired by the JPS 2003.

4. Also Gen. 6.8; 29.31-32; Exod. 4.31; 1 Sam. 16.7; Hab. 1.13; Ps. 32.8; Prov. 15.3; Job 34.21; 1 Pet. 3.12.

5. Translation adapted from the translation by Howell 2013: 192.

6. The concept of 'flow', as a defining characteristic of broadcast television, has been described as the continuous experience of watching TV by British cultural historian Raymond Williams (2003).

and relationship. Seeing, therefore, be it by the Divine or by the worshipper, is an outward-reaching process that connects the one seeing with the one being seen. The worshipper raises their eyes to YHWH, and this has been identified as 'expectant' (Goldingay 2008: 471), one of 'entreaty and dependence' (Mays 1994: 395), a gesture of prayer (Alter 2007: 441), of yearning and longing (Kraus 1989: 122). I agree that 'raising eyes to God' is inclusive of all that, but I also suggest that the worshipper is not a *passive* recipient but an active participant in this exchange/interaction, which begins with the journey to the abode of God. That journey is intentional and with purpose. The worshipper is hopeful; and is enabled to absorb, through the eyes and seeing, something of the attributes, the energy/power of the Divine, as well as God's own power of sight/seeing.

Using the first-person plural, the psalmist uses a double simile to describe the relation between the devotee and the Divine:

> As the eyes of servants look to the hand of their master, as the eyes of a maid to the hand of her mistress, so our eyes look to the LORD our God, until God has mercy upon us. (v. 2)[7]

A word picture is painted of how the psalmist sees the community's relationship to YHWH – a master–servant, slave–mistress relationship, a familiar construct, inclusive of men and women. The relationship is hierarchical, one of total subservience, and absolute dependence on the favor, goodness, graciousness, and mercy of the master/mistress. The worshipper looks to God in a similar vein, anxious to see signs of grace/pity,[8] which is seen as appropriate to the situation and the posture of prayer (Allen 1987: 217). The plea for attention and mercy is clear.

The possible harshness of this hierarchical relationship is softened by suggesting that this was part of the covenantal relationship – 'slaves before their Divine master' (Allen 1987: 217), and that it was a relationship of 'mutual commitment' (Goldingay 2008: 472), awaiting 'the generous hand of their master' (Kraus 1989: 122). The reader's social location has some impact on how these master–slave similes are received. They are troublesome in the Indian context of the hierarchical caste structure and need some explanation. The relationship between a Dalit and a dominant caste landlord/master in this servant–master relationship is fraught with oppressive elements. Caste regulations do not allow Dalit servants to enter the house of an upper caste household. Dalits are used for duties outside the house. 'Slaves from the upper caste were clearly differentiated from Dalit slaves.'[9] Slaves allowed/used within the home were those drawn from the same caste as that of the master/mistress. For example, *Vellala* (a caste group in South

---

7. Translation inspired by the RSV.
8. The LXX translates the Hebrew here, שיחננו (from *ḥānan*) as 'pity'.
9. Kolappan 2017, see https://www.thehindu.com/news/national/tamil-nadu/once-dalits-were-landowners-vellalas-slaves/article18405606.ece (accessed 28 August 2022).

India) women slaves, known as *vellatis*, were used for housekeeping and to serve their *Vellala* mistresses (Koppalan 2017). Those were women who had been sold due to poverty or because they had contravened caste rules. However, slaves were completely under the subjugation of their owners; and the relationship between these slaves and masters/mistresses is complex, with harsh and violent penalties for resistance. There was no mutuality of obligations here or choice for the slaves, who were completely at the mercy of the owners.

From a dominant caste perspective, submitting oneself to a higher Divine power in the likeness of a master–slave relationship is construed as a pious and humble posture, a sign of complete submission to God, a high form of faith. Dalits, on the other hand, know what this is all about. They too espouse this hierarchical relationship with the Divine, but they replace the earthly master with an alternate understanding of God as master/mistress. They seek to resist the theology of the powerful and use their theological senses, which enable them to picture God as being on the side of the powerless, kind, just, merciful, and gracious. They also believe that YHWH will curse those who curse them (Gen. 12.3), for the look of the Divine is not always beneficent, merciful, or compassionate. It can also be destructive.

The oppressed worshippers approach God and look up with the hope that God will see them and show *mercy and compassion*, intervene, and bring to fruition the promise made in Genesis 12. I take inspiration for this interpretation from the following verses of Psalm 123:

> Have mercy on us YHWH, have mercy on us, for we have had more than enough of contempt. Long enough have we endured the scorn of the complacent, the contempt of the haughty. (vv. 3-4, JPS)

The contempt that the psalmist has endured is understood to be the scorn and disdain of imperial colonizers under whose control the Israelites were during the exile, and this makes sense (Allen 1987: 216; Kraus 1989: 122). The Dalit would understand this as the contempt that comes of being born a Dalit and considered polluting, unclean, untouchable, sinful, marginalized and oppressed: a centuries-long contempt that has denied them their humanity and dignity and life in its fullness. They have reached breaking point, since they are now saturated in it.

They have come to YHWH for help. In the presence of God and the visual interaction, the beauty, the splendor, and the majesty of YHWH enthroned, YHWH's abode, the temple, transcend everything that has been hitherto seen and experienced. Also implicit in this interaction is the worshippers' belief that they will undergo transformation, a change in how they perceive of themselves, their experience, the world around them and the Divine.

In Valmiki's autobiography, *Joothan* (2003), he narrates an incident in which his mother, a menial worker in the home of an upper caste landlord, is given a basketful of used banana leaf plates after a wedding feast. She and her children were supposedly expected to eat the scraps of food left on these leaves. She is further insulted when she makes a request to the landlord for fresh food for herself and her children. Valmiki writes, 'That night the mother goddess Durga[10] entered my mother's eyes. It was the first time that I saw my mother get so angry. She emptied the basket...my mother had confronted him like a lioness. Without being afraid.'[11]

The worshippers, perhaps slaves and servants, are seeking something that is not easily found or experienced in their world, namely compassion/mercy/grace (Mays 1994: 395) and justice. They do believe that YHWH, in all of YHWH's power and majesty, functions first and foremost from a place of grace and compassion and not violent power. Through their upward looking eyes, they seek to absorb something of what their God, YHWH, represents, empowering them to cope with the onslaught of contempt in all its varied and painful facets. They hope therefore that, in the return gaze of this gracious God, they will be blessed by a grace that will equip the worshipper with the power to resist and reject the contempt and scorn of the haughty and the complacent.

The Psalter has been tamed and domesticated, at least within the communities that I represent, and I do not necessarily see the justice and injustice potential within the psalms. I am drawn to the psalms that are considered nondescript, not necessarily popular, or seem uninteresting on the surface – and discovered within them a fascinating and powerful, radical, and revolutionary message when carefully and contextually read. Among the many psalms that I like, and those that speak forcefully to the experiences of women, is Psalm 140, which has stood out for me as one that speaks passionately when placed on the lips of abused and raped women (Melanchton 2014).

Monica Jyotsna Melanchthon is Associate Professor, Hebrew Bible/Old Testament Studies at the Pilgrim Theological College, University of Divinity, in Melbourne, Australia. She has also taught at the Gurukul Lutheran Theological College in Chennai, India

References

Allen, Leslie C. (1987), *Psalms 101–150*, WBC 21, Waco: Word.
Alter, Robert (2007), *The Book of Psalms: A Translation with Commentary*, New York: W.W. Norton.
Goldingay, John (2008), *Psalms 90–150*, Grand Rapids: Baker Academic.
Howell, Brian C. (2013), *In the Eyes of God: A Metaphorical Approach to Biblical Anthropomorphic Language*, London: The Lutterworth Press, James Clarke & Co.

---

10. *Durga*, a principal form of feminine energy (*Shakti*), the power of nature, the power that enables all creatures to exist, to feel, think, act and react, who triumphs over all who attempt to subjugate her.
11. Valmiki 2003: 12 (Kindle Edition).

Kolappan, B. (2017), 'When Dalits were also Landowners and Vellalas were slaves,' *The Hindu* (Chennai, 8 May 2017), https://www.thehindu.com/news/national/tamil-nadu/once-dalits-were-landowners-vellalas-slaves/article18405606.ece (accessed 28 August 2022).

Kraus, Hans-Joakim (1989), *Psalms: 60–150*, trans. Hilton C. Oswald, Minneapolis: Augsburg Fortress.

Mays, James L. (1994), *Psalms: A Commentary for Teaching and Preaching*, Interpretation, Louisville: John Knox.

Melanchthon, Monica Jyotsna (2014), '"Protect me from those who are violent!" – Psalm 140: A Cry for Justice, A Song of Hope', in Kenneth Mtata, Karl-Wilhelm Niebuhr and Miriam Rose (eds), *Singing the Songs of the Lord in Foreign Lands: Psalms in Contemporary Lutheran Interpretation*, 33–58. LWF Documentation Series (59/2014), Leipzig: Evangelische Verlagsanstalt (EVA).

Rajendran, Abilash (2017), 'Why Do Idols of Certain Hindu Gods have Big Eyes?', *Hindu Blog* (September 2017), https://www.hindu-blog.com/2017/09/why-do-idols-of-certain-hindu-gods-have.html.

Raman, Ratna (2020), 'Shabari of Ramayana: The Woman who Broke Norms', *The Hindu: Business Line* (9 October 2020), https://www.thehindubusinessline.com/blink/explore/shabari-of-ramayana-the-woman-who-broke-norms/article32810973.ece (accessed 28 August 2022).

Valmiki, Omprakash (2003), *Joothan: An Untouchable's Life,* trans. Arun Prabha Mukherjee, New York: Columbia University Press.

Williams, Raymond (2003), *Television: Technology and Cultural Form*, London: Routledge.

PSALM 126
WEEPING, REAPING, AND DINING

Adele Reinhartz

I have chosen to write about Psalm 126, the seventh of fifteen so-called Songs of Ascent included in the biblical book of Psalms. My choice is not based on a thorough reading of the entire book of psalms and careful weighing of criteria and considerations. Rather, it is based on a deep familiarity engendered by sheer repetition. For the past four decades and more, I have recited, or, more precisely, sung, Psalm 126 countless times. This is because this psalm serves as the introduction to the blessing after meals (*birkat ha-mazon*) after each of the three sabbath meals (dinner on Friday evening, lunch and supper on Saturday) and throughout the year on the festivals.

The psalm is short enough to quote in full. Below is the NRSV translation.

A Song of Ascents

126.1 When the LORD restored the fortunes of Zion, we were like those who dream.
126.2 Then our mouth was filled with laughter, and our tongue with shouts of joy; then it was said among the nations, 'The LORD has done great things for them'.
126.3 The LORD has done great things for us, and we rejoiced.
126.4 Restore our fortunes, O LORD, like the watercourses in the Negeb.
126.5 May those who sow in tears reap with shouts of joy.
126.6 Those who go out weeping, bearing the seed for sowing, shall come home with shouts of joy, carrying their sheaves.

The psalm has been dated to the post-exilic period, on the assumption that the Lord's restoration of fortunes mentioned in v. 1 was the return from Babylonian exile in the late sixth century BCE (Keck 2009: 4:1195). This interpretation is disputed by Mitchell Dahood, who points out that the terminology used in this verse is also attested in the pre-exilic period. In Dahood's view, no specific referent is needed (Dahhod 1970: 217).

The main interpretive problem in this short psalm concerns the tenses of the verbs used in vv. 1-3. The NRSV translation, quoted above, uses the past tense in its English rendition of these verses. The JPS, however, views the entire psalm as being oriented towards the future:

A Song of Ascents

>   126.1   When the LORD restores the fortunes of Zion we see it as in a dream. (*Lit.: 'we are veritable dreamers'*)
>   126.2   our mouths shall be filled with laughter, our tongues, with songs of joy. Then shall they say among the nations, 'The LORD has done great things for them!'
>   126.3   The LORD will do great things for us and we shall rejoice.

The difficulty in pinning down the verb tenses may frustrate attempts to situate the psalm's time of composition. For my purposes, however, this matter is not a problem but an opportunity to engage in a multivalent reading of the psalm.

The psalm is easily divided into two stanzas of equal length. If we read the entire psalm as a gesture towards the future, the first stanza, vv. 1-3, describes how 'we' will feel at the time of future restoration: as if we are in a wonderful dream filled with laughter and joy. This restoration is recognized not only by 'us' who will experience it, but also by the nations among whom we live. The second stanza, vv. 4-6, calls upon God to hasten this future restoration, and describes again the joyous response that will ensue, when weeping will turn to joy and the harvest will be abundant. This reading is appealing and uplifting for it maintains a hopeful, optimistic, joyful mood throughout by 'us' – as a joyful dream. If so, vv. 4-6, whose future orientation is not disputed, calls upon God

The psalm becomes more complex, however, and therefore more interesting, if we read the verbs in vv. 1-3 as references to a past restoration. This restoration was experienced to enact another restoration, so that 'we' can be joyful again.

Like the verb tenses, the timing of this restoration is also difficult to determine. Those who are eschatologically inclined may wish to read the second part as a reference to a messianic future, in which food and joy will abound. But I prefer to read the psalm in this-worldly terms. The cycle of adversity and relief from adversity is one that we follow throughout our lives. Many of our adversities are minor, some are major, but relief is welcome in both cases.

I therefore prefer to read the first stanza as focusing on the past, and the second stanza as focusing on the future. Missing is the hinge between past and future, namely, the present. This absence frustrates any attempt to know the precise circumstances for which or out of which the psalm was composed. At the same time, it leaves space for listeners and readers to insert their own present situation. Indeed, it is this gap that allows the psalm to remain relevant and therefore unimpeded by our distance in time and space from its author and the context that prompted it.

As I have mentioned, however, my own experience of the psalm is very much anchored to a specific situation: the sabbath meal. It is not immediately obvious why this psalm was chosen to introduce the grace that is said after sabbath and festival meals. According to one orthodox rabbi, Rabbi Uriel Romano, the practice of reciting this psalm was a Cabbalistic innovation in Safed, Israel, in the late sixteenth–early seventeenth century.[1] The first reference to the practice is in the book *Seder HaYom* (1599) of the mystic Moshe ben Machir in Safed. Rabbi Romano suggests that the recitation of this psalm, which concerns restoration after catastrophe, reflects the Jewish practice of recalling the exile from Jerusalem and the Land of Israel even at the most joyous moments, much like the practice of breaking a glass at the conclusion of the Jewish wedding ceremony. This explanation draws upon the traditional identification of the exile and return as the catastrophe and restoration alluded to in the psalm.

It is not surprising that mystics attached this psalm to the sabbath. Sabbath is a time out of time, a respite from the real world, a foretaste of the world to come, graced by the messianic banquet at which all desires are fulfilled. From a mystical perspective, singing a song of ascent allows the soul to rise to the heavenly spheres to enjoy communion with the divine, who is especially close on this seventh day. The eschatological undertones that one can read into the psalm's references to joy and abundance cohere well with this understanding of the sabbath.

Not having a mystical bent, I have fashioned my own, far more mundane, connections between the psalm and the sabbath meal. On the most basic level, the psalm speaks about food, both figuratively and literally. Psalm 126.2 refers to mouths filled with laughter and tongues that give voice to shouts of joy. The abundance that spills over onto the page can foreshadow the plenitude of the messianic age, but it also describes the sabbath table, which traditionally is the most elaborate, the most special set of meals of the week. Similarly, vv. 5 and 6 describe the labor of sowing, followed by the joy of reaping, a sequence not unlike the toil involved in sabbath preparation, followed by the day of rest when no work is done. It feels right to chant a psalm that refers to planting and consuming food as a prelude to the blessings of appreciation for the sabbath meal we have just enjoyed.

When chanting this psalm at the sabbath table each week, however, I am rarely thinking about the meaning of its words. The psalm signifies the end of the sabbath meal and the transition to whatever activity, or non-activity, will follow. As we sing the opening words, I am often looking forward to a walk, a nap, or an opportunity to sink into a novel. It is the situation – and the melody – more than the words that move me each time I sing them.[2]

---

1. This online resource can be found at https://urielromano.com/wp-content/uploads/2017/05/1-way-do-we-sing-psalm-126-before-the-birkat-hamazon.pdf.

2. Although there is a traditional melody that is well-known throughout the Jewish world, contemporary composers of Jewish music have introduced other melodies into our

My second choice would have been Psalm 130, solely on the basis of its creative use in M. Night Shyamalan's engaging 1999 horror film, *The Sixth Sense*.

Adele Reinhartz is Distinguished University Professor at the University of Ottawa, Canada, where she is also professor in the Department of Classics and Religious Studies. She specializes in early Jewish-Christian relations, and Bible and Film.

References

Dahood, Mitchell J. (1970), *Psalms III: 101–150*, AB 17A, Garden City: Doubleday.

Keck, Leander E. (2009), *The New Interpreter's Bible General Articles & Introduction, Commentary, & Reflections for Each Book of the Bible Including the Apocryphal/Deuterocanonical Books; in Twelve Volumes, 4.4*, Nashville: Abingdon.

family repertoire. One of my favorites is the tune composed by Debbie Friedman, which can be heard at https://www.shazam.com/track/54129572/shir-hama-alot. Another, more recent addition to our repertoire was composed by Joey Weisenberg, which can be found at https://joeyweisenberg.bandcamp.com/track/shir-hamaalot.

PSALM 126
COMMEMORATING THE DEAD DURING THE LOCKDOWN, 2020

Ingeborg Löwisch

In the first days of the Covid lockdown in spring 2020, my turn in the emergency pastoral care team brought me to a family in the outskirts of Hamburg. A boy had suffered a seizure in the tub and suffered oxygen deprivation. When I arrived, the ambulance had just left for the hospital with little hope for his life to be saved. A young relative stood in the door and provided disinfectant to the people who crowded in the hall and I admired his responsibility. Other relatives were about to leave for driving to the hospital. Of course, getting close, providing care and securing parents and siblings in the larger family net, was an evident thing to do. Only much later, when I was on my way back home, did I realize that none of them would be allowed to enter the hospital. If lucky, both parents would have been allowed to see their son.

I don't know what happened to the boy and his family. In the emergency care system other people take over. But in my own neighbourhood and parish located in the centre of Hamburg, similar situations occurred. They shed a light on the situation in hospitals during the lockdown. Patients were often alone and isolated. Relatives could not visit them or only one person was allowed to come. Larger family or friendship connections were interrupted and became partly dysfunctional. Friends and family were denied the opportunity to care for a loved one, to offer the solace of touch to the dying, to say good-bye. Numbers of participants were restricted at funerals. Funeral feasts and visits were suspended.

Experiencing the despair, anger and also inhumanness of pandemic death culture, our parish decided to perform the ritual of commemorating the dead on Eternity Sunday, even though services on site were still exceptional in Hamburg at this point of the pandemic. In the Protestant church in Germany, Eternity Sunday is celebrated at the end of November. On the last Sunday of the liturgical year before advent, we read out the names of the dead of the previous year and light candles for them. Performing an in-person ritual in November 2020 was meant to restore a sense of dignity, the comfort of participation and also normality in individual and social dealing with death, as well as to enable bereaved ones to enter a process of mourning. The service was extremely intense and concentrated. For a long time, I felt that it was the most sensible and meaningful thing we did as parish in the lockdown – for the individual participants as well as for the neighbourhood and greater communities.

After this powerful experience, I wondered what made the service so significant. Of course, the ritual of names and candles is always meaningful. Of course, providing the church room as public space in a situation in which people were so strongly thrown back on their selves, was revealing. Of course, the music was beautiful. But in the end, I felt that reciting Psalm 126 made the difference. The ritual was strong in bestowing dignity unto the deceased and unto the bereaved. But the words of Psalm 126 opened an emotional space in which consolation was given.

Psalm 126 is an inherent part of the texts of Eternity Sunday. On first glance, this is due to Luther's translation for v. 1, which comes as a view on eternal life:

Wenn der HERR *die Gefangenen Zions erlösen wird,*
so werden wir sein wie die Träumenden.

To translate Luther's translation into English:

When the Lord will redeem the captives of Zions, we shall be as dreamers.

Indeed, Luther's phrasing is a beautiful way of expressing the longing for, as well as the promise of, a future for both the living and the dead. However, Luther's translation does not entirely overwrite the psalm's reference to a very particular past. The NRSV translates v. 1,

When the LORD *restored the fortunes of Zion, we were like those who dream*

– or alternatively,

When the LORD brought back those who returned to Zion...

and thus particularly refers to the return from the Babylonian exile. The Hebrew text allows for both foci – a view toward the future and a reference to the past (Zenger and Hossfeld 2008: 499-512). It initiates a motion between looking ahead and looking back, between anticipation and experience. Thus Psalm 126 has a proper place in the ritual of honouring the dead. Its dream about a future in which the situation of *our mouth shall be full of laughter and our tongues full of praise* (*LU*17, v. 2) is grounded in the experience of God's liberating action. In the space that opens between dream and recall, contemporary readers can find themselves.

Psalm 126 is structured in two parts. These parts are structured through the signal verb שוב, *šwb*, 'restore', in v. 1 and v. 4. Verses 1-3 deal with the history between God and His people as it resonates between past and future; vv. 4-6 focus on the present request of restoring anew one's fortunes. On Eternity Sunday 2020 this would be the request that those who are torn out of traditions that usually help to deal with death, would be restored to entering a path of mourning and coping.

The potential of Psalm 126 to help restore people to a path of mourning also has to do with the psalm's form, which is linked to a way (up). Psalm 126 belongs to the collection of Songs of Ascent (Pss. 120–134). The 'ascent' may have referred to the actual ascent to Jerusalem for annual feasts or pilgrimage, or to climbing the Temple steps. Metaphorical meanings such as the way of life, or the path of mourning, likewise resonate with the headline, שיר המעלות, 'A song of Ascents'. Verse 6 takes this up when it states that 'those who go out weeping… shall come home with shouts of joy' (NRSV). However, the Hebrew verbs הלך, *hlk*, and בוא, *bwʾ* (both in the *Qal* formation) do not emphasise a movement of going out and coming back, but rather mark the beginning and end of one single way (Deeg and Schüle 2018: 497). Psalm 126 envisions a path that holds different and even controversial experiences: those who go forth weeping shall come along with songs of joy. Likewise, despair and hope belong to one's life; grief and hope belong to a single, one mourning process; doubt and trust belong to one heart.

Between longing for the future and recalling the past, on an ascent that inheres weeping as well as joy, the outcry of the psalmist is rendered in two strong images. *Restore our fortunes, O LORD, like the watercourses in the Negeb* (NRSV, v. 4). The first image of water coursing through the Negeb brings about the issue of strong feelings. The watercourses of desert wadis are not gentle, harmless streams through creeks but come suddenly and with might. They bring intense blossoming and growth. However, the intense vegetation only endures for a certain period. Being seasonal streams, the Negev watercourses inhere rhythm. After a period of growth, the desert takes over again. In the context of commemorating and mourning, strong feelings are virulent, yet not always welcome. Emotions such as anxiety, anger, grief or guilt might be feared. At the same time emotions such as relief, blossoming and growth or even *joie de vivre* might be felt as inadequate or a sort of betrayal. Within the storm of bereavement, both the intensity and the rhythm of this image may bring relief and comfort.

Rhythm hums through the second image as well. *May those who sow in tears, reap with shouts of joy* (NRSV, v. 5). In an urban German perspective, sowing and reaping often comes as a rather romantic image. However, with climate change, it is generally understood that in many places sowing becomes an increasingly hard and uncertain work. Will the seed rise up to a harvest and the promise of seasonal rhythm hold? More and more often, sowing is related to a state of shortage and the agonizing decision to give away something one needs in the present for an uncertain future.

In the context of loss, I picture clasped hands that hold tight onto feelings, regrets or hopes that would need to be given away in order to rise up. Yet they are too crucial to the present to be given away. Mourning companion and author Chris Paul, in her work with people who lost someone to suicide, did research on the feeling of guilt after a close person takes their own life. At the beginning, her work focused on how people could unload the feeling of guilt, which she identified as a demoralizing and destructive emotion. Later, she came to understand various functions of guilt, for example, as an emotion with a strong bonding quality that can also help keep in touch with the beloved one (Paul 2016: 69). Guilt, she argues, is something one might have to hold onto in order to withstand the situation. A feeling to keep inside one's clasped hands. Giving up guilt, one would have to let go the intensity of the bonding it induces and become exposed to underlying, possibly threatening feelings. Sowing involves releasing the clasped hands in order to let go and scatter the seed. Releasing hands and hearts in order to let go of feelings that have functions one does not want to lose is something I can relate to in the image of sowing in tears. In Chris Paul's terms, sowing in tears would be a form of memory work. She suggests recalling and sharing memories as a way towards gaining a differentiated bond with and relationship to the lost ones. Memories would then be like seed. Sharing memories would be the process of opening hands in order to let go and scatter them in tears. Hopefully, the harvest of mourning includes weeping and singing, holding tight and letting go, feeling refreshed and feeling arid, all experiences of life and living.

My second choice for the volume would have been Psalm 57.

Dr. Ingeborg Löwisch studied Bible at the Universiteit van Amsterdam and received her PhD from Utrecht University, both in The Netherlands. She works as a pastor in a Protestant parish in the centre of Hamburg, Germany. Her focus is on working with children and families, as well as community-oriented work in the neighbourhood.

References

Deeg, A. and A. Schüle (2018), *Die neuen alttestamentlichen Perikopentexte: Exegetische und homiletisch-liturgische Zugänge*, Leipzig: Evangelische Verlagsanstalt.
Evangelische Kirche in Deutschland / Foundation Deutsche Bibelgesellschaft (2017), *Neue Lutherbibel 2017*, Stuttgart, Germany (*LU*17).
Paul, C. (2016), *Schuld | Macht | Sinn: Arbeitsbuch für die Begleitung von Schuldfragen im Trauerprozess*, Gütersloh: Gütersloher Verlagshaus.
Zenger, E. and F.-L. Hossfeld (2008), *Psalmen 101–150*, Freiburg: Verlag Herder.

PSALM 126
THOSE WHO SOW SHALL REAP IN TEARS

Assnat Bartor

Childhood

All of us who grew up in the Israeli education system, from kindergarten to high school, celebrated every year the 'Israeli holidays'. These are the traditional Jewish holidays originating from the Bible, mainly the three pilgrimage festivals: Passover, Shavuot and Sukkot. These celebrations were supplemented with content that reflected the new Jewish-Zionist ethos, and the agricultural aspects that exist in the biblical holidays were given a central place, expressing the people's longed-for connection to the country and to their land. Each year, as children and as young adults, wearing white shirts and with gleaming eyes, we participated in these festive processions and ceremonies. The songs, dances and speeches composed to honor these occasions established the Zionist holiday tradition.

The collective ceremonies, which originated and developed in the agricultural settings (*kibbutzim* and *moshavim*), were held as well in urban localities within the educational frameworks (kindergartens and schools). On Passover, the Festival of Spring, a ceremony of bringing the עמר, *'omer* (Lev. 23.10) was held, symbolizing the beginning of the harvest. On Shavuot, the harvest festival, a ceremony of bringing the first fruits was held, symbolizing the conclusion of the wheat harvest (this was my favorite ceremony, because the wreath of flowers placed on my head was also my birthday bouquet). On Sukkot, the end-feast of harvest time, we welcomed the new agricultural year with songs and dances. Among the many sayings recited at these ceremonies, I particularly remember two biblical verses:

> May those who sow in tears reap with shouts of joy. Those who go out weeping, bearing the seed for sowing shall come home with shouts of joy, carrying their sheaves. (Ps. 126.5-6)[1]

---

1. Citations taken from the NRSV unless otherwise stated.

These verses were read, and are read to this day, in the ceremony for Shavuot. We also recited them as we danced the harvest celebration dance, and later I discovered them and Psalm 126 in its entirety in the Passover Haggadah of the kibbutz movement.

The two verses, probably belonging to the genre of 'labor songs,' and which may even have been taken from one of the ancient 'harvest songs' (see Isa. 9.2), are incorporated into 'The Song of Ascents,' one of fifteen post-exilic psalms, probably belonging to the genre of 'songs of pilgrimage,' whose common background is the return of the exiles from Babylon to the Land of Israel:[2]

> A Song of Ascents. When the LORD restored the fortunes of Zion,[3] we were like those who dream.[4] Then our mouth was filled with laughter and our tongue with shouts of joy; then it was said among the nations, 'The LORD has done great things for them.' The LORD has done great things for us, and we rejoiced. Restore our fortunes, O LORD, like the watercourses in the Negeb.[5] (vv. 1-4)

Joy is a central theme in the chant. Joy over the return of the captive-exiles to the land, or joy over the restoration of the land to its state as it was prior to the destruction and exile. The meaning depends on the interpretation of the words שיבת, *šibat*, and שבותנו/שביתנו, *šbitenu/šbutenu*, in vv. 1 and 4.[6] Perhaps the joy is twofold, both for the return of the captives-exiles (when v. 4 describes the stream of exiles who will come to the land) and for the restoration of the land itself (as can be understood in v. 1). Either way, the joy involves returning to the homeland, represented in the second part of the psalm through the quintessential image of the farmer. This is an image based on the daily life of the one who works the land, the one who sows and reaps, which symbolizes and illustrates the restoration of the condition to its former state, to the natural state of the land and its inhabitants. The choice to integrate the two verses from the 'reapers' singing' in the psalm also allows the poet to make an analogy between the joy of return and the joy of the harvest (by chaining the words 'shouts of joy,' which appear three times, in both parts of the psalm). The ordinary joy of the reaper, when toil and efforts have borne fruit, will be doubled and multiplied with the reward of the crop, for it

---

2. Goulder 1998: 27–30; Ross 2016: 663; Amzallag 2021: 589.

3. LXX translates: 'When the Lord returned the captivity of Zion.'

4. LXX and the Vulgate translate: 'we became like people comforted.' The Aramaic Targum reads: 'we became like the sick who are cured.' The Qumran Scroll (the big Qumran Psalms scroll, 11QPsᵃ) appears to agree with the Greek and Aramaic translations, for it has the form חלומים, *ḥalumim*, reflecting the other meaning of the root חלם, *ḥlm*, which is 'to recover health.'

5. LXX translates: 'Return our captivity, O Lord, like Wadis in the south.'

6. The first interpretation is reflected, for example, in Jer. 48.46-47; the second, more widespread interpretation, is reflected in Jer. 33.11b and Job 42.10.

proves the success in reviving the desolate land: the land which has been neglected due to the prolonged absence of the people. The joy of returning to the land of Israel, the revival of the land, the renewal of the earth, the joy of work, which yields crops – Psalm 126 is the essence of the Zionist ethos.

Reality

In 2009, I joined the legal department of *Yesh Din* (Heb. 'There is Law'), a human rights organization. *Yesh Din* is an NGO dealing with complaints from Palestinians, residents of the West Bank, about legal violations perpetrated by soldiers, policemen and settlers – the three groups representing the Israeli occupation in the occupied territories. The prolonged occupation, which began in 1967, causes significant harm to Palestinian residents on a daily basis. The occupation deprives Palestinians of fundamental rights, imposes on them decrees that make their lives unbearable, and uses various forms of violence against them, all while systematically violating the rules of International Humanitarian Law. *Yesh Din* strives to help Palestinians deal with these injustices both on a personal and on a systemic level. Working within the Israeli law enforcement system, *Yesh Din* argues cases where legal and human rights violations occur.

Agriculture is the main source of livelihood for the Palestinians in the West Bank. This source of livelihood suffered a fatal blow with the establishment of the Israeli settlements, on hundreds of thousands of dunams of agricultural land. To this are compounded the orders prohibiting Palestinian farmers from entering their land, and the repeated invasions of settlers into these lands. These actions prevent Palestinian farmers from cultivating their fields and orchards. The looting of the lands and the prevention of access to them are joined by the settlers' daily attacks, which take place in Palestinian agricultural areas: displacement of seedlings, felling of fruit trees (mainly olive trees), burning fields and orchards, theft of crops (mainly olives), destruction of fences, pollution of wells, and more severe damage to the farmers' property.[7]

It is there, in the looted fields and burned orchards, among the uprooted trees and felled branches, that I saw before my eyes 'those who sow in tears, those who go out weeping, bearing the seed for sowing.' I saw them weep over their bitter fate and the bitter fate of their land. The biblical image of the sowers and reapers, which accompanied my childhood and has blurred over the years – for in the State of Israel, the agricultural-technological power, the Israeli farmer has not walked in his own fields for a long time; and foreign workers, forced to exile from their own homeland in the search of livelihood, provide the agricultural labor for the Israeli landowner – reappeared, receiving a new context. Unfortunately, the main concern of Palestinian farmers is not with the fertility of the land, with the amount of precipitation and other environmental conditions that affect their

---

7. See on *Yesh Din* website, 'A Summary of the 2021 Olive Harvest Season': https://www.yesh-din.org/en/a-summary-of-the-2021-olive-harvest-season/.

crops, but with the incessant harassment by Jewish settlers and the destruction they sow, which in many cases deny Palestinian farmers an opportunity to harvest their crops. Only the tears remain, tears shed for the destruction of crops, for the prevention of access to land, for the restriction of freedom of movement, for the violation of property rights.

It is possible to sail to other symbolic places, to which Psalm 126 invites us, and think about the right of return; of those who have been privileged to return to their homeland; and of those whose right is denied to them.

The Sublime

Johannes Brahms was not a farmer. The Land of Israel was not part of his childhood landscape and the Return to Zion was not the ethos on which he grew up. Yet, in the first chapter of *The German Requiem* (*Ein deutsches Requiem*),[8] after the opening verse, taken from the Sermon on the Mount (Mt. 5.4) – *Selig sind, die da Leid tragen, denn sie sollen getröstet warden* ('Blessed are they that mourn, for they shall be comforted')[9] – it is quite understandable why Brahms chose this verse to present his concept of death and of the appropriate emotional response to death, there appear the two Psalm 126 verses which are discussed here:

> *Die mit Tränen säen, werden mit Freuden ernten. Sie gehen hin und weinen und tragen edlen Samen, und kommen mit Freuden und bringen ihre Garben.*

> They who sow in tears shall reap in joy. He that goeth forth and weepeth, bearing precious seed, shall doubtless come again with rejoicing, bringing his sheaves with him.

And the choice to use them is less self-evident, although it can be explained.

Unlike the Catholic Requiem, which is a Mass to commemorate the dead and pray for the souls of those who had died (*Missa pro Defunctis*), the German Requiem addresses those who live. It speaks to those who have lost loved ones, and it seeks to give them comfort (Musgrave 1996: 1; Van Camp 2002: 2). The text focuses on comfort, hope, reassurance, and reward for personal efforts, and one of

---

8. Brahms' Requiem is called 'German' because it is sung in the German language, not in Latin, the language of the Catholic Requiem Mass. Brahms not only chose the spoken language and abandoned the liturgical language but also deviated from the familiar pattern of the burial prayer. Instead of its regular texts he composed a textual sequence, consisting of verses he chose from the Old and New Testament and from books of the Apocrypha. In 1867, two years before completing the work, he wrote to the organist of Bremen Cathedral: 'I will admit that I could happily omit the "German" and simply say "Human".'

9. The text of the German Requiem is taken from the original text of Luther's Bible, and the official English translation is taken from the King James Bible.

the main motifs is that sorrow is (or will be) turned into joy. Those in sorrow shall reap joy; those who weep shall rejoice. Therefore, the poetic proverb (v. 5) and its narrative illustration (v. 6)[10] fit the spirit of things, even though their context is not death or mourning individuals' death.[11]

In May 2015, I sang the German Requiem for the first time. It was at a concert presented by my choir, the Tel Aviv Collegium Singers (since then we have sung it only one other time). We finished singing the heavenly opening: *Selig sind, die da Leid tragen*. The woodwinds played the two measures transitioning to the next theme. The tenors and basses began to sing *Die mit Tränen säen*; the strings accompanied the singers; and when the harp joined we, the alto singers, also joined, with the repetition of *mit Tränen säen*. I choked up with emotion, which did not go well with the sound I produced, but I felt elated. And with a strangled throat and eyes glistening with tears I remembered the girl in the white shirt, the garland of flowers on her head and her eyes shining, and I heard her recite the verses in Hebrew. As a child, I did not know that these verses would come back to affect me so deeply, in a way which made me feel part of something sublime.

My Second Choice of Psalm

> Let sinners be consumed from the earth, and let the wicked be no more.
> Bless the LORD, O my soul. Praise the LORD! (Ps. 104.35)

I have a list of many sins and many sinners that deserve to be wiped off the face of the earth. On the day this miracle happens even a hard-core secular person such as I will find myself blessing the Lord.

Dr. Assnat Bartor lectures in Biblical Studies at Tel Aviv University, specializing in biblical law. She is also a criminal attorney and lawyer specializing in human rights, and a member of a semi-professional choir of classical choral singing.

References

Amzallag, N. (2021), 'Psalm 120 and the Question of Authorship of the Songs of Ascents', *JSOT* 45: 588–604.

Goulder, M.D. (1998), *The Psalms of the Return, Book V, Psalms 107–150*, Sheffield: Sheffield Academic.

Lategan, B.C. (1980), 'Ein Deutsches Requiem: Notes on Brahms's Selection of Biblical Texts', *Scriptura, Journal for Biblical, Theological and Contextual Hermeneutics* 1: 29–41.

---

10. See also Amos 9.13.

11. 'In a very striking metaphor, the *tears* of the mourners become the *seed* of the harvest of joy': Lategan 1980: 36.

Musgrave, M. (1996), *Brahms, A German Requiem*, Cambridge: Cambridge Music Handbooks.
Ross, A.P. (2016), *A Commentary on the Psalms*, Vol. 3, Grand Rapids: Kregel Academic & Professional.
Van Camp, L. (2002), *A Practical Guide for Performing, Teaching and Singing the Brahms Requiem*, New York: Alfred Publishing.

PSALM 127.2
HE GIVETH UNTO HIS BELOVED IN SLEEP – *AND WHAT ABOUT ME?*
A PERSONAL STORY OF PSALM 127

Sabine Dievenkorn

My grandmother was not really a religious person. Nor was she an intellectual, not at all an academic. She was rather pragmatic. She was the tenth of twelve children in the countryside somewhere in the former East Prussia, near the Baltic Sea, where the grass is low and the horizon wide. War and post-war times, expulsion and annihilation had shaped the 1913-born woman. Wisdom of life as well as a mixture of loss and trust were her guides. And she communicated large parts of her wisdom in silence, that is, in deed rather than words. She was not a woman of many words. There are few words I remember. I was a child when I was her granddaughter. Today I would say that my grandmother was a woman of great words. They often came in the guise of brisk sayings. Wisdom of life in aphorism form. And she was a Bible connoisseur, as I later discovered. Among the proverbs with which she descriptively mastered the challenges of life were many sentences from the Bible. *Den Seinen gibt's der Herr im Schlaf, He giveth unto His beloved in sleep*,[1] was one of them.[2]

---

1. The English version used here is the *JPS The Holy Scriptures, Tanakh 1917 edition according to the Masoretic text*: https://biblehub.com/jps/psalms/127.htm. This is an exact parallel to the German that my grandmother quoted which can be found today in the German Translation *Einheitsübersetzung, 1980*. The old JPS Tanakh translation has an interesting history and connections to Christian Protestant Bible versions. See https://jps.org/books/holy-scriptures-tanakh-1917-edition/.

2. Cf. the difficult MT text, כן יתן לידידו שנא. *BHS* suggests, כן יתן לידידיו ש[י]נה. Most English translations render as 'for he gives sleep to his beloved' or similar. But the JPS, not just the 1917 version but even the 1985 version, is closer to the rendering here quoted from the German: 'He provides as much for His loved ones while they sleep', with the latter adding a note: 'meaning of the Hebrew uncertain'.

As a child, I hated this saying. I also remember feeling that when I was told this sentence, either I did not understand my grandmother or else she did not understand the situation. If something failed me, something did not go well, something could not be forced, if I wanted to make something, build, paint, tinker – and what I wanted and how I wanted it could not be implemented in this or any other way – my grandmother knew how to comment: *He giveth unto His beloved in sleep.* My grandmother seemed to overlook the fact that I – maybe six, seven or eight years old – neither slept nor wanted anything in my sleep: what should you want or get in sleep, when all you want is to put your project into practice here and now? The fact that my grandmother gently stroked my head while talking solidified my childish opinion that the older generation really understands very little about the problems that ours struggles with.

Presumably, after this description, it goes without saying that my granddaughter–grandma relationship meant that I could not have asked my grandmother about the meaning of her saying or started a conversation regarding the sense and nonsense of her remark. *He giveth unto His beloved in sleep...*

Left alone with the theological challenge of this verse from Psalm 127, I found not only that my grandmother missed the heart of my drama, that she did not understand or want to understand what it was all about, but that it also seems completely useless to have a Lord who does not help you when you need help. A Lord who somehow seems to acknowledge that help, and giving help, is necessary, but who only affords it – if at all – if you do not notice anything about it? Only in your sleep? Why believe in a God who only does things the way He likes them and not the way I need them?

A difficult theological question. Not only for children. Never mind. At the time, I did not dare give up faith in God. For whatever reason, this solution was not an option for the granddaughter I was then. Under the premise that my grandmother perhaps understood more than I assumed, and with the axiom that God not only existed but also valued effort and work, I was looking for a meaning. Why had I not achieved what I wanted to achieve even with the greatest childlike effort? Why had the glued picture not hold on the wall? Why did the watercolors on the paper simply flow beyond the boundaries I thought I had set for them? Why did the nail keep bending when being hammered? Why had the cat not come when I called her? ... The list of childish frustrations following intensive efforts could easily be continued.

He giveth unto His beloved in sleep... Then all of a sudden, I had it, the solution, the bitter one: I don't belong to His beloved. Because they get what they want, or even need, in their sleep. His beloved don't even need to make an effort. What I'm struggling to do, they get for free. Just like that.

How mean, I thought as a child, and a long-lasting feeling of lack of belonging was born in me. And that was so all-encompassing, so final and immovable in these seven words that the theological-childlike interpretation contained a certain rigor and brutality, which I still feel today when reading this verse. To be excluded. For ever and ever. And never to belong. This collided with my not-only childlike longing for belonging and home.

When I came across the biblical context of this, my grandmother's saying, later, much later, it did not make the situation any better. On the contrary. The first verse and a half of Psalm 127 describe exactly my childhood drama. Now as a dilemma of adults. And much clearer, culminating in the words *in vain*.

> Except the LORD build the house, they labour in vain that build it; except the LORD keep the city, the watchman waketh but in vain. It is vain for you that ye rise early, and sit up late, ye that eat the bread of toil; so He giveth unto His beloved in sleep. (127.1-2)

I am still learning that success is not a measure or indication of closeness to, acceptance by, and belonging to God. I now understand the promise that can be read in these lines – by 'His beloved'. Even today, against every intellectual, academic-theological effort, I feel strongly the mercilessness of being excluded. I have had to understand through the Bible, the religions that are based on it, and cultures that also live completely independently of biblical dogmas and norms, that belonging is something that cannot be established by those who seek it. Membership in a community is granted to you from without. The one who desires it can neither produce it nor acquire affiliation or even force it against the will of others.

Of course, it is clear to me that you do not have to focus on reading these verses of Psalm 127 as I do here, as containing politics of chosenness and exclusion. However, I deem it important that the potential of exclusion that may lurk under the surface of biblical statements should not be overlooked. Especially in Christian traditions and theologies, which aspire to appear so open, the bearers of an ever-lasting culture of welcoming and hosting, all the more so with the examples of the New Testament: the outcasts, impure, sick, nonbelievers, tax collectors, whores, and drunkards are all welcome by Jesus… And then, as a Christian theologian, you read St Augustine and understand his discussion of the visible and invisible Church: despite all the culture of welcome, there is a limit, an insurmountable one; there is true and real belonging. Even if the entrance gate is made as large as possible, it remains part of a wall. Better yet, there is no gate without a wall. There can be no talk of belonging without exclusion. Sure, the Lord does not give unto all of *us* in *our* sleep, no: He giveth unto *His beloved* in *their* sleep. Perhaps with continuous and daily efforts, outsiders can conceal their non-belonging. There are also projects that succeed. Nails that hold on to the wood and watercolors that correspond to the intentions of the painter. Why not attribute these results of effort and work to the Lord's blessing? However, what is the value of appearances when one longs for inclusion and being?

Certainly, my grandmother did not tell me this verse in order to increase my childlike dilemma or to add a fundamental exclusion of my personally felt failure in my work. For her, my belonging to *His beloved*, to herself, to 'us', was beyond doubt, a given fact in the universe. Therefore, she believed she could cheer me up with this saying, true to the motto: What you are does not depend on what you do and how. Or, in modern terms: self-worth and work success are not two sides of the same coin. And one's worth can neither be produced nor invented. Our worth is our being.

This grandmotherly conviction probably needs a good portion of life wisdom for becoming a life maxim. In the end, belonging isn't about how you are seen from the outside. It's about what you feel. What is felt deep inside. Being chosen is wonderful when you know you are chosen. Chosenness, however, remains an absolutely passive act and ordination for both the chosen and the non-chosen. On which a whole life can depend.

My second choice would have been a part of Psalm 90, vv. 3 to 6, especially 5 and 6. These verses are almost always quoted in our (Lutheran) funeral tradition. The German version translates the difficult Hebrew word זרמתם of v. 5 into 'stream [them]' instead of 'flood', as in the KJV. I have a corresponding picture for such a 'stream' in my childhood. The words became descriptions of a reality, by which I tried to understand the phenomenon of death. Not far from my grandmother's house flowed a water stream, pulling softly but firmly at the grass growing on its banks. The strong young grass was being washed around, green and invigorated; while the old, colorless yellow was taken away by the water, softly carried to an unknown place of death at the then-unknown end of the stream.

Sabine Dievenkorn, PhD in Theology (Universität Hamburg, Germany), is Professor and Director of the Academia de Teología in Santiago de Chile. An ordained reverend of the Lutheran Church, she serves as the European Society of Women in Theological Research (ESWTR) representative in Israel and Palestine. She grew up in a Christian Jewish family that told its stories in hidden pictures and silent gestures. She lives in Israel part of every year.

PSALMS 127-128
WHOSE LABOR? WHOSE HANDS?

Gale A. Yee

As a former Roman Catholic, psalms have always been a special part of my life, as it has been for many convents, monasteries, and abbeys down through the ages. The psalms of Gregorian chant encouraged me through the times when my mind blanked while writing my PhD dissertation. I would begin my teaching days at morning prayer where the psalms were sung. When I taught psalms, I would expose my students to the many different recordings of psalms that I collected. Because I have not previously written an exegesis of the psalms,[1] I chose Psalms 127–128 because they provide different viewpoints on the topic of labor or work, which has been a Marxist/materialist interest of mine, particularly with respect to gender.

Psalms 127–128 are often paired together, both as psalms of ascents and as Wisdom psalms. They have a shared vocabulary (Miller 1982: 128–30; Van Niekerk 1995; Viviers 2019: 436; McCann, Jr 1996: 1200):

- sons (בנים, *bānîm*): 127.3-4//128.3, 6
- man (גבר, *geber*): 127.5//128.4
- fruit (פרי, *pěrî*): 127.3//128.3
- house (בית, *bayit*): 127.1//128.3

Moreover, a chiastic arrangement interconnects both psalms (Allen 1983: 179; Viviers 2019: 436):

A   127.1: Lord, House, City
B   127.3-4: Many sons, Womb (wife)
C   127.5: Happy (אשרי, *'ašrê*), blessed with sons
C' 128.1: Happy (אשרי, *'ašrê*)
B' 128.3: Wife, blessed with sons
A' 128.5: Lord, Zion, Jerusalem

---

1. My previous work on the psalms was primarily geared to praying and preaching them (Yee 2022). English translations are from the NRSV unless otherwise noted.

'A' of the chiasmus warns the reader/hearers that unless they put their trust in Yhwh, they labor in vain, whether building a house, guarding a city, or eating bread produced by tedious labor. 'House' is a multivalent word that not only connotes a material building but also family and dynasty (for instance 2 Sam. 7.5, 11). The blessing of a large family of sons is the thrust of both psalms (B, C, C', B'). In 127.4-5, sons are like a quiver full of arrows to a man blessed with them. In 128.3-4, sons are like olive shoots around a table to a man, similarly blessed in being fearful of Yhwh (ירא, yĕrē' Yhwh). The locus of the blessing shifts from the family to the larger community and back again in C': Yhwh will issue his blessings from the material houses and buildings of Zion/Jerusalem to the familial lineages of one's children's children. The chiasmus ends by picking up the sequence, שלם (šlm) from ירושלם (Jerusalem) in 128.5 by summoning 'peace' (שלום, šālôm) upon Israel in v. 6.

Psalms 127-128 provide two different interpretations of labor/work, from materialist and gendered perspectives. I begin first with Psalm 128. Although Psalm 128 declares inclusively that 'Happy is *everyone* who fears the LORD, who walks in his ways', it presumes a male audience and a male agrarian setting in its imagery (Brettler 1998: 29-30). According to Gen. 3.18-19, God tell the man (האדם, hā'ādām) that he will eat food 'by the sweat of your face', farmed in soil filled with 'thorns and thistles'. When the psalmist simply states that the reader/hearer 'shall eat the fruit of the labor (יגיע, yĕgî'a) of your hands' (v. 2), he is putting a positive spin on the demanding male labor of cereal-crop plow agriculture. The psalmist, however, does not consider the equally arduous labor by women processing this food for eating: grinding grain, baking bread, drying fruits and legumes, as well as caring for the animals that pull the plows (Carol Meyers 2013: 128-35; Carol L. Meyers 1998: 254).

Instead, the psalm highlights the primary labor that women perform in the reproduction of children. According to 128.3, 'Your wife will be a fruitful vine within your house' (בירכתי ביתך, bĕyarkĕtê bêtekā). Although the NIV and NRSV translate the construction בירכתי ביתך, bĕyarkĕtê bêtekā simply as 'within your house', it has been rendered variously as 'innermost parts of thy house' (ASV), 'inner parts of your house' (CJB),[2] 'in the very heart of your house' (NKJV). Although Brettler interprets the expression as a 'peripheralization of women' (Brettler 1998: 35), archaeological investigations of the standard four-room house of Israelite farmers may provide us with clues here. Several of the rooms were multipurpose, fluctuating in the various phases of the domestic life cycles experienced by a family (Stager 1985: 17). The rectangular broad room that runs across at the rear of the house often served as storage or for other household activities (Carol Meyers 2013: 106-7). However, in the context of this psalm, *bĕyarkĕtê bêtekā* may refer to the back room in which children were born, a cult corner where females were ritually celebrated for their first menses, and a place where they gathered during their subsequent ones (Ebeling 2010: 30-31, 61-63, 69-71).

2. Complete Jewish Bible.

The 'inner-most part of the house' is thus the locus of women's reproductive cycles that will issue forth in the children who will be 'like the olive shoots around your table', thus blessing the man 'who fears the LORD' (128.3-4).

As one of the songs of ascents, v. 5 presumes that the addressee has not yet reached Jerusalem, but is still going up to the city.[3] The blessing from Zion is that he will eventually 'see' the prosperity of Jerusalem all the days of his life. Perhaps this (pilgrim) farmer is seeing the city for the first time, because the ambiance of Psalm 127 is completely rural. The focus of the psalm is on the agrarian labor of the man and the implicit reproductive labor of his wife, which result in the flourishing of his sons around his household table. In contrast to Psalm 127, there are no references to urban architecture. The farmer who fears YHWH has all he needs for his rural subsistence lifestyle: land to till, a house, and a fertile wife who will give him sons.

Psalm 127 exhibits a different tone from Psalm 128. The labor (עמל, *'āmāl*) described in Psalm 127 (v. 1) is of building (from the verb בנה, *bānāh*) a house, guarding (from the verb שמר, *šāmar*) the city (עיר, *'îr*), rising up early and retiring late just to eat the bread of anxious toil (עצב, *'eṣeb*). The superscription attributes this psalm to Solomon. The building of the 'house', therefore, could refer to the construction of the temple in the city of Jerusalem (McCann, Jr 1996: 1198–99). The psalmist warns that such labor and toil will be 'in vain' (שוא, *šāw'*) if YHWH is not completely involved. The three-fold repetition of שוא (*šāw'*) in vv. 1-2 underscores the pointlessness of these endeavors. In contrast to the rural agrarian labor (יגיע, *yĕgî'a*) of Ps. 128.2, the labor (עמל, *'āmāl*) and anxious toil (עצב, *'eṣeb*) of 127.1-2 describe work in an urban environment of houses, guards, cities, and gates (127.5).

Sons are extolled as a heritage from God (נחלת YHWH, *naḥălat Yhwh*) in 127.3, just as sons are a blessing for the man in 128.4. However, the reproductive wife of 128.3 is simply reduced to a baby-making womb (בטן, *beṭen*) in 127.3. The images of sons in 127.4-5 are not the agrarian 'olive shoots around the table' that describe the sons of 128.3. Instead, the sons become the masculine, phallic arrows in quivers held by warriors of the city's standing army. These sons provide the muscular leverage needed when their father must negotiate with 'enemies at the city gates' and not be humiliated or 'put to shame' (127.5, לא יבשו, *lō' yēbōšû*).

Psalms 127 and 128 offer two understandings of labor or work, dependent upon their social setting. The God-fearing agrarian farmer of Psalm 128 shall eat of the fruit of his labor (יגיע, *yĕgî'a*) and be happy and prosper. Highlighting the rural imagery, his wife will be a fruitful vine in the innermost part of his house, giving birth to sons who are likened to olive shoots around his table. He will be blessed by the number of children and blessed also in his pilgrimage up to Jerusalem, where he is promised of seeing his children's children all the days of his life. On the other hand, Psalm 127 warns of the futility of labor (עמל, *'āmāl*) and toil (עצב, *'eṣeb*) in the urban context of houses, cities, gates, and armies, if this toil and

---

3. I am assuming that Ps. 128 is a pilgrimage song.

labor does not include the deity. While the man is blessed in the number of sons, his wife simply becomes the aperture from which they issue. The sons themselves become a weapon in their father's hand when he confronts the enemy at the city gate.

Because Psalms 127–128 reduce women to their reproductive functions, Psalm 127 even demoting women to a bodily organ, I present in the following a re-reading of Psalm 127 by incarcerated women inmates:

> A home built without the Lord's presence
>   is built in vain.
> Without God by your side,
>   your efforts go to waste.
> You can work all day, all night
>   and it will be for naught.
>
> Daughters are made in the image of God;
>   our children are our reward.
> What arrows are to a warrior,
>   a child is in a mother's arms.
> Happy is a woman surrounded by family,
>   just as a warrior is happy
>   with a quiver full of arrows.
> Proud is a woman who stands at the gate
>   with God and her children by her side. (Women inmates 2011: 253)

If I had to choose a second psalm, I would pick Psalm 42, 'as a doe longs for running streams', because I have heard so many musical versions of this psalm that have spoken to my soul.

Gale A. Yee is Nancy W. King Professor of Biblical Studies *emerita* of Episcopal Divinity School. She identifies herself as an Asian American intersectional scholar, living in a retirement community in Claremont, CA, noted for its social activism.

References

Allen, Leslie C. (1983), *Psalms 101–150*, WBC 21, Waco: Word.
Brettler, Marc Zvi (1998), 'Women and Psalms: Toward an Understanding of the Role of Women's Prayer in the Israelite Cult', in Victor H. Matthews *et al.* (ed.), *Gender and Law in the Hebrew Bible and the Ancient Near East*, 25–56, Sheffield: Sheffield Academic.
Ebeling, Jennie R. (2010), *Women's Lives in Biblical Times*, New York: T&T Clark International.
McCann, Jr, J. Clinton (1996), 'The Book of Psalms: Introduction, Commentary, and Reflections', *The New Interpreter's Bible* 4: 640–1280.

Meyers, Carol L. (1998), 'Everyday Life: Women in the Period of the Hebrew Bible', in Carol A. Newsom and Sharon H. Ringe (eds), *Women's Bible Commentary*, 251–59, Louisville: Westminster John Knox, expanded edn.

Meyers, Carol L. (2013), *Rediscovering Eve: Ancient Israelite Women in Context*, New York: Oxford University Press.

Miller, Patrick D. (1982), 'Psalm 127: The House that Yahweh Builds', *JSOT* 7: 119–32.

Stager, Lawrence (1985), 'The Archaeology of the Family in Ancient Israel', *Bulletin of the American Schools of Oriental Research* 260: 1–36.

Van Niekerk, M.J.H. (1995), 'Psalms 127 and 128: Examples of Divergent Wisdom Views on Life', *OTE* 8: 414–24.

Viviers, Hendrik (2019), 'The Psychology of Place Attachment and Psalm 128', *OTE* 32: 426–43.

Women inmates (2011), 'Psalm 127', in Andrea. Ayvazian (ed.), *Psalms in Ordinary Voices: A Reinterpretation of the 150 Psalms by Women, Men and Children*, 253, Amherst: White River Press.

Yee, Gale A. (2022), 'Cast Your Burden on the Lord: Praying the Psalms', in Young Lee Hertig (ed.), *A Biblical Study Guide for Equal Pulpits*, 27–39, Eugene: Cascade.

PSALM 132
LIFEGIVING CONVERSATIONS WITH A PSALM

Melody D. Knowles

For most readers, Psalm 132 is hardly a familiar text. 'Lord remember David, and all his afflictions…', as the KJV renders the first verse, is not usually recited at weddings or funerals and appears rarely in any lectionary. Perhaps the clearest indication of the text's relative invisibility in contemporary contexts is in its most typical liturgical use: at the ordination of priests, at which time a select few of the Christian church join their voices with the text to repeat God's ancient promise to 'clothe' the priests of Zion with salvation (132.16).[1]

This liturgical invisibility of Psalm 132 stands in contrast to its textual neighbors, the 'Songs of Ascents' (Psalms 120–134), which are some of the favorite and most well-used texts in the Psalter. Read together, it is clear that Psalm 132 doesn't include many of the other striking poetic features that have propelled the popularity of this collection. For example, absent from Psalm 132 are any of the beautiful phrases that weave throughout the grouping, such as 'maker of heaven and earth' and 'the LORD bless you out of Zion'. Further, it marshals unfamiliar vocabulary and place names to evoke a moment in a time now difficult to pinpoint. 'Behold, we heard of it in Ephrathah, We found it in the field of Jaar,' the text declares in v. 6. Yet neither the 'we' nor the 'it' are described anywhere, and the place names are not easily recognized. Ultimately, the reader is baffled in the attempt to make sense of the action, the speakers, and the context.

For all of this, the elements that *are* clear in Psalm 132 are startling. Although David is named in nearly half of the superscriptions in the Psalter, he appears as a significant feature in the body of only three psalms: 78, 89, and 132. Exceptionally, in Psalm 132 he appears and even speaks in order to vow his efforts in securing an

---

1. Psalm 132, along with Psalms 40 and 135, are listed as texts to be used in the service of ordination to the priesthood in the Roman Catholic Church and the Church of England. Unless indicated, the translation of the text is my own.

earthly dwelling for God. Further, given that psalms are mostly prayers *to* God, it comes as no surprise that God rarely speaks in the Psalter. Yet no less than half of Psalm 132 is a direct quote from God that includes promises to David's line and to Zion (vv. 11-18). Threaded between these unusual speeches are prayers of the community that plead for God to claim a residence on earth and to support the Davidic line.

Politics and religion, land and theology – Psalm 132 makes core claims about communal identity mostly in direct quotes from God and David. Significantly, these claims emerge dialogically. That is, God sets out the astounding promises only *after* the human community has prayed for them, sometimes even picking up and repeating their very words. First, David vows to God to establish a 'place for YHWH', and the people pray:

> Let your priests be clothed with righteousness,
> and let your godly ones sing for joy. (v. 9)

God then responds to these requests emphatically and expansively. God first vows to David to set his children upon the throne and claims Zion to be 'my resting place forever' (v. 14). Then God promises:

> I will also clothe its priests with salvation,
> and its godly ones will sing aloud for joy. (v. 16)

Psalm 132 thus promotes a theology of divine responsiveness in which human prayer is answered by a sympathetic and generous deity. David and the congregation model something for God in that God's promises are closely shaped by their prayers even as they develop and expand them. In this way, core religious and political features emerge not as a result of a cosmic battle as in Psalm 46, or a prior idea in the mind of God as in Psalm 89, or even a rejoinder to David alone as in 2 Samuel 7, but in response to the prayers of David and the community. In the dialogical presentation of Psalm 132, the acts and prayers of the human community are valorized as influential on the divine world.

Several years ago my doctoral advisor asked me to write on Book V of the Psalter for the *Illuminations* commentary series. Although I was honored, I also assumed that I'd respectfully decline the commission. Writing commentaries seemed like a marathon exercise of lonely toil, and I had other more interesting academic conversations that I wanted to pursue as well as a very young family to raise. But the chance to work alongside the other scholars writing on Books I–IV was intriguing, and the reception history approach would allow me to study works from a broad spectrum. Daunted and slightly terrified, I said 'yes'. But how does one begin to write a commentary? Somewhat counterintuitively, I began by writing another book – a monograph on Psalm 132. Given the text's striking and significant claims, I thought that it might be able to fund a book-length study in reception history while exposing me to the key sources needed for the larger commentary on the rest of Book V. As it happened, I was correct in these assumptions. What I didn't see at all was the many ways that my work with this one dialogical text would involve so many wonderful dialogical conversations with which a scholar engages in order to do her long and lonely labor.

The work itself occurred in fits and starts, buffered by the academic calendar, access to resources, and childcare. Married to an academic and with two young children, I kept my teaching position in Chicago even when we moved to Poughkeepsie so that my husband could take up a tenure-track position. My first sabbatical in this context came as a welcome relief from regular travel, even as it also meant that I would be working in a library curated for undergraduate students and rich in everything, it seemed, except biblical studies. Compelled to explore beyond my usual call numbers, I stumbled onto Books of Hours from early modern Europe. Previously I had only considered their beautiful and sometimes whimsical images as works of visual art. With a new set of questions, I started thinking about who actually looked at these images, and which psalms were part of those people's prayers. Even though Psalm 132 was not as frequently included in these volumes as the other Psalms of Ascents, its presence in sections devoted to the Gradual Psalms meant that it had been prayed daily by individuals for hundreds of years. The ownership inscriptions and images confirmed that some of these individuals were women, and the charts of the alphabet sometimes found in the initial pages indicated that the books were primers for teaching children to read, some of whom apparently didn't wash their hands before their lessons and left fingerprint smudges on the page.

Thinking of the psalms as a vehicle for women's literacy was new for me, and I soon came to realize that they were also vehicles for women's literary production and political engagement. In Elizabethan England, Mary Sidney Herbert, Duchess of Pembroke (1561–1621), took up the project that had begun by her brother Philip to paraphrase the entire Psalter in verse of the highest literary art.[2] Unpublished and neglected for centuries, her work was just then receiving attention from literary scholars, and it was a delight to bring her work to bear on biblical studies as well (although I did have one colleague tease me that, with my focus on the literary work of the Duchess of Pembroke, I was moving feminist studies into lady-ist spheres!). It was also fascinating to uncover the political project in play. Sidney's intricate poetry aimed to demonstrate that the newly Protestant England could fund its own cultural resources apart from its Catholic heritage and its Protestant neighbors. In her paraphrase of Psalm 132, Mary Sidney reworked God's promises to David and his heirs into a thorough-going defense of her childless Protestant queen, Elizabeth I.

---

2. See, for instance, in: https://trinitycollegelibrarycambridge.wordpress.com/2019/03/08/the-sidney-psalms-and-mary-herbert-countess-of-pembroke/; for her works in the public domain, see, for instance, https://archive.org/details/thepsalmesofdavid_2012_librivox.

At the same time that my own material concerns relating to family and career were at the forefront of my considerations, I was also coming to see the significance of the materiality of the texts I was studying. I took up an administrative position at Virginia Theological Seminary and we moved to Alexandria. In another counterintuitive move, I soon realized that the position allowed me to be more physically present with the kids even as I could also apply for funds to support research travel. I was thus able to travel to England to examine most of the twenty-two extant manuscripts of Mary Sidney's paraphrases in person. In so doing, I came to realize that even though her project progressed Protestant ideology, it nevertheless maintained a traditional Catholic visual presentation. With the use of Latin *incipets* (initial sequence) and limitation of production to only manuscript form, the volumes physically harkened back to the past even as the ideology clearly promoted the emerging Protestant age. In hindsight, taking the physicality of the text seriously now seems obvious, but I had never before considered it in much depth. Through travel, my prior dialogue with intangible ideas now expanded to consider physical objects and real-world questions of how to lay out words on a page.

Throughout my research, I found myself grateful for the many communities and conversations that promote such considerations. These include families that support travel and talk at dinner about the laying out of words on a page, as well as institutions that support scholarship. They also include the librarians who care for and promote access to resources. There is just something so utterly serious in presenting a letter of support from the librarian at one's own institution to librarians at other institutions, having them read it carefully and gravely assess one's project and person, and finally grant access to their collections. In the case of the Bodleian Library (Oxford), this was only after I read aloud an oath in which I promised that I would 'not bring into the Library or kindle therein any fire or flame'. In another library, the manuscript I had requested to examine was brought into a separate room containing only a desk and a librarian whose only job that day apparently was to keep an eye on me. Mary Sidney made the choice to limit circulation of her writing 500 years ago, but librarians and travel funds and supportive families permit ongoing access to such treasures.

Psalm 132 is my favorite psalm because studying it wove me into conversations that made me bigger than was when I began. Having expanded my theology with its vision of a generous and responsive God, I see now that the text also expanded my experience by ushering me into conversations with so many others. The monograph still isn't complete, and this fall I'm planning out yet another academic year aiming to integrate writing and research with administration as well as family considerations.

I finish this reflection having just arrived back home after dropping my daughter off for her first year at college, and I am grateful that Psalm 132 and its generous and responsive God was in the background of our years together, quietly promoting the kind of engagement with others that promotes life and change.

I chose Psalm 132 as my favorite psalm because of its expansive influence on my own life as a human and a scholar. If I were to choose another one it would be Psalm 85, because of its dialogical vision that presents an astounding and gladdening future where righteousness and peace kiss, and truth springs up from the ground.

Melody D. Knowles is Vice President of Academic Affairs and Associate Professor of Old Testament at the Virginia Theological Seminary, USA.

PSALM 136
THE POWER OF A LIST

Diana Lipton

In 1973, Bryan Ferry released a recording of 'These Foolish Things', a song from the 1930s that recalls lost love by means of a list of the 'foolish things' that remind him of her.[1] Instantly, it became, and has remained, one of my favorite songs. I was 13 years old and had never been to Paris, but I could smell the Gardenia perfume, taste the wild strawberries, see the gulls around the Ile de France, and hear the waiters whistling as the last bar closes. I was deeply nostalgic for a past I hadn't experienced.

Fast forward to c. 1980 and I was sitting in a bar with Seamus Heaney. He'd given a reading to the Oxford Literary Society, of which I was at the time President, and I was asking him for a copy of the brilliant, then unpublished, translation he'd just read of a Middle English poem called 'The Names of the Hare'. This poem consists mainly of a list: 77 epithets to ward off bad luck when encountering hares: 'The hare, call him scotart, big-fellow, bouchart, the O'Hare, the jumper, the rascal, the racer, beat-the-pad, white-face, funk-the-ditch...'[2] By then, I understood the secret of 'These Foolish Things': the power of a list.

In an essay on epiphany in literature, Teju Cole cites parts of a page-and-a-half long list from Orhan Pamuk's *Istanbul: Memories and the City*.

> I am speaking of the evenings when the sun sets early, of the fathers under the streetlamps in the back streets returning home carrying plastic bags. Of the old Bosphorus ferries moored to deserted stations in the middle of winter, where sleepy sailors scrub the decks, pail in hand and one eye on the black-and-white television in the distance; of the old booksellers who

---

1. Composed in 1937 by Eric Maschwitz (lyrics) and Jack Strachey (music), the song has been recorded by Billie Holiday, Ella Fitzgerald and Frank Sinatra among others, but for me, Bryan Ferry best captures its spirit.

2. He generously gave me a copy. A couple of years later, 'The Names of the Hare' appeared in Heaney and Hughes 1982.

lurch from one financial crisis to the next and then wait shivering all day for a customer to appear; of the barbers who complain that men don't shave as much after an economic crisis; of children who play ball between the cars on cobblestoned streets; of the covered women who stand at remote bus stops clutching plastic shopping bags and speak to no-one as they wait for the bus that never arrives; of the empty boathouses of the old Bosphorus villas...[3]

For this writing to work, we must be aware, if only subconsciously, that Pamuk isn't gazing at Istanbul spread out before him and reporting what he sees. Rather, he's creating a list of recollections. In combination with the hypnotic repetition of 'of the', which Cole compares to biblical 'begats', it's our knowledge that we're reading an inventory of what Pamuk remembers that enables us to share, in a limited sense, his experience of 'the melancholia specific to Istanbul and Turkish history itself' that is his main subject in this passage (Cole 2021: 186–87).

My favorite psalm, Psalm 136, is also an inventory – of the great deeds God performed as tokens of his eternal steadfast love.[4] The much shorter preceding psalm, 135, praises God for a combination of continuing actions, such as making lightning and sending forth wind; and complete past actions, such as striking down Egypt's first-born. In Psalm 136 – aside from vv. 1-3 and 26, which exhort the reader to thank God; v. 4, which may refer to God's continuing interventions in creation (cf. Job 5.9 and 37.5); and v. 25, which speaks of his ongoing gift of food to all living beings (we'll return to this) – the psalmist is concerned with completed actions. From the first acts of creation, through bringing the Israelites out of Egypt and protecting them in the wilderness, to giving them the land of Israel, the psalmist provides us with a list of God's past deeds.

One might object that, since these deeds are specified in the order in which they occurred – creation, exodus, wilderness, land – Psalm 136 is less a list than a narrative. But lists often have organizing principles that simultaneously reflect the circumstances in or the purpose for which they were compiled and serve as aides memoire. A shopping list, for example, may follow the layout of a supermarket, which both determines its structure and helps the shopper to remember items without constantly referring to the list. A list of actions or events can be organized chronologically. In Psalm 136, I think, the psalmist uses the list as a device to draw close his audience. To paraphrase Teju Cole on a list in Virginia Woolf's *Mrs. Dalloway*, Psalm 136 'does not bring some staggering moment of insight. What it does is cook a list, nourish the eye and ear, and bring us closer to Mrs. Dalloway's [in our case, the psalmist's] consciousness and ours' (Cole 2021: 183).

---

3. Cole 2021: 186–87. Cole is citing Orhan Pamuk's *Istanbul: Memories and the City*.
4. In this article, I refer to the *JPS Tanakh* translation (1999). Following the Septuagint, Christian translations of Ps. 136 include a clause about bringing forth water from the rock (v. 16); this does not appear in the Hebrew text.

Psalm 136 is one of the *pesukei d'zimra*, verses of songs, recited during Shabbat morning prayers. In terms of frequency, that's my primary exposure to Psalm 136, but my most powerful experience of it comes once a year at the Passover *Seder*, where it appears in the Haggadah in its capacity as the *hallel ha'gadol*, the Great *Hallel*.[5] With six of its 25 verses devoted to the exodus from Egypt – from the death of the first-born to the crossing of the Reed Sea – it's a natural fit for the Haggadah. And it's fitting in another way too. Psalm 136 is for the most part a list of remembered acts, and memory and remembering are central concepts in the Passover Haggadah: 'Remember the exodus from Egypt as if you yourself were slaves in Egypt'.

For fifteen years or so, I was a leader of the Reform Jewish community in Cambridge, England, where I played a significant role in shaping synagogue services. One innovation I introduced was that we sang the entire *Hallel*, the set of six psalms (113–118) that feature in the festival liturgy. Most communities sing just the first couple of verses of each psalm or start singing *Hallel* towards the end of the *Seder*, but I wanted us to sing every word from start to finish. In those pre-YouTube days, if neither I, nor anyone I knew, knew a tune for the part of the liturgy I wanted to sing, I made one up. This process did not deserve to be called composition. Sometimes, I woke up in the morning with a tune in my head. Sometimes, I opened the *siddur* and looked long and hard at the words until a tune came. The tunes were simple and sounded quite traditional.

More than the regular *Hallel* psalms, Psalm 136, the Great *Hallel*, cries out to be sung. It has a 'chorus', the repeated כי לעולם חסדו, 'for his steadfast love is eternal', at the end of each verse. Except for v. 9, where it's necessary to cram in את הירח והכוכבים, 'the moon and stars', each verse has about the same number of syllables. And it's a list, and thus invites performance improvisations, such as variations in tempo and volume. Elizabeth Minchin compared Homer's ship-lists – a list of names with their own logic and aesthetic appeal – to the list-songs used by modern folk-musicians to showcase their skill as performers (Minchin 1996). Closer to home, readers of the Esther Scroll at Purim traditionally attempt to chant a short list – the names of Haman's ten sons in Est. 9.7-10 – in one breath. Improvisation showcases skill, but it also enables performers to emphasize or de-emphasize passages according to their needs and preferences. When singing Psalm 136 at our *Seder* – to a tune I made up – we gradually accelerate during vv. 1 through 14, then slow down dramatically and raise our voices for v. 15, in which God hurls Pharaoh and his army into the sea. As well as being particularly relevant at Passover, this verse happens to mark the end of one of the discrete sections into which Psalm 136 is divided.[6]

---

5. Various proposals are made about precisely which psalm(s) constitute(s) the Great *Hallel* (see *b. Pesaḥim* 118a), but all agree that it includes Ps. 136.

6. Different divisions have been proposed. I tentatively favor vv. 1-3, 4-9, 10-15, 16-22, 23-24, 25, 26.

Speaking of finales brings me to my last comment, on v. 25, the penultimate verse of Psalm 136. Along with lists come categories, order, a sense of what does and does not belong and what belongs where. The items listed in Psalm 136 tend to the dramatic: The LORD is the 'God of gods' (v. 2), who alone worked great marvels (v. 4), spread the earth over the water (v. 6), brought Israel out of Egypt (v. 11), struck down great kings (v. 17), brought us into the land, and rescued us from our enemies (v. 24). Decidedly non-dramatic and, as noted, different too for being ongoing as opposed to a past act, is v. 25: 'who gives food to all flesh'. Why did the psalmist end with a deed that doesn't seem to belong with the others, and that could even be seen as an anti-climax?

I have two answers to this question. The first appears in the Babylonian Talmud, *Pesaḥim* 118a. For the psalmist, daily bread was a miracle on a par with creating the universe and bringing Israel out of Egypt.[7] By mentioning it at the end of a list of seemingly more dramatic interventions, he shows us that a guaranteed food supply is at least as dramatic as creating the world, parting the sea and so forth, and deserves to be mentioned in the same breath as them. My second answer is that Psalm 136's penultimate verse forces us to re-evaluate the whole psalm. It would be so easy to see creation in Psalm 136 (as in the Bible as a whole) as little more than a striking backdrop for our real interest: Israel. But 'all flesh', which surely refers to all living beings, animals as well as humans (cf. Gen. 6.12, 13, 17, 19; 7.15, 16, 21; 8.17; 9.11, 15, 17), takes us full circle back to creation. Psalm 136 could have been so particularist, but its penultimate verse – its pinnacle, one might say – leaves no room for doubt: we must never lose sight of the big picture of which we are a part.

When Athalya Brenner-Idan graciously invited me to contribute to this commentary, I had no hesitation in choosing Psalm 136. My second choice, partly because I've sung its opening verse (in Hebrew) so many times in so many places to so many tunes with so many people who are important to me, but mostly because of its message, would have been Psalm 133,

הנה מה טוב ומה נעים שבת אחים גם יחד

How good and how pleasant it is when brothers dwell together. (133.1b)

Before *Dr. Diana Lipton* moved to Israel in 2011, she was a Fellow of Newnham College, Cambridge (1997–2006), and a Reader in Hebrew Bible and Jewish Studies at King's College London (2007–2011). In Israel, she's taught at the

---

7. 'The *Gemara* asks: And why is this section called the great *hallel*? Rabbi Yoḥanan said: Because this passage states that the Holy One, Blessed be He, sits in the heights of the universe and dispenses food to every creature. The whole world praises God for His kindness through the great *hallel*, which includes the verse: "Who gives food to all flesh" (Ps 136:25)', The William Davidson Talmud edition via Sefaria online (link to the Hebrew: https://www.sefaria.org.il/Pesachim.118a.2?lang=he).

Jerusalem Hebrew University's International School and, currently, in the Department of Biblical Studies at Tel Aviv University. She gives a weekly *shiur* (lesson) on the weekly Bible *parasha* at Beit Moses home for the elderly in Jerusalem. She serves on the Boards of Jerusalem Culture Unlimited (JCU) and Hassadna Jerusalem Music Conservatory.

References

Heaney, Seamus and Ted Hughes, eds (1982), 'The Names of the Hare', in *The Rattle Bag*, 305–306. London: Faber & Faber.

Cole, Teju (2021), *Black Paper: Writing in a Dark Time*, Chicago: University of Chicago Press.

Minchin, Elizabeth (1996), 'The Performance of Lists and Catalogues in the Homeric Epics', in Ian Worthington (ed.), *Voice into Text: Orality and Literacy in Ancient Greece*, 3–20, Leiden: Brill.

PSALM 137
A *KAU'I-TALANOA* READING*

Nāsili Vaka'uta

This reading of Psalm 137 seeks to be *interruptive*; to *kau'i-talanoa*. *Kau'i-talanoa* refers to the act of 'joining (kau) a conversation (talanoa)' or 'interrupting the flow of a *talanoa*'. In Tongan culture, kau'i-talanoa is considered disrespectful, unwanted, and improper. Underlying this attitude is a cultural view that one's right to a speaking turn is sacrosanct. Everyone is expected to know when to speak and what to speak about. What is largely ignored in the discourse of *kau'i-talanoa* is the fact that it is considered improper/*tapu* only by those who are in positions of power and privilege. Authoritarian parents do not expect their children to interrupt them when they are engaged in a conversation. We can find similar instances in religious and educational settings, especially when *kau'i-talanoa* is more intrusive than cooperative.[1]

If *talanoa* is perceived to be the right of the powerful and privileged, *kau'i-talanoa can be viewed as a means by which the powerless, the excluded, the oppressed, the marginalized, and the ignored tell their stories.* Kau'i-talanoa provides an opportunity to recover and retell one's story in one's own way, rather than being told by others. *Kau'i-talanoa* is about projecting one's voice, and recovering lost voices. It is about declaring one's presence and reclaiming absence. *Kau'i-talanoa* carries a plea to be considered, and acknowledged. It expresses a desire to be included, to be counted (*kau-he-lau*) and to belong (*lau-he-kau*). *Kau'i-talanoa* seeks to make a difference, and to open up new avenues for dialogue. But it does not ask for permission and offers no apologies. *Kau'i-talanoa* in this sense is *transformative interruption*! It does not merely interrupt for interruption's sake;

---

* This is a revised version of a Bible study on Ps. 137 for the General Assembly of the Pacific Conference of Churches, Auckland, New Zealand (29 October 2018).

1. Nāsili Vaka'uta, 'Kau'i-talanoa: Interruptive Reading/Reading Interruptions', a paper presented at the 2012 Meeting of the Oceania Biblical Studies Association, Nuku'alofa, Tonga. See also 'Kau'italanoa on Gender Justice', Keynote Address, Gender Justice Workshop, Council for World Mission, Nadi, Fiji, 1–5 June 2015.

it interrupts for the sake of transformation. *Kau'i-talanoa* can be cooperative or intrusive, but the goal is to transform. It enters the interpretation process to disrupt any narrative of exclusion and oppression.

This *kau'i-talanoa* reading of Psalm 137 is woven to allow the ignored and unheard the opportunities to speak up and speak out, to interrupt, to (re)claim their presence.

Psalm 137 is located in a situation of *displacement, loss and trauma*; the ideas it shares need to be read within that context. It opens with a group of exiled Judeans sitting by the rivers of Babylon (their new home; an empire), weeping and remembering Zion (their former home; destroyed and gone). What causes them to weep is not clear; perhaps the memories of what once was. *Memories can be painful! Why the need to remember at all?*

The psalm closes (v. 9) with a call for violence against Babylonian *babies/children* (infanticide): a discomforting call that is rooted in a need for revenge, first, against Edomites who not only failed to help them in times of suffering, but also called for sexual violation (i.e. 'strip her, strip her to her very foundations', JPS, v. 7). Second, it calls for violence against Babylonians for their brutality and barbarity, especially when they destroyed Jerusalem.

Memories of such events can be violent and can cause violence! But why do babies/children have to suffer for the sins of their parents? How might we deal with such violent texts?

Between the opening and ending, lies the following:

- The exiles are retreating from making music (lyres hung up)
- The exiles are refusing to sing (despite being asked to sing by their oppressors). It is important to note that the request is for *a song of Zion* (attached to a place, perhaps to mock the exiles). The response is about *a song of the Lord* (attached to a person). Does this imply that every song of Zion is the Lord's song? If so, are the exiles only allowed to sing in the Lord's land, and not anywhere else? But isn't the Lord's land now owned by the Babylonians?
- The central question is (v. 4): *How can we sing a song of the LORD on alien soil?* But one might also ask:
  - Which/whose song is the Lord's?
  - Isn't Zion an alien soil as well?
- The exiles pledge not to forget Zion
  - What is Zion to the exiles? A home?
  - What is a home?
  - Is it a place? Is it an imagined space?
  - Is home a fixed, immobile place?

The overarching orientation of the psalm is to remind the readers the significance of Zion/Jerusalem as their homeland. Yet, this is far from being the only exilic voice in the Bible. Jeremiah 29.4-7 offers a different voice,

⁴Thus said the LORD of Hosts, the God of Israel, to the whole community which I exiled from Jerusalem to Babylon: ⁵'*Build houses and live in them, plant gardens and eat their fruit. ⁶Take wives and beget sons and daughters; and take wives for your sons, and give your daughters to husbands, that they may bear sons and daughters. Multiply there, do not decrease. ⁷And seek the welfare of the city to which I have exiled you and pray to the LORD in its behalf; for in its prosperity you shall prosper.*' (JPS)

Whereas in Psalm 137 the call is for exclusion, non-conformity and violence, Jeremiah 29 urges immersion, integration, and co-existence. Whereas Psalm 137 puts emphasis on the memory of Zion, their homeland, Jeremiah 29 encourages the building of new homes in their new host-land regardless of what happened. Whereas in Psalm 137 home is a place to remember and return to, home in Jeremiah 29 is something you *negotiate on the move*, and *not a place of return*.

So, *what are the implications of these two biblical positions on exile and home for Pacific migrants in various places, and for Pacific migrant churches in particular? What might be our position on migrants and refugees – those who seek to find shelter amongst us in our midst?*

I will return to these questions shortly, but let me bring your attention back to some very important issues that have emerged from the text (and I will deal with them very briefly because I do not have the luxury of space) here.

Migration Is Our Story

The story of humanity is one of movement and migration; we are all migrants! That is who we are! We constantly participate in the ongoing cycle of *departure, travel and arrival*. And we never settle! Once we arrive, we depart! That is what makes life exciting!

The stories recorded in the Bible are migrant stories – of people seeking refuge, of people looking for a new life, of people exploring new possibilities, of people seeking new opportunities, of people venturing into the unknown for its own sake, of people being forced to move, of people whose only option is to escape from slavery, violence and oppression, and so forth.

Among these people is a Migrant God whom we find in their midst – a God who moves with them, wanders with them, crosses boundaries with them, confronts oppression with them, breaks traditions of death with them, shares bread of life with them, dwells with the least of them, resists hegemonies among them, endures hardships with them, and ultimately, for some, dies and lives for them! That is what a Migrant God looks like! So should be migrant churches!

It is important to be mindful of migrants whose humanity is constantly questioned by heartless political leaders around the world. For examples, the refugees from Central America who flocked to the US seeking a safer place for their children; or Syrian refugees and those from war-torn countries in various parts of the world. Closer to home are refugees in Nauru and Manus islands, who have been denied entry into Australia on nonsensical grounds.[2] There are also those who are victims of human trafficking, those constantly moved against their will to serve the interests of greedy and evil traffickers.

Memory Is Our Link

Migration is the condition for memory. We yearn to remember because we shift and move constantly, and as such, we are linked to places, peoples and events by our memories. Psalm 137 repeatedly mentions memory and remembrance with reference to Zion, Jerusalem and God. Israel is called upon to remember who they are not only as chosen people, but also as former slaves delivered by God.

Memories, however, differ from one person/group to another. Our ability to remember is not the same. Sometimes we have selective memory. We remember only that which we choose to remember. And not all memories are pleasant; some need to be ignored, otherwise they will cause more harm than good.

Memory is not a perfect reconstruction of the past. At best we have distorted memories. Whatever we recreate/clone will also be imperfect. Memory can be violent and vengeful (Ps. 137.9).

Most migrants are holding on to memories of places, ideas, traditions and practices that belong to a bygone era and as such unable to embrace what is new, relevant and life-affirming. Our memories need checking!

Home Is Built Enroute

Home is negotiated on the move, and cannot be fixed. Why? Because we cannot return to the same home twice!

I migrated from Tonga to New Zealand about eighteen years ago. Every time I go back, Tonga is no longer the same place I left behind. It has evolved and changed so much in every way. To be nostalgic about the Tonga I knew then would make me feel foolish because that Tonga no longer exists.

So are the communities of yesterday and yester-years. We build migrant communities wherever we move, but instead of embracing what is new we in most cases still seek to emulate the communities we have left behind as if they are incapable of changing.

The options for Pacific migrant communities is either to clone replicas of their home overseas and render irrelevant to the new generation of Pacific Islanders, or to adopt Jeremiah's alternative: mingle with the new and promote what's on the ground, for in their prosperity, you shall prosper!

Violence Is Not Ok!

Violence is prevalent in religions and in sacred texts, including the Church and the Bible. The #MeToo movement against sexual violence exposes the barbarity of

---

2. See, for instance, http://www.refugeeaction.org.au/?page_id=4528.

the issue and the complicity of churches, Christian leaders, and their sacred texts. To go along with texts that call for stripping and bashing of women and children, like Psalm 137, is to commit violence in the name of God and religion, and that is totally unacceptable. Violence of any kind must be resisted, and any violent-supportive systems (like patriarchy and empire) must be demolished.

The following questions need further *kau'i-talanoa*:

- How might we, as members of Pacific churches, respond to this issue of violence in our midst?
- How safe are our Church spaces for our children, women and those who are vulnerable to such acts of violence?
- How might we weave ourselves together in a way that respects and promotes the dignity and humanity of those subjugated by oppressive systems like patriarchy/capitalism?

The challenge for Pacific churches both inside and outside the region is to envision a future that is life-giving for everyone. Such a future begins with the courage to move beyond the borders of our own ethnic, cultural and denominational boundaries. It involves empowering people to speak truth to power, speak the truth about power, and strive for justice, equality and fullness of life.

That is the Lord's song, and that is the song worth-singing wherever we are!

My second psalm choice would be Psalm 88. My attention is always captured by the fact that the psalmist suffers, yet has the strength to utter this prayer and speak out. Where in other lament psalms there is a glimpse of hope or redemption, this one still lurks in the 'shadow of death'.

Nāsili Vaka'uta is Principal and Ranston Lecturer in Biblical Studies, Trinity Theological College, Auckland, New Zealand. He is a proud Tongan native and an advocate for Moana hermeneutics and epistemologies. He co-founded the Oceania Biblical Studies Association (OBSA). Among his published works is a new volume he co-edited (with Jione Havea and Emily Colgan), *Theology as Threshold: Invitations from Aotearoa New Zealand* (Lexington, 2022).

PSALM 137
EMOTIONS OF THE EXILES IN A FOREIGN LAND

Wei Huang

Among all the psalms, Psalm 137 attracted my attention immediately when I had my first look at the book. It conveys strong feelings. I am quite touched by the nostalgic tone in the poem, when the captives answer the demand addressed to them by refusing to sing YHWH's song in a foreign land. I cannot help asking myself: how could I comprehend the emotional expressions in the poem when I do not either belong to this historical exilic community, or possess an identity as a descendant of those exiles? As a Chinese, can I explain to myself the fluctuations in emotion I get from reading the poem?

The poem's narrated setting is the Babylonian exile. The opening verses present the sorrows using the grammatical first-person plural, showing a vivid image of a group of homesick captives sitting and crying by the rivers of Babylon. Their sorrows are sharply contrasted with the scenario that follows, when the Babylonians request the Judean deportees to sing a homeland song for pleasure (or, most likely, for reasons of exotic curiosity on the latter's side?). Undoubtedly, the captors do not understand the captives' sorrows, and are making the request joyfully. Yet the contrast between sorrow and joy causes the Judean deportees even stronger longings for their homeland. Certainly, the sorrows are so deep that the captives express their refusal to sing. The last section of the poem implies the bitter memory of the destruction of Jerusalem. It then arouses further the anger of the people who have lost their country. The rage is against their political and military oppressors. Therefore, in the end a wishful revenge is called out to praise those who would violently attack even the most vulnerable: the newborns of their enemies.

I agree with the opinion that the poem was historically non-specific, even if it is set as if the narration happens in Babylon (Brenner 2003: 86). The strong emotions in the poem form an assumed exile experience, which participates in making a collective memory of the Judean deportees and later the Jewish identity. While I feel the psalmist's sorrow, I share, alter and reproduce the pain of losing one's country. With my identity as a Chinese reader, I cannot resist relating the sorrow for losing one's country with my own cultural texts.

My first example is *The Book of Poetry* (*Shijing*), which is the earliest anthology of poems in China, compiled more than 2500 years ago. The book consists of 305 poems collected by royal musicians. It was highly appraised by later generations and became one of the six classical canons of Confucianism, thus as the textbook for Chinese intellectuals in the following thousands of years. Confucius said, 'If you do not learn the Odes [=*The Book of Poetry*], you will not be fit to converse with' (*The Analects*: Book XVI. Ke She 13.3; Legge 1893; the note in brackets is my rendering).[1]

Depending on the occasion in which the poems of the *Book* were used, there are three types:

1. Ballads sung by the people in 15 feudal states.
2. Odes sung by the nobles at court or at banquets.
3. Hymns used during sacrifice to the gods and ancestors.

Both the odes and hymns, some of which usually praise the military prowess of the king and the victory of the campaign against the frontier tribes, in fact might have been sung in the presence of the feudal princes and the king. However, in the collection of ballads we find that poems would rather describe the chaos and sufferings of wars, and also the great sadness over the desolation of one's homeland. In the piece titled 'Shu Li' ('Rows of Millet'), the poet expresses his feelings for his homeland. The poem reiterates a description of the millet with its drooping heads, and sorghum that is growing. Instead of enjoying the joy of a great harvest, the poet must leave his homeland. Repeatedly, the poet addresses his mournful cry out to Heaven. Similarly, pieces such as 'A Wife Waiting' and 'My Man is Away' voice the anxiety and longing of a wife whose husband is on military duty and serves on the frontier. 'Complaint of a Soldier', 'The Ruined Capital', 'In Garrison', 'A Refuge', and 'A Homesick Warrior'[2] – to name but a few soldiers' songs – express the sorrows of soldiers for being away from their homeland and their complaints about the cruel wars.

I would like to introduce another piece of literature as well, 'The Siege of Gaixia', in order to illustrate how emotions may become prominent in historical writings. This piece is included in the *Records of the Grand Historian*, a work by Sima Qian (ca. 135–86 BCE), the so-called Chinese Herodotus. The historical background of the account is the period of the demise of the powerful Qin Empire and the rivalry of regional kingdoms. Xiang Yu of Chu and Liu Bang of Han were powerful contenders for the imperial throne. They had been engaged in war for more than four years. 'The Siege of Gaixia' narrates the final battle of the Chu and Han. By the time of the siege, Liu Bang (of Han) had already managed to have all the other rivals of Xiang Yu (of Chu) join his alliance. And yet, the Han army was outnumbered about threefold by the Chu army. The situation called for a trick. At

---

1. For another take on some parts of *The Book of Poetry* see further Lee's article on Ps. 78 in this volume, pp. 101–108.
2. The English titles quoted here are from Xu Yuanchong's translation (Xu 2013).

night, Liu Bang instructed the Han army to loudly sing songs from the kingdom of Chu. Xiang Yu was agitated and despondent by hearing the Chu songs from the Han army: he speculated that the Han army had already captured many soldiers from the region of Chu. In the company of his consort, the fierce and arrogant warrior Xiang Yu had to face his final failure. He sang a song lamenting his failure and the fate that would befall his beautiful Concubine Yu. This is how a military defeat emotionally was summed up by a private affair.

And indeed, this emotional piece later became one of the most popular episodes of the Beijing Opera, in which Xiang Yu and his Concubine Yu are created as much more legendary figures than in the *Records of the Grand Historian* itself. Thus, the 'cult' film *Farewell My Concubine* (1993), directed by Chen Kaige, follows the lives of two Beijing Opera performers, who are famous for playing the episode of *Farewell My Concubine*. The film was awarded the Palm d'Or at the Cannes Film Festival. The story from ancient times certainly touched present readers/audience in its emotional rather than historical form.

Having such texts in mind, I notice that the Chinese translation of Psalms by John C.H. Wu is an excellent example of relocating the biblical texts to the Chinese literary traditions (Hong 2022). So let me return to Psalm 137. Like the poems in the *Shijing*, Wu came up with a title for each piece in the book of Psalms, and Psalm 137 is entitled 'Remembering the Past'. It is not uncommon to find more than one Chinese poem with this title throughout history. Wu also adopts the classical Chinese poetry styles in his translation of Psalm 137. By doing so, Wu's version looks very much like a genuine ancient Chinese poem.

It is worth noting that eponyms/toponyms mentioned in the text, such as 'Babylon', 'Zion', and 'Jerusalem' are usually transcribed phonetically, in Chinese characters. The only exception is the name 'Edom'. In the currently dominant Union Version,[3] the two Chinese characters for 'Edom' do not create any meanings. But Wu skillfully chose the two Chinese characters, *Yi* and *Dong*, that roughly correspond to the pronunciation of *E-dom*. On the other hand, *Yi Dong/ Dong Yi* is an existing Chinese idiom, referring to the ethnic groups east of the Central Plains of China. It literally means 'foreigners from the East'. I believe that Wu brought this idiom into his translation deliberately. The resentment of *Dong Yi* by Chinese readers thus adds another layer of emotions and comprehension, not to mention contemporaneous relevance, to the Chinese reading of the translated psalm.

From the above examples, I conclude that:

1. Emotions are part of historical meaning-making.
2. Cultural circumstances have a notable effect on emotional experience.
3. Cultural differences in linguistic expressions shape our emotions.
4. Emotions are crucial to the understanding of human experience.

3. For the origin of the Chinese Union translation of the Bible (CUV), see Strand 2018 (ChinaSPPource | The Origins of the Chinese Union Version Bible). For the Chinese Union Version translation of the psalm, go to Hong Kong Bible Society Online Bible: http://rcuv.hkbs.org.hk/RCUV1/PSA/137/.

Expressing emotions does not always alleviate them. The reason why emotions are shared in texts (or visual art) is that the infinite reproduction of emotions turns all readers (or audience) into the carrier of emotions. What I gain by reading Psalm 137 is not only getting to understand other traditions through emotions, but to comprehend more about myself. As in what Confucius commented on the *Book of Poetry*. Here is what the master said,

> The Odes serve to stimulate the mind. They may be used for purposes of self-contemplation. They teach the art of sociability. They show how to regulate feelings of resentment. From them you learn the more immediate duty of serving one's father, and the remoter one of serving one's prince. (The *Analects*: Book XVII. Yang Ho 9:2-5; Legge 1893)

If I were asked to choose another psalm, I would choose Psalm 129. I like the unique and graphic metaphors in this concise piece. 'The plow', 'the cord', 'the grass on roofs', all together form the background of the agricultural world which can be shared with my cultural texts.

Dr. Wei Huang is an assistant professor of World History in the Department of History, Shanghai University. She serves in the committee of the Society of Asian Biblical Studies (SABS). Huang is interested in reading the Hebrew Bible together with the Chinese classics. Currently she is conducting a research project on the history of ancient Israelite religion.

References

Brenner, A. (2003), '"On the Rivers of Babylon" (Psalm 137), or between Victim and Perpetrator', in J. Bekkenkamp and Y. Sherwood (eds), *Sanctified Aggression: Legacies of Biblical and Post-Biblical Vocabularies of Violence*, 76–91, The Bible in the Twenty-First Century 3, London: T&T Clark.

Hong, Xiaochun (2022), 'The Bible between Literary Traditions: John C.H. Wu's Chinese Translation of the Psalms', *Religions* 13 (10): 937.

Legge, James, trans. (first published 1879), *The Shih King or Book of Poetry* (online: https://www.gutenberg.org/cache/epub/9394/pg9394-images.html).

Legge, James, trans. (first published 1893), 'Confucian Analects', in *The Chinese Classics: With a Translation, Critical and Exegetical Notes, Prolegomena, and Copious Indexes*. Vol. 1 (online: https://www.gutenberg.org/cache/epub/4094/pg4094-images.html).

Strand, Mark (2018), 'The Origins of the Chinese Union Version of the Bible' (ChinaSource | The Origins of the Chinese Union Version Bible).

Wu, John C.H. (吳經熊) (1946), *The First Draft of Paraphrasing the Psalms. With Comments by Chairman Chiang* (聖詠義譯初稿:蔣主席手訂), Shanghai: The Commercial Press.

Xu, Yuanchong (许渊冲), trans. (2013), *The Book of Poetry: An English Translation with Chinese Text* (诗经:汉英对照), Beijing: Haitun Publishing (北京:海豚出版社).

PSALM 137
SONG OF A BROKEN HEART

Hemchand Gossai

Introduction

We are living in a time when some leaders in communities and states across the US are banning books in classrooms and libraries, employing the dubious argument that the subject matter creates discomfort for students. In doing so a wide swath of history is excised and discarded, particularly if the subject matter forces us to have serious moments of introspection and the remembrance of a painful past. As important as historical foundations are, we read the texts and hear stories from where we are, defined in part by who we are and our experiences. Interpreters reading alongside each other, but coming from different circumstances, will invariably explore texts differently, and that certainly enriches and widens the scope of the discourse. The conclusions may be different even as the lenses are different.

Psalm 137

> Happy shall they be who take your little ones
>   and dash them against the rock! (Ps. 137.9, NRSV)

The deep resonance of Psalm 137 for me as a first-generation immigrant to the US has to do with a sense of longing and belonging. It is not any specific parallel with the experience of exile, but rather the remembrance of home that brought tears and nostalgia of a time that was lost, snatched away. Being alone in a foreign land in the midst of taunts that generated a longing for a home not as an actual place but an idea.

I have been drawn to Psalm 137 for a while now and even though the themes are painful, difficult, challenging, poignant and where the last verse might justifiably be described as odious and abhorrent. Yet, the last verse is an integral part of the psalm and it cannot, must not, be redacted for the sake of comfort. To redact the closing verse of Psalm 137 is to discard the deep and poignant emotions of an exiled and enslaved people. Excising such memory has a particular pernicious and re-enslavement quality to it. Themes such as imperial power, exile, despair, betrayal, mockery and heartfelt anger, among others, have ongoing universal pertinence and applicability. Psalm 137 captures the brutal existence of the exiles' experience, and the longing for what was. The military and political reach of the Babylonian Empire has left, and continues to leave, its mark on society. One of the protracted and persistent themes in Psalm 137 is the idea of how to balance the need for cultural assimilation while ensuring that one's religious and national identity is maintained. Further, how to ensure that the voice of the exiles is not muted or silenced, so that they are able to complain and appeal to God with searing cries, and not resort to violence acts.

Reading Psalm 137 in isolation might very well lead one to conclude that it was one incident or issue that was the generating factor that brought about the culmination in v. 9. Collectively, however, we witness the range of interconnected issues that set in motion this moment. It is not an overnight guilt or isolated act that has brought the exile into being, by any measure; it seems to be a level of punishment that spans time and space. With this as a backdrop, the healing and restoration that will be necessary will not eventuate in one moment either. The exiles will be stripped bare, and if not literally in this instance, certainly in other ways, as they seek to forge, survive and live out a new identity. The idea of seeking revenge is a deep-rooted human impulse, and nowhere in this psalm is this impulse more aggressively stated than in the final verse. But this is not only 'an eye for an eye' but the violence against the most painful loss, namely one's child, and therefore one's future. It is important to note that Psalm 137, with its brutal imagery in v. 9, is placed firmly in the canonical context of psalms of praise and thanksgiving.

The psalm begins with weeping and is punctuated by the memory of what once was, a deep chasm between longing and belonging, one that will never be bridged. Jerusalem is on the minds and hearts of the exiles, and the sharpness of their memory brings a particular kind of melancholia. In this state of stark honesty and heartbrokenness, the exiles believe that they cannot sing songs of home. Not because they are incapable, but because memory coupled with the taunts by their captors make it impossible to be joyful. While their tormentors ask for joy, the exiles are in a state of despair. Despite the divine promise of a homecoming in time, in the present exilic reality joy has retreated in the distance. Fear and anger, despair and longing all make for an expression of violence that is shocking. Yet, in this context it is an appeal to God. Revenge and pain are borne out of the depth of suffering and a sense of betrayal and abandonment in the exilic experience. As much as any other moment in Psalm 137, v. 9 is a devastating reminder of their own children, and with that a future that will never be.

As much as any other text of lamentation, it is Psalm 137 that provides a backdrop of what exile is like in Babylon. The qualities of life; the range of emotions; the grasp of a lost existence; the evaporating of hopes and aspirations; the loss of belonging and home – all have left an indelible mark on the exiles. Yet, this psalm is not only about unrestrained violent revenge. In the midst of extraordinary and life-transforming despair, the exiles' memory will not allow them to neglect or forget the history of their relationship with God and Jerusalem. Thus, the canonical placement of Psalm 137 alongside psalms of praise and lament is not in any way inappropriate. Rather, this is an appeal to God in the midst of the suffering brought about by God and sanctioned by God. The heart of the exiles cries out, and this serves as a reminder that the suffering and despair of the exiles come from their hearts, hidden from the world but known to God. These tears will continue, and the belief is that God might still respond. For the audience, then and now, the idea of crying from the heart, or being 'heartbroken', is acutely understood with a sense that what comes from the heart comes from the core of who one is, stripped of all pretenses, and only God ultimately knows. The exiles know that the Babylonian exile will not last forever, and as much as the temptation to seek revenge is present, it is the memory of the exiles and their appeal to God that contextualizes the climactic verse. One of the definable elements that is borne out of the Babylonian influence is the painful reality of loss of life as captives and exiles.

Psalm 137 stands as a sharp recollection of those who have caused the exiles pain, and the juxtaposition of both covenantal kin and enemy. It underlines the unbridled freedom to question and challenge God, knowing that in so doing they will not nullify the covenant relationship. I think of James Baldwin's words, 'I love America more than any other country in the world, and exactly for this reason, I insist on the right to criticize her perpetually' (*Notes of a Native Son*, 1955). Thus, we have the terrifying vision of smashing heads of Babylonian children, and perhaps this also indirectly indicts God on allowing the devastating violence against the Jewish children. We know that trauma does not leave one untouched and there are certainly intended and unintended consequences.

Moreover, literally and as a figurative representation of imperial power in a distinct and discernable demonstration, the Empire is not beyond mercy and redemption. Even though Nebuchadnezzar might not feel compelled to show mercy to the exiles, both king and Empire will be held accountable, and this would be one of the foundational factors for indictment and punishment. Compassion begets compassion. While in exile, the Jews are expected to be shown compassion and mercy. What the Babylonian Empire has exemplified with clarity is the fact that compassion, mercy and justice are not narrowly construed and located in an exclusive geography. However, whatever might have been said or understood to be expected is not practiced. Two ideas converge at this point. First, it is possible that mercy and righteousness are both within the parameters of an imperial government, and that these realities are not mutually exclusive. Second, there is the pronounced notion that those with power who choose to rule with force, but without a sense of justice, mercy and righteousness may for a while feel the quality of permanence in their potency, but such self-assurance will not last. Ultimately empires collapse under such an unsustainable burden of unfiltered power, as in fact the Babylonian Empire did.

In the Babylonian exile, the Jews are called upon to redefine their identity, and they are told that their very identity will be inextricably interwoven with that of the Babylonians. This will not be the people's choice, but rather a divine and prophetic mandate. This exile becomes, among many things, an occasion for a sharp redefining of how imperial power, which posits itself as invincible, will potentially be reshaped in the face of a newly construed peace ethic.

We know that historically migration happens for a variety of reasons, and the biblical memory constitutes forced migration. Could this experience of Babylonian captivity aid in defining the manner in which refugees and others might be welcomed in a community? Equally aligned is the notion of how a community or nation welcomes the exiled and migrants who seek refuge. Such a template for refugee status has had extraordinary implications and impetus for centuries, as refugees and migrants from a variety of geographical contexts, and with a spectrum of particularities including religion, ethnicity, nationality, caste, political affiliations, economics and perhaps most notably war, have sought haven. While a development of forced migration and the ensuing trauma generated by such migration is beyond the scope of this essay, it is an area that is being addressed by scholars.

In particular, we might reflect on those persons whose lives were defined by an exilic experience in which they were made voiceless through the actions of those with human power. Many may be called the 'in between' generation, as the exiles in Babylon might have been classified. Their lives had to be acculturated to the extent that they embrace the mores of Babylon while seeking the welfare extended by their captors. Given the duration of the Babylonian exile, many of the 'in between' generation would know only Babylon as their home. It is a common hallmark for exiles and refugees that for a while they may have a longing for 'home', but invariably 'home' may very well be the idea of belonging, and not necessarily a geographical location.

Care for the other will challenge the narrowly construed rebuilding of Jerusalem and the reconstituting of a community of faith. The exilic experience established the inextricable connection between one's welfare and that of the other, particularly when the other's identity is that of oppressor and enemy. Such a principle is not guided by nationality, religion, ethnicity, status, station in life, etc. The exile in Babylon underlines the philosophical and practical approach to governing and the politics of government.

My second choice would have been Psalm 30. Grief comes to us in a variety of ways but is never the last word.

Dr. Hemchand Gossai is Associate Dean of Humanities and Social Sciences at Northern Virginia Community College, US, and Professor of Hebrew Bible. He is the author of several scholarly volumes and two memoirs.

PSALM 139
FULLY KNOWN*

Margaret Aymer

A Brief Description of the Psalm

In the fifth and final division of the book, Psalms 138–145 stand apart as a collection of Davidic Psalms (DeClaissé-Walford 2020: 253; DeClaissé-Walford, Jacobson, and Tanner 2014: 748). Psalm 139, the second of this collection, is my favorite psalm. Scholars debate about the nature and purpose of this psalm, alternatively considering it a prayer of confidence and trust (Goldingay 2008: 626), a psalm of lament (Longman 2014: 452), a psalm of thanksgiving (DeClaissé-Walford 2020: 258), and even simply a wisdom meditation (Hossfeld and Zenger 2011). The psalm is bounded in vv. 1 and 23 by the words 'search' (חקר, *ḥqr Qal*) and 'know' (ידע, *ydʿ Qal*), words that bracket the psalm in a poetic form called an *inclusio*.

Psalm 139 consists of four strophes, or sections, of six verses each. The first asserts God's omniscience. The poet confesses that God knows them and surrounds them fully.[1] They underscore the fullness of God's knowledge by using pairs of contrasts, or merisms, to indicate the extent to which God knows them. The poet confesses God knows when they sit and when they rise, their walking path and their lying down (139.2-3). That is, God is aware of all their movements. God discerns even what they are going to say before they speak it (139.4). Indeed, God's presence is binding, from the Hebrew verb צור (*ṣwr Qal*) that can have the negative connotation of 'bind' or 'besiege'. God's knowledge cannot be escaped, says the poet.

Strophe two, 139.7-12, moves from divine omniscience to omnipresence. The poet confesses God's presence in all places and circumstances: heaven or Sheol, darkness or light. These merisms underscore that God is inescapable, even in places where people might go to hide. The similarities here to the story in Jonah 1 about his flight from God, the storm and his being swallowed by a big fish have

---

* All English translations come from the NRSVue.
1. I am using gender-neutral pronouns for the poet.

not been lost on scholars of this psalm. Nevertheless, I do not agree with Frank Hossfeld that the psalmist wishes to flee from God (Hossfeld and Zenger 2011: 540). The psalmist appears to be confessing the impossibility of escape, rather than lamenting it.

Strophe three, 139.13-18, imagines God as omnitemporal – that is, existing throughout all time. The poet's own temporality is bounded by their lifespan, but God predates their birth and holds their length of days, never abandoning them from conception until the moment of death. While this strophe often gets maladroitly deployed by those calling themselves 'pro-life,' the poet's words do not prescribe fetal gestation. Instead, the poet describes a God who wove together the poet's 'unformed substance' (139.15-16). The word the poet uses for 'my unformed substance,' גָּלְמִי (*golmî*), occurs only once in the entire Bible and seems to have been borrowed from a cognate language, Babylonian Aramaic (DeClaissé-Walford 2014: 750). This word does not mean 'embryo' or 'fetus' but rather something more like a 'formless mass'. Here, the poet evokes images of God forming humanity from the humus of the earth (Gen. 2).

The final strophe, 139.19-24, can be jarring for the contemporary reader. The poet first yearns for God's destruction of the wicked, proclaiming hatred toward God's enemies. Such sentiments often arise from those who find themselves oppressed by forces bigger than themselves, and as such seem out of place from the lips of a David, to whom the psalm is attributed. More likely this poem emerges from the lips of exiles unable to fight 'the bloodthirsty' and those who 'lift themselves up against' God (and presumably God's people) 'for evil' (139.19-20). Echoes of these sorts of feelings may be found in other art forms of the oppressed, such as the African American sorrow songs. The poet, however, does not end vindictively but reflectively. Returning to the original themes in 139.23-24, God is once again invited to 'search' and 'know' the poet, and to lead them 'in the way everlasting.'

The Immigrants' Daughter Speaks

Immigration is a form of deracination. This remains true whether one immigrates willingly or is a subject of forced migration. The act of moving removes one physically, culturally, and psychosocially from the 'ground' of one's being. I am an immigrant and the daughter of immigrants. At the age of nine, my parents left Caribbean soil to immigrate to the United States, toward otherwise unavailable academic opportunities. And, as my sisters and I were minors, we came too.

We entered an aeroplane (British spelling) in the Caribbean and stepped out of an airplane (American spelling) in New Jersey onto unfamiliar ground where flats had become apartments, cars had trunks not boots, people cheered for football, not cricket, and adults played spades, not dominoes. We landed in a world where children dressed up in strange costumes in late October, and television came in color. Moreover, we stepped through the veil of race, going from majority people to minoritized others, neither Black enough for those groups into which we would be racialized, nor white at all. There were few ties to our past: our parents, yes, but precious few others. Where before we had been known by our parents, known to our community, known in our schools, now we were strangers, foreigners for the first time in our lives.

O Lord, YOU have searched me out! O Lord, YOU know me! Our one tether was faith, the practices of Christianity which traveled with us through the clouds and descended to the tarmac of Newark Airport in our hearts, in our minds, in the words we recited from the Christian scriptures even as children. We had come to a place where we would spend years being unknown, misunderstood, and misrepresented. Our family lived in other lands. Our friends were left behind. But still we relied on the One who searched us out, the One who knew us.

This psalm reminded us, reminds me still, even in this place between heaven and Sheol called the United States, that I am not removed from God's presence, nor from God's spirit. Rather, like the poet, I find myself trusting that even here, wherever here is at this moment, God is nearby to guide, to take hold, to hem me in behind and before. Unlike others who have read these lines as controlling (cf. the excursus in DeClaissé-Walford 2020: 266), I hear them as the inspiration of St. Patrick's Breastplate, that Irish prayer of God's protection that imagines one being surrounded by Christ: 'behind me', 'before me', 'beneath me', 'above me' (Alexander 1889).

The psalmist also reminds me to love myself, my flesh, for I am God's own weaving, God's own handiwork. *I praise you because I am fearfully and wonderfully made*: big-bellied, brown-skinned, with a head full of curly-nappy hair. Here, in our place of deracination, we found ourselves swept up in a world that disdained our fearfully, wonderfully made bodies, that were too large, with hairs on our heads that refused to hang completely straight even when malformed by chemical processes that left us scalp-sore and rain-wary. This world questioned the capacities of our fearfully, wonderfully made brains that had been reading since we turned three, that had been doing mental math for five years before we were expected to be less than others. We found ourselves in a world where Black girls were not supposed to be excellent students, but were supposed to understand basketball and cheerleading and gospel music, a world where we were anomalies, curiosities, always already suspicious to the others around us of every color. Our pepper pot of Caribana admixture, at once African and British, Indian[2] and Latinx, informed by drums without sticks and curry and syncopated rhythms so 'exotic' to the American ear, caused confusion, hilarity, scorn. Yet the poet reminds me, reminds us: *I am, we are, fearfully and wonderfully made. That we know full well.*

And what of the imprecations at the end of the psalm? In truth, I probably did not know them as a younger child. However, as I progressed through adolescence and faced the bullying that often accompanies difference in culture, accent, and economic class, I certainly would have known occasions to pray for God's protection, perhaps not in these words but with a similar passion and, sometimes, even

---

2. Approximately 20,000 laborers from India came to Jamaica as indentured servants to harvest sugar cane after African emancipation, among them my great-grandparents.

similar vitriol. I cannot remember ever praying for God's vengeance upon others, but for my own safety – yes, the psalmist spoke for me.

And still the poet speaks. As I have aged with this psalm, I have found myself praying it differently. As a mother of a white male child watching the radicalization of white men into terrorists capable of racist acts of bloodshed and murder, I have prayed for protection from the bloodthirsty many times – protection for him whom I love as though I gave him birth, and protection for me also.

And since there is no place between Sheol and heaven that God cannot be, here in this place I accepted the call to Christian ordination in the Presbyterian church. Once again rose the prayer of the ancient poet, as I discerned my sense of call and vocation: 'Search me and know my heart, test me and know my thoughts. See if there is any wicked way in me, and lead me in the way everlasting' (139.23-24).

I am still on the move. Years after our family deracinated from the Islands, I have found myself transplanted many times. My sojourn has taken me from the northeast to the south and now deep into the heart of Texas. And yet, I have found the psalmist to be true: even here God's hand leads me. Even here, the right hand of God continues to hold me fast.

Were I to choose a second psalm, it would perhaps be Psalm 19. I cannot help but hear Haydn's majestic chorus as the psalm begins,[3] but that chorus also reminds me, when I am feeling most displaced, to look up. For the heavens declare God's glory, regardless of where on earth you stand. At its center, the psalm reminds me to turn once more to the scriptures of my faith, for revival and wisdom, joy and enlightenment (19.7-9). I turn not as a naïve reader, but as a scholar of texts, both faithful and critical, being both instructed by these ancient writings and warned by the places in which they fail. Psalm 19 ends with the prayer that begins almost every one of my sermons, a prayer repeated by many around the world: 'Let the words of my mouth and the meditation of my heart be acceptable to you, O Lord, my rock and my redeemer'.

Margaret Aymer is an ordained Minister of Word and Sacrament in the Presbyterian Church (U.S.A), and serves Austin Presbyterian Theological Seminary in Austin, Texas, as Academic Dean and First Presbyterian Church, Shreveport, D. Thomason Professor of New Testament Studies.

References

Alexander, Cecil Frances (1889), 'I bind unto myself today', in *The Writings of St. Patrick*, edited by Charles Wright, London: Religious Tract Society, https://www.hymnologyarchive.com/patricks-hymn.

---

3. See, for instance, https://bibleasmusic-com.translate.goog/die-himmel-erzahlen-die-ehre-gottes-the-heavens-are-telling-the-glory-of-god-from-die-schopfung-the-creation-psalm-19-1-3-joseph-haydn/?_x_tr_sl=en&_x_tr_tl=iw&_x_tr_hl=iw&_x_tr_pto=sc.

Clifford, Richard J. (2002), *Psalms 1–72*, Abingdon Old Testament Commentaries, Nashville: Abingdon

DeClaissé-Walford, Nancy L. (2020), *Psalms: Books 4–5*, Wisdom Commentary 22, Collegeville, MN: Liturgical Press.

DeClaissé-Walford, Nancy L., Rolf A. Jacobson, and Beth Laneel Tanner (2014), *The Book of Psalms*, The New International Commentary to the Old Testament, Grand Rapids: Eerdmans.

Goldingay, John (2008), *Psalms 90–150*, Baker Commentary on the Old Testament, Grand Rapids: Baker Academic.

Hossfeld, F.L. and E. Zenger (2011), *Psalms 3*, Hermeneia, Minneapolis: Fortress.

Longman, Tremper, III (2014), *Psalms: An Introduction and Commentary*, Tyndale Old Testament Commentaries, Downers Grove: InterVarsity Academic.

PSALM 146
A NATIVE RESTORYING OF THE PSALM UNDER TSUNAMI AND COVID WAVES

Jione Havea

As the Psalter draws to a close, a confident poet praises Yhwh and admonishes their[1] (for the poet) own soul (נפשׁ, *nefesh*) to disregard princes and mortals ('son of man') – princes and mortals are not to be trusted, there is no help in them (Ps. 146.1-2).[2] On the day that princes and mortals die, their thoughts and plans perish with their breaths and their bodies return to dust (146.3-4). Yhwh the god of Jacob is different – Yhwh is more superior, worthier, dependable, and durable. The people who locate their hope upon Yhwh find happiness in their lifetime (146.5; cf. Ps. 1). The poet supports their personal admonishment with traditional theological explanations:

- Yhwh created the sky, earth, and sea, along with their cohorts;
- Yhwh keeps truth, forever (146.6).
- Yhwh executes justice for the oppressed, and provides food for the hungry;
- Yhwh sets prisoners free (146.7).
- Yhwh heals the blind, and assists the downtrodden;
- Yhwh loves the righteous (146.8).
- Yhwh keeps the strangers, and upholds the fatherless and widows;
- Yhwh brings the wicked to ruin (146.9).
- Yhwh will reign forever, and for all generations,
- Hallelujah (146.10).

In closing, the poet praises Yhwh and thus opens the Doxological Hallels (Pss. 146–150). I imagine that the poet's soul, and whomever might have overheard

---

1. The author of this essay uses gender-neutral pronouns here.
2. Translations from the Hebrew are the author's unless otherwise stated.

their meditation (which could have been spoken out in the open, in public),[3] would have responded with their own 'Hallelujah' and 'Praise Yah'.

reStorying

This reflection diverts from the usual paths for doing contextual interpretation (Havea and Lau 2020). Instead of using concepts and realities *from* our living contexts to unpack Psalm 146 (for other readers, near and far), or seeking to make sense of Psalm 146 *for* our people, i[4] *talk-back-and-forth* (*talanoa*)[5] with the poet's assertions. Would the poet's assertions in Psalm 146 work in Pasifika (Pacific, Oceania)? What do the assertions reveal or conceal? How do the assertions help, empower, trouble and/or irritate us? Do the assertions encourage hope or illusion? This reflection is another version of my native reading (Havea 2020), for which I coined the label 'reStorying' (Havea 2021).[6]

In reStorying, I do not privilege the biblical texts. My starting point is the affirmation that the Bible is a foreign book – brought to Pasifika by missionaries and colonizers. To borrow the words of the Black Caribbean queer feminist Audre Lorde, the Bible is the tool of the master. In reStorying, I engage the depictions and worldviews in biblical texts as blueprints for constructing, approving, and maintaining the Master's House. My aim in talking-back-and-forth with biblical texts is to make space in the master's house for the depictions and worldviews of natives, which are – nonetheless – not free of power dynamics, idiosyncrasies, and blind-spots. Hence a more appropriate descriptor for the reStorying approach is that it is (at this point in its journey) an attempt to break into the master's house.

I stage two features of the reStorying approach in this reflection. First, in reStorying one reads *with* both the text and the contexts. The text is not an *object* for readers to decipher, but an (un/willing) accessory with which readers *conceive* realities and worldviews in both texts and contexts. In this regard, contexts are not empty destinations where readers unload and unpack texts, but rather *contexts are texts* that can be made to talk-back-and-forth with biblical texts.[7]

---

3. Compared to the communal tones of the following hallelujah psalms (see, e.g., references to 'our Lord' in 147.5, angels and hosts in 148.2, Israel and children of Zion in 149.2, and 'everything that breathes' in 150.6), this song is an individual hallelujah meditation, between the poet and their soul.

4. This writer uses a lower-case first-person sg. pronoun intentionally.

5. The term *talanoa* (Havea 2016) is used in many, but not all, native Pasifika communities to refer to three events: story, telling (of story), conversation (storyweaving). I use 'talk-back-and-forth' here in reference to the three events of *talanoa*, and cf. Vaka'uta's essay in this volume, pp. 231–35.

6. In 2022 we held a conference around this mode of thinking (https://sites.google.com/a/nomoa.com/talanoa/2022; accessed 29 August 2022).

7. In *talanoa*, orality and oratory cultures confluent and hence readers can talk-back-and-forth with a text. This would be challenging for bookish cultures, as Callahan discussed in *The Talking Book: African Americans and the Bible* (2008).

Second, texts and contexts are not tidy, clean, and calm spaces. Rather, texts and contexts are lively and messy. I begin with the second feature in the following reStorying.

Lively and Messy

Behind Psalm 146, the context feels messy. Princes and mortals are responsible for the mess, by deceiving people to think that help and hope are in them. In the poet's confident opinion, the devices of princes and mortals add up to a big fat lie. The extensive explanations in 146.6-10 – reaching back to creation and forward to eternity – suggest that the poet's soul too was deceived. The poet consequently directs their soul onto the right and proper path, where they will make the correct decisions – which simply requires that they come under the wings of Yhwh.

The parallelisms in 146.6-10, according to the structuring given above, hint at the messy situation in which the poet's soul was: Yhwh may have been the creator, but has Yhwh been *keeping faith* (146.6 NRSV; אמת, *'emeth*)? In the Assyrian and Babylonian exiles, and in contexts similar to those of Job and Lamentations, the answer would be messy – any experience of displacement or innocent suffering undermines the poet's confidence that Yhwh was keeping faith *forever*. In such contexts, a theology of theodicy is appropriate: suffering is evidence that creator Yhwh was not keeping faith. In other words, if Yhwh had been keeping faith, then creation would not have been broken. This theology emerges from the expectation that Yhwh would be responsible and sovereign.

The popular meaning of *'emeth* renders the poet's assertion in 146.6 to be about Yhwh *keeping truth*, and invites another question on account of 146.7: Did the poet's soul see the oppressed experience justice, the hungry eat food (from the hands of Yhwh), and the prisoners go free? I cannot answer this question with confidence, but it gives a utopian feel to the poet's assertions. The poet appears to dwell in the world of hope and illusion, rather than in the real inhabited worlds where injustice, hunger, and imprisonment are the daily food of minoritized people.

The poet's utopian world is for righteous people. However, it is not clear in 146.8 who the righteous people are – the blind or the blind who have been healed, the downtrodden or the downtrodden who have been lifted up – and how. Traditional understandings assumes the blind and downtrodden are righteous; but do they lose their righteousness when they are healed? It is also not clear, in the next verse, who or how some people have become wicked. These messy views are drawn from 146.9, which may be rendered as follows:

> Yhwh watches the strangers
> the fatherless and widows he upholds
> and the way of the wicked he makes crooked.

Two readings of this rendering are possible: first, Yhwh punishes the wicked, by straightening their crooked way; second, Yhwh is the one who made the way of the wicked crooked. The verse is messy, and the image of the wicked in 146.9, along with the image of the righteous person in 146.8, are not clearcut. Despite the messy situation, the poet still expects Yhwh to reign forever, unto all generations (146.10). This may be read as expression of deep hope; and it may also be read as evidence of blind[ing] illusion.

The above talk-back-and-forth with the poet's assertions engaged the texts, which I found messy. The texts are messy, on their own. Not only are the texts messy, but so is the context behind the text – the context that the text makes present. The foregoing reflection demonstrates one of the features of reStorying.

Reading with

Like other readers, I am located at several contexts – physical, ideological, emotional, spiritual etc. – and those contexts are texts that can (with my urgings) talk-back-and-forth with biblical texts. Moreover, each of the contexts from which I reStory biblical texts are also messy. To demonstrate what *reading with* involves, I draw attention to a recent messy event.

On 15 January 2022, during bright daylight, one of my contexts (Tonga) was waggled by an underwater volcanic eruption (The Visual Journalism Team 2022; Boscaini 2022) – in between two islands, Hunga Tonga and Hunga Ha'apai – followed by tsunami waves that destroyed nearby islands and parts of the capital island, Tongatapu. Three human lives were lost due to the tsunami (it could have been more if the waves came at night), but many more lives were disturbed and displaced, with the inhabitants of four islands (Mango, Fonoifua, Nomuka, 'Atatā) having to be resettled to other islands. The damage to other life forms, on the islands and in the sea (Olley 2022), are yet to be assessed but are expected to be tremendous; and the recovery from this 'unprecedented disaster' (according to the Tongan government) will take several years.

The 2022 eruption was unprecedented but not inexplicable. The Tonga group of islands sits on the Pacific Rim of Fire, so we have frequent earthquakes, and we have legends about Māui bringing up fire from the deep. And tsunami is not novel to us (Young 2010). We had one in 2009, in the dark before the dawn of 29 September, in which nine lives were lost and extensive damages was caused to the ecology and life cycles of Niuatoutapu. Ecological disasters are destructive in and to our islands, but the natives have learned to cope and prevail.

When the 2022 eruption and tsunami came, the Tonga group was still free of Covid. And as our families, friends and neighbours in diaspora rushed to collect and send help – clothes, food, water, tents, tools, money etc. – our main fear was with the possibility that aid will bring Covid to our shores. And so it happened: barely two weeks after the tsunami, Covid came in the bodies of helpers who came in solidarity (BBC 2022). Covid is thereby a reminder of our colonial past, when the carriers of the Christian good news also infected Pasifika bodies with viruses and pandemics, among many other disgraces and 'shitstems' (Havea 2022).

Ecological disasters and Covid are realities in the present time. Set alongside Psalm 146, these realities affirm the admonishments of the poet: from the side of the biblical *texts*, we should not trust princes and mortals because their devices gave rise to, and spread the waves of, ecological disasters and Covid. And from the side of Pasifika *contexts*, the natural explanations for our ecological situations and the colonial memories awakened by Covid mess up the poet's theology. We may look up to Yhwh God for help, and sing hallelujah, but we should not therefore assume that help will come from above or without. The more reliable help will come from within, among us. And we could still be happy in our lifetime, even if there are no help and hope in Yhwh God (cf. 146.5).

So What?

I favor reStorying as one of the tools of native Pasifika people. I used it in this reflection to break into the (textual and contextual) house that the poet of Psalm 146 contributes to its construction and maintenance, and i made some space in that house for our native perceptions and worldviews. Our lively and messy living situations in Pasifika need more than the help and hope that the Psalter and the Bible offer, and i expect that this longing is shared by other readers in and beyond Pasifika. Hallelujah!

Jione Havea is co-parent for Diya Lākai, native pastor (Methodist Church in Tonga), migrant to Naarm (renamed as Melbourne by colonizers of the cluster of islands now known as Australia), and research fellow with Trinity Methodist Theological College (Aotearoa New Zealand) and with Australian Centre for Christianity and Culture (Charles Sturt University). Jione seeks opportunities for collaboration and theological (broadly conceived) revol-u-ting. Recent works include *Losing Ground: Reading Ruth in the Pacific* (2021), *Bordered Bodies, Bothered Voices: Native and Migrant Theologies* (ed. 2022).

References

BBC (2022), 'Tonga enters Covid lockdown after aid delivered', *BBC News* (2 February), https://www.bbc.com/news/world-asia-60210867 (31 August 2022).

Boscaini, Joshua (2022), 'Tonga volcanic eruption confirmed as the largest explosion recorded since 1883', *ABC News* (16 May), https://www.abc.net.au/news/2022-05-16/tonga-volcanic-eruption-largest-recorded/101069416 (31 Aug 2022).

Callahan, Allen Dwight (2008), *The Talking Book: African Americans and the Bible*, New Haven: Yale University Press.

Havea, Jione (2013), 'Diaspora Contexted: Talanoa, Reading, and Theologizing, as Migrants', *Black Theology* 11 (2): 185–200.

Havea, Jione (2016), 'Reading islandly', in R.S. Sugirtharajah (ed.), *Voices from the Margin: Interpreting the Bible in the Third World*, 77–92, New York: Orbis.

Havea, Jione (2020), 'Repatriation of Native Minds', in Jione Havea (ed.), *Mission and Context*, 1–13, Lanham: Lexington / Fortress Academic.

Havea, Jione (2021), 'Going Native: reStorying Theology and Hermeneutics', *Modern Believing* 62 (4): 349–57.

Havea, Jione (2022), 'Covid, Climate, Coloniality: Theological (in)verses from Pasifika', in Dorothea Erbele-Küster and Volker Küster (eds), *Between Pandemonium and Pandemethics: Responses to Covid-19 in Theology and Religion*, 131–42, Leipzig: Evangelische Verlagsanstalt.

Havea, Jione and Peter H.W. Lau (2020), 'Context Matters: Reading from Asia and Pasifika', in Jione Havea and Peter H.W. Lau (eds), *Reading Ecclesiastes from Asia and Pasifika*, 1–11, Atlanta: SBL.

Olley, Sam (2022), 'Will Hunga Tonga-Hunga Ha'apai reefs recover post-eruption?', *RNZ* (21 January), https://www.rnz.co.nz/news/national/459937/will-hunga-tonga-hunga-ha-apai-reefs-recover-post-eruption (31 August 2022).

The Visual Journalism Team (2022), 'Tonga tsunami: Before and after eruption', *BBC News* (18 January), https://www.bbc.com/news/world-australia-60039542 (accessed 31 August 2022).

Young, Lani Wendt (2010), *Pacific Tsunami 'Galu Afi'*, Apia: Marfleet.

PSALM 150
HALLELU, HALLELU, HALLELUJAH

Dominic Mattos

When Athalya and Gale reached out to me for a contribution to this volume I was somewhat taken aback. Publishers do not often find themselves within the volumes that appear on their lists, and there are probably a number of very good reasons for that.[1] The request was, however, that I write something from the perspective of the other side of my life, as a professional musician. I am a countertenor and work from time-to-time in opera and oratorio, alongside my publishing work. I had a think and could only come up with something dry on Handel's *Dixit Dominus*, or something more circumspect and half-baked that would have attempted to link King David with Orpheus. These ideas both ticked the music box, but did not seem to make a valuable contribution when it came to reflecting a unique – or even particularly personal – context.

Therefore, I spent some time thinking about the verses of, or allusions to, the Psalms that jumped out at me as having been important in my own context, that of a Roman Catholic from a middle-class background, born in the south of England in the 1980s. I tried to think of how the Psalms had impacted me in this environment, and more specifically about how the use of music in worship had been part of my life and ongoing development as a musician.

The Roman Catholic Church of the post-Vatican II[2] era is not renowned for the splendour of its musical output. Rather, this outpt may be considered notorious for its banality, and so I felt it would take me a while to hit upon something. But the Psalms, of course, are a specific type of musical engagement with worship.

---

1. It is important to me to point out that this piece has been included at the request of the volume editors, and subject to their independent review. Its inclusion in the volume is on this basis, and not because of my own hectoring. It is a personal piece, which unashamedly reflects on a specific context of personal faith and community. It may also add a certain piquancy to the record to note that it was the publisher who delivered his piece almost last, and after much chasing.

2. The second ecumenical council of the Roman Catholic Church, 1962–65.

They are musical prayer and praise, whether because many of them are/have always been sung in contexts of worship, or because they represent a culture of Hebrew poetry that is musical in its very rhythms and structures. These musical prayers have been prayed through the centuries by a wide range of professionals: musicians, priests, or both, whether vicariously or in person. Many are sung by highly trained singers, in worship, or in concerts in front of well-heeled audiences. This is all intended to be very beautiful, and indeed the beauty of music is what gives it the power to transcend. Beauty is easy enough to define in human/secular terms, as something pretty, or nice…but both of these terms seem a little banal themselves, and we must also remember the old adage that beauty lies 'in the eye of the beholder', so perhaps defining beauty is a little more complicated than at first thought. When linked to the divine it becomes harder still. For Hans Urs von Balthasar, in his monumental work on theological aesthetics, *The Glory of the Lord*, beauty is inextricably intertwined with the glory of God, and as such is an essential part of the human condition and of humanity's response to God. Balthasar writes: 'Whoever sneers at beauty's name as if she were the ornament of a bourgeois past – whether he admits it or not – can no longer pray, and soon will no longer be able to love' (Von Balthasar 1982: 18).

But this is not merely/only a 'traditional' or easily perceived beauty, and Von Balthasar is clear that neither the beauty nor the Glory of God can truly be defined. The beauty of God demands adoration (Von Balthasar 1982: 321): it demands engagement at a profound level, and it is within this context that what may be deemed most pleasing or beautiful to God may be located. It also cannot be separated from truth, or in more simple terms, from sincerity. It is a slippery term. Both beauty and glory are present within God's creation, and it is within creation that Von Balthasar sees the ever-greater glory of God being manifest in the response of human beings to and within the already existing beauty of creation.

If we apply this to music, and to the beauty of music in the praise of God in creation, then it perhaps follows that there must be something of the primeval about it. As classical singers we are taught about the importance of 'engaging with our primal', of trying to return to primal noises in order to find the healthiest and most physically engaged means of making a sound that can fill a concert-hall without amplification, or that can cut across a seventy-piece orchestra. We are taught to think of babies crying, who never need any assistance in being heard. We are taught that there is value to understanding our sound in the realms of what might traditionally be thought of as ugly, or at the very least as messy.[3] In the case of singing opera, it is a heightened connection to the primal in terms of what may be regarded as a refined primal noise, but more than that: it is – at best – also a connection to primal and visceral emotions that might move an audience, even though that audience might not understand the words.

Put simply, music connects us to our primal selves, and it stands to reason that it can do so most powerfully, and most meaningfully, in situations where it

---

3. See the great vocal pedagogue Chapman (Chapman 2011).

is used to bring a community together. This, I would venture, is particularly true in a community of different ages, experiences and abilities. It is in such a context that I believe there is good potential for an articulation of the complicated metaphysical beauty that Von Balthasar talks of, and upon which I wish to gently reflect in this piece.[4] I wish to reflect, in particular, on a community environment that was pivotal for me. This is personal, indeed as this is a contextual piece it is deeply personal, and it involves one of the most significant figures in my life, my aunt.

My aunt has learning disabilities.[5] My aunt is also an adult woman with 60 plus years of life experience, who has lived a complexed life, initially living with my grandparents before moving to residential care a few years after my grandmother died in 1993. My parents have in many ways stepped into a role *in loco parentis* for her, and to me (an only child) she is in some ways now a little bit like a sibling. During my own development she was there to do art projects with me, to spar with, to snigger with over rude words (such as 'knickers'), and she was also not above pinching my toys (which was probably very good for me). In her own way, she has also always steadfastly looked after me, always asks about my life, and always helps me to prepare the vegetables for Christmas dinner, even though supervision is required. I mention these aspects of my aunt and her life because I do not want to fall into the trap of attempting to define or reduce my aunt in such a crass, outdated term such as 'mental age'. Rather, I want to give a sense of how she approaches the world, and the various situations she encounters. She loves Disney. She loves colour and is immensely creative with it, and she is a woman of strong, and easily accessed, emotions. My aunt is the third of four children on my mother's side of the family (my mother is the eldest). She takes very much after my grandmother, who was a do-er, full of life and activity, at times infuriatingly optimistic, and not to be crossed.

One of the things my grandmother 'did' was to run a group for those with learning disabilities and their families to pray together. The group was part of the Faith and Light movement founded by Jean Vanier and Marie-Hélène Mathieu

---

4. I am aware that many have and will use Von Balthasar's writings to refer to far more highbrow musical experiences/styles than related in this piece and would – indeed – use them to condemn the exact thing I am writing about as nothing more than ugly noise. I think the crucial point here is the sincerity/truthfulness of the situation and how it can be seen as giving glory to God. I also think the slipperiness of beauty as a theological concept is useful in this discussion.

5. I wish to clarify that I am no expert in writing about learning disabilities, or people with learning disabilities. I am writing this piece from a personal perspective, and it relates to a specific member of my family whose permission has been obtained for writing about her. My hope is that this piece offers a means by which someone with learning disabilities can offer a contribution to this discussion of contextual interpretation of the Psalms. Anyone wishing to understand and engage more with people with learning disabilities should begin with the resources offered by a charity such as Mencap: http://www.mencap.org.uk/learning-disability-explained .

in 1971.[6] The group met once a month in the church hall, and the proceedings would usually involve arts and crafts, and drama activities around the Bible readings of the given Sunday, a Mass, and a thwomping great shared afternoon tea to finish things off (it was England, after all). And music. Lots of music. Singing in procession – both tuneful and untuneful – tambourines, drums, whistles and bells. My own contribution, as a very small child, was to strum a Kermit-the-Frog miniature guitar with no concern whatsoever for the actual chords or notes required by the hymn at hand. In many ways, as an adult, I have shied away from this sort of musical event in favour of more polished offerings and more silent prayer,[7] but there was definitely order to the noise of those moments of worship. I also certainly don't mean to downplay the work of the few excellent musicians in our midst who held everything together. Rather, I want to talk-up the other voices, the other contributions, the raw noise, the connectedness, and the joy of it all. This brings me to Psalm 150 in particular, and to my reasons for selecting it for this piece.

One of the songs that we sang at Faith and Light was the popular praise song '*Hallelu, hallelu, hallelu, hallelujah*! Praise ye the Lord!'.[8] These are the only words, and they are repeated over-and-over to a simple, up-beat, tune. I cannot find out who wrote the song, but it is very well known. We would often sing it after the tea, as a final hurrah, and before a closing prayer that focused on the different but valuable abilities of all. It would be sung antiphonally, getting increasingly louder, with one side of the table standing to sing the '*Hallelus*' and then sitting quickly as the other rose for 'Praise ye the Lord!' The song is not a deliberate setting of Psalm 150, but I see it as a significant part of a community event in which, as a whole, I discern a realization of Psalm 150.

Indeed, if we look closely at Psalm 150 we have not only the repeated '*Hallelus*' of the praise song, but also many of the instruments described above as being part of our worship/community event ('trumpet, lute, harp, tambourine, strings and pipe', vv. 4-5). The music suggested by these instruments is loud noise: 'clanging/crashing cymbals' (v. 5). It is also not necessarily organized noise. Goldingay points out that while the instruments in the psalm include Priestly and Levitical ones (horn, harp, lyre and cymbals), they also include instruments used by the 'laity' (tambourine, strings and pipe). Furthermore, 'all the emphasis lays on noise' (Goldingay 2008: 748). The psalm may reflect Priestly Temple activity, as several commentators have noted, but it also unambiguously suggests the unification

---

6. For more details see: http://www.laici.va/content/laici/en/profilo.html. In addition, Vanier was also the co-founder of L'Arche and it is sad to have to note that, after his death in 2019, L'Arche concluded that Vanier had engaged in emotional abuse and manipulation/coercive sexual abuse of several women in the context of giving spiritual direction.

7. Indeed, it's humbling to realize that I have often used Von Balthasar to decry 'happy clappy' music.

8. There are many, easily findable, versions on YouTube, or on kids' praise compilations/playlists etc. Here is version on YouTube: https://www.youtube.com/watch?v=BrlEuIv5nrA (accessed 8 January 2023).

of Temple worship with broader, more encompassing praise; 'Let everything that has breath praise the Lord' (v. 6, NIV). Human also refers to the blending of 'cultic' with 'profane' instruments as suggesting/confirming that the psalm's original context was not as part of any specific cultic act; and goes on to talk of the 'universal character' rendered to the psalm by v. 6, and its 'open-ended wish that all life should praise Yah' (Human 2011).

There are clear allusions to Genesis here (as pointed out by Human and others). The entire created order is exhorted to use its breath (רוח, *rūaḥ*) to praise Yhwh in his 'firmament' (רקיע, *rāqīʿa*). This same breath has been given to creation by Yhwh himself in Genesis 1–2, and now the psalmist portrays creation praising him – indeed exhorts creation to praise him – in the same firmament that he 'hammered out'[9] in the cacophonous act of creation itself. This is the freedom of the loud, of the noisy: the creative voice in the created giving praise to the creator. There are no value judgments, the sound is raw, it reflects the primal breath of creation. It is the beauty of the imperfect.

My aunt, as it happens, has a beautiful voice, and she truly loves to sing hymns and does so with great gusto…but she is not always able to remember, read, or understand the words. And yet, undeniably singing is for her an act of community and of worship, but it really *is* the *music* and *not* the 'libretto' (as we classical singers would call it) that is at the root of her engagement within her own context, and with the contexts of others who may be singing the same piece with her, according to their own abilities. It is the noise-making, and the experiential elements of music-making that are the act of communal worship, identity, praise.

Reflecting on this from my own perspective as a singer who often works in the very cerebral (singing very complicated music in foreign languages, with difficult staging), it is arresting to realize the importance of the simple. I have also come to be a classical musician rather later than most who try this strange way of life. As a result, within my family we often wonder: 'Where did it all come from?… we do not have any other singers in the family'. But my aunt sings, with an ability to remain unerringly in tune and in time (which is more than can be said for many a member of many a church choir); and yet, we do not often truly consider that if 'it' came from anywhere, 'it' could have come from my aunt. It is strange, and moving, to realize that a lot of who I am as a musician comes from the freedom and joy of the haphazard music-making at the Faith and Light meetings of my childhood. It was in this context in my childhood that there was always music, and it was here that music was unifying in a very profound way.

This is not an academic piece, and it makes no pretensions to be so, but what I hope it has done is provide a little of the context of a very special person in my life who would not have been able to make this contribution herself. More than that: I hope it has gently made the point that there are many different ways to make a beautiful noise, and that sometimes the least organized are the most beautiful. When we all sang at Faith and Light it was beautiful to me, but I believe it was

---

9. *rāqīʿa* is derived from the root *rqʿ*, which (in the *Qal* formation) means 'to beat or spread out thinly' (BDB: 955)

still yet more beautiful to God. For me, in the context of my family and my childhood, that is what the sheer noise demanded by Psalm 150 is all about. It is about a profound and unifying physical experience of the beauty and glory of God, which takes us back to Von Balthasar, who writes of the necessity of physicality in appreciating beauty and developing faith: 'Everything depends on the effects of seeing, hearing, tasting, smelling, and especially touching the Word of Life, all of which culminates with the placing of the fingers in the wound on the side' (1982: 313). In this context there is the imperfection of the wounded beauty of God, in which everyone can find a place, and in which all can be glorified with the creator.

To conclude. In the consciously and performatively inclusive social environment in which we live, it is at times startling to note that the contributions of those with learning disabilities remain marginalized, and that those with learning disabilities often cannot record their thoughts or feelings about their own contexts or share them with the world.

Experiencing the Covid-19 lockdowns, in the UK at least, and the lack of compassion with which these lockdowns often treated those with learning disabilities and their needs, underlined how little modern societies can value people who have unique contributions to make. It is sad to note, and I feel I must note it, that the isolation and enforced deprivation from family that my aunt experienced during the Covid lockdowns caused her untold pain and mental anguish, and that she is a changed person because of them, but just as this is not an academic piece, it is also not a piece of activism. The only point I am trying to make is that my aunt's contribution, her context, matters. I'm grateful to have had the opportunity to share that context in this volume, a context that celebrates the power and freedom of shared noise made with the breath of the creator, a breath that sits deeply in each of us whatever our ability, and is the gift we can offer both to each other and to God.

As a second choice I think I would have gone with the *De Profundis* (Ps. 130), for all its penitential and liturgical uses, and musical settings. It is also a psalm that features regularly in my own prayer.

Dominic Mattos read Theology at St. Benet's Hall Oxford and studied singing at the Royal Northern College of Music. He is Senior Publisher of T&T Clark, an imprint of Bloomsbury Publishing.

References

Von Balthasar, Hans Urs (1982), *The Glory of God: A Theological Aesthetics*, Vol. 1, Edinburgh: T&T Clark. Originally in German, Johannes Verlag, 1961–67.

Chapman, Janice (2011), *Singing and Teaching Singing: A Holistic Approach to Classical Voice*, San Diego: Plural Publishing Inc.

Goldingay, John (2008), *Psalms 90–150*, Grand Rapids: Baker Academic.

Human, Dirk J. (2011), '"Praise beyond Words": Psalm 150 as Grand Finale of the Crescendo in the Psalter', *HTS Theologiese Studies/Theological Studies* 67 (1), Art. #917, 10 pages.

INDEX OF BIBLICAL REFERENCES

HEBREW BIBLE/
OLD TESTAMENT
Genesis
1–3	158
1–2	26, 259
1	37
1.1	37
1.6-7	37
1.7	124
1.9	124
1.11	124
1.15	124
1.26-28	6, 19
1.28	143
2–3	93
2	245
2.7	121, 122
2.15	21
2.18	71
3	117
3.6	110
3.17-19	147
3.18-19	217
3.19	117
4	67
4.17-22	139
5	93
6.3	93
6.8	193
6.12	229
6.13	229
6.17	229
6.19	229
7.15	229
7.16	229
7.21	229
8.17	229
9.11	229
9.15	229
9.17	229
12.3	195
16.13	193
17.1	126
19.4	92
21	139
24	124
24.30	124
25.1-10	116
25.8	92
27–28	139
27.33	110
29.31-32	193
30.8	110
32–33	139
35.29	92
48.15	48

Exodus
3.14	126
4.31	193
118	165, 166
118.10-12	166, 167
118.13-14	166
118.15-16	165–67
118.18	165
13.14	134
14–15	165
15.1-19	165
15.2	167
15.6	166
15.18	167
17.1-7	158
19.5-6	157
19.18	157
20.5	94, 121
31.18	25
32.15-16	25
34.6-7	161
34.6	161
34.7	121

Leviticus
5.10	110
7.12	133
19.32	94
23.10	206
25.7	24
26.6	24

Numbers
6.24-26	188
10.36	123
15.20	186
20.1-13	158

Deuteronomy
5.16	94
6.16	127
21.18-21	94
21.18	94
33.7	30

Joshua
4.19	139
18.1	19

Judges
5.11	24
6.1	30
8.22	19
11.40	24

Index of Biblical References

1 Samuel		66.21	30	1.2	61
2.1-10	88			1.3	61
16.7	193	*Jeremiah*		2	127
17.49	30	2.22	79	2.2	102
22.5	48	4.14	79	3–41	63
28	15	6.20	79	3–14	63
		7.22	79	4	4, 129
2 Samuel		9.1-2	71	5	4
7	222	29	233	6	14, 16
7.5	217	29.4-7	232	6.1	14, 15
7.11	217	31	79	6.2	15
7.14-15	107	33.11	207	6.2 MT	14, 15
8.11	19	48.46-47	207	6.3 MT	15
11–12	8, 79			6.4	15, 16
11	67	*Ezekiel*		6.5	15
12	82	36	79	6.5 MT	15, 16
15.16	67			6.6	14
16.20-22	67	*Hosea*		6.6 MT	15
22	28	6.6	79	6.7	14
22.35	29	10.1	65	6.7 MT	14
		12.3-4	139	6.8	MT 14
1 Kings				6.8-9	16
4.21	19	*Amos*		6.9-10 MT	16
12	92	1.11-12	139	7	4
		5.21-22	79	8	3, 4, 6, 18, 20, 22, 140
2 Kings		9.13	210		
17	107			8.1	18
19.3	42	*Jonah*		8.2	26
		4.4	65	8.3-4	18
Isaiah				8.3	25
1–39	177	*Micah*		8.4	26
1–4	176	4.4	63	8.5	18
1.11-13	79			8.6	18, 19
1.18	79	*Habakkuk*		10	100
2.1-4	176	1.13	193	11.2	30
5.12	30			15–24	63
6	177	*Zechariah*		16	11
6.9-10	177	5.11	30	17	11
7.9	77	8.4	92	18	8, 28, 32, 45
9.2	207				
29.12	30	*Malachi*		18.1	45
30.29	30	1.1-5	139	18.30	30
37.3	42			18.35	28, 29, 33
42.1	162	*Psalms*		19	26, 36–41, 247
49.16	161	1–2	108		
51.9	158	1	61, 108, 127, 167, 249	19.1	39, 121
54.12	30			19.2	37
61.1	110			19.3	37
65	79	1.1	1	19.4	37

Index of Biblical References

19.5	37, 38	37	6, 59, 61–63	39.9	65
19.7-9	38, 247			39.10-12	66
19.7	37	37.1-11	60	39.10	66
19.10	40	37.1-8	60	39.12	66, 67
19.11	40	37.1	62	39.13-14	66
19.12-14	38	37.3-4	62	39.13	66
19.13-14	38	37.3	64	39.14	66
19.15	30	37.7	62	40–41	63
20	7, 42–45	37.8	62	40	9, 221
20.1-5	42	37.9-22	60	40.18	63
20.1	42	37.9	61, 63	41.4	30
20.2	42	37.11	61, 63	42	219
20.3	42, 45	37.12-20	60	44.2	30
20.4	42, 45	37.12	62	45	127, 190
20.7	102	37.14	62, 63	45.13 Eng.	190
20.9	43	37.16	64	45.14 Heb.	190
22.4	24	37.21-29	60	46	70–72, 222
23	3, 5, 6, 9, 10, 47, 50, 52–54, 56–58, 115, 184	37.21	62	46.2-4	70
		37.22	61, 63	46.2	71
		37.23-26	61	46.3-4	71
		37.24	62	46.6	72
		37.27-34	60	46.7	72
23.1-3	49	37.29	61, 63	46.8-10	73
23.1	115	37.30-31	61	46.9	72
23.2	48	37.30	62	46.10	72
23.3	48, 49	37.31	64	46.11-12	73
23.4-5	49	37.32	62	49	75, 76, 78, 88
23.4	47–49	37.33	62		
23.5	48, 49, 56	37.34	61, 63	49.2-5	76
23.6	47, 49, 56	37.35-36	61	49.4	77, 88
24.1	121	37.35	62	49.5	76
25–34	63	37.37-40	61	49.12	77
30	243	37.39-40	62	49.13	76, 77
30.1-12	136	37.39	64	49.14-21	76
30.1	3	39	65, 67	49.16	77, 78
30.3	16	39.2-6	65, 66	49.20	77
30.4	MT 16	39.2-4	66	49.21	76, 77
30.5	136	39.2	65, 66	51	8, 10, 79, 80, 83
30.6-7	17	39.3	65, 66		
30.7-8 MT	17	39.4-6	66	51.1-2	79
32.8	193	39.4	66	51.1	80
33	11	39.5-14	66	51.2	80, 81
33.2-3	4	39.5	65, 66	51.3-19	79
33.4	160	39.6	66, 67	51.3-11	80
34	63	39.7-12	66	51.3-4	80
34.1	30	39.7-9	66	51.3	80
35–41	63	39.7	66, 67	51.4	80
35	63	39.8-12	66	51.5-8	80
35.1	63	39.8	66	51.5-6	81

Psalms (cont.)		68.24-25	87	84.1 MT	109
51.5	80, 83	68.25	87	84.2	109
51.6	80, 81, 83	68.27	87	84.3	110, 111, 114
51.7	80, 83	68.28	87		
51.8	81	68.29	87	84.4	111
51.9	80	68.30	87	84.4 MT	5, 110, 111, 114
51.10	80, 81	68.33	86		
51.11	80	68.35	87	84.5 MT	111
51.12-19	80	70.1-2	30	84.8	102
51.12-14	80	71	4, 91, 92	84.10	109
51.12	81	71.8-9	90, 91	84.11 MT	109
51.13	81	71.9	90, 95	84.11-12	109
51.15	80, 81	71.18	90, 91, 94	84.12	30
51.16-19	80	72	11, 80, 127	84.12 MT	114
51.16	81	73	8, 97, 100	84.12-13 MT	109
51.18	79, 81	73.1	100	85	225
51.19	81	73.2	98, 100	86.2-3	30
51.20-21	79	73.4-9	98	87.1	3
57	205	73.10	98	88	235
57.9	4	73.12	98	89	107, 127, 221
63.2	48	73.13-14	98		
64.2	30	73.14	98	89.3	102
65	153	73.16	99	89.20	102
65.11	30	73.21-22	99	89.30-34	106
65.17-25	72	73.27-28	99	89.35	102
67.1	3	73.27	100	89.38	102
68	4, 85–88	73.28	100	89.51	102
68.1-3	87	78	101, 104–107, 149, 221	90	3, 7, 116–20, 127, 215
68.1-2	87				
68.1	3				
68.2	87	78.1-8	105	90.1-2	116
68.4-6	87	78.8	105	90.1	125, 142
68.4	86	78.9-11	105	90.2-3	120
68.5-6	87	78.17-31	105	90.2	119–21, 123
68.7-10	86, 87	78.37-39	30		
68.7	87	78.40-41	105	90.3-6	215
68.10	87	78.56-58	105	90.3	117, 121
68.11-14	87	78.60	106	90.4	121
68.11-12	87	78.67-72	101	90.5-6	116, 117
68.14	86, 87	78.67	105, 106	90.5	117, 122, 215
68.15-18	87	78.68-72	105		
68.15-16	86	78.68-70	106	90.6	122, 123, 215
68.17-18	87	78.68	106		
68.17	86	78.70-72	102	90.7-9	119, 120
68.19-23	87	78.70	106	90.10	116–19, 122
68.22-23	87	81.34	4		
68.22	86	84	109, 110, 114	90.11	119, 122
68.24-35	87			90.12-17	116

Index of Biblical References

90.12	119, 123	100.4-5	133, 135	104.35	138–40, 147, 148, 210
90.13	122	100.4	135		
90.14	123	100.5	135		
90.16	123	103.7	142	105	151
90.17	121, 123	104	3, 4, 6, 11, 137–39, 142–44, 146–49	105.26	142
91-11-13	128			106	135, 150, 151, 153
91	4, 125–27, 129, 130			106.1-5	151
91.1-4	126	104.1-4	138	106.2-3	151
91.1-2	125	104.2-4	142	106.4-5	151
91.1	130	104.2	144	106.6-49	151
91.3-13	126	104.5-9	138	106.6	150, 152
91.3-6	126	104.5-6	142	106.16	142
91.3	130	104.5	145	106.23	142
91.4-5	127	104.6-9	138	106.32	142
91.4	128	104.7-10	142	106.47-48	151
91.5-8	126	104.10-18	138	107	151
91.5-6	127	104.11	142	107.1	151
91.5	129, 130	104.12	142	108.3	4
91.6	126	104.13	142, 144	110	127
91.7-13	126	104.14-23	140	111-116	161
91.7	130	104.14-15	142, 147	113-118	5, 155, 161, 228
91.9-10	125	104.14	137, 143–45		
91.11-12	127			113	159
91.11	127, 128	104.15	143	113.1	161
91.12-15	126	104.16	142	113.9	161
91.12	128	104.17	137, 142	114	5, 50, 155, 158, 159
91.13	127–30	104.18	142, 145		
91.14-16	126	104.19-23	138	114.1	155–57
91.16	126, 127	104.19-20	142	114.2	155, 156
92	125, 145	104.20-23	147	114.3	155
92.1	3	104.20-22	142	114.4	155
92.4	4	104.20	143	114.5	50, 156
92.12-13	125	104.23	142, 143	114.6	156
92.12	145	104.24-27	138	114.7	156
92.13	145	104.24-26	138	114.8	156
93–98	142	104.24	142, 145, 147	115	124
93.1-2	124			115.18	161
96	133	104.25-26	138, 142	116	161
98.1	3	104.26	147	116.19	161
98.4-6	134	104.27-31	138	117	7, 68, 160–62
99	133	104.27-30	140		
99.6	142	104.27	144, 145	117.1	160
100	5, 133, 135	104.28-30	138	117.2	161
100.1-3	133, 134	104.28	144	118	8, 164
100.1	134	104.30	147, 148	118.1-18	164, 167
100.2	134	104.33-34	143	118.1-3	164
100.3	134, 135	104.33	148	118.19-29	164

Index of Biblical References

Psalms (cont.)
118.28	167	126.2	41, 198–200, 203	135.6	221		
118.29	167			135.14	160		
119	11, 11, 34	126.3	198, 199	136	5, 9, 227–29		
119.100	48	126.4-6	199, 203				
120-134	192, 204, 221	126.4-5	7	136.1-3	227, 228		
		126.4	198, 203, 204, 207	136.1	160, 228		
121-134	3			136.2	229		
121	3–5, 7, 41, 169–73, 175, 176, 178, 180, 182, 184, 186, 187, 189, 190	126.5-6	206	136.4-9	228		
		126.5	198, 200, 204	136.4	227, 229		
				136.6	229		
		126.6	198	136.9	228		
		127-128	6, 216, 217, 219	136.10-15	228		
				136.11	229		
		127	3, 212–14, 218, 219	136.14	228		
				136.16-22	228		
121.1-4	184	127.1-2	214, 218	136.17	229		
121.1-2	175, 187	127.1	216, 218	136.23-24	228		
121.1	4, 171, 172, 175, 183	127.2	5, 212	136.24	229		
		127.3-4	216	136.25	227–29		
121.2	171, 172, 181–84, 188	127.3	216, 218	136.26	227, 228		
		127.4-58	217	137	3, 6, 8–10, 41, 119, 127, 231–36, 238, 240–42
		127.4-5	218		
121.3-8	175	127.5	216, 218		
121.3-6	187	128	217, 218		
121.3-4	171	128.1	216		
121.3	183, 184, 188	128.2	217, 218	137.4	232
		128.3-4	217, 218	137.7	232
121.4	183, 188	128.3	216–18	137.9	119, 232, 234, 240, 241
121.5-6	171	128.4	216, 218		
121.5	181, 183, 188	128.5	216–18		
		128.6	216, 217	138–145	244
121.6	183, 188	129	239	139	6, 83, 244
121.7-8	187, 188	130	11, 201	139.1	244
121.7	171, 184	132	6, 221–25	139.2-3	244
121.8	171, 181, 188	132.1	102	139.4	244
		132.9	222	139.7-12	244
123	8, 192, 195	132.10	102	139.13-18	245
123.1	193	132.11-18	222	139.15-16	245
123.2	194	132.12	106	139.19-24	245
123.3-4	195	132.14	222	139.19-20	245
126	3, 5, 41, 198, 202–204, 206–209	132.16	221, 222	139.21-22	144
		132.17	102	139.23-24	245, 247
		133	229	139.23	244
		133.1	229	140	196
126.1-4	207	134	129	144.9	4
126.1-3	199, 203	135	221	144.10	102
126.1	198, 199, 203, 207	135.4	160	145	6
		135.5	160	146–150	249

146	249, 250, 253	*Job* 5.9	227	NEW TESTAMENT *Matthew*	
146.1-2	249	26.12-13	158	4.6	127
146.3-4	249	34.21	193	4.7	127
146.5	249, 253	37.5	227	5.4	209
146.6-10	251	38–41	143	5.5	61
146.6	249, 251	42.10	207		
146.7	249, 251			*Mark*	
146.8	249, 251	*Esther*		12.26-27	16
146.9	249, 251	9.7-10	228		
146.10	249, 251			*Luke*	
147.5	249	*Qoheleth*		1	67
148	22	11.7	30	4.11	127
149.2	249	12	94	4.12	127
149.3	4	12.1-7	90	16.19-31	82
150	8, 11, 58, 95, 255, 258, 260	*Daniel* 3.5-10	4	18.9-14 *Romans* 1–3	17 40
150.1	58, 95				
150.2	58	*Ezra*			
150.3-5	4, 58	3.11	135	*1 Peter*	
150.4-5	258			3.12	193
150.5-6	95	*1 Chronicles*			
150.5	258	16.34	151		
150.6	1, 58, 162, 249, 259	*2 Chronicles* 10	92		
Proverbs		12.13	92		
8.22-31	142				
15.3	193				
26.2	111				
31.1-9	67				

INDEX OF AUTHORS

Adamo, D.T. 86, 88, 89, 171–73
Albright, W.E. 88
Alexander, C.F. 247
Allen, L.C. 142, 145, 147, 149, 160, 161, 163, 187, 190, 194–96, 216, 219
Alonso-Schökel, L. 67, 68
Alter, R. 24–26, 48–50, 150, 154, 181, 185, 194, 196
Amit, Y. 4
Amzallag, N. 207, 210
An, Z. 102
Arnold, C. 134, 136
Asamoah-Gyadu, K. 172, 173
Asumang, A. 58
Avineri, S. 113, 115
Aymer, M. 6

Bacher, W. 178, 179
Bal, M. ix
Ballentine, D.S. 158, 159
Barker, D.G. 187, 190
Barr, J. 38, 41
Barth, K. 98, 100
Bartor, A. 7
Bauckham, R. 19, 22, 143, 145
Beckwith, R.T. 126, 131
Begrich, J. 147, 149
Beit-Hallahmi, B. 186, 190
Beller, S. 115
Bellinger, W.H., Jr 37, 41, 60, 64, 151, 154, 175, 179
Berlin, A. 85, 88, 133, 136
Berry, D.K. 29, 34
Bilu, Y. 186, 190
Blustain, S. 182, 185
Boer, R. 110, 115
Booij, T. 117, 119

Boscaini, J. 252, 253
Bowman, R. 43, 46
Braude, W.C. 30, 31, 34, 48–50, 127, 131
Breed, B. 125, 127, 129–31
Bremer, J. 63, 64
Brenner-Idan, A. 1, 4, 10, 93, 96, 118, 186, 190, 229, 235, 239
Brettler, M.Z. 5, 133, 136, 155, 159, 217, 219
Briggs, C.A. 30, 34, 65, 66, 68, 86, 88
Briggs, E.G. 34, 65, 66, 68, 86, 88
Brinkman, J.M. 48, 51
Brison, O. 5, 186, 190
Brown, W.P. 126, 131, 138, 140, 142, 143, 145
Brueggemann, W. 37, 41, 60, 64, 97, 100, 151, 154, 175, 179, 187, 190
Butler, J. 82, 83
Buttenwieser, M. 29, 34, 37

Callahan, A.D. 253
Carroll, R. 105, 108
Carson, D.A. xiii
Celan, P. 26
Chapman, C.R. 110, 115
Chapman, J. 256, 260
Chau, K. 8
Chen, Z. 102, 108
Cheng, Y. 119
Childs, B.S. 18, 22, 85, 88
Chiu, M.M. 105, 108
Clackson, J. 111, 115
Cleath, L. 7, 153, 154
Clifford, R.J. 66, 68, 248
Clines, D.J.A. 29, 34
Cohen, A. 133, 136
Cohen, S.Y. 96

Cole, R.L. 109, 115
Cole, T. 227, 230
Coleman, O. 87, 89
Connell, R.W. 82, 83
Cooley, J.L. 37, 41
Craigie, P.C. 37, 38, 41
Crenshaw, J.L. 66, 68
Crissy, K. 31, 34
Cross, F.M. 85–87, 89
Crow, L.D. 190
Culler, J. 164, 165, 168

Dahood, M.J. 34, 37, 41, 66, 68, 75, 78, 85, 89, 187, 190, 199, 201
Dahouh-Halevi, D. 33, 34
Damati, E. 33, 35
David, I. 59, 64
Davis, E. 127, 131
Day, J. 187, 190
Deeg, A. 204, 205
de Moor, J.C. 75, 78
DeClaissé-Walford, N. vii, ix, 6, 43, 46, 68, 69, 117, 119, 145, 161, 163, 244, 245, 248
Dievenkorn, S. 5
Dobbs-Allsopp, F.W. 167, 168
Dowling Long, S. 128, 131
Dube, M.W. xii, 5, 52, 57, 58, 173

Ebeling, J.R. 217, 219
Efthimiadis-Keith, H. 68
Ehud Bannai 51
Eissfeldt, O. 126, 131
Elon, A. 113, 115
Elvin-Nowak, Y. 82, 83
Ephros, G. 180, 182, 183, 185
Evans, C.A. 126, 131
Ewald, H. 34

Fagles, R. 31, 32, 34
Falk, A. 113, 115
Feldman, L.H. 31, 34
Finkelstein, I. 106, 108
Flesher, P.V.M. 29, 34
Forti, T. 65, 68
Freedman, D.N. 85, 87–89

García Bachmann, M.L. 7
Gärtner, J. 151, 154

Gerstenberger, E.S. 65, 68, 164, 168, 175, 179
Gese, H. 81, 83
Gilat, Y.D. 178, 179
Gilbert, W.B. 58
Gillingham, S. 8, 37–39, 41, 43, 46, 80, 83, 125, 127, 129, 131
Gilson, E. 138, 140
Goldingay Scott, J. 17
Goldingay, J. 7, 17, 29, 34, 38, 41, 43, 46, 194, 196, 244, 248, 258, 260
Goodblatt, D. 179
Gossai, H. 6
Gosse, B. 151, 154
Gottwald, N.K. 170, 171, 174
Goulder, M.D. 207, 210
Gray, A.R. 30, 34
Greenspoon, L. 20, 22
Gruber, M.I. 29, 30, 34, 127, 131
Gunkel, H. 29, 34, 77, 78, 85, 89, 147, 149

Hakham, A. 147, 149
Hasan-Rokem, G. 32, 34
Havea, J. xii, xiii, 6, 235, 250, 253, 254
Heaney, S. 230
Hebron, S. 128, 131
Heller, R.T. 49, 51
Hertz, J.H. 129, 131
Herzi, T. 115
Hoffman, Y. 147–49
Holm, T. 43, 46
Holmberg, C. 82, 84
Hong, X. 238, 239
Horkheimer, M. 131
Hossfeld, F.-L. 65, 66, 68, 89, 142, 145, 151, 152, 154, 164, 165, 168, 175, 179, 203, 205, 244, 245, 248
Howell, B.C. 193, 196
Hughes, T. 230
Human, D.J. 259, 260
Hunter, A.G. 24, 27
Hunziker-Rodewald, R. 125, 131
Hurvitz, A. 159
Huxley, W. 131

Idelsohn, A.Z. 180, 182, 185
Ilan, Z. 33, 35, 108

Jacobson, H. 32, 35
Jacobson, R. 46, 66, 244, 248
Jacobson, R.A. 65, 69
Jakobson, R. 85, 89
Jastrow, M. 30, 31, 35
Jenkins, P. 125, 129–31
Johnson, A.R. 106, 108

Kalimi, I. 32, 35
Kamin, S. 29, 35
Kamionkowsky, S.T. 68, 69
Kaulbach, E.N. 127, 131
Kay, J. 19, 22
Keck, L.E. 198, 201
Kim, J. 20, 22
Knight, D.A. 93, 96
Knowles, M.D. 6
Kolappan, B. 194, 195, 197
Kraus, H.J. 43, 46, 80, 84, 102, 108, 194, 195, 197
Kraus, T.J. 131
Kritzinger, J.N.J. 172–74
Krondorfer, B. 138, 140
Kuang, K. 117, 119
Kugel, J. 85, 89
Kushelevsky, R. 30, 35
Kynes, W. 60, 64

Landy, F. 25, 27
Larsson, M. 8, 82, 84
Lategan, B.C. 210
Lau, P.H.W. xii, xiii, 250, 254
Lee, A.C.C. 1, 8
LeFebvre, M. 61, 64
Legge, J. 236, 239
Leneman, H. 4
Lewis, C.S. 129, 131, 139
Lewis, H.O. 140
Lichtheim, M. 147, 149
Liebrich, L.J. 190
Limburg, J. 187, 190
Limmer, S.M. 32, 35
Lioy, D. 138, 140
Lipton, D. 5
Lissoni, A. 139, 140
Littledale, R.F. 129, 131
Litweiler, J. 89
Longman, T., III 244, 248

Lovelace, V. 5
Löwisch, I. 6
Lugt, W. van der 75, 78

Ma Chiying 103, 108
MacMillan, J.D. 48, 49, 51
Mack, H. 29, 35
Mamdani, M. 139, 140
Manus, C. 22
Martin, M.W. 156, 159
Masenya, M. 58
Mattos, D. 8
Mays, J.L. 37, 38, 41, 145, 194, 196, 197
Mbuvi, A.M. xii
Mbuwayesango, D.R. xii
McCann, J.C. 142, 145, 216, 218, 219
Meer, W. van der 75, 78
Mehlman, B.H. 32, 35
Melanchthon, M.J. 196, 197
Mellet, P.T. 139, 140
Mettinger, T.N.D. 108
Meyer, B.U. 99, 100
Meyers, C.L. 217, 220
Miller, P.D. 216, 220
Minchin, E. 228, 230
Mofokeng, T. 170, 174
Morgenstern, J. 49, 51, 190
Mosala, I.J. 171, 174
Mowinckel, S. 85, 89
Muilenburg, J. 85, 89
Murphy, K. 83, 84
Murrell, N.S. 86, 89
Musgrave, M. 209, 211

Nam, R. 7
Neale, J.M. 129, 131
Newsom, C.A. xiii
Niehoff, M.R. 31, 35
Nims, C.F. 43, 46
Nir, S. 8, 29, 35
Nowell, I. 160, 163

O'Connor, M.P. 156, 159
Obioma, D. 22
Olley, S. 252, 254

Packenham, T. 139, 141
Page, H.R., Jr 4, 86, 87, 89

Index of Authors

Patte, D. xiii
Paul, C. 205
Penner, T. xiv
Perkinson, J.W. 140, 141
Perry, M. 146, 149
Polliack, M. 5
Premnath, D.N. 7

Rajendran, A. 192, 197
Raman, R. 193, 197
Ready, J.L. 31, 35
Reid, B. 7
Reinhartz, A. 5
Reizel, A. 32, 35
Rhoads, D. xii, xiv
Ringe, S.H. xiii
Ross, A.P. 207, 211
Rothberg, M. 141
Rubin, A.D. 156, 159
Ruth, P.J. 132

Samet, R.E. 135, 136
Sasson, G. 32, 35
Saunders, C. 139, 141
Sawyer, J.F.A. 128, 131
Schaefer, K. 136
Schüle, A. 204, 205
Schuller, E.M. 32, 35
Schwartz, B.I. 104, 105, 108
Scobie, C.H.H. 107, 108
Sebidi, L. 170, 174
Segovia, F.F. x, xiv
Shaked, M. 190
Shannon, D.T. 86, 89
Shenan, A. 29, 35
Shewell-Cooper, W.E. 122, 124
Simon, U. 191
Sjöberg, M. 83, 84
Smelik, K. 46
Smith-Christopher, D. 152, 154
Sneed, M. 60, 64
Snyman, G.F. 6, 138, 141
Sokoloff, M. 30, 35
Sommer, B.D. 37, 41
Spronk, K. 4, 75, 76, 78
Stager, L. 217, 220
Stec, D.M. 127, 132
Steiner, R.C. 43, 46

Steinsaltz, A. 191
Stern, M. 128, 132
Sternberg, M. 116, 119
Stinson, M.A. 152, 154
Strand, M. 238, 239
Suderman, W.D. 86, 89
Sweeney, M.A. 4, 176-79

Tanner, B.L. 6, 46, 69, 119, 244, 248
Tate, M.E. 119, 133, 136
Teugels, L. 6
Thiselton, A.C. 171, 174
Tilford, N.L. 6
Tlhagale, B. 171, 174
Tolbert, x, xiv
Tournay, R. 42, 46
Trinka, E.M. 111, 115
Tripp, J. 119
Tsevat, M. 117, 119
Tupamahu, E. 8

Vaka'uta, N. xii, xiv, 5, 8
Valmiki, O. 195, 197
Van Camp, L. 209, 211
van der Ploeg, J.P.M. 126, 132
van der Toorn, K. 43, 46
Van Niekerk, M.J.H. 216, 220
Van Wolde, E. 138, 141
Vander Hart, M. 20, 22
Vander Stichele, C. xiv
Viviers, H. 140, 141, 216, 220
Vleeming, S.P. 43, 46
Von Balthasar, H.U. 256, 260
Vosloo, R. 170, 174

Waley, A. 102, 108
Wallace, R.E. 109, 115
Waltke, B.K. 156, 159
Warrior, R.A. 138, 141
Weber, B. 151, 154
Wei Huang 8
Weinfeld, M. 118, 119
Weiser, A. 37, 41, 43, 46, 86, 89
Weiss, M. 148, 149, 191
Welshman, F.H. 130, 132
Wesselius, J.W. 43, 46
West, G. 7
Westermann, C. 187, 191

White, L., Jr 19, 22
Wieder, N. 191
Willems, B. 187, 191
Williams, R. 193, 197
Wilson, G. 61, 64
Wilson, G.H. 109, 115
Wolff, H.W. 27
Wu, J.C.H. 239
Wyatt, N. 78

Xeravits, G.G. 32, 35
Xu Yuanchong 102, 108
Xu, Y. 237, 239

Yanjing Qu 8
Yao Jiheng 102, 108
Yassif, E. 30, 32, 35
Ye, R. 119
Yee, G.A. 1, 5, 12, 89, 216, 220
Young, K. 87, 89
Young, L.W. 252, 254

Zenger, E. 80, 84, 86, 89, 142, 145, 151, 152, 154, 164, 165, 168, 175, 179, 203, 205, 244, 245, 248
Zevit, Z. 43, 46

www.ingramcontent.com/pod-product-compliance
Lightning Source LLC
Chambersburg PA
CBHW071240230426
43668CB00011B/1514